"*Rebirth of a Nation* charts the story of how the United States consistently has failed to become a true democracy, both in terms of its policy and ideological development. It also points forcefully toward the crucial steps that must be taken to reverse that failure and produce a racially fair and just society."

—**William A. Darity Jr.**
coauthor of *From Here to Equality:*
Reparations for Black Americans in the Twenty-First Century

"*Rebirth of a Nation* makes a powerful case for historical reckoning in America. Goza's faith in, and bearing witness to the beauty of, Black resistance to systemic oppression reminds us that the soul of this nation can and must be redeemed. Everyone should read this book."

—**Khalil Gibran Muhammad**
author of *The Condemnation of Blackness:*
Race, Crime, and the Making of Modern Urban America

"*Rebirth of a Nation* is simultaneously thought-provoking, somber, enraging, yet surprisingly hopeful. Goza powerfully and convincingly calls for reparations as a key pathway from our historical and current state of systemic racial inequality and injustice. The book envisions an American rebirth as a viable democracy no longer wracked by the legacies of slavery, Jim Crow, colorblind racism, and the hatred unleashed after 2016."

—**Carol Anderson**
author of *White Rage: The Unspoken Truth of Our Racial Divide*

"*Rebirth of a Nation* takes its readers on an emotional and transformative journey. In an engaging narrative, Joel Edward Goza chronicles indisputable facts to explain religious and scientific justifications to dehumanize people of African descent. He connects these to the structure of US systems, policies, and laws used to violently exploit, oppress, and lock African Americans out of myriad opportunities. In his well-documented and well-argued case for economic restitution and soul repair, he presents a call to those who have benefited from unequal advantages baked into a race-based caste system. He outlines how leaving the cocoon of denial and precarious comfort to right centuries of wrong will benefit everyone. His ideas can lead to the creation of a more perfect union."

—**Michelle Duster,**
great-granddaughter of Ida B. Wells,
author of *Ida B. Wells: Voice of Truth*

"A powerful blend of history, meditation, and social commentary, Joel Edward Goza's *Rebirth of a Nation* documents the persistence of white supremacy in the United States and considers what it has cost us as a nation. This thoughtful and compelling book offers a way forward for anyone seeking to advance social justice."

—**Keisha N. Blain,**
author of *Set the World on Fire: Black Nationalist Women and the*
Global Struggle for Freedom and coeditor of *Four Hundred Souls:*
A Community History of African America, 1619–2019

"In *Rebirth of a Nation*, Joel Goza powerfully explains how Thomas Jefferson perpetuated white supremacy and how Abraham Lincoln, evolving in the face of military necessity, somewhat mitigated it. He helps us to understand why we have not eradicated white supremacy even in the aftermath of the civil rights movement of the 1950s and 1960s. He also pulls back the curtain on how Ronald Reagan, one of our country's most popular presidents, perpetuated and heightened white supremacy. The book effectively achieves part of the work that must be done if we are ever to have reparative justice for our country's racial wrongs."

—**Mary Frances Berry,**
Geraldine Segal Professor of American Social Thought, professor
emerita of history and Africana studies,
University of Pennsylvania

"Goza is an esteemed scholar of African American history. In this book, he offers us his prodigious knowledge of racial inequality and systemic racism. In spite of our country's dark history, Goza is hopeful. He offers us a vision for a new America, one where true equality exists, and he has a practical plan for achieving this vision. This is an important book that will influence both individual lives and public policy."

—**Mary Pipher,**
author of *Writing to Change the World*

"In *Rebirth of a Nation*, Joel Edward Goza gives us a historically grounded and deeply discerning look into the enduring power of white supremacy. He teaches, yes, but also makes a compelling case that learning is not enough: we must act upon what we know, and not just move toward reconciliation but repair the damage that America has inflicted upon its own citizens, its own best lights, and its own destiny."

—**Timothy B. Tyson,**
author of *The Blood of Emmett Till*

"The derision and hostility that too often greet the very idea of repair, where racial oppression is concerned, rest on lack of historical knowledge, dulling of moral sensibility, and failure of political imagination. Goza's impassioned and intelligent study addresses all three of these deficiencies in accessible, concrete, and moving ways."

—**David Roediger,**
author of *How Race Survived U.S. History*

Rebirth of a Nation

Reparations and Remaking America

Joel Edward Goza

WILLIAM B. EERDMANS PUBLISHING COMPANY

GRAND RAPIDS, MICHIGAN

Wm. B. Eerdmans Publishing Co.
4035 Park East Court SE, Grand Rapids, Michigan 49546
www.eerdmans.com

Book design by Lydia Hall

Printed in the United States of America

30 29 28 27 26 25 24   1 2 3 4 5 6 7

ISBN 978-0-8028-8431-2

Library of Congress Cataloging-in-Publication Data

A catalog record for this book is available from the Library of Congress.

Author proceeds go to the benefit of Black-led organizations.

Contents

Foreword by William J. Barber II   vii

A Letter to My Children on Inheritance   ix

Preface   xi

Introduction   1

PART I: SHACKLES   13

1. The Evolution of White Supremacy   15
   Racial Myths and Making America

2. Thomas Jefferson   19
   The Man and Mind That Helped Make America

3. Abraham Lincoln   39
   The Emancipator and His Two Proclamations

4. The Lasting Legacy of Shackles   60
   Establishing America's Racial Hierarchy

PART II: LYNCHINGS   65

5. Slavery without Paternalism   67
   From Shackles to Lynchings

6. Thomas Dixon   78
   Burning Down Uncle Tom's Cabin

7. Madison Grant   101
    Eugenics and Purifying the Republic

8. The Lasting Legacy of Lynchings   130
    Racial Terrorism, Scientific Racism, and the American Way

    PART III: PRISONS AND POVERTY   137

9. Two Roads Diverge   139
    Pathological Black Families or White Racism

10. Fighting a King   153
    Ronald Reagan and Rejecting Civil Rights

11. The Reagan Revolution   186
    Fighting the Dream, 1980–1988

12. The Lasting Legacy of "Colorblindness"   221
    Deepening America's Divides

    PART IV: REMAKING AMERICA   231

13. Birthing Pains   233

14. Repentance   240

15. Repayment   260

16. Repair   269

17. Rebirth   289

    Acknowledgments   293

    Notes   295

    Bibliography   333

    Index   351

Foreword

As a preacher, I've always been drawn to the story of Nicodemus that is recorded in John's Gospel. It's the occasion when Jesus suggests to his nighttime visitor that he must be "born again," but American Christians too often think they know what Jesus meant apart from the story. In the text, Nicodemus comes to Jesus at night because he has heard enough to know that what Jesus is saying is powerful, but he also knows it could be dangerous for someone like him. Nicodemus was someone who had status in the society of his day. He knew people with power, had connections, and used those connections to protect the people he loved. A movement that threatened to change the status quo was a challenge to Nicodemus. But Nicodemus understood that change was needed—not just for the people who were flocking to Jesus for healing, but also for someone like him.

Joel Goza reminds me of Nicodemus. Having been formed as a white man in America, he has spent his adult life being re-formed by relationships built in the trenches of living and working in some of America's poorest communities. From Houston's Fifth Ward to Louisville's Westside and the HBCU Simmons College of Kentucky, where he teaches poor Black and white men and women behind Kentucky's prison bars, Joel's perspective has been honed within communities deeply wounded by our nation's misplaced priorities. It's from this place that he has learned to imagine what it might mean for America to be born again.

There is a long and proud tradition of Black Americans who have demanded reparations as a matter of justice for the descendants of people who were held as property with the legal sanction of the federal government. But just as Nicodemus saw that Jesus's message of "good news to the poor" meant freedom for him as well, Joel sees clearly how repair is needed for people like him. "Reparations is about resurrecting liberty, justice, and equality in a land where these democratic possibilities were killed long before they were ever born," he writes. "It is the work to harmonize our life together with the demands of human decency, dignity, and democracy. Repentance, repayment, and repair: this is the work of reparations. Reimagining our past and future: this is the work of reparations. Providing a path to an antiracist and interracial democracy: this is the work of reparations. Reparations is about healing our racial wounds and a rare opportunity for our nation to begin anew."

But, as Nicodemus recognized in his talk with Jesus, we cannot imagine a new future without going back and facing the stories that have shaped us into the people we are. "Not everything that is faced can be changed," James Baldwin reminds us, "but nothing can be changed until it is faced." Joel takes us back to the eighteenth century to show how Thomas Jefferson's *Notes on the State of Virginia* provided a playbook of racial myths to entrench slavery in American life. In the age of Jim Crow, those same myths were repurposed to justify white terrorism. But it didn't stop there. Ronald Reagan deployed Jefferson's racial myths to justify intensifying poverty and mass incarceration. By the end of Joel's narrative, we can see that those living in America today have not only inherited a traumatized history; we have made decisions that perpetuate national crimes.

When Joel moves to envision reparations, he does so with the two ingredients essential to social change—idealism and pragmatism—showing us not only what can happen but also how, and what each of us can do. We can do the work of making political change possible and creating a context where the crimes of the past cannot move into the future. We have the resources to do it, and we know the kinds of policies that work. Joel offers a vision for how we can reimagine the political infrastructure and social awareness of our poorest communities and build the collective will for transformative change, which is what we lack.

I thank God for Joel, and I celebrate this book as an important intellectual contribution to the work of repairing this nation's breaches. May the Spirit renew your mind as you read it, and may it help grow a movement for a Third Reconstruction in our time.

WILLIAM J. BARBER II
NEW HAVEN, CONNECTICUT

A Letter to My Children on Inheritance

Dear children,

When I write, I often feel you and your mother gazing over my shoulder. You and your mother are who matter most to me, and I feel your presence even as I labor all alone. Though you are young, I am dedicating this book on reparations to you. I write, in part, from a debt of gratitude to Black communities and people who deeply love us. In part, my writing is a process of learning how to take responsibility for our inheritance and to deal with our nation's racial wounds with dignity, wisdom, and grace.

I share this letter with others because in these traumatizing times now rattling our nation resides a precious opportunity to transform our future by honestly reckoning with our present and our past. I open this letter because we are not the only white people needing to learn how to respond to the inheritance we received. For far too long the indifference of white families has placed the burden of our country's racial sins on Black people's backs to bear all alone. Our country yearns for a better way.

So I need you to know that in your veins flows the blood I gave you that came from poor Confederate soldiers who went to war to kill, suffer, and die to perpetuate Southern people's power to shackle mothers, fathers, and children. I also gave you the blood of Southern enslavers whose wealth reduced *other people* to *our property*. From your mother, you received the blood of Northern enslavers and Klansmen whose chains, rituals, and robes demonstrated that white supremacy united—not divided—white America. I hope you inherit more from us than this. I am certain you will never inherit less.

White families usually refuse to share the secrets of our racial past with our children. We prefer to protect you by shading America's racial realities with half-truths and whole lies that we pass down to every generation. When white politics placed Black people in chains and segregated spaces, we lied to ourselves and said white politics harmonized with the demands of Black biology. After slavery and segregation, we continued believing in racial myths and supported public policies that placed Black people in prison and entrapped entire communities in dire poverty. These policies destroyed Black neighborhoods, families, and people. Yet too often, white people believed Black suffering resulted from *Black* culture and *Black* proclivities rather than from our nation's brutal treatment of Black people.

But despite our family's complicity in white supremacy, our loved ones never consisted of convenient caricatures. Your family knows love. We know pain. We know life is hard. People are good, people are bad. We know that people and life are complicated. But intertwined with everything your family knows are truths we prefer to deny and a history we would rather bury than face. By refusing to own our nation and family's racial history, we pass our racial ways to children like you. We ask you to accept our family's fictions of innocence as an act of love and loyalty. Remember, children, loyalty is love—until it isn't.

So this is what I need you to understand about how white supremacy is tethered to history. History, every act of compassion and every act of violence, is made of flesh and blood. Your forefathers were neither gods nor demons. Humans are beautiful. Humans are broken. Humans heal. Humans kill. Humans hate. Humans love. White supremacy is demonic. But those possessed by white supremacy are humans just like you. This is why intentionality with *your* life, with *your* wounds, with *your* words—intentionality with *our* inheritance—matters.

The time to begin reparations for Black America is at hand. Our family and nation need a process of repentance and atonement. Always remember that repentance that provides no atonement is only posturing.

Children, there is nothing I love more than you. And when I see you, I see my family in you. Your mother often feels that in raising you, my daughter, she is raising my mother because you are your grandmother sixty-five years ago. And you, my son, carry the name of the grandfather and great-grandfather you never met because I wanted my fathers to be with you everywhere you go. The best I can give you I learned from them. Yet, we are people with a history. And to live and navigate our present challenges, we must learn from our history—from what brings us pride *and* what brings us pain.

In the pages that follow, I detail the racial history we inherited as white people in America. What you read may make you feel mad, feel sad, feel shame, but know that we are never whole when we fail to own our history. I desire your wholeness—for I love you with all my heart.

FOREVER YOUR FATHER,
Joel Edward Goza
Houston's Fifth Ward

Preface

Like many white Americans, for a long time I believed it was possible to support Black people's struggle for equality and work to heal the nation's wounds while rejecting the very idea of reparations as both impractical and a distraction from the real work of racial justice and democratic engagement. *Rebirth of a Nation* details why I was wrong.

For twenty years now, I have lived and worked in impoverished communities. For most of this time, I have worked in Black organizations ranging from a church to a nonprofit to a media company to a historically Black college. Through my work, I have received opportunities to collaborate with leading urban researchers and practitioners who have committed their lives to transforming poor Black communities through education, health care, and housing, as well as with activists and religious leaders seeking to stitch together our nation's social divides. Through this work, we have experienced meaningful victories and many more heartrending defeats. Over the years, I have watched as the young people of my community have aged far too fast, and I have attended many funerals of friends far too young to be fitted for a coffin. During this time, our nation grew increasingly divided, and hope was hard to find.

As the suffering of my community intensified and our culture became more toxic, I began to thirst for a better way. My thirst led me to examine our nation's history and the Black Freedom Movement and, eventually, to write on the work of reparations. Through my research and writing as well as my struggles and failures, I became convinced that any effort to heal our nation's wounds without a robust program of reparations is designed to fail.

Rebirth of a Nation invites readers on a journey to see the interconnections between the violence of slavery and the racial violence we continue to perpetuate—to see how this history of racial violence shapes the people and nation we have become. But because *Rebirth of a Nation* is about reparations, it is not a tragedy. *Rebirth of a Nation* is about our nation's pain—but it is also about our nation's possibilities. Navigating the pain of the past and working to realize a reparative future is the difficult and costly work of hope. By helping us see the racial crimes we continue to commit, I desire to help us not only to understand the urgency of reparations but also to embrace our responsibility to produce the political will necessary for realizing them.

As someone whose life is deeply entwined with community activism, I am committed to rigorous research. But *Rebirth of a Nation* is not focused primarily on the economic and social statistics of racial inequality. Statistics are essential to the work of reparations. But stats without stories often get the life sucked out of them. We must always remember that names are more important than numbers.

So rather than rehashing statistics, *Rebirth of a Nation* revisits specific racial myths, ideas, and men that painted Black Americans as pathological and innately inferior from the times of George Washington to George Floyd. These myths and men were essential components of a racial system that evolved from enslavement to the ritual of lynching to the practice of placing Black Americans in prison and entrapping them in poverty. Through the stories *Rebirth* shares, we see how white supremacy took on life on American soil.

"What it means to be a Negro in America," wrote James Baldwin in the wake of the lynching of Emmett Till, "can perhaps be suggested by an examination of the myths we perpetuate about him."[1] To create a framework for our conversation on reparations, *Rebirth* focuses on four racial myths: myths about Black sexuality and Black families, myths about Black sloth and Black dependence, myths about the intellectual inferiority of Black people, and myths about Black men as criminal beasts. Taken together, these myths display how the racial logics that once justified slavery and lynching continue today to war against our nation's potential to realize an interracial democracy marked by economic equity and racial justice.

Part I, "Shackles," focuses on the lives of Thomas Jefferson and Abraham Lincoln as it reexamines the age of slavery. "Shackles" details not only how Jefferson and Lincoln fought to create and preserve America, but also how they simultaneously created and preserved America's commitment to white supremacy and Black debasement. "Shackles" shows how white supremacy was meticulously crafted to make racial injustice appear as a necessary consequence of Black people's innate inferiority. By making racial injustice seem natural, white supremacy was perfectly engineered to outlive the institution of slavery. Indeed, slavery turned out to be only the first act of a three-act play.

Part II, "Lynchings," focuses on the second act: slavery's afterlife during the days of Jim Crow–styled segregation. In the aftershock of slavery's demise, America entered the birthing pains of a new racial age with the opportunity to pursue human equality. But this opportunity was explicitly rejected. Through the writings of Thomas Dixon and Madison Grant, Part II focuses on how we chose to christen white terrorism rather than risk realizing an interracial democracy. Today, Dixon and Grant are not popularly known writers and intellectuals, but they possess few equals in shaping America's racial imagination during the era of segregation. Through the work of Dixon and Grant, we will examine how an express aim of those seeking to protect white superiority and racial purity under Jim Crow's reign was not merely the preservation of a segregated society but the *eradication* of Black America. Jim Crow was not about Whites Only signs. Instead, it was eerily reminiscent of Germany's "Final Solution" for the Jewish people.

After the fall of segregation, the nation once again began crafting a new racial age. We received another opportunity to pursue an interracial and egalitarian democracy. But once again, rather than fully embracing a commitment to Black justice, white supremacy was reentrenched.

Part III, "Prisons and Poverty," details the evolution of white supremacy during the "Colorblind Age" by focusing on the work of Ronald Reagan from the 1940s through his presidency. It was in the aftermath of the Civil Rights era that Reagan and a bipartisan constituency of American leaders heralded America's realization of an age of equal opportunity for people of all races while explicitly trying to roll back every achievement of the Civil Rights Movement. The racial rhetoric of the Colorblind Age represented a deliberate refusal to acknowledge systemic racism in American life—past or present. Yet outlawing the specific mention of race only intensified the inequalities that slavery and segregation engineered. Under Reagan's watch, skyrocketing rates of incarceration and racial inequalities secured white supremacy and Black degradation in an era proclaiming racial progress. The Colorblind Age never dulled the edges of America's racial violence; it simply sugarcoated the razor.

Through these stories, *Rebirth of a Nation* empowers readers to feel in their bones the violence of our nation's racial injustices and commit to joining the work to eradicate America's racial inequality. Critically examining the roles of national "heroes" in perpetuating America's racial mythologies is not an attempt to use history as a progressive form of white self-hate or self-flagellation. The point of self-examination is to foster the self-awareness that the work of repair requires.

In Part IV, "Remaking America," we move from America's racial past to our present moment as we bring into being a new racial age that offers an opportunity to heal our racial wounds and reimagine our nation's future. Part IV looks to the future to explore the essential features of a "Reparative Age." The word "age" is important here. Reparations is the work of a generation, not an election cycle. The vision of reparations cast in *Rebirth of a Nation* provides no silver bullets. *Rebirth of a Nation* is pragmatic and seeks to help readers forge the imagination and commitment to stay in the saddle through the struggle, setbacks, evolution, and improvisation inherent in the journey of transformation.

Part IV envisions three essential elements of the work of reparations: *repentance, repayment,* and *repair.* First, repentance. It is through the work of repentance that we can transform our nation's political possibilities. Penitence is not impotence; it is the power to heal, to transform, and to humanize. Repentance empowers people and societies to begin again. Second, repayment. Repayment continues the work of repentance through monetary atonement to erase the racial wealth gap. Lastly, repair explores remediating systemic and institutional racism through reimagining and restructuring American society and reinvesting in Black communities. Through repentance, repayment, and repair, reparations begins a voyage not only to tend to the racial wounds Black people bear but also to restore pieces of humanity many white Americans lost somewhere along the way.

Reparations offers an opportunity to salvage our history and pull an antiracist future from a remarkably racist past. Implementing that opportunity depends on the ability to reimagine how different America's story could and should be. For this reimagining, *Rebirth of a Nation* uses as guides through each racial era the wisdom and witness of Black activists, writers, and intellectuals of the Black Freedom Movement who continually wooed America toward an interracial and egalitarian democracy. The Black historian Vincent Harding envisioned this tradition as a river traveling through time and space. "The river of black struggle is people," Harding wrote, "but it is also the hope, the movement, the transformative power that humans create and that creates them, us, and makes them, us, new persons."[2]

As white supremacy evolved and re-created itself, so did the Black Freedom Movement. Never one-dimensional or monolithic, the river always consists of currents and crosscurrents. The tactics of Frederick Douglass were not the tactics of Ida B. Wells; Martin Luther King Jr.'s strategy differed from Stokely Carmichael's; and today, William Barber II's work differs from Stacey

Abrams's. Yet, the revolutionary work that unites Douglass, Wells, King, Carmichael, Barber, and Abrams is the shared mission to make Black lives matter through the fight to create an interracial and egalitarian democracy.

Black activists, writers, and intellectuals have revealed white supremacy as much more than a war against Black America. Black people have consistently painted white supremacy as an insanity that wars against America's soul and every tenet of democracy, human dignity, and equality—an insanity void of compassion for the needs most Americans hold in common.

By rejecting white supremacy, it has been Black activists, writers, and researchers who have challenged America to see an expansive and poignant spectrum of political possibilities. The Black Freedom Movement sees through America's self-deception to the radical possibilities within American democracy simply because Black activists, writers, and researchers know that Black people are merely and yet wholly human. That one truth uncovers the lies that limit our life together. The world has yet to experience an egalitarian, interracial, antiracist democracy. And yet it is precisely this radical vision that many Black communities have sought to nurture and empower throughout our nation's life together.

As we listen to our guides, we may come to recognize that our racial nightmare continues not because we lack practical ways to address America's racial crisis but because we have continually rejected Black wisdom. In the days of slavery, we rejected the wisdom of the enslaved. In the days of segregation, we rejected the wisdom of the community Jim Crow sought to lynch. Today, to reject America's need for reparations and a national rebirth is not only to reject the wisdom of today's Black Freedom Movement but also to reject the collective wisdom of Sojourner Truth, Frederick Douglass, Harriet Tubman, Callie House, Ida B. Wells, W. E. B. Du Bois, Queen Mother Moore, Martin Luther King Jr., Stokely Carmichael, and John Lewis. This is the line through which the river of Black America's struggle flows toward the work of reparations.

Throughout our history, resistance to racial justice and Black wisdom has depended on deceptive framing, racial logics, historical amnesia, and superficial thinking. What those committed to resisting Black justice could never afford is a serious public conversation about America's racial history and a vulnerable public consideration of pragmatic public policies to begin reversing the way white America's indifference perpetuates Black America's suffering. And this is particularly true regarding the rejection of reparations. As Guy Emerson Mount writes, "America seems intent on a reparations policy driven [by] a popular *Simpsons* meme: 'We've tried nothing, and we're all out of ideas.'"[3]

But reparations is not a utopian dream. It is practical, pragmatic, and long-game politics to begin healing our nation from hundreds of years of our traumatic racial history. Reparations is about resurrecting liberty, justice, and equality in a land where these democratic possibilities were killed long before they were ever born. It is the work to harmonize our life together with the demands of human decency, dignity, and democracy. Repentance, repayment, and repair: this is the work of reparations. Reimagining our past and future: this is the work of reparations. Providing a path to an antiracist and interracial democracy: this is the work of reparations. Reparations is about healing our racial wounds and a rare opportunity for our nation to begin anew.

Introduction

> One is not attempting to save twenty-two million people. One is
> attempting to save an entire country, and that means an entire
> civilization, and the price for that is high. The price for that is to
> understand oneself.
>
> —James Baldwin, *The Artist's Struggle for Integrity*, 1963

BREATHE. JUST BREATHE. Many pages in this book hurt. And hope is here
too. *Rebirth of a Nation* is about an unbroken chain of racial ideas, practices,
and public policies that have devastated Black people, families, and communities. This chain was forged in the days of slavery, reforged in the era of
lynching, and reimagined after legal segregation ended to cage Black communities in poverty and Black people in prisons. *Rebirth of a Nation* details
not only how this unbroken chain enslaved Black America but also how the
cost of forging that chain was our nation's very soul.

But *Rebirth of a Nation* is more than that. It is an urgent call to embrace
the hope of radical change. And it is a call to action. In previous eras, our
racial crisis called us to end slavery and segregation. Today, our racial crisis
calls us to finish the work of abolition and the struggle for civil rights by
striving to end our racial crimes and repair our democracy. This work is the
work of reparations. Reparations is about reckoning with the racial crimes
of our past and the profound inequality of our present. And it is also about
healing our nation's soul and crafting a future where racial solidarity replaces
our ritual sacrificing of Black people and communities.

Opening the Caskets

Over sixty-five years ago, a tragic spark ignited the Civil Rights Movement
and led to a national reckoning. On the morning of August 29, 1955, Mamie

Till-Mobley received news about the kidnapping of her son, Emmett Till, who had left Chicago to visit relatives in Mississippi earlier that summer. Her life would never be the same. And neither could America's. Almost immediately, Ms. Till-Mobley began working the phone lines to alert the press and gather allies. Yet, while she worked, her worst nightmare was realized as Emmett's lifeless body surfaced in Mississippi's Tallahatchie River.

White authorities worked to quickly bury Emmett's body to erase the evidence of Southern savagery. But Emmett's mother outmaneuvered Mississippi and managed to get the remains of her son back to Chicago. When she witnessed the way *America* mutilated her beloved child, Ms. Till-Mobley resolved that Emmett's funeral not only serve as a memorial for his life but also force the world to see and reckon with the brutal handiwork of American racism.

Ms. Till-Mobley was convinced that the crime against her son implicated more than just the hands that took his life. His broken body bore the fingerprints of a sadistic society. Mamie Till-Mobley believed that if she could make America see what she saw, feel, in some measure, what she felt, her son's death would not be in vain. So she told the mortician that her son needed no makeup. "I took the privacy of my own grief and turned it into a public issue, a political issue," Ms. Till-Mobley remembered, "one which set in motion the dynamic force that ultimately led to a generation of social and legal progress for this country."[1] And she opened Emmett's casket to the world.

No one knew the consequences of opening the casket of a tortured child. All Ms. Till-Mobley knew for certain was that if the casket closed, Emmett's broken and mutilated body could never challenge America's indifference to Black suffering. If the casket closed, Mississippi would never cease breaking the bodies and hearts of Black sons and fathers, mothers and daughters. From the president to the people, Mamie Till-Mobley demanded that America *see* the truth about its soul that her son's mangled body revealed.

And see, we did. Hundreds of thousands filed by Emmett Till's glass-sealed casket in person, which was adorned with three of Mamie Till-Mobley's favorite photos of him. She wanted the world to see Emmett through her eyes and haunt our nation through the beauty of the boy she lost. In time, hundreds of millions witnessed his remains in magazines, newspapers, textbooks, and the newly created medium of television. "Mass media and massive protest may have made his murder the most notorious racial incident in the history of the world," writes historian Tim Tyson. "His lynching, his mother's decision to open the casket to the world, . . . spun the country, and arguably the world, in a different direction."[2]

When Ms. Till-Mobley opened Emmett's casket, she entered a long and sacred tradition in Black America's struggle for racial justice. When white America has worked to bury, forget, misremember, and downplay the violence of our racial ways, courageous Black Americans have demanded our nation deal transparently with America's racial past and present. They have forced white America to reckon with the truths about our nation that Black caskets reveal. Perhaps only when white Americans are ready to look directly into the face of Black death can we begin to confront the realities that shape Black lives.

As I worked on *Rebirth of a Nation*, a photo of Emmett Till hung above my desk. I desired my work to take shape underneath his gaze. The longer I sat under Emmett's photo, the more deeply I came to believe the hope of our future depends on our readiness to keep the caskets of our past open and vulnerably engage with the horror. If white America finds the courage to face our racial past and the wisdom to listen to and learn from the Black struggle, then we might develop the political, moral, and spiritual will necessary to respond to our racial crimes in a manner that provides a path into an antiracist future. If we embrace the process and pain's transformative work, we might begin to understand the necessity of reparations—not only for the sake of Black America but for the salvation of white America as well.

Reparations is about keeping the caskets of America's racial past and present open and publicly, politically, economically, and spiritually tending to our racial wounds with the hope of remaking our nation. We cannot change our past, but we can reckon with it. And that reckoning can be reparative. Reparations is about the work of repentance that can change our political possibilities. Reparations is about the work of repayment and repair that can transform our life together and redeem our future. Reparations is what the work of our democracy is all about—a never-ending journey toward a more perfect union.

Bearing Witness: My Story

Growing up, everything I thought I knew about Black people I learned from Ronald Reagan. In my suburban neighborhood, we learned to love Black heroes after they were safely dead and their messages were edited into irrelevancy. We learned to love Black babies until they were born and to fear how

Black people's addiction to welfare was ruining our nation. My community often believed we understood the problems of Black people and neighborhoods without needing to risk the intimacy required to truly know either.

Yet, sometimes life forces us to question everything we learned from those who loved us most, and we enter a season of growing pains that can happen when the life we are living hits a dead end. There was nothing particularly interesting about the season of personal crisis that occurred in my early twenties. Despite my best-laid plans, in my twenties my most cherished relationships left me traumatized, undiagnosed diabetes wrecked my health, and I dropped out of graduate school. I moved back home and started working. But my career began imploding before it could really get going. My dreams were haunted and nights were often restless. When I awoke, there was no peace either. Sometimes our nightmares intensify during waking hours.

And so it was that during a season of personal crisis, a friend who taught in Houston's Fifth Ward invited my college roommates and me to move into the community where he worked. The Fifth Ward is Houston's poorest Black and Brown community. It was there that I sought to place my life back together. And it was there that I was forced for the first time to face our nation's racial nightmare.

Established in the aftershock of the Emancipation Proclamation, Houston's Fifth Ward is marked by both the beauty and the brokenness of Black Americans' struggle for justice. As with other Black communities, slavery carved the Fifth Ward's original wounds. But after slavery, white politics poured an endless stream of salt on those wounds through racist public policies and practices.

Beginning in the 1930s, redlining began in neighborhoods like the Fifth Ward to rob Black communities of the financial infrastructure required to fully thrive. In the 1950s, the Federal-Aid Highway Act plowed freeways through the hearts of Black communities across the nation, attacking their physical infrastructure. City planners bulldozed two intersecting freeways through the Fifth Ward's main artery, destroying its business district and forming the shape of a cross. People who remember the freeways' horrific placement refer to it as Fifth Ward's crucifixion.

In the following decade, "integration" did many things in America. But it never created a two-way street that robustly pursued racial justice. Instead, Black businesses and Black schools across America were devastated, and the suffering of Black communities often intensified. The few Black businesses that survived the crucifixions on the cross of racist freeways depended on a near monopoly of Black patrons. When Houston's commerce "integrated,"

Black people were free to shop in white stores. And they did. But white people showed no interest in returning the favor by shopping at Black businesses. The Fifth Ward's Black stores began to fail and fold as more Black money was placed in white pockets.

When Houston's public schools integrated, a select few of the Black communities' most gifted students and teachers flowed to the better-funded white schools. But additional funds, gifted white students, and high-performing white teachers rarely entered communities like the Fifth Ward. It is not that integration failed to provide positive changes and opportunities. It did. But for many residents of the Fifth Ward, America's explicit aim to achieve racial integration without an equally explicit aim to achieve racial justice failed to repair the wounds of America's unequal racial worlds.

So it was that in the 1970s, the implosion of the Fifth Ward community began in earnest. Most middle-class Black families who could get out did as Black flight followed on the heels of white flight. The Fifth Ward's infrastructure went into rapid decline until the landscape consisted largely of dilapidated houses, abandoned properties, liquor stores, underfunded schools, and churches that continued to shake and sway on Sundays. In the second half of the 1970s, the Fifth Ward became ground zero for America's war against crime, but that war only made matters worse.

In the 1980s, the crack epidemic hit the Fifth Ward and Houston flooded the community with additional cops acting as "holy warriors" as the War on Crime intensified into the War on Drugs. The cops deployed search-and-destroy tactics that left behind a neighborhood of scorched earth. In the 1990s, the community began gathering the resources and know-how that redevelopment required. But today, community-centered redevelopment fights against gentrification that too often represents a slow Black communal lynching in twenty-first-century form.[3]

Of course, that is only one side of the story. From within the Fifth Ward, one sees interlaced within the vicious cycles of this history the heroic struggle of people who refuse to be broken. In 1979, the year of my birth, *Texas Monthly* moved investigative journalist Richard West into the Fifth Ward. For West, the neighborhood was a different universe. But what he found surprised him: "a community determined that life should win over death, hope over despair, pride over poverty." West titled his article "Only the Strong Survive." "And I don't mean just physical strength," West wrote. "I mean the strength that is in quick wits, friendship, family, religion, love, and hard work. Two worlds—life at its worst and life at its best—exist side by side, beginning just outside my window . . . a rip-roaring place—tough, brutal, savage, yet full of life."[4]

The community's moxie that West wrote about proved true when I moved into the neighborhood twenty years ago, and it still proves true today. When I first moved in, I was working at one of the world's largest accounting firms. My friends and I got to work flipping a house, and as the house came together, slowly but surely my life did as well. By 2006, I had completed grad school and began working for a Black church in the Fifth Ward with a long history of spearheading the neighborhood's community-based development and political engagement. For the next ten years, I was immersed in the community's religious life and the fight for essential community services ranging from education to health care to affordable housing.

One day at a time, my life and family intertwined with the community's life and families. From the Fifth Ward, I witnessed the struggles of the Johnson, Roberts, and Combs families. Through the Johnson family, I felt the violence of the racist public policies that shape our health care and criminal justice systems. Like too many other impoverished African American women, Jamarcus and James Johnson's mother died at a very young age, never receiving the quality care she needed to save her life. The brothers were not young men. They were small children.[5]

Jamarcus is an extrovert. James is an introvert. Yet what separates these brothers is not their personalities. The dividing line was drawn over a decade ago when Jamarcus encountered the criminal justice system as a middle schooler. Once Jamarcus had a criminal record, the criminal record had Jamarcus. On paper, stealing a bike was Jamarcus's crime. Yet, to understand the predatory nature of America's criminal justice system is to understand that Jamarcus's imprisonment resulted ultimately from Black poverty, not a stolen BMX.

After losing his mother and brother to racism in systemic form, James sharpened his survival skills as a young boy. He navigated his way out of the Fifth Ward's failing schools, schools that James said were places "where dreams went to die." He attended magnet programs that required an hour-long commute on multiple city buses to attend. James is brilliant, gifted, disciplined, and he beat the odds. He survived. James graduated from college with a degree in aerospace engineering. But James's exceptionalism encapsulates the tragedy. We should know the rules of the game are rigged when survival requires exceptionalism.

I met Lamar Roberts through James when he was beginning middle school. Lamar's mother loved him but couldn't afford to pay the bills. After their lights went out and their water ran dry, Lamar's mother took him to stay at a friend's home. What she didn't know is that it was a home where sexual predators prowled. After he was molested, her son was never the same.

In the Fifth Ward, I also met Grandma Combs and her family. In communities victimized by racial injustice, wherever there are children on the playground there are often grandparents in the background. Grandma Combs's son-in-law was murdered. Her daughter's drug addictions deepened, and she landed in prison instead of rehab. Grandma Combs's grandchildren came to live with her in her apartment.

When they moved in, Grandma Combs received no funding for the care her grandchildren required. Without adequate public assistance, she could not afford to stay home to tend to the family she loved. More children meant more bills. More bills meant endless hours working for menial wages. Rather than giving her grandchildren all the love, nurture, and support she desired and they required, Grandma Combs worked multiple jobs as a home health provider.

For over a decade, I watched as her grandchildren worked diligently to unleash their gifts in the world. And though they were *greatly* gifted, the price they paid for the murder of their father, the incarceration of their mother, and the refusal of our nation to support their grandmother's efforts on their behalf often proved unbearable.[6]

Over the years, I learned that the stories of the Johnsons, the Robertses, and the Combses are not the exceptions to America's racial rules. Instead, they epitomize the struggles Black families face in impoverished communities across our nation. *Rebirth of a Nation* bears witness to the price our nation pays for its racism through lost sons and daughters, sisters and brothers, parents, and grandparents. It bears witness to the dignity of people seeking to thrive despite a remarkably racist world. The Johnson, Roberts, and Combs families of the Fifth Ward are more than victims of our nation's racial history and racist policies. They are survivors of our nation's war against poor Black people. Such survivors and communities are worthy of our profound respect. And, as I would later learn, they are worthy of reparations as well.

From Good Intentions to Reparations

After a decade of navigating America's racial nightmare with families and friends from the Fifth Ward, devastating personal losses led me into another season of growing pains and a grueling career transition out of the church and nonprofit world. I remained in the community, but the hodgepodge of my talents and expertise offered no clear path forward, and I entered a long season of unemployment. As I knocked on doors that refused to open, I began writing as well. Years of living in the Fifth Ward and working between institutions of power and the community convinced me that the game we were playing was rigged—that the racial devastation that marked both Houston and our nation was destruction by design.

I desired to understand how we had become a nation and a city capable of placing a white person on the moon while proving either unwilling or unable to help Black working families flourish. I wanted to understand how white churches saved white souls without creating solidarity with Black justice. How was it possible that a city and a nation of such wealth, innovation, and pious people had destroyed so many of its Black citizens by denying them an adequate education, livable wages, and social services? As my unemployment continued, my search for understanding culminated in my first book, which focused on enlightenment philosophers who harmonized American democracy and Christianity with slavery and racial inequality. I titled the book *America's Unholy Ghosts: The Racist Roots of Our Faith and Politics*.

America's Unholy Ghosts was published in the spring of 2019. Following the book's release, I was interviewed in George Floyd's Third Ward neighborhood by prominent pastor, DJ, and community activist Dr. D. Z. Cofield. Cofield began his radio show *Real World, Real Talk* with the golden voice of a seasoned DJ. He introduced *America's Unholy Ghosts* with high praise. "I believe this book," he selected his words carefully, "can shake our nation's political order by providing a context to discuss the work of reparations."

I sat dumbstruck. Despite my experiences in the Fifth Ward, reparations seemed like nothing more than the wistful fantasies of fanatics. When Cofield linked my writing to reparations, my resistance proved so instantaneous and reflexive that it nearly produced an out-of-body experience. I tried to slow down, to breathe, and to process Cofield's words and my violent reaction to them. I am familiar enough with my own racial instincts that I recognized the violence within me as white supremacy at work—it was the recoil that happens when Black hands take the steering wheel and direct conversations on race to places where well-intentioned white folks like me fear to go.

That summer, I repeatedly processed my time with Cofield. The more I processed, the more clearly I came to see how white supremacy not only created racial crimes but also *perpetuates* our racial criminality by fostering resistance to Black people's pursuit of racial justice. The action, reaction, and analysis called me into the work this book required.

Today, many people recognize the reality of stark racial inequalities and the role of racism in creating that injustice. Yet, while more than three out of four Black people support reparations, almost three out of four white people reject them.[7] White Americans often desire innocence more than justice, so we pretend that all the moral and financial debts our ancestors incurred vanished and no personal or communal profit was pocketed. But since the past is always present, when we claim to be innocent of the sins of previous generations, what we really mean is simple: we would rather Black people continue to suffer as second-class citizens than pay the price required to tend our nation's racial wounds.

For four hundred of the four hundred years since slavery's inception, our nation has perpetuated a domestic war along racial lines that exploited Black bodies for white profit. During slavery, the cornerstone of the racial profiteering was the auction block. Following slavery, when Black bodies became expendable in the pursuit of white profit, they were—and that proved profitable too. From convict leasing schemes and for-profit prisons, to unjust and unlivable wages and mass unemployment, Black people have been routinely sacrificed to protect white wealth. Despite this ongoing ritual, our nation continually refuses to repent or recognize that the dehumanizing racial project that slavery began is one we choose to perpetuate.

As I began processing our nation's responsibility to those we enslaved and continue to pillage, Ta-Nehisi Coates's "The Case for Reparations," published by the *Atlantic* in 2014, proved pivotal. Despite the horror slavery wrought, the accent of Coates's argument for reparations is placed not on the racial crimes of slavery but on the atrocities of slavery's afterlife in modern America. His case for reparations focuses on racist public policies of the twentieth century that "plundered" Black Americans in the land of the living. Coates seeks to instill in his readers the social depth perception that the work of reparations requires. "When we think of white supremacy, we picture COLORED ONLY signs," Coates writes, "but we should picture pirate flags."

Coates demands his readers face the fact that we are "a country whose existence was predicated on the torture of black fathers, on the rape of black mothers, on the sale of black children."[8] The colors of America's racial pathologies are not Black; they are red, white, and blue. Today, the average wealth of a Black family amounts to less than a dime to white America's dollar.

After dissecting the twentieth century's racialized economic exploitation and social degradation, Coates turns his pen to envision the future and lays the soul of his argument bare:

And so we must imagine a new country. Reparations—by which I mean the full acceptance of *our collective biography* and its consequences—is the price we must pay to see ourselves squarely. . . . What I'm talking about is more than recompense for past injustices. . . . What I'm talking about is a national reckoning that would lead to spiritual renewal. . . . I believe that wrestling publicly with these questions matters as much as—if not more than—the specific answers that might be produced.[9]

For Coates, even if reparations fail to economically balance America's racial ledger, the process embodies an act of love in the public square that just might humanize our nation and our future. Coates is but one brilliant voice within a chorus committed to the struggle to realize reparations. And this chorus is calling our nation past the self-soothing paradigm of good intentions and into the more costly economic and societal work capable of transforming our nation into a land of liberty and justice for all. For only a radical commitment to reparations can begin the work of national healing and transformation that our wounds demand.

Reparations is soul work. It is a clarion call that justice can replace injustice and that our nation's racial future need not repeat the crimes of our nation's past. Reparations is about Thomas Paine's revolutionary truth of 1776: "We have it in our power to *begin the world over again." All* of this is the work of reparations.

Hope for the Journey

In the pages that follow, I hope that opening the caskets of our racial past and seeing white supremacy's vicious toll on American lives empowers people from *different* backgrounds and perspectives to consider reparations and America's future from a *common* framework. What we must understand as we begin is that *this history matters.* How history lives, moves, and breathes in our present moment matters. Our savage racial history has a gravity we cannot rise above. But we must salvage our story and repurpose it to begin crafting a reparative future.

Such work calls us to a deep and more radical hope. And that type of hope is never far from danger. When it comes to seeking hope for our nation's future, American history often proves salt water for the thirsty. Knowledge of our history, of our inheritance, easily leads to despair. When I chose to write on reparations, it was not hope that drove me but desperation. Yet, the journey surprised me. What surprised me most in researching the ideas, work, and history of reparations was not only the remarkable consistency of hope embedded in the Black Freedom Movement but also its determined nature. W. E. B. Du Bois described Black hope as "a hope not hopeless but unhopeful."[10] Howard Thurman wrote of a "despairing hope and groping faith."[11] And indeed, the vast majority of Black thinkers and activists have fiercely held to this deeper and dangerous hope. With heavy hearts, they have hoped against hope that our nation can be *reborn*, that we can *revise* our founding documents by holding them accountable to their own words, and *restructure* American democracy by ridding it of anti-Black racism. It is that deep, determined, and heavy hope against hope that has inspired the struggle to continue, even after optimism lost its lure.

Empowered by their daring hopes, Black America endured the hatred of their fellow citizens and the abandonment of their allies and withstood the bewilderment of the vicious backlash that every step of racial progress produced. Yet, those who committed themselves to life within "the river," as Vincent Harding dubbed it, proved incapable of unfeeling the future they felt in their bones or unseeing the visions they saw when they were immersed in the river's forward flow. And at every step in America's history, that river invited our nation to embrace the sacrifices and struggles necessary to begin writing a different future here and now. With notable exceptions, white America consistently refused the invitation to stand in solidarity with the struggle. And Black America was left to fight for racial justice without much help.

Nonetheless, the struggle instilled a hope in Black sojourners that the American experiment could not drown—no matter how hard it tried. The hope of the struggle for Black justice is rooted in the reality that our future is not predetermined, but rather is utterly contingent on the choices—the sacrifices and struggles—of today. "Hope," as James Baldwin said, "is invented every day."[12]

Over the course of this project, I found myself drawn time and again to walk the sacred grounds of the Fifth Ward's oldest cemetery. It is sandwiched between the freeway that violently cut the Fifth Ward in two long ago and a low-income housing complex named in honor of the Black poet Phillis Wheatley. Many who are buried in the cemetery were born into slavery. Most were born in the era of Reconstruction. All died during Jim Crow.

When I am in the Fifth Ward's cemetery or her public housing projects, my writing feels like a woefully inadequate offering for such an urgent moment. But we are living in a time that demands that each of us lay the best we can give on the altar. And as in Jesus's lesson of the poor widow, each mite matters. As I offered my writing and research to the cause of reparative justice, I began to experience the silhouette of the deeper and more determined hope of which I read. Somewhere along the journey, I began to believe that white Americans who accept the invitation to, in the words of the old Negro spiritual, "wade in the water" can begin again. And it will not take many white Americans hearing the choir's invitation beckoning us to the river for the lethal grip of white supremacy to break. Then we will be free at last to begin our nation anew.

Will white America accept the invitation into the river's waters, the invitation to die to be reborn? Or will America's future be the same as it ever was? I do not know. But we are not alone. The struggle started long ago. The river will flow long after we are gone. New works in an old struggle will emerge, and as long as the river flows and the choir sings, the hope that inspires the struggle will remain. Struggle and hope, for whatever else they are, are by their very natures inseparable. As long as either one lives, neither one can remain dead long.

I

SHACKLES

The Mythology of Black Pathology
from the Declaration to the Emancipation

Mr. Jefferson . . . has in truth injured us more, and has
been as great a barrier to our emancipation as anything
that has ever been advanced against us. . . . Mr. Jefferson's
remarks respecting us, have sunk deep into the hearts
of millions of the whites, and never will be removed this
side of eternity.

—David Walker, *Appeal,* September 28, 1829

Abraham Lincoln was not . . . either our man or our
model. . . . In his habits of thought, and in his prejudices, he was a white man. He was preeminently the
white man's President, entirely devoted to the welfare
of white men. He was ready . . . to deny, postpone, and
sacrifice the rights of humanity in the colored people to
promote the welfare of the white people of this country.

—Frederick Douglass,
"Oration in Memory of Abraham Lincoln,"
April 14, 1876

1

The Evolution of White Supremacy

Racial Myths and Making America

> You can't solve a problem with the consciousness that created it. The antiquated belief that some groups of people are better than others distorts our politics, drains our economy, and erodes everything Americans have in common. . . . And everything we believe comes from a story we've been told.
>
> —Heather McGhee, *The Sum of Us*, 2021

At our inception, America attempted to harmonize democracy and the idea of human equality with the institution of slavery. That attempt was a sin against America's soul and began an unending tradition of racist ideas and public policies that divided the nation along racial lines. From slavery to segregation and through the Colorblind Age, such ideas and policies perverted our nation's potential by preying on Black people, families, and communities.

As white supremacy evolved, it consistently acted like an addictive drug that numbed white America from the pain of our nation's racial nightmare. Narcotics perform powerful work on people. But for all their ability to dissociate us from reality, they possess no ability to heal our wounds or the history from which we hide. White supremacy made too many white people feel both exceptional in our place in the world and comfortable with the injustices that shape our life together. Hope and healing never emerge through exceptional comfort.

In every American age, white America received repeated opportunities to repent of our addiction to white supremacy. Instead, we doubled down on denial and refilled our toxic prescription. The nightmare of loving an addict is that addicts often choose self-destruction over detox. For some addicts, self-destruction makes sense. The price of sobriety is high. It demands you deal with your demons, demands enduring addiction's death and embracing the birthing pains that new life always entails.

Though time and time again, America chose destruction, this can change if we cling to the conviction that reckonings can be redemptive. Like the abolitionist and civil rights movements of yesteryear, the reparations movement provides yet another opportunity to tend to our nation's wounds and begin a committed journey into a Reparative Age and a national rebirth.

One way we transmit white supremacy is through stories that simplify and romanticize American history in a way that leads to national self-deception instead of self-understanding. Too often, America's mainstream self-awareness is embedded in the "great men" histories focused on leaders such as Washington, Jefferson, Lincoln, the Roosevelts, Kennedy, and Reagan. We learn that these men's virtues made America a city on a hill and light to the world. Yet, if their virtues left an indelible impact on the country, so did their vices. It is a basic fact from which we often flee that all these men were complicit in creating and perpetuating a nation divided along racial lines. Tragically, what is required to make sense of today's racial tragedies and trauma are the historical and social realities we were never allowed to learn. And by failing to reckon with how interlaced our inheritance is with white supremacy, we not only fail to remember how different our story should have been but also lose the ability to imagine how different our future can be.

As we reexamine America's history and heroes with a focus on the realities revealed by the open caskets of Black Americans, white supremacy's violence becomes more visible and central to the story of our life together. And the more visible the violence of white supremacy becomes, the more details regarding the evolution of white supremacy on American soil are revealed. The devil is in the details, and it is in the details that distinctive patterns in this evolution arise. White supremacy was not simply about the truths we buried about cherished white leaders. Throughout America's history, white supremacy arose with racial lies about nonwhite people—and Black people in particular. As racial lies gained traction, they inspired racial legends, myths, and caricatures that painted Black people as pathological and innately inferior. These racial legends, myths, and pathological caricatures gave life to vicious racial logics and ideas. And eventually, these racial logics and ideas metastasized into racist practices and public policies that preyed on Black people.

At the beginning of white supremacy's evolution in America, at least three lies blamed Black people for their place at the bottom of America's social and economic ladder. The first lie claimed Black sexuality was depraved and Black families were dysfunctional. The second lie suggested Black people were slothful and lacked the inner drive self-reliance required. The third lie insisted that Black people lacked brainpower. In every era of America's life, these racial myths ingrained the conviction of Black people's innate inferiority to justify the intensity of Black America's suffering.

These racial myths performed precisely the work their authors intended by limiting America's political imagination and shriveling the political, economic, and spiritual will democracy requires. White supremacy intoxicated white America until a racial hierarchy seemed to harmonize with the very laws of nature. Once racial divides felt natural, the fight for racial equality seemed to be rooted in a utopian fantasy rather than our most essential democratic convictions.

As we begin to construct a framework to understand the urgency of reparations, we start with the age of slavery and the shackles that attempted to lock Black America in subservience. The myths white supremacists crafted during slavery to portray Black people as pathological and requiring shackles were absurd, yet they proved persuasive in every American age. By detailing how racial lies gave birth to racial legends and how those legends led to dehumanizing racial practices, we begin to see how America became fertile ground for a racial nightmare that haunts our nation's every waking hour.

"Shackles" examines two of the most cherished presidents during the era of slavery: Thomas Jefferson and Abraham Lincoln. It is hard to think of two American presidents more different in that era than Jefferson and Lincoln. Jefferson was a child of privilege, a product and prophet of the Enlightenment, and a beloved son of Virginia's slavocracy who reigned over his plantation from the mansion of Monticello. Lincoln's family also traced their roots to Virginia, but they were of a different pedigree. His mother, Nancy, is believed to have been born out of wedlock and, according to early biographers, developed a reputation as "a bold—reckless—daredevil kind of a woman, stepping to the very verge of propriety."[1] Due to her reputation, the paternity of Abraham Lincoln was always in question. But what was not in question was that Nancy was married to Thomas Lincoln.

Thomas was also born in Virginia. His family moved to Kentucky when he was a young child, and there, at the age of eight, Thomas witnessed his father murdered by Native Americans. By the time Nancy and Thomas had their first son, Abraham, they were poor, illiterate, antislavery Kentuckians living in a log cabin. While Jefferson's extraordinary wealth enabled a life of extraordinary luxuries that devolved into extraordinary debts, much of Lincoln's life was marked by the struggle to survive and was lived within an arm's reach of poverty.

Despite class differences, both men reflected the most troubling aspects of their age and helped frame America's racial future, forever placing their fingerprints on the American imagination through their almost magical power with the written word. Their signature pieces, the Declaration of Independence and the Emancipation Proclamation, fueled America's quest for equality while also revealing how that same quest was rooted firmly in ideologies of white supremacy and a lethal vision of racial division, exclusion, and deprivation. Understanding these documents and the men who penned them is how we can begin to understand the role white supremacy played in shaping America's soul. What is frightening is how the racial lies and logic promoted during slavery continue to provide the foundation of America's racial imagination today.

2

THOMAS JEFFERSON

The Man and Mind That Helped Make America

> Thomas Jefferson was one of the wildest and most irresponsible of the people who developed the ideology of racial superiority and inferiority.
>
> —John Hope Franklin, C-SPAN, April 15, 2007

WRITING ABOUT THOMAS JEFFERSON IS DIFFICULT. Jefferson was thoroughly versed in the art of deception. He posed as a bachelor, a simple farmer, and a prophet of equality while living a life completely contradictory to this carefully crafted image. However, the difficulty of accurately analyzing Jefferson lies deeper than the contradictions between his lived life and the ideologies he espoused. What compounds the difficulty in interpreting Jefferson is the tendency he had to dodge conflict by nimbly articulating his beliefs to harmonize with what his audience hoped to hear, employing rhetoric that intentionally masked his political aims. Through this habit, Jefferson produced conflicting evidence of his convictions on many topics, and this is particularly true on the issue of slavery.

Jefferson made the notion that "all men are created equal" synonymous with the American experiment. Yet his book *Notes on the State of Virginia*, released in 1785, made him one of the leading theorists of white supremacy of his era. And in that unmentioned conflict between the ideologies of equality and white supremacy, Jefferson ingrained a self-deception in the American imagination that still tears at our national fabric today.

Born into a family of privilege, Jefferson recalled his earliest memory was of being carried on a pillow by a person his family enslaved. As a young man, he fell in love with and married Martha Skelton. The marriage proved both passionate and intimate, but its practical implications reached further.

Martha's wealth far outpaced Jefferson's. Their marriage tripled the number of people Jefferson enslaved, and his radical increase in wealth gave him the freedom to focus on his intellectual and political passions full-time. But tragedy seemed nearly ever present in the home of the young couple. Together, they bore six children, with only two surviving to adulthood. Perhaps the greatest blow was Martha's passing from this life only four months after the birth of their final child. She was only thirty-three and her husband thirty-nine. As she died, she got Jefferson to commit to never remarry. It was a commitment he kept, and, as we shall see, it was a commitment that played a leading role in complicating his legacy ever after.[1]

But Jefferson's story runs much deeper than the tragedies he endured and is indiscernible apart from three of his masterpieces: the Declaration of Independence, *Notes on the State of Virginia*, and his Monticello mansion. We begin with Monticello. To enter Monticello is to enter a mind that helped make America. Monticello, all eleven thousand square feet and forty-three rooms of it, was more than Jefferson's home.[2] Monticello also provided a means for Jefferson to celebrate the life of the mind as well as the men who shaped his political and philosophical thinking. Monticello's entranceway greeted guests with busts of Hamilton in marble and Voltaire in plaster. As the guests moved through the entrance to the public parlor and dining room, portraits of groundbreaking geniuses, such as Isaac Newton, Francis Bacon, and John Locke, adorned the walls. Other paintings in the sitting room featured scenes from the Gospels, Greek mythology, and the American Revolution. But the most sacred space of his mansion was his library. "I cannot live without my books,"[3] Jefferson confessed. And he gathered to himself the largest individual collection of books in America at the time.

Like Jefferson himself, there is more to Monticello than what appears on the manicured surface. To drive to Monticello today is to be greeted by signs that herald a "Journey through Hallowed Ground." But if Monticello is hallowed ground, it is also haunted ground. To the untrained eye, neither white supremacy nor slavery are easily discernible at Monticello, but both were and are omnipresent. With illusion in mind, Jefferson intentionally designed Monticello to hide from his audience the slavery that was its lifeblood.[4] Yet, to examine the ideas in Jefferson's library and the people portrayed in the sculptures and paintings is to realize that Jefferson hid white supremacy in plain sight. The books range from the ancient Greeks up through the Enlightenment. But it is the artworks that provide the road map from the library to the minds that mattered most to the master of Monticello. And it is important to understand that much of Monticello's art enshrines the Enlightenment philosophers responsible for resurrecting ancient Greece's justifications of classism and slavery and tailoring them for a world being made modern. Harmonizing democracy with inequality and slavery was a passion project for America's founding generation, and no founder was more passionate or influential in that mission than Jefferson.

To read the Declaration of Independence in light of Monticello and the ideas that inspired it uncovers the intricate work occurring between every line and letter. As slave labor permeates every aspect of the crafting of Monticello, white supremacy permeates every aspect of the Declaration of Independence. So much so that when Jefferson writes, "All men are created equal," he is implicitly, but intentionally, calling into question the very humanity of Black Americans.

As Benjamin Isaac explores in his remarkable work *The Invention of Racism in Classical Antiquity*, the West's addiction to myths of human superiority and inferiority extends all the way back to the ancient Greeks, who also crafted rationalizations to justify slavery and inequality. Jefferson was intimate with these myths and their most famous Greek promoters: Plato and Aristotle.[5]

In the *Republic*, Plato imagines "a noble lie" to indoctrinate citizens to believe that some Athenians are created by gold, some silver, and others iron to protect class distinctions in a democratic society. This laid the groundwork to argue for a human hierarchy. Aristotle went on to imagine slavery as an institution that was mutually beneficial for the enslaver and the enslaved and went further still by imagining slaves as animals. Jefferson was intimate with such stories and logic, and they informed his understanding of how to promote deeply entrenched racial distinctions in a society defined by democratic ideals.

But Jefferson's thinking was also shaped by the racial ideologies of the Enlightenment. When the philosophers of the Enlightenment examined the Greek myths and rationalizations that justified class segregation and slavery, they proved inspirational. The Greek philosophies and mythologies of inherent superiority and inferiority needed to evolve from a hierarchy completely unrelated to the color of skin and physical features to a worldview obsessed with the physical distinctions between Europeans and non-Europeans. And, of course, the primary target was repeatedly the physical distinctions of Africans. Thus, when the Enlightenment philosophers seized the Greeks' myths that undergirded their conceptions of a human hierarchy, they *radicalized* the myths by *racializing* them. The myths proved a powerful weapon in the colonial tool belt. Jefferson was entranced by how Enlightened racists customized Greek myths to modern demands. In turn, he sharpened the most racist aspects of Europe's Enlightenment for the racial infrastructure at the heart of the new American experiment.

One particularly compelling legend for Jefferson mashed up mythologies of sex and the animalistic nature of slaves, and then aimed that myth at Africa. Crafting this mythology was the most influential philosopher for Jefferson's thinking on equality: John Locke, the father of classical liberalism. In Locke's *Essay on Human Understanding*, he writes that all men are created equal. But that statement only raises a question. What exactly is "man"? We don't really know because the "real essence . . . is impossible to know." Locke often takes gold as an example. Not everything that glitters is gold. So too, not everything that looks human meets the gold standard for full humanity. "Take my word for it," Locke writes as he takes an ancient insult and begins sowing the seeds that cast Africans as animals and African women as sexually depraved, that there are creatures in the world that look human but have "hairy tails." "If history lie not, women have conceived by drills [baboons]." Locke continues: "We have reason to think this not impossible since mules . . . from the mixture of an ass and a mare . . . are so frequent in the world."[6]

For Locke, Africans are, at least potentially, the offspring of sexual liaisons between humans and monkeys. What to do with those with different skin colors and hair textures whose nature might lean closer to that of monkeys than that of Europeans? For Locke, that is a "new question" for a world being made modern.[7] And this question was in no way merely philosophical speculation but was intentionally etched onto America's collective consciousness and cultural common sense. If you ever wondered why people who shared European and African descent were referred to as "mulatto"—the Spanish word for mule—this is it. The very word our forebears used to refer to interracial community members signified their conviction that interracial meant less than fully human and implies that interracial sex itself is a moral crime akin to bestiality.

And so it was that Greek thinkers like Plato and Aristotle first imagined a human hierarchy to justify slavery, segregation, and inequality within a democratic state. And as the Western world modernized, thinkers such as John Locke radicalized that hierarchy by racializing it, placing Europeans on top and Africans on the bottom.[8] This racialization did not ease or erase class distinctions within white society. Indeed, white supremacy would be designed to make class distinctions within white society deeper still.

Collectively, these philosophers helped Thomas Jefferson harmonize the ideologies of democracy and human equality with the realities of slavery and pervasive destitution in America. When Jefferson penned "All men are created equal," the assumptions of class distinctions, white supremacy, and slavery ran through each word. Political rhetoric regularly hides the true aims of political power players. Transparency is rarely the path to power, and the Revolutionary generation understood this. Despite the rhetoric of freedom, equality, and liberty for all, a nation divided along both economic and racial lines was by *design* from the very beginning. In both explicit and implicit ways, this was an essential aim of the founders' revolution. And they sincerely believed the aim of their work harmonized with the grain of the universe. Through their work, they believed history itself was progressing in a new and profound way.[9]

Through the Declaration of Independence, Jefferson placed the mask of equality on the face of white supremacy. Then, only a few years after the document's signing, Jefferson got to work penning *Notes on the State Virginia*, in which he is remarkably transparent with his racial ideologies. Jefferson wrote *Notes* to respond to questions posed by France's François Barbé-Marbois in 1780. *Notes* would be published in 1785, roughly nine years after the signing of the Declaration of Independence but two years before the Constitutional Convention. Jefferson organized his responses to Barbé-Marbois by topics with the goal of portraying Virginia as a preeminent example of Enlightened ideals while writing in a manner that allowed for mass consumption.

Jefferson could not discuss Virginia without writing about slavery. But in typical Jeffersonian fashion, he posed as a humanitarian by portraying slavery as a moral monstrosity. In *Notes*, Jefferson writes at length about emancipation, and his critiques of slavery prove nothing less than scathing. He shudders: "Indeed I tremble for my country when I reflect that God is just: that his justice cannot sleep for ever. . . . The Almighty has no attribute which can take side with us."[10] However, the more Jefferson bemoans slavery's barbarism and cruelty, the more he is compelled to sharpen white supremacy's racism to justify slavery's existence in America as a current political necessity. For Jefferson, slavery is a crime against both justice and nature, but its greatest victims are not the inferior race of the enslaved but the superior race of masters who must cruelly enforce it.

Despite slavery's long history in America, when Jefferson wrote *Notes* in the 1780s, slavery was much less entrenched than it would become in the nineteenth century when cotton became king.[11] In fact, when *Notes* was published in 1785, both the abolition of slavery and reparations were real possibilities, not utopian fantasies. In 1783, Belinda Sutton, who had been enslaved in the Royall house, won her case pursuing reparations, setting a precedent that racial justice need not wait.[12] And it is the reality of those possibilities that makes the timing and influence of *Notes* so tragic. In writing *Notes*, Jefferson entered into the fray on slavery's future by providing a bible of eighteenth-century perceptions of those whom America enslaved. From depraved Black sex, to sloth and dependence, to the inferiority of Black intelligence, *Notes* provides the racial lies and ideas that not only informed the Three-Fifths Compromise but that continue to uphold America's racial imagination today. Due, in part, to *Notes'* influence in securing slavery's future and shaping its afterlife, it is considered one of the most influential books colonial America ever produced.[13]

In "Query XIV" of *Notes*, Jefferson reveals the inner workings of his racial imagination. He provides the perfect frame for his conversation by imagining a future for Virginia without slavery *and* without the formerly enslaved. Jefferson was convinced that after slavery, an interracial Virginia was an impossibility, because after the horrors of slavery, an interracial Virginia would produce "convulsions which will probably never end but in the extermination of the one or the other race."[14] Running deeper than that prediction, Jefferson adds "objections . . . physical and moral," explicitly arguing for the racial hierarchy of white supremacy in a way that not only supported slavery in the present but ensured white supremacy long after slavery's shackles were shattered.

Jefferson begins by rooting African inferiority in notions of beauty. For Jefferson and many racist minds of his era, whiteness is beauty and Blackness is beauty's opposite. Everything related to the white body and its biology—such as hair, and even glands and kidneys—approaches physical perfection. Everything related to Black people's bodies and biology is beastly. "The circumstance of superior beauty," Jefferson notes, "is thought worthy attention in the propagation of our horses, dogs, and other domestic animals; why not in that of man?"[15]

Racist critiques of Black beauty encapsulate more than personal preferences and are never just skin-deep. They are political and cut to the bone. As Nell Irvin Painter reminds us in her brilliant book *The History of White People*, for racial theorists of Jefferson's era, "beauty and ugliness . . . led to different fates." White beauty personified human perfection and superiority—a perfection and superiority that characterized every aspect of white people and their civilization. Blackness personified humanity's debasement, and "inferior peoples' inferiority justified, even required, their enslavement and the use of despotism for their control."[16]

As Jefferson philosophizes about the enslaved, he moves from disparaging Black beauty to racist myths about Black sex. With a nod to his hero John Locke, Jefferson mythologizes that the orangutans' sexual desire is "uniformly . . . for the black women."[17] In the writings of Locke, Blackness is merely implied in the sexual intimacies between women and baboons. But Jefferson makes Blackness explicit in that coupling.

For the myth to perform precise political and social functions, such explicitness was demanded. Behind the dehumanizing mythology of Black women's ravenous sexual appetites that led to acts of bestiality was the pervasive reality of white men engaging in sex with the women they enslaved. Even in colonial America, sexual relationships transcended racial divides. But consistently, the context of white men's sex with Black women was the brutality of rape, not interracial intimacy. Enslavers' freedom to rape the women they enslaved was often considered a birthright. And it was a birthright with the potential to increase one's wealth through the children the sexual violence produced. By the time of the Civil War, it is estimated that as much as 80 percent of the enslaved population shared in the family line of their enslavers.[18]

Toward the end of "Query XIV," Jefferson becomes more direct regarding the fears that drove his writing. The greatest threat of Black female sexuality was found not in his fantasies about orangutans in the jungle but in the potential for interracial sex to corrupt white society's racial purity by "staining the blood" of the "master."[19] For Jefferson, such intermingling of blood represented a crime against the very laws of nature.

Every crime needs a criminal. By creating the myth of the sexually deviant Black woman, Jefferson and other racial theorists painted Black women as the villains rather than the victims of interracial sexual encounters. In Jefferson's racist view, a white republic simply could not survive in a nation whose darker vixens demanded sex from anything that moves. Such she-devils threatened to darken the white republic and denigrate its virtue and genius.[20] In future years, that fear would be labeled "miscegenation." Miscegenation named the pervasive fear, from Jefferson to today, that the white republic might become more like its Black people.[21]

For interracial sex in America to not call into question the nation's racial hierarchy, a rationalization was needed. And this is precisely what Jefferson's writing intentionally provides—vilifying Black women and the children they bore whose physical features were reminiscent of their oppressors. In doing so, Jefferson crafted a caricature that provided cover to both the reality of the enslavers' sexual violence and the possibility of humanizing interracial intimacy. For white supremacists, interracial children were not a sign of white perditions or Black equality; rather, they embodied, in the flesh, the threat that Black women's sexual desires posed to America's racial purity. Long before Reagan's infamous welfare queen, Jefferson's caricature of oversexed Black women sought to justify society's indifference toward Black women's agony and the misery of the families they mothered.

After demonizing the sexuality of Black women, Jefferson then sets his gaze on enslaved male sexuality. "They are more ardent after their female," Jefferson writes, "but love seems with them to be more an eager desire, than a tender delicate mixture of sentiment and sensation" common to white lovers.[22] For Jefferson, Black men may prove themselves energetic and exotic lovers in bed but are emotionally incapable of fulfilling the more meaningful roles of loving husbands and fathers.

Through such sentences, Jefferson helped create a racialized spectrum of sexual and family values that was central to white supremacy's racial hierarchy. At the spectrum's virtuous end resided pure white ladies of disciplined chastity and monogamy and white men whose sexual virility harmonized with the deeper virtues that made intimate family relationships possible. At the spectrum's carnal end resided Black women and men whose appetite for sex is insatiable but whose emotional maturity and desire for relational intimacy are nonexistent. The assertion that Black sexuality was driven by carnality rather than the deepest and most intimate forms of human connectedness enabled whites to claim that Black family bonds lacked a sacred essence. Black families were reduced to carnal sexuality run amok. When slave societies tore families asunder—husband from wife, parents from children—they often believed they committed no crime. The self-deception inherent in white supremacy's racialized spectrum of sexual virtue empowered enslaving societies to believe themselves the paragons of godly, family-oriented virtues while believing that those they enslaved were ridden with animalistic vices that demanded their bondage.

Myths about Black sexual depravity were integral to justifying the auction block. At the auction block, some Black women were sold as "breeders" for their ability to bear children. Some were sold as laborers for their ability to work the field or the house. But the highest prices went for the "fancies"— beautiful Black women whom white men used as sex slaves.[23] Time and again, when the auction block severed sacred Black family ties, Black people experienced total physical, emotional, and psychological breakdowns. In *Narrative of the Life and Adventures of Henry Bibb, an American Slave*, Bibb narrates the horrific scene he witnessed at an enslavers' auction:

> She pleaded for mercy in the name of God. But the child was torn from the arms of its mother amid the most heart-rending shrieks . . . while she was sacrificed to the highest bidder. In this way the sale was carried on from beginning to end. . . . And while bathing each other with tears of sorrow on the verge of their final separation, their eloquent appeals in prayer to the Most High seemed to cause an unpleasant sensation upon the ears of their tyrants, who ordered them to rise and make ready their limbs for the caffles.[24]

White society tried to not understand the horror their eyes saw and their ears heard because any honesty regarding the essential humanity of Black people and sacredness of Black family bonds threatened to sever the convictions that tied their racialized world together.

It is unclear how many orangutans opened up to Jefferson about their sexual preferences. What is clear is the cutting irony that one of America's earliest racial myths about the pathologies of Black sex and families, about lusty Black ladies and derelict Black dads, was penned by a man who took the bodies of those he enslaved and kept his own lover and children in bondage.[25] That irony, however, failed to prevent Jefferson's racial legends and logics about the pathologies of Black sexuality and families from shaping public policies ever after.

For Black abolitionist David Walker, the monstrosity of such racist ideologies separated American slavery from its historical predecessors:

> I call upon the very tyrant himself, to show me a page of history, either sacred or profane, on which a verse can be found, which maintains that the Egyptians heaped the insupportable insult upon the children of Israel, by telling them that they were not of the human family. Can the whites deny this charge? Have they not, after having reduced us to the deplorable condition of slaves under their feet, held us up as descending originally from the tribes of Monkeys or Orang-Outangs? O! My God![26]

"Oh my God!" indeed.

The intersection of race and sexuality proved explosive, and we continue to live within the blast radius of Jefferson's racist caricatures. From slavery, through segregation, to today, caricatures of Black sex and Black families were deemed root causes for Black suffering and justified white indifference. The truth that white society sanctioned the raping and forceful breeding of the enslaved and the rending of sacred family bonds rarely led white people to question their supposed moral superiority. Instead, throughout American history, white society added insult to injury by assuming that the suffering that white supremacy produces was a symptom of Black people's moral inferiority—a just and true consequence of Black depravity.[27]

After deliberately denigrating Black beauty and demonizing Black sexuality, Jefferson writes a concise paragraph that ricochets between denigrating Black suffering, work ethic, and intelligence. He begins with Black people's alleged high pain tolerance. To numb the conscience of an entire slave society—from those wielding the master's whip, to those bidding at the auction block, to those who simply stood silent—Jefferson riffs on the fiction that Black people prove incapable of truly suffering. "Their griefs are transient," he writes. "Numberless afflictions . . . are less felt, and sooner forgotten."[28] Slavery demanded a cruel society. A cruel society demanded callousing white consciences. And callousing white consciences demanded dehumanizing Black suffering. What was necessary for cruelty, callousness, and dehumanization was creating a divide in white minds between the *poignancy* of white people's emotional and physical pain and the *impossibility* of Black people fully entering into the depths of human agony. So Jefferson begins stenciling this differentiation into white America's psyche.

During slavery and after, the myth of Black people's pain tolerance made white hearts hard to the soul-rending cries of Black people. Even into the nineteenth and twentieth centuries, American medicine and science often perpetuated the myth.[29] It became so ingrained that by 2011, the study "Racism and the Empathy for Pain on Our Skin" revealed that when white people witnessed Black people in pain, white people's neurological responses failed to register any empathy at all. It was as if, in white minds, Black pain was not the pain of a fellow human. Believing Black people cannot feel pain never increased the pain tolerance of Black people. But that racist belief did increase the ability of white people to inflict and tolerate the excruciating pain Black people were forced to bear. And that, after all, was the aim of the racist lie.

Nothing demands reparations more than the crimes that envelop the auction block. What happened at that block was a crime against humanity. It displayed more than the theft of labor and the corruption of white consciences. The auction block displayed the perversion of an entire society, which was inherently complicit in the attempt to transform vulnerable people into valuable pieces of private property. The nature of the crime demands a commitment to a Reparative Age—demands repentance, repayment, and repair. Anything less than this represents an inadequate understanding of what is required to pursue a more perfect union in a nation with so haunted a history.

As Jefferson continues the same paragraph in *Notes on the State of Virginia*, he begins expanding the encyclopedia of racial folklore and ties Black pain tolerance to Black sloth and then Black sloth to a lack of Black brilliance. In so doing, Jefferson hints that slavery is indeed a positive good. Just as Black people were possessed by a deep love for carnal sex, they also were possessed by a "disposition to sleep." "An animal whose body is at rest," Jefferson writes, "and who does not reflect, must be disposed to sleep of course." Comparing Africans to sleepy animals is not sufficient for Jefferson, and so he begins to further dissect Black brilliance. "Comparing them by their faculties of memory, reason, and imagination," Jefferson writes, "it appears to me, that in memory they are equal to the whites, in reason much inferior. . . . In imagination they are dull, tasteless, and anomalous." It seems for Jefferson that since enslaved people's "reason is inferior" and "nature has been less bountiful to them in the endowments of the head,"[30] the sweat of the brow is the best way for them to bless the world. Here is how Jefferson's logic works: as the slave driver's whip is unleashed on people who are unable to suffer but who seemingly need motivation to work, the slave driver becomes an essential instrument of industry required to unleash the potential of Black people and help the nation flourish.

Of course, Jefferson was quite aware of the abundant, well-known examples of Black brilliance of his day. But no such evidence debunked myths about Black people's inferior intellect for Jefferson. Instead, believing in Black people's inherent inferiority simply made evidence of Black brilliance and wisdom easy to dismiss. And this was particularly true when it came to Black perspectives on how to remedy their plight in America. Perhaps the best example of how Jefferson's white supremacy made him immune to evidence of Black equality is his correspondence with Benjamin Banneker. Banneker was a Black freeman who labored as a mathematician and astronomer. He desired to use his brilliance as leverage for the liberation and benefit of Black people. He believed slavery's future, at least in part, hinged on proving the intellectual equality of Black people, and he committed himself to making as many white converts as possible. And though he made many converts, Jefferson was not among them.

On Friday, August 19, 1791, Banneker wrote from Maryland to Jefferson in Philadelphia. In a heartfelt letter that reads with all the intensity of someone in a holy struggle for the soul of his nation, Banneker solicits Jefferson to aid the suffering of "a race of Beings who . . . have long been considered rather as brutish than human, and Scarcely capable of mental endowments." "Lend your aid," Banneker beseeches, and "readily embrace every opportunity to eradicate that train of absurd and false ideas and opinions." To buttress his argument, Banneker not only uses Jefferson's own words that "all people are created equal" but moves further to provide evidence of Black brilliance by including an almanac he authored. Through argument and evidence, he fights not only for Jefferson's mind and emotions but also for human connection as he urges Jefferson and his fellow enslavers onto the path of salvation by renouncing their racism and standing in solidarity with the enslaved. "Put your souls," Banneker pleads, "in their souls' stead."[31] Banneker's vulnerability is breathtaking.

Though Jefferson proved hospitable, he also proved remarkably hard-hearted. Despite holding evidence of Black brilliance in hand, Jefferson chose to deny the evidence, accused Banneker of plagiarism, and continued to embrace white supremacy over Black equality. Jefferson's indifference to Banneker's brilliance is but a fruit of Jefferson's more deeply rooted indifference to Black people's intrinsic humanity. From Jefferson to today, white supremacy often makes its hosts not only impervious to Black people's suffering but also immune to every tangible evidence of Black humanity's equality.[32]

As Jefferson brings "Query XIV" to an end, he sets the stage for the debates of white supremacy and Black inferiority for more than the next two centuries. Jefferson concludes: "I advance it therefore as a suspicion only, that the blacks, whether originally a distinct race, or made distinct by time and circumstances, are inferior to the whites in the endowments both of body and mind."[33] For Jefferson, as for the vast majority of Enlightened thinkers of his age and the ages to come, the belief in the innate inferiority of Black people provided the lynchpin of white supremacy's dogma. Jefferson's indelible shaping of the racial lies and legends that made America not only justified the racial injustice of slavery but also provided the critical ingredients of slavery's afterlife. "Query XIV" is a small pill. Much of his work is accomplished in a few brief paragraphs. But they are paragraphs that prove once again Jefferson's ability to fashion the American imagination with only a few words.

Four years after publishing *Notes on the State of Virginia* and seven years after the death of his wife, Jefferson entered into a sexual liaison with Sally Hemings, whom he enslaved till the day he died. It is unlikely that Sally represented Jefferson's first sexual foray with someone he enslaved. As a young man, he wrote a friend about enslavers' ability to live contentedly as bachelors due to their sexual relationships with those they enslave.[34]

But Hemings was unique. She entered the Jefferson household through his marriage to Martha. She was Martha's enslaved half sister and bore a striking resemblance to her. Since Jefferson and Hemings's relationship was shrouded in secrecy, it is impossible to know how to characterize it. But for four decades, dating from around 1789 to July 4, 1826, Jefferson lived out the reality of the interracial sex he demonized with such vigor. At the beginning of their relationship, Hemings was fourteen and Jefferson was forty-four. Through their liaison, Jefferson's worst fears in *Notes* took on flesh in his own family. He fathered six children with the enslaved Hemings, four of whom—William Beverly Hemings, Harriet Hemings, James Madison Hemings, and Thomas Eston Hemings—lived into adulthood. They were a talented clan of artisans and artists. Two of Jefferson's children fled for their freedom. Two stayed, living as enslaved people along with their mother until Jefferson's death.

After fathering an interracial family, Jefferson refused to risk the intimacy that would complicate the master-father dichotomy with his children or challenge his notions of Black inferiority. "He was not," reported his son, James Madison Hemings, "in the habit of showing partiality or fatherly affection to us children. We were the only children of his by a slave woman."[35] With such indifference to his own flesh and blood, perhaps it is unsurprising that Jefferson never publicly recanted his fear that mixture "stain[s] the blood of [the] master."[36] By the time of his passing, Jefferson had enslaved his lover and children for a cumulative 125 years. Jefferson was the master of Monticello. His lover and children were the help—for they lacked the pure blood the Jefferson name required.

In addition to reading *Notes* in relation to the Hemings family, we must also wrestle with *Notes* in relation to the Declaration of Independence, the Founding Fathers, and the trajectory of white supremacy in America. First, it is critical to repeat that Jefferson never perceived any conflicts between the

Declaration of Independence's ideology of equality and the racist convictions in *Notes*. Neither Jefferson, nor the vast majority of Enlightenment thinkers, ever placed Africans into their equations of human equality.

On August 25, 1814, Jefferson penned a reply to Edward Coles, who had invited Jefferson into his work to abolish slavery, starting with freeing the enslaved of Monticello and relocating them to present-day Illinois. Though Jefferson wished Coles's experiment success, he demurred from participating. Jefferson professed hope for a future emancipation. "Time," Jefferson said, "has only served to give . . . stronger root" to his convictions concerning the need for emancipation expressed in *Notes*. But time had also fortified Jefferson's white supremacy. The enslaved, Jefferson wrote,

> are by their habits rendered as incapable as children of taking care of themselves and are extinguished promptly whenever industry is necessary. . . . They are pests in society by their idleness, and the depredations to which this leads them. Their amalgamation with the other color produces a degradation to which no lover of his country, no lover of excellence in the human character can innocently consent.[37]

White supremacy made nearly all convictions of equality that Jefferson expressed in the Declaration of Independence impotent. Yet, Jefferson's notions of equality rarely robbed any convictions of white supremacy expressed in *Notes* of their power.

Second, and equally problematic, though some Founding Fathers opposed slavery, *Notes* is one of the most significant documents critiquing slavery to be published by any of the Founding Fathers.[38] America's Founders were so enmeshed in white supremacy that Jefferson's writings passed as progressive racial ideas.[39] Jefferson would provide the text to his friend John Adams. When Adams, one of America's most ardent antislavery Founders, posed for his portrait at his writing desk, he had a quill and paper in hand, and Jefferson's *Notes on the State of Virginia* prominently on display to the side.[40] Adams wrote to Jefferson regarding *Notes*: "I thank you kindly for your Book. It is our Meditation all the Day long. . . . I think it will do its Author and his Country great Honour. The Passages upon Slavery, are worth Diamonds."[41]

When it comes to white supremacy's future, the Constitutional Convention was held two years following the publication of *Notes on the State of Virginia*. All racial compromises within the convention happened on the grounds of white supremacy. The Three-Fifths Compromise not only wove white supremacy into America's DNA but also established the precedent for the future racial compromises America would make rejecting Black humanity, dignity, and equality. Instead of shaping a nation of freedom, liberty, and justice for *all*, the convention stripped Blacks of any leverage in their fight for justice and equality.[42]

In 1790, after the Constitution was ratified, the debate on slavery first came to the congressional floor. When the debate arrived, the spokesmen for the South stood ready with Jefferson's book in hand. Representative James Jackson of Georgia highlighted for his colleagues Jefferson's belief that if freed, Black people would represent the greatest threat that white America had ever known. Following Jackson, South Carolina's William Loughton Smith highlighted Jefferson's fear that beyond the physical threat Black people represented was the preeminent threat that emancipation was the path to "stain the blood of the whites."[43] And who could argue with the most famous advocate of equality?

Jackson's and Smith's arguments revealed the precision of Jefferson's marksmanship. For Jefferson penned *Notes* to deepen white supremacy's hold on America's moral imagination and position his ideas not only to shape the terms of America's racial debates but also to shape what was and is considered politically possible on American soil. The more entrenched white supremacy became, the more impossible and utopian it was deemed for America's public policies to even *aim* to realize racial equality.

After *Notes*, Jefferson quieted his call for the abolition of slavery. "As it is," he later wrote, "*we* have the *wolf* by the ears, and we can neither hold him, nor safely let him go. Justice is in one scale, and self-preservation in the other."[44] That Jefferson saw the enslaved, rather than the enslavers, as the wolf, displays just how perversely he read the nation's predicament and who posed the dangers to the republic's future following emancipation.

As the years passed, Jefferson moved into a more philosophical indifference and refused any meaningful pursuit of liberty for the enslaved. He developed a two-step dance to avoid personal responsibility. The first step placed the blame for slavery on the enslaving ancestors, and the next step deferred the responsibility for emancipation to generations yet to come. Like many in white America, Jefferson saw himself as victimized by the responsibilities stemming from his racial inheritance, yet he held high hopes for racial justice in a future generation.[45] Unlike others, Jefferson systematized his thinking to absolve himself of accountability to work for racial justice in the present.

Step 1: In a letter to James Madison, the father of the Constitution and Bill of Rights, Jefferson wrote: "I set out on this ground, which I suppose to be self-evident, *'that the earth belongs . . . to the living'*: that the dead have neither powers nor rights over it." The bounties of the earth flow naturally to the next generation, and "that generation receives it clear of the debts and encumbrances."[46] Jefferson desired to cut the cords between the sins of the past and the responsibilities of the present—to inherit the plunder and disinherit any accountability to the plundered.[47]

White America today is perhaps less philosophical than Jefferson. But what we often hold in common with him is our continuing to claim the right to inherit the privileges that slavery and its vestiges produced, while rejecting reparations to those who paid the highest price for our nation's prosperity. Claiming inheritance and rejecting reparations shows just how much today's racial logic shares with that of our slaveholding forefathers.

Step 2: Despite rejecting responsibility, Jefferson comforted himself in the self-deception that a future generation would be better positioned to realize racial justice than his own. "With one foot in the grave, and the other uplifted to follow it," he wrote to Francis Wright regarding abolition in the summer of 1825, "the march of events has not been such as to render its completion practicable within the limits of time allotted to me; and I leave its accomplishment as the work of another generation. And I am cheered . . ."[48]

This is typical Jefferson. Yet, the truth was, time itself was running in an ominous direction. When racial injustice runs rampant, time compounds rather than simplifies the problems. Despite his posturing, Jefferson understood this in 1825. As mentioned earlier, Jefferson wrote extensively on emancipation in *Notes*. Since he considered emancipation exclusively through the logic of white supremacy, like many aristocrats in America, he imagined emancipation as the trickiest business imaginable. From *Notes* through his final writings on the subject, Jefferson embraced a vision of a gradual emancipation framed by two demands: *compensating enslavers* and *colonizing the freed*.

Details matter. And what is critical to understand about Jefferson's framework for emancipation is its intentional design. Taken together, compensation and colonization acted as barriers, not practical pathways, to emancipation in America.[49] They were nearly as impossible to implement as they were to square with justice. Jefferson was not a political dunce. He was a genius. By supporting an impossible schematic for emancipation—a schematic that got more costly every year—Jefferson's proposal secured the shackles of those who lived at the end of Monticello's lash. Compensating enslavers embodied the perversity of reparations in reverse. However, such perverse reparations troubled the Jeffersonian imagination so little that he felt no need to justify it.

In 1824, Jefferson put pen to paper to calculate the cost of emancipating and expatriating America's 1.5 million slaves over the course of twenty-five years. He estimated the costs at $900 million, which made it "impossible to look at this question a second time."[50] Over and over again, Jefferson's sentimentalism freed him to dream of a day when slavery would end without feeling compelled to stand in solidarity with those who were ready to pay the price such a transformation entailed. Like many other enslavers, Jefferson professed a desire to end slavery but also labored to ensure that emancipation would never happen in his lifetime.

Underneath his sentimentalism, the truth was that Jefferson possessed an insatiable need to dominate. If any moment revealed how deep that need ran, it was when the repeal of the Missouri Compromise threatened to tear the Union asunder. Some demanded freedom on Missouri's soil, others slavery, and still others championed popular sovereignty that allowed new states to determine slavery's destiny within their borders. Rather than taking sides, Jefferson demanded that the federal government stand down in the fight over slavery's future. In a letter to a friend, Jefferson counseled patience "with our brethren" despite their overreach in Missouri. Yet, the time of patience was also a time of preparation. If forced to choose between secession and accepting federal fingerprints to limit the extension of slavery, Jefferson warned, "between these two evils when we must make a choice, *there can be no hesitation.*" Jefferson would rather see the nation torn in two than witness the federal government attain the power to stop the spread of slavery or liberate those who lived under the lash. When slavery and patriotism threatened to diverge, Jefferson sided with the venerated rights of enslavers rather than the sacredness of the Union.[51]

Missouri epitomized the nature of America's racial negotiations between the Revolutionary and Civil Wars—negotiations that continually broke toward the perpetuation and entrenchment of keeping people in shackles. The system that Jefferson and the founding generation put into motion brokered no compromise with white supremacy. From the Three-Fifths Compromise to 1857's *Dred Scott* decision, time and again, the ideologies of liberty and justice for all bowed to the preservation of white power.[52] Of all the compromises America brokered, none proved more repellent to Frederick Douglass than the Fugitive Slave Act of 1850. Looking back, Douglass wrote, "We had been drugged nearly to death by proslavery compromises."[53] The Fugitive Slave Act lit a fuse that would burn for a decade before blowing the nation apart.

Little more than six months after he penned his lament on federal interventions into Missouri affairs, Thomas Jefferson drew his last breath on July 4, 1826.[54] Pulitzer Prize–winning historian Joseph Ellis notes the significant irony of Jefferson's final moments. Just as Jefferson's first memory was of being carried on a pillow by someone his family enslaved, his last request was answered by Burwell Colbert, his personal butler and the younger brother of Sally Hemings. Colbert understood Jefferson's desire and adjusted the pillow Jefferson was lying on to ease his suffering. Pillows and slavery provide fitting bookends to a life whose luxuries were derived from human bondage. And, as I will discuss in detail in Part IV's proposal for reparations, it is in the tension between those two bookends—between America's richest white families and an entire race of people those families enslaved—that the nation Jefferson helped midwife into existence still lives, moves, and has its being.[55]

It is difficult to grasp the full impact of Jefferson on America's racial imagination. As the dominant and most influential thinker of the era, Jefferson helped harmonize the racist instincts of the Founding Fathers with political pronouncements that centered on liberty, equality, and justice. The European Enlightenment based its political vision on the assumptions of white supremacy and Black inferiority. And Jefferson helped Enlightened racism secure a home in the American Revolution through his myths about Black sex and families, Black sloth, and Black intelligence.

In the early nineteenth century, David Walker provided some of Black America's most searing analysis of Jefferson as he lamented: "Mr. Jefferson's remarks respecting us, have sunk deep into the hearts of millions of the whites, and never will be removed this side of eternity."[56] Walker understood that in colonial America, as well as the America to come, racist fictions from leaders such as Jefferson carried the weight of racial facts. Walker understood that Jefferson's power to influence was rare in world history and what it meant that Jefferson chose to unleash his most persuasive powers to reinforce racial distinctions rather than unwrite them. Walker understood that once Jefferson's racist lies were written onto white hearts, they would prove nearly impossible to erase.

But more than that, Walker understood a central truth that we must reclaim. And that is that Jefferson received repeated opportunities to choose a different path—and so did America. Yet Jefferson ignored, dismissed, and devalued every Black person in America who sought to entice him to reject his racism. From Benjamin Banneker, the poet Phillis Wheatley, and the essayist Ignatius Sancho, to the Hemings side of his own family, no evidence of Black equality challenged his commitment to enforcing white supremacy. The pleas and arguments of white abolitionists like Anthony Benezet, Edward Coles, and Timothy Dwight IV fared no better. Jefferson's white supremacy made resistance to racial justice a central legacy of his life and of the nation he helped birth.

If David Walker helped provide Black America's analysis of Jefferson's legacy, decades later, in 1857, Chief Justice Roger B. Taney provided white America's definitive analysis in the majority opinion of *Dred Scott v. Sandford*. Scott sued for his freedom and the freedom of his family because he had lived for four years in Illinois and Wisconsin, where slavery was illegal. Justice Taney made explicit what Jefferson's Declaration only implied. With stark clarity, Justice Taney wrote: "The men who framed the Declaration of Independence and established the State Constitutions and Governments . . . show that a perpetual and impassable barrier was intended to be erected between the white race and the one which they had reduced to slavery in a manner too plain to be mistaken." The Founders carved a "stigma of the deepest degradation . . . upon the whole race." Rather than dodge, downplay, or deny, these realities "proved too clear for dispute." Black Americans, whether freed or slaves, "had for more than a century before been regarded as beings of an inferior order . . . so far inferior that they had no rights which the white man was bound to respect." For Justice Taney, whether the case's technicalities provided Scott a solid legal argument mattered not at all. The tragedy of Dred Scott's verdict was not that it was unfaithful to our Founding Fathers' intentions. The tragedy was how well it encapsulated the Founders' designs.

By inscribing racist thought into the American mind, Jefferson narrowed the spectrum of democratic possibilities to those that harmonized with white supremacy. By doing so, Jefferson not only helped secure slavery for decades to come but also, more importantly, ingrained white supremacy in America's DNA, providing a racial ideology that would long outlive slavery. America's vision of equality slowly advanced. But the more expansive the vision of equality grew, the more in conflict with the original author of American equality and his intentions it became. After the ideology of equality crossed the color line in the popular imagination, Jefferson continued to receive a lion's share of credit for a concept so noble it apparently possessed the power to realize the exact opposite of its original political aims.

When the American experiment could no longer bear the yoke of slavery, the children and grandchildren of the Revolutionary generation paid for their sins in flesh and blood. In the article "Who Divided This House?," John Hope Franklin writes of the lesson the Revolutionary generation left for those who follow in their footsteps. "If there is one lesson we should learn from this, it is to face up to our staggering problems now and not put them off for some unknowing, innocent generation. It would cost infinitely more to solve the problems we leave than it would cost us to face up to them and solve them now."[57]

3

Abraham Lincoln

The Emancipator and His Two Proclamations

> In most respects Lincoln's attitude toward Negroes was that of
> other average white Americans. He did not really know them. . . .
> He saw black folk from afar as comical, shiftless, and ugly. But he
> was a man of deep sympathy. . . . When as President he came to
> know Negroes as men, he dared to treat them as such.
>
> —W. E. B. Du Bois, "Abraham Lincoln and the Negro," 1922

In Thomas Jefferson's final month as president in 1809, Abraham Lincoln was born into an impoverished family in a log cabin in the backwoods of Kentucky. Over the coming decades, the house the Founders divided began rapidly deteriorating. In 1861, it would fall to Lincoln to face the reckoning the Revolutionary generation had set in motion.

Lincoln was not the most obvious choice for such a momentous challenge. His background was unremarkable. His political history proved a bewildering hodgepodge. Lincoln's political commitments were antislavery, *antiabolition*, and deeply shaped by anti-Black racism. Though in time he earned the respect of Black America, neither his candidacy nor much of his presidency inspired confidence among the Black masses or their leaders. However, as became clear in time, there was more to Lincoln than what appeared on his gangly surface. The traumatic times in which he lived revealed what ordinary times may not have uncovered. Grasping Lincoln's impact on the trajectory of racial justice in America demands careful attention to his leadership in crafting not one but two proclamations: the Emancipation Proclamation and the Proclamation of Amnesty and Reconstruction. One ended chattel slavery in America. The other left the racial hierarchy in the South intact and laid the groundwork for perpetuating Black poverty and disenfranchisement for the next one hundred years. Just as Jefferson's legacy demands reparations, so too does Lincoln's.

Before delving into Lincoln's leadership, perhaps an overview of the lay of the land is in order. From Andrew Jackson's Indian Removal Act and Trail of Tears to the expansionist policies and machinations of enslavers, the United States by the early 1850s stood on the brink of disunion. As Lincoln came of age, white supremacy placed America at war with itself. Among both rich and poor, white supremacy was endemic in America. Yet the North and the South envisioned two different and irreconcilable racial and economic futures. The North envisioned a segregated society and an economy in which every worker was free to use their labor to improve their lot in life. But the Southern oligarchy insisted slavery shape society's every aspect. Despite the similarities in Black folks' place in the equation, the differing visions between free and slave labor placed the Northern and Southern trains on a collision course, and each train was picking up speed.

By the time of Southern secession, more millionaires per capita called Mississippi home than any other state in the Union and seven of the eight wealthiest states were located in the South.[1] Cotton was king, but cotton was not a king that was benevolent to all. In his masterpiece *Black Reconstruction in America*, W. E. B. Du Bois estimates that while four million Black people lived in chains, the vast majority of the South's five million white people lived in squalor. The moneymakers' club was a small oligarchy limited to about, according to Du Bois, eight thousand planters. The planter class shaped everything in Southern culture—politics, education, economics, religion—and increasingly held considerable power at the national level. "On the eve of the Civil War," writes James M. McPherson, "plantation agriculture was more profitable, slavery more entrenched, slave owners more prosperous, and the 'Slave Power' more dominant within the South, if not in the nation at large, than it had ever been."[2] In Southern states, the addiction to the enslaving way of life grew deeper with every passing year.

Enslaved people in the South learned to look northward for freedom land. If the North was Black folks' heaven, it was also a reminder of how thin the veil between heaven and hell was. "Canaan was a strange place," writes Vincent Harding:

> The land created in songs and dreams of black hope in the South bore little resemblance to the cold and disappointing realities developing in the states of the North. . . . The demise of legal slavery in the North had actually ripped the mask from the . . . self-righteous white racism, rapacious economic greed, and deep-seated, irrational fear of blackness.[3]

Prior to and following the war, the North's anti-Black hatred proved nearly equal to their Southern brethren's. A free Black man said it simply: "This northern freedom is nothing but a nickname for northern slavery."[4]

Rather than slavery, Black Laws laid the racist train lines in the North. Prefiguring aspects of the Jim Crow South, the Black Laws of Northern states inverted the Bill of Rights and segregated everything: housing, entertainment, religious worship, education, voting booths, labor laws, criminal justice systems, transportation, orphanages, and health care. Northern segregation extended from the land of the living to the cemeteries that entombed the dead.[5] Midwestern states made Black Americans' entrance across their borders a crime. The typical reception of Black people in the Midwest was emblazoned into the name of a piece of Illinois legislation: Act to Prevent Free Negroes into this State.[6]

Anti-Black racism was also the law in the Northeast. In *Force and Freedom*, Kellie Carter Jackson examines Philadelphia's racial atmosphere. "The 'city of brotherly love,'" she writes, "experienced seven major antiblack and anti-abolitionist riots over the course of the 1830s and 1840s."[7] A full fifty years after Pennsylvania embraced the Gradual Abolition Act of 1780 to end slavery in the state, Philadelphia was no haven for Black America but instead a dangerous mix of abolitionist allies and racist vigilantes.

In New York City, whose wealth was derived from cotton, Mayor Fernando Wood recommended joining the South in secession. It was this economic self-interest and racial vitriol that made the New York riots of 1863 possible. The spark that lit the explosion was the Emancipation Proclamation and Lincoln's decision to inaugurate a draft. What started as an attack on a conscription office devolved into a race to kill Black people as cruelly as possible and destroy their property. Abolitionist Mattie Griffith recalled the horror: "A child of 3 years of age was thrown from a 4th story window and instantly killed. A woman . . . was set upon and beat with her tender baby in her arms. . . . Children were torn from their mothers' embrace and their brains blown out in the very face of the afflicted mother. Men were burnt by slow fires."[8] From Black Laws to an atmosphere ripe for racialized riots and mass murder, the train tracks of white supremacy in the North, as in the South, were made of steel.

Yet, to say America was united in its white supremacy and racial violence in no way suggests that white supremacy led to Black submission. Inspired by the successful Black Haitian Revolution from 1791 to 1804, revolution was brewing in Black America. Gabriel Prosser led a revolt in Richmond, Virginia, in 1800; Denmark Vesey led one in Charleston, South Carolina, in 1822; and perhaps the most famous of all was Nat Turner's Revolt in Southampton

County, Virginia, in 1831. Black protest raged, and Black people refused to submit to their captivity. On an annual basis, nearly fifty thousand broke their chains of bondage.[9] Despite having the chips stacked against them, mothers and fathers, sisters and brothers continued to risk everything and gambled their lives for but a taste of freedom.

The Black fight for freedom in the South led to radical acts of solidarity in the North. In oppressed Black communities in the North, civil disobedience was written in the blood of slave catchers. "The only way to make the Fugitive Slave Law a dead letter," mused Frederick Douglass to an audience in Pittsburgh, "is to make half a dozen or more dead kidnappers."[10] And kill slave catchers they did. The effectiveness of the Fugitive Slave Act, the specific law upon which white union depended, crumpled as Black defiance in both the North and the South hastened a national reckoning.

President Lincoln received this powder keg of a nation as he traveled from Illinois to Washington, DC. But what type of leader was America getting in President Lincoln to see her through the days of disaster? Lincoln was both a gentle and hardscrabble man, or, in the more famous words of Carl Sandburg, a man made of "both steel and velvet."[11] Yet, neither the struggle to survive in a log cabin on Kentucky's frontier nor the antislavery leaning of his family made Lincoln immune to anti-Black racism and white supremacy's seduction.

Unlike Jefferson, the education Lincoln received for his future calling was homespun. He was a "constant and . . . stubborn" reader who learned the power of words and how to employ them largely by reading and rereading Scripture and Shakespeare. Often lacking paper to rehearse the lines of these masterpieces, he instead penciled them onto pieces of scrap wood. When the pencil lead eventually made the wood illegible, he shaved the wood and started again.[12] Lincoln proved to be a lifelong learner. Through an education that began with scrap wood, Scripture, and Shakespeare, Lincoln learned to etch words and ideas into the souls and minds of Americans with simplicity, brevity, and grace.

Lincoln was a lawyer by trade. In particular ways, his mind was remarkably legalistic. And it was legalism that often pitted him against both the demands of justice and the Black and white abolitionists who fought for its realization. More than most men, Lincoln needed intellectual and moral surety to dictate his actions. In his early years, one of the few things Lincoln found surety in was the Constitution. Abolitionists disagreed. William Lloyd Garrison called the Constitution "the most subtle and atrocious compromise ever made to gratify power and selfishness! . . . a libel on Democracy."[13] Frederick Douglass was more moderate but still demanded that the document mature. He believed the Constitution possessed the potential to be an antiracist document if it were rightly amended to align the document's soul and structure with its preamble's promise to "form a more perfect Union, establish Justice, insure domestic Tranquility."[14]

Lincoln, on the other hand, believed the document embodied perfection without the need to amend its Three-Fifths Compromise or fugitive slave clauses. Instead, Lincoln thought it "better to habituate ourselves to think of it as unalterable. It can scarcely be better than it is."[15] And so Lincoln worked with the law as if it were written in stone and attempted to find loopholes that harmonized the letters of the law with the demands of justice. Such stances took remarkable moral flexibility.

In 1854, Lincoln gave a speech in Peoria, Illinois, responding to the Kansas-Nebraska Act that extended slavery into new territory. Lincoln looked toward the Revolutionary generation, and Jefferson in particular, for leadership clues on how to bend morality without breaking it: "The plain unmistakable spirit of that age, towards slavery," he declared, "was hostility to the PRINCIPLE, and toleration, ONLY BY NECESSITY."[16] Lincoln's vision simply never harmonized with the facts.[17] But it did provide a paradigm through which Lincoln operated until the final years of his life. For Lincoln, "toleration by necessity" translated to "toleration by any means necessary," as too often the law's letters proved more powerful for Lincoln than justice's demands. Following in the footsteps of Jefferson and the Revolutionary generation, Lincoln continued to place his faith in the deadly political art of deferring racial justice even as the crisis threatened to tear the Union asunder.

"My mind is like a piece of steel, very hard to scratch anything on it," Lincoln admitted, and then with a smirk added, "and almost impossible after you get it there to rub it out."[18] If in time Lincoln's steadfast nature garnered worthy and lavish praise, during the Civil War the agonizingly slow pace of writing principles on the steel of Lincoln's mind garnered equally worthy and scathing criticism. Until a principle was written on Lincoln's mind with clarity, it was a principle prone to be compromised whenever compromise was convenient.

Wednesday, May 3, 1837, was one such occasion. As Illinois's winter gave way to spring, Lincoln, in his late twenties, was an emerging state legislator in the Whig Party. He and a colleague wrote a remarkable sentence denouncing slavery: "The institution is founded on both injustice and bad policy." Yet, the authors were not done until they denounced abolition with equal vigor. "The promulgation of abolition doctrines," they wrote, "tends rather . . . to increase than abate [slavery's] evils."[19] Despite its thin opposition to slavery, Lincoln's Illinois was ardently antiabolitionist. Indeed, only six months after Lincoln's peculiar proclamation, the radical abolitionist Elijah Lovejoy was murdered in Alton, Illinois, on November 7. Winter had returned to Illinois. Yet, the blood of the martyr left Lincoln largely unmoved in his ideological commitments, and he continued to oppose abolition even as Lovejoy's murder shook the nation.[20]

The compromises continued. Ten years later in 1847, as Lincoln was making his living as a lawyer, he proved ready to work to keep a family enslaved and prepared their sale to the cruelties of the Deep South.[21] Everyone needs to make their nickel, and Lincoln proved ready to help enslave a family to pay his bills.

One last example of shameful compromise comes from Lincoln's days as a US Congressman, when he authored legislation that called for both abolition of slavery in the nation's capital *and* honoring the Fugitive Slave Act that reenslaved people whose thirst for freedom led them to risk life and limb. Proposing to return to enslavement those who, like Frederick Douglass, Sojourner Truth, and Harriet Tubman, risked everything for their freedom earned Lincoln the nickname among abolitionists "that slave hound from Illinois."[22] "I confess," wrote Lincoln to a friend, "I hate to see the poor creatures hunted down, and caught, and carried back to their stripes, and unrewarded toils, but I bite my lip and keep quiet."[23] From his days as a lawyer through his first years as president, slavery was a moral monstrosity Lincoln proved more than ready to do business with. As often as not, Lincoln followed in the footsteps of America's Founding Fathers and allowed the monster to dictate the terms.

His confidence in and commitment to an unaltered Constitution was complemented by his confidence in and commitment to white supremacy—and it is there where the roots of Lincoln's moral flexibility resided. In his famous debates with Stephen Douglas, Lincoln declared: "I am not, nor ever have been, in favor of bringing about in any way the social and political equality of white and black races." In words that rhymed with the racial logic of Southern segregationists of the twentieth century, Lincoln continued, "I am not nor ever have been in favor of making voters or jurors of the negroes, nor qualifying them to hold office, nor to intermarry with white people." Lincoln pushed further still: "There is a physical difference between the white and black races which *will forever* forbid the two races living together on terms of social and political equality. . . . While they do remain together, there must be the position of superior and inferior. I am as much as any other man in favor of having the superior position assigned to the white race."[24]

Here is the significance: Following the lead of racial theorists from both the North and the South, Lincoln believed the very pursuit of racial equality violated the dictates of nature in the same way that slavery violated the dictates of justice. Another way of saying that is that Lincoln seemed to fear the pursuit of equality as much as, if not more than, the institution of slavery.[25] For Lincoln, slavery was a tragic necessity within the current political and economic landscape. The pursuit of equality, on the other hand, went against the very grain of the universe. Such legalism, moral convictions, and compromises were the political gospel upon which Lincoln based nearly the entirety of his career.

Yet, while Lincoln peddled Negro inferiority, segregation, and the tolerance of slavery by any means necessary, the work of abolition was reaching a fever pitch, and a creative and interracial minority was ready to raise hell. They demanded immediate abolition and a different, more radical political gospel rooted in democracy, rooted in freedom, liberty, and justice for *all*. Beginning in the 1830s, a coalition of Black and white abolitionists laid their bodies on the line to realize a nonviolent end to American slavery. Perhaps the most prominent expression of this work was the American Anti-Slavery Society, founded by William Lloyd Garrison and Arthur Tappan in 1833. Frederick Douglass became one of the society's leading voices, and its work proved pivotal in the careers of future leaders like Sojourner Truth and Harriet Beecher Stowe.

The society's pursuit of abolition relied on a moral suasion rooted in religion and personal testimonies of slavery's horrors to stir the conscience of the nation in the hope that we would repent and renounce slavery.[26] And though Black and white abolitionists provided America every opportunity to embrace a nonviolent abolition, after two decades of struggle, no repentance was forthcoming. The number of the enslaved doubled, and no meaningful progress toward abolition was made.

Yet, rather than the failure of nonviolent abolition taming the movement, it radicalized it. After America rejected Garrison and Stowe and Douglass and Truth during their pacifist days, Black America believed the time for the politics of Nat Turner and John Brown had dawned. The abolitionist movement transitioned, in Kellie Carter Jackson's words, "from prayers to pistols."[27] In an atmosphere of ever deepening desperation, Black abolitionist

Henry Highland Garnet epitomized the emerging mood of the 1850s when he demanded that his people "USE *EVERY* MEANS, BOTH MORAL, IN-TELLECTUAL, AND PHYSICAL, THAT PROMISES SUCCESS." Neither he nor his people lusted for blood, yet "however much . . . all of us may desire it," Garnet lamented, "there is not much hope of redemption without the shedding of blood."[28] Many Black leaders, including Harriet Tubman and Frederick Douglass, came to believe that Garrison's nonviolence toward enslavers would never end the enslavers' violence against Black America. Through sacrifice and strife, abolitionists came to recognize that the sadistic nature of white supremacy refused to negotiate with, in Lincoln's hopeful rhetoric, "the better angels of our nature."[29]

When Lincoln won the presidential office, the question hanging in the air for abolitionists during the transition of power was if the incoming president would make any room for the enslaved and use the power of his office to place the nation on the path to freedom. For many, the introduction to Abraham Lincoln came through his first inaugural address. Lincoln highlighted his promises to protect slavery and his respect for states' rights. Lincoln aimed to soothe Southern anxieties and let Southern states know that "there has never been any reasonable cause for such apprehension." He quoted himself from previous speeches: "I have no purpose, directly or indirectly, to interfere with the institution of slavery in the States where it exists. I believe I have no right to do so, and I have no inclination to do so." At nearly every turn, Lincoln promised to tilt the nation toward a Southern way of life in an effort to preserve the Union. He doubled down on the status quo of slavery and the Fugitive Slave Act. Despite believing in the Constitution's perfection, he even promised to consider a constitutional amendment to provide slavery even more robust constitutional protections.

In the aftershock of Lincoln's soul-crushing speech, Frederick Douglass shook his head at America's inability to produce leadership with moral fiber. To express his resentment at the first inaugural's remarkably callous legalism, Douglass turned to one of Lincoln's favorite writers: Shakespeare. When it came to the enslaved, Douglass quipped, Lincoln "will have the pound of flesh, blood or no blood, be it more or less, a just pound or not." Douglass resurrected Lincoln's old nickname of "slave hound" and designated him as "the most dangerous advocate of slave-hunting and slave-catching in the land." Rather than protecting the pillaged, the first inaugural address's primary promise was greater protection for the "pirates," Douglass wrote to his readers.[30]

Beginning with the inauguration and while the nation's body count rose throughout much of his first term, Lincoln's moral compromises produced self-inflicted wounds instead of national unity. Lincoln drew too clear a line between presidential powers and personal convictions. His compromises elicited a profound personal toll. For years, slavery had made him "miserable." He spoke of needing to "crucify [his] feelings" to stay faithful to the Constitution and the Union.[31] Lincoln confided to a friend: "I am naturally anti-slavery. If slavery is not wrong, nothing is wrong. I cannot remember when I did not so think, and feel." Yet despite these convictions, he continued: "I aver that, to this day, I have done no official act in mere deference to my abstract judgment and feeling on slavery."[32] That slavery continued to slip into a gray zone of abstract judgment in Lincoln's mind reveals the transformation he still needed to undergo to become the person his moment in history demanded.

After the shots rang out from Fort Sumter, Lincoln's propensity to compromise on anything regarding slavery accelerated through his first years as a wartime president. As the war began to rage, the river of people fleeing to freedom behind Union lines widened. Generals David Hunter and John C. Frémont proved more radical than their commander in chief, as they provided haven for the enslaved and promised freedom to those who fled for their lives to Union lines. This enraged Lincoln. "The General should never have dragged the Negro into the war," he fumed. "It is a war for a great national object, and the Negro has nothing to do with it."[33]

Significantly, Lincoln's first move regarding Black liberation was to nullify his generals' emancipation orders and reinscribe the enslavement of those who risked their lives by placing themselves in Union hands. As with many people in the North, what was sacred for Lincoln was not Black life but white union. The Union was for Lincoln and the North what slavery was for the South: the greatest principle that every other principle must bend to protect.

As the war dragged into 1862 and the body count rose, Lincoln continued to surrender moral ground by resurrecting the call for reparations in reverse, leading the passing of a declaration that the United States stood ready to pay the South for the freedom of those they enslaved. If the South renounced secession and planned for the gradual abolition of slavery, the United States would "compensate for the inconveniences, public and private, produced by such change of system."[34] But in 1862, neither compensation nor compromise was on Southern minds.

As the North experienced defeat after defeat, abolitionists saw Lincoln's refusal to place abolition as the center point of his political calculus for the self-defeating madness it was. For Douglass, both morally and strategically, slavery provided "the grand hinge of American politics"[35] and "the pivot on which turns all the machinery of this tremendous war."[36] For Tubman, slavery was *the* snake that needed killing. "God won't let Master Lincoln beat the South till he does *the right thing*. He can do it by setting the Negroes free," she declared. "Master Lincoln, he's a great man, and I'm a poor Negro, but this Negro can tell Master Lincoln how to save money and young men." She provided a parable:

> Suppose that was an awful big snake down there, on the floor. He bite you. Folks all scared, because you die. You send for a doctor to cut the bite; but the snake, he rolled up there, and while the doctor doing it, he bite you again. The doctor dug out *that* bite; but while the doctor doing it, the snake, he bite you *again*. The doctor dug out *that* bite; but while the doctor doing it, the snake, he spring up and bite you again; so he *keep* doing it, till you kill *him*. That's what Master Lincoln ought to know.[37]

Yet, for all their disappointment in Lincoln's waffling, for all the wounds he inflicted on Black America, Black leaders possessed a mysterious clarity and confidence that history was changing our nation *and* its president. In the midst of his most fiery critiques, Douglass perceived a larger frame of reference than the failure of the moment. "Time and practice will improve the President as they improve other men," Douglass confessed. "He is tall and strong but he is not done growing, he grows as the nation grows."[38]

To grow into his moment, the president needed all the pain his Black critics could bring. But grow he did—slowly and painfully. As he and the nation waded through rivers of blood, Lincoln slowly embraced emancipation as a military rather than moral necessity. "Things have gone from bad to worse," Lincoln recalled later, "until I felt that we had reached the end of our rope on the plan of operations we had been pursuing; that we had about played our last card, and must change our tactics, or lose the game!"[39] Against his will, the goal of preserving the Union led Lincoln to consider how to construct and leverage a threat of emancipation to hasten the rebellion's end and restore the Union.

As the spring of 1862 gave way to summer, Lincoln believed the moment of military necessity had arrived and he made up his mind that it was time to change the rules of the game. On July 22, the Cabinet gathered and received the first reading of the Emancipation Proclamation. There would be conversation but not debate. Lincoln "had resolved upon this step, and had not called them together to ask their advice."[40] The first draft was brief. By restricting emancipation to states that refused to return to the Union by January 1, 1863, the proclamation was designed as a doomsday device that provided both the South and the border states the opportunity to restore the Union with slavery *intact*. The question that hung in the air on July 22, 1862, was not whether to make the Emancipation Proclamation public, but when. Of the collective wisdom in the room, Lincoln's closest ally, William Henry Seward's, proved the most persuasive—urging Lincoln to pocket the proclamation for the moment and make it public against a background of Union victories rather than the current context of defeat and despair.

In Lincoln's pocket, the Emancipation Proclamation evolved in tandem with his thinking that summer. Two ideas that he had long heralded and that can be traced to Jefferson took on a more central role in the proclamation: the need to *compensate* enslavers and *colonize* the formerly enslaved. By August 1862, compensation and colonization joined military necessity and the restriction of emancipation to rebellious states to complete the framework of Lincoln's thinking concerning the Emancipation Proclamation. The deadline of January 1, 1863, for reunification was left unchanged.

To lay the groundwork for the emancipation to come and the colonization to follow, in August Lincoln invited a delegation of Black Americans to the White House to win support for the wisdom of his colonization scheme.[41] It was the first such invitation in the mansion's history, and it proved as tragic as it was historic. Instead of providing Black wisdom a platform, Lincoln used the gathering to give a lecture saturated in the white supremacist logic of his age. "You and we are different races," he told the group. "This physical difference is a great disadvantage to us both, as I think your race suffers very greatly . . . *while ours suffers from your presence*. . . . If this be admitted, it affords a reason at least why we should be separated."[42]

A little over fifty years had passed since Jefferson held court in the Oval Office. Yet, as America's racial imagination evolved from the Revolutionary age to the era of the Civil War, white supremacy became only more entrenched.[43] Lincoln's meeting might have been the first of its kind, but it was certainly not the last gathering where white arrogance undermined the potential of an interracial alliance. If Lincoln was determined to provide the lecture, Douglass was determined to provide the last word. Regarding the meeting, Douglass wrote to his monthly readers: "Mr. Lincoln is quite a genuine representative of American prejudice and Negro hatred and far more concerned for the preservation of slavery . . . than for any sentiment of magnanimity or principle."[44]

As the proclamation evolved during the summer of 1862, the issue of slavery continued as a pawn in Lincoln's game for union. Lincoln made his stance abundantly clear, not only in private meetings and correspondence but also publicly and, perhaps most infamously, through his open letter to the *New York Tribune* only eight days after his meeting with the Black delegation on colonization. "My paramount object in this struggle *is* to save the Union, and it is *not* either to save or to destroy slavery," Lincoln wrote. Striving to be crystal clear, he continued: "If I could save the Union without freeing *any* slave, I would do it, and if I could save it by freeing *all* the slaves, I would do it; and if I could save it by freeing some and leaving others alone, I would also do that. What I do about slavery, and the colored race, I do because I believe it helps to save the Union."[45] With the proclamation on his mind and in his pocket, Lincoln knew the rules of the game would soon change. The aims of the war would not, at least not yet.[46]

As summer turned to fall, the tide of the war shifted. This shift provided the slight crack Lincoln needed to make his proclamation national policy. On September 17, 1862, with the Battle of Antietam still raging, Lincoln presented the latest draft to his Cabinet:

> I have . . . thought a great deal about the relation of the War to slavery. . . .
> I determined, as soon as [the Confederate army] should be driven out of Maryland, . . . to issue a Proclamation of Emancipation. . . . I said nothing to anyone; but I made the promise to myself, and (hesitating a little) to my Maker. . . . I have got you together to hear what I have written down. I do not wish your advice about the main matter—for that I have determined for myself.[47]

Lincoln was that rare man who could make a deal between himself and God and keep it even when the chips were high and the odds stacked against him. On September 22, 1862, the Emancipation Proclamation became public. The date for the South to return to the Union (with slavery intact) remained January 1, 1863, but the proclamation now included the provisos "that *the effort to colonize persons of African descent* . . . will be continued" and "that citizens of the United States who shall have remained loyal throughout the rebellion . . . *shall be compensated* for all losses by acts of the United States, *including the loss of slaves*" (emphasis mine).

After nearly a year and a half of war, Lincoln—on his own terms—placed the war and the Union itself on a collision course with slavery. As of September 22, Lincoln's deepest hope for the proclamation was that it would act as the threat that protected slavery by ending the war and not the fiat to begin abolition in America. By then, however, Lincoln likely understood that the emancipation would end the possibility of restoring the Union of old. The emancipation itself revealed the character of Lincoln's mixed commitments, but nonetheless, he committed.

During the 101 days between September 22, 1862, and January 1, 1863, deepening commitments were being etched onto the steel of Lincoln's mind, and there would be no rubbing them out. The meaning of the emancipation and the specific aim of the war evolved rapidly as the sparks of controversy surrounded Lincoln. Day by bloody day, his resolve to end slavery deepened until it became the primary mission of the nation's struggle. As the flames encircled Lincoln, many abolitionists feared he would vacillate on his commitment. Yet on the first day of 1863, Lincoln took pen in hand and professed, "I never, in my life, felt more certain that I was doing right than I do in signing this paper."[48] Though the final draft of the Emancipation Proclamation continued to aim exclusively at the rebellious states and excluded nearly every province under the Union umbrella, the clauses concerning colonization and compensation were nowhere to be found.[49]

What changed within Abraham Lincoln? Certainly the world was changing at a remarkable rate, and history itself was demanding a response to the convulsing tides of war. Both the continual push for freedom from the enslaved and the North's deepening need for Black troops to win the war placed pressure on Lincoln in a manner that aligned the demands of national survival with the demands of racial justice. Thus, what started as a military necessity began taking a moral turn that transformed Lincoln at the core of his being.

And just as Black leaders foretold, as the nature of the war changed, so too did the momentum. When the crisis the enslaved people helped create provided an opportunity to take up arms against their oppressors, they fought. The people the South enslaved fought for freedom and our nation's perfection. Through these heroics, Black America played the indispensable role of saving the nation from itself. The contribution of Black America proved so decisive that in a paper that later became famous, historian Robert F. Engs asks, "Who freed the slaves?" The most honest answer Engs can find is: "The slaves freed themselves."[50]

One month after the Emancipation Proclamation, the 54th Massachusetts Infantry Regiment began receiving its first recruits. Nearly two hundred thousand Black Americans joined the Union cause through military service, revolutionizing the Civil War into a fight for Black freedom. No longer desiring to keep Black people in bondage, Lincoln came to see Black freedom as the heartbeat of the war's moral meaning. And his transformation from antiabolitionist to emancipationist forced the nation to begin reimagining its racial commitments. After January 1, 1863, Lincoln proved increasingly unwilling to make the presidential office complicit in perpetuating slavery.

Yet, in a foreshadowing of future injustices, Black America's readiness to fight for freedom and the nation's readiness to make abolition the aim of the war was not matched by the Union's willingness to provide equal pay for Black soldiering. As Black America fought for freedom, the Union fought to preserve the cherished racial hierarchy in its own ranks. Black soldiers received only seven dollars per month to the white soldiers' thirteen dollars. The Constitution's Three-Fifths Compromise valued Black Americans at 60 percent of their white counterparts. The Union army reduced that estimate, valuing Black soldiers at only 54 percent of white soldiers.

In August 1863, Frederick Douglass brought the complaints of Black soldiers to the presidential mansion. No input had been solicited from Douglass, but he nonetheless joined the line of daily patronage seekers who simply hoped for a chance to gain the president's ear. Upon learning that Frederick Douglass was at the White House, Lincoln requested that Douglass be pulled from the line and escorted to his office. The two leaders engaged in open and frank discussion. Lincoln defended racist public policies that underwrote the inferior treatment and pay that Black Union soldiers received. Ever the politician, Lincoln said that as president, he was required to consider "public popular prejudice" and that racial inequality was "a necessary concession" for Black America to bear arms in the Union army.[51] Such callous political compromises regarding men who were sacrificing their lives to save our nation were surely salt water for Douglass's thirst for national leadership possessed by democratic convictions. Yet, the Black statesman nonetheless continued to discern continued growth in the character of our president and planned on actively spurring Lincoln toward greater moral maturity.

It would not be the last time Abraham Lincoln and Frederick Douglass met. In August 1864, almost exactly a year after their original encounter, a second meeting occurred. This time, Lincoln initiated getting together. He did so in response to blistering public criticism from Douglass. Douglass's criticism centered on the hypocrisy of Lincoln's public policies that treated

Black soldiers as second-class citizens while offering proposals for Reconstruction that welcomed home treasonous Southerners as equals who had committed no crime. "Policy, policy, everlasting policy," Douglass bemoaned, "has robbed our statesmanship of all soul-moving utterances."[52]

What was both remarkable and moving about this second meeting of minds was that Lincoln framed their time together in a manner that positioned Douglass as a friend and an adviser, not as a critic to be silenced. In Lincoln's words: "I want to have a long talk with my friend Frederick Douglass."[53] Together, Lincoln and Douglass strategized how to unleash the spirit of John Brown throughout the South and build armed bands of freed people to spread the good news of emancipation. As the "slave hound from Illinois" sought wisdom from a runaway slave, he embodied the radical political possibilities that arise when political calculations are no longer subservient to the demands of white control. As Lincoln moved from lecturing Black America to becoming perhaps the first president in US history to seek Black wisdom, he secured the transformation of the war's goal from preserving the Union to perfecting it through the eradication of slavery. In so doing, Lincoln matured from a legalist committed to enforcing the letter of law to the rare revolutionary committed to paying the price to rewrite the very rules of the game.[54]

Just as Lincoln took a pencil to scrap wood long ago, in Lincoln's post-Proclamation years, he began to write his words on the hearts and minds of the American people with a new and profound power. This new power was on vivid display on Gettysburg's sacred grounds. In the now famous words from November 19, 1863, Lincoln began:

> Four score and seven years ago our fathers brought forth on this continent a new nation, conceived in Liberty, and dedicated to the proposition that all men are created equal. Now we are engaged in a great civil war, testing whether that nation, or any nation so conceived and so dedicated, can long endure.[55]

As Lincoln endowed the Civil War with the moral gravity of human equality, he saw in the war a bloody "new birth of freedom." With this new aim, the Civil War had taken on cosmic meaning for Lincoln, becoming exactly what it always was for Black America: the beginning of a second revolution and the rebirth of our nation.

In his third annual message to Congress, Lincoln was nearing the pinnacle of his moral and political maturity. His reelection the following year was anything but certain. Yet, for the Congress that he once badgered to consider strengthening slavery's security, Lincoln now drew a line in the sand. "While I remain in my present position," he announced, "I shall not attempt to retract or modify the Emancipation Proclamation."[56] In his fourth annual message, he reiterated his position: "If the people should, by whatever mode or means, make it an Executive duty to re-enslave such persons, another, and not I, must be their instrument to perform it."[57] Beginning in 1863, Lincoln's metamorphosis proved nothing less than remarkable. A politician who only a few short years earlier ran for president on a white supremacist platform, who stood ready to allow the South to dictate slavery's future, became a leader of conviction who made the end of slavery the sine qua non for peace and his continued service as president.

Yet for all Lincoln's steadfast commitment to eradicate slavery after the Emancipation Proclamation, for all the remarkable moral clarity of his Gettysburg Address, a wide chasm remained between Lincoln's vision of the future and the demands of Black America and their radical white allies. For both Black America and white radical abolitionists, the end goal of the struggle was never a mere end to the institution of slavery. The aim had to be the realization of Black equality and the birth of an interracial democracy on American soil. The chasm between Lincoln and radical abolitionists was best captured by Lincoln's second proclamation: the Proclamation of Amnesty and Reconstruction.

Lincoln released this proclamation on Tuesday December 8, 1863, only three weeks after his visit to Gettysburg. Lincoln's second proclamation is not as well remembered as the Emancipation Proclamation or the Gettysburg Address. But history shows that its significance in molding America's racial future has few equals. The remarkable significance of the proclamation is not in its moral clarity but in its tragic political expediencies.

Lincoln offered the Proclamation of Amnesty and Reconstruction as an evolving vision, but the proclamation had a fundamentally flawed framework. In desiring to design a document that hastened the end of the war and the restoration of the Union, Lincoln's proclamation promised to return power to unrepentant Southern enslavers following the war. "I, Abraham Lincoln, President of the United States, do proclaim, declare, and make known to all persons who have . . . participated in the rebellion," he wrote, "that a full pardon is hereby granted them and each of them, with restoration of all rights of property, except slaves."[58] Though Lincoln provided a list of people to except from his proclamation, in practice, Lincoln placed the bar for reunion so low that it reempowered the entire Confederate social order. Lacking both national and Southern repentance and devoid of any demands for racial justice, Lincoln's vision was perfectly designed to perpetuate white supremacy and create two separate and unequal Americas following the war.

If the Emancipation Proclamation radiated Lincoln's late light, the Proclamation of Amnesty and Reconstruction was a masterpiece of misplaced magnanimity that cast a cloud over the hopes of Black equality. Lincoln's proposal of amnesty reempowered the Southern aristocracy while ignoring the needs of the freed people who were "a laboring, landless, and homeless class."[59] Just as the *clarity* of the Emancipation Proclamation sealed the fate of slavery, the *ambiguity* concerning how to provide for the necessities of the freed people in his second proclamation threatened to place Black people back into the hands of those seeking to reenslave them.

It is important to highlight how Lincoln's vision displayed just how far his racial convictions lagged behind those of his more radical contemporaries who demanded that Reconstruction provide an infrastructure for an interracial democracy. For example, abolitionist Wendell Phillips insisted that Reconstruction could never be complete until Blacks had been guaranteed education, access to land, and the ballot.[60] Instead of the Proclamation of Amnesty and Reconstruction making real the promise of the Emancipation Proclamation, Phillips quipped that Lincoln "frees the slave and ignores the negro."[61] Likewise, Frederick Douglass demanded that Reconstruction include civil rights, just wages, and military protection to create a context for meaningful Black freedom. Douglass wrote that Lincoln's plan for the freedman was "to hand him back to the political power of his master, without a single element of strength to shield himself from the vindictive spirit sure to be roused against the whole colored race."[62]

In one swipe, Lincoln found the courage to strike at slavery's heart by "henceforth and forever more" freeing 3.3 million enslaved people of the South. His second proclamation provided the opportunity to strike at the heart of white supremacy itself by striking at the nation's racial hierarchy and committing to a vision for an interracial democracy that opposed all forms of racial inequality. But in his second proclamation, Lincoln stilled his hand and refused to strike. The South was not ready for racial equality. And neither was the North. And neither was Lincoln.

If Lincoln had included sufficient Black political and economic provisions in his proclamation and held Southern enslavers accountable for their treason, the proclamation would have provided a powerful blueprint for a fundamentally different future for the entire nation. Such provisions would have dealt a devastating blow to white supremacy on both sides of the Mason-Dixon line. When Lincoln penned his final proclamation, he had it in his power to bury the Southern aristocracy and protect and empower both Black America and the white poor. Instead, nearly eighteen months before the Civil War's cease-fire, Lincoln's failure to strike positioned the president who took power following his assassination to partner with an unrepentant South in designing a new society equally committed to white supremacy and Black degradation.

It radically underestimates Lincoln to see his failures in providing Black America political independence (through the ballot) and economic independence (through land and capital) as a tragic oversight. The conversations over land, property, protection, and enfranchisement permeated the Civil War struggle. The Proclamation of Amnesty and Reconstruction was meticulously engineered and part of Lincoln's long-game strategy to appease the Southern power structure even at the expense of Black dignity and equal citizenship. Even after the Emancipation Proclamation, such a devastating compromise was what Lincoln saw as the price of the ticket to preserve the Union. That Lincoln was ready to pay that price cannot be divorced from the anti-Black racism of both the South and the North that viewed the pursuit of racial equality as a violation of the very dictates of nature. As historian Christopher Bonner notes in the television docuseries *Lincoln: Divided We Stand*: "If we know that Lincoln can imagine a different future for slavery, we shouldn't let him off the hook for failing to imagine a different future for racial relations in the country."[63]

If Lincoln should not be let off the hook, neither should our nation. Our nation paid a ghastly price to receive an opportunity to begin again and create an interracial democracy committed to human dignity. It was an opportunity our nation rejected. The case for national reparations is rooted in our collective responsibility for that rejection.

In the final year of the war, which also turned out to be the final year of Lincoln's life, Lincoln's metamorphosis continued, and his emerging clarity of vision shaped quite a different inaugural address following his reelection. At his second inauguration, Lincoln displayed his determination to include the nation in the moral transformation he was undergoing. He spoke as a man wrestling with his conscience and his God. "If we shall suppose that American slavery is one of those offenses which in the providence of God must needs come but which having continued through His appointed time He now wills to remove and that He gives to both North and South this terrible war as the woe due to those by whom the offense came," confessed Lincoln with a solemn gravity and grace, "shall we discern therein any departure from those divine attributes which the believers in a living God always ascribe to Him?" With the fervency of a man all too intimate with the price the nation paid for its sins, he continued:

> Fondly do we hope—fervently do we pray—that this mighty scourge of war may speedily pass away. Yet, if God wills that it continue, until all the wealth piled by the bond-man's two hundred and fifty years of unrequited toil shall be sunk, and until every drop of blood drawn with the lash shall be paid by another drawn with the sword, as was said three thousand years ago, so still it must be said "the judgments of the Lord are true and righteous altogether."[64]

Rather than attempting to comfort the nation—North or South—in its acquiescence to slavery, Lincoln submitted himself and the nation's soul to the purification of God's wrath. If in his first inaugural address Lincoln was not the leader the nation needed, the brutality of the war, the embrace of emancipation, and the responsibility of establishing a foundation for a new birth of freedom acted as a refiner's fire. Confessing the nation's guilt, Lincoln repented, and through the flame of the Civil War years, he became a revolutionary leader who in a meaningful—but far from perfect—way opened the door for the nation to begin again.

As the months dragged by in the war's final year, as more mothers became childless and more children became fatherless, Lincoln continued to mature. Time failed to provide Lincoln the luxury to perfect the Proclamation of Amnesty and Reconstruction, but it did provide an opportunity for him to bring the work that the Emancipation Proclamation began into the Constitution itself by passing the Thirteenth Amendment. "The passage of this amendment," Lincoln declared, "will clinch the whole subject; it will bring the war, I have no doubt, rapidly to a close." And Lincoln fully committed. In *And There Was Light*, Jon Meacham narrates the moment:

> Federal appointments, legislative favors, even bribes were rumored to be on offer. "Money will certainly do it, if patriotism fails," one of [Secretary of State William H.] Seward's agents said. "The greatest measure of the nineteenth century," Thaddeus Stevens remarked, "was passed by corruption, aided and abetted by the purest man in America"—Lincoln himself. . . .
>
> [Lincoln] had finally learned that, in the battle against slavery, winning the game was more important than following the rules. On April 8th, 1864, Lincoln maneuvered the 13th Amendment through the Senate.[65]

The evolution of Lincoln's moral imagination was picking up speed, and with each passing day he was sounding more and more like the radical abolitionists he had long dismissed. Lincoln began to consider lending his support for the previously unthinkable: education for freed people and enfranchisement to freedmen. Together, the possibilities possessed the potential to provide the cornerstones for an interracial democracy. And it was through this radicalization that Lincoln established the trajectory that led to the Fourteenth and Fifteenth Amendments, which provided Black America her first constitutional protections.

Perhaps Lincoln's transformation was perceived most clearly by those who welcomed it the least. On April 11, 1865, a little over a month after Lincoln's second inaugural address and two days following General Robert E. Lee's surrender, Lincoln faced a jubilant crowd to share what became his final words with the nation. It was Tuesday of Holy Week as Lincoln looked to the future, turning south to herald the example of Louisiana, a state that embraced the vision to enfranchise and educate the formerly enslaved. It was a vision of peace and reconstruction much more radical than his own Proclamation of Amnesty and Reconstruction. In the words of one particularly disgruntled man in the audience that day: "That means nigger citizenship. That is the last speech he will ever make."[66] That man was John Wilkes Booth, and Good Friday was only three days away.

We will never know what would have been without Booth's bullet. But what is clear is that Lincoln and his Emancipation Proclamation opened the door to reimagining race in America even as his Proclamation of Amnesty and Reconstruction provided the possibility for white supremacy to resurrect in new forms. Lincoln's legacy cannot and should not be divorced from his anti-Black racism, which molded his political career and shaped the future of Black America in ways almost too profound to imagine.

Like Jefferson, Lincoln was not merely a man of his time. To play down his white supremacy says much more about the white supremacy of our own time than his. Antiracism was often less than ideologically pure in Lincoln's time, but it was more alive and more radical than at any other point in American history. Many white women committed their lives to the cause, including abolitionists Sarah Grimke, Angelina Grimke, Lucretia Mott, and Delia Webster. The courage of these women was matched by leaders ranging from William Lloyd Garrison to Elijah Lovejoy, Thaddeus Stevens, Charles

Sumner, John Brown, and the less-known but equally self-sacrificial Calvin Fairbank, who worked the Underground Railroad. In this era, the creative white minority provided some of the strongest white antiracist leadership our nation has ever experienced.[67]

For nearly all his life, Lincoln held more in common with the morality of the enslavers than with the moral vision of radical abolitionists—Black or white. For everything noble about Lincoln, like most men who attain power, he possessed a sinister side that reflected the worst of his era. Lincoln's sinister side consistently led him to placate rather than eradicate slavery and racism in America. In Lincoln's day, far too many lost their lives due to his wavering. Every day that Lincoln hesitated on emancipation made the South more powerful and the war more deadly. We live with the lasting consequences of those instincts. To the extent that Black suffering in America following the Civil War can be traced to individual men, Lincoln bears a significant amount of responsibility—for no man was better positioned to end white supremacy in America than Lincoln after he ended slavery.

Yet, Lincoln was never a morally static man, and neither was his anti-Black racism. What separated Lincoln from most people was how he grew and changed not only to meet the demands of his time but also to address his own failures and shortcomings. If we learn anything from US history, it is how uncommon it is for our leaders to confront the moral significance of white supremacy and the institutionalization of America's racism. No president before or since has matched the depth of Abraham Lincoln's repentance over the depravity of our nation's racial practices. And no president went through the moral transformation he endured. Lincoln left a lasting testimony to the expansive possibilities repentance produces.

In his eulogy of Abraham Lincoln, Frederick Douglass pulled no punches. Wounds were remembered and imperfections recalled. Yet, like for so many others in the Black Freedom Movement, Lincoln became to Douglass "the first martyr President of the United States" whose death was inseparable from his fight to give liberty life.[68] For all his failures and shortcomings, Lincoln changed. And changed dramatically. Lincoln, for W. E. B. Du Bois, represented the best hope for white America. "The world is full of people born hating and despising their fellows," wrote Du Bois. "To these I love to say: See this man. He was one of you and yet he became Abraham Lincoln."[69]

4

THE LASTING LEGACY OF SHACKLES

Establishing America's Racial Hierarchy

Slavery is the next thing to hell.

—Harriet Tubman to Benjamin Drew, St. Catharines,
Ontario, Canada, 1855

SINCE AMERICA'S INCEPTION, WHITE SUPREMACY has waged its war against hope by making racial injustice feel immutable. America's founding generation understood that to give racial injustices the semblance of immutability, those injustices needed to seem to flow from innate racial differences. Dissecting the logic of racial sciences in the nineteenth century in *The History of White People*, Nell Irvin Painter writes: "Innate qualities are needed to prove the justice—the naturalness and inalterability—of the status quo."[1] And it has been precisely this function—to make America's racial hierarchy seem immutable, natural, unalterable—that racist ideas have played from the days of slavery to today. Once racial difference became innate in the minds of white America, white supremacy provided the racial paradigm that divided the nation along racial lines ever after. This history is the foundation of today's racial crisis. Until that foundation is faced and repaired, all attempts to address today's democratic and racial crises build upon a broken bedrock.

As we consider reparations and the racial legacies of Jefferson and Lincoln together, we see both the role of America's aristocracy in crafting white supremacy and how the ideologies of white supremacy trickled down to infect white Americans of every class and political persuasion. Not even a poor boy from Kentucky who hated slavery proved immune. Just as white supremacy infects its individual hosts in mind, body, and spirit, so too white supremacy infects every aspect of our nation's conscience and consciousness.

The founding generation entrenched a lasting vision of Black Americans. From pathological Black sex and Black families, to Black sloth and Black dependence, to Black people devoid of brainpower, Jefferson provided the particulars of the supposed inferiorities of Black people. Despite their long history, Jefferson's rationalizations were forged in the fires of absurdity with the explicit intent of numbing our nation's moral sensibilities. *Every* mythology that rationalized slavery was rooted in violent racial lies and caricatures. And as these lies and caricatures became America's common sense, they took on a life of their own by justifying dehumanizing racial malpractices. American slavery's plunder, rape, and terrorism was never an unavoidable evil. It was an evil of choice that Jefferson and America's aristocracy meticulously justified. The more we dodge the depth of the depravity of American slavery, the deeper we dig ourselves into racial mythologies with no basis in truth.

When we think of Jefferson's place in history, we often think of him as a father of equality, but that understanding has more to do with Jefferson's mastery of illusion than the essence of his ideologies. The very words "all men are created equal" were themselves undergirded by classist and racist ideas. When it came to realizing equality along either racial or economic lines, Jefferson's leadership often proved lethal. His fingerprints remain all over America's greatest moral failures: the slavery of the eighteenth and nineteenth centuries, segregation and the eugenics movement of the twentieth, and the radical racial inequality of the twenty-first. Jefferson's mythologies of Black pathology and white supremacy cost America nearly 700,000 of her children in the Civil War and more than 135 million years from her people in slavery.[2] Jefferson never ingrained a commitment to equality into America's DNA, but he certainly ingrained a commitment to design the entire American enterprise around demonic and undemocratic understandings of racial differences. Jefferson's self-deception—his illusions of innocence and his racial paradigms—long outlived the age of slavery, becoming constitutive of America's identity and self-understanding. When we rightly read Jefferson in the annals of history, we just might start to see the same instincts in ourselves—and it is those instincts that reparations seek to challenge and change.

Abraham Lincoln was not Thomas Jefferson. Lincoln did not share equally in the privileges of white supremacy with his aristocratic contemporaries or America's Founding Fathers. Yet, he was thoroughly formed by white supremacy's racial instincts and rejected repeated opportunities to strike at America's racial hierarchy. For nearly his entire life, Lincoln was as anti-Black as he was antislavery. Rather than fighting for the highest moral ground of equality, ground that radical abolitionists occupied, Lincoln's anti-Blackness led him to continually treat Black liberation as a weapon for political leverage for white union. When Lincoln did strike slavery, he did so with force and courage despite his mixed motives. But when the opportunity arose to strike at white supremacy, Lincoln did nothing. In that sin of omission, Lincoln perpetuated the worst aspects of the founding generation he idolized. Following Lincoln's lead, no moment of reckoning or repentance ever arose in the wake of the Civil War. Unlike with the Nuremberg trials that held Nazi criminals to account following World War II and in so doing provided a devastating blow to Nazi ideals, no trial was held for the Confederates or the national ideologies that made their atrocities possible.[3]

In time, Lincoln learned that neither empathy nor political compromise with the institutional forms white supremacy takes *ever* leads to a more perfect union. A more perfect union began to emerge on American soil only when such empathy and compromises were *rejected*. Only because Black folks fled and fought for their freedom, only because Lincoln stood his ground and *refused* to compromise on emancipation, did an opportunity open for America to pursue an interracial democracy. The more Lincoln embraced the wisdom of Black America and the politics and strategies of John Brown, the more he became the leader America's moment required.

Lincoln's anti-Black racism stains his legacy and indelibly shaped Black America's postslavery suffering. Yet, he nonetheless provided the nation an opportunity to improve upon his work and redeem his shortcomings. When shackles started breaking from the feet, wrists, and necks of Black folks, shackles began breaking from the minds and hearts of white folks as well. A moment materialized that allowed America to question everything she thought she knew about herself and those she enslaved. A moment materialized to make an interracial democracy a living reality.

As we begin considering reparations for Black America for the sins of slavery and the perpetuation of radical racial inequalities, any meaningful conversation must include making reparations for the uncompensated labor and the land that Black Americans purchased through blood, sweat, and tears. If America, from the time of the colonies and throughout the Civil War, could calculate making reparations to enslavers, it is not too early to imagine how to begin making the many trillions of dollars in reparations for lost land and labor that we owe the descendants of the enslaved.

But reparations must reach deeper than economic recompense. Thomas Jefferson and the founding generation's convictions and compromises warped America's soul, and that warping has never been remolded. The end of slavery could have been the end of white supremacy, but our failure to enter a process of repentance and fully embrace our responsibilities to repair our nation ensured that it was not. Until we repent and atone, we will not be able to free our nation from the grasp of the racial crimes that slavey began. Until we reconstruct our moral imagination, the auction block will continue to serve as a cornerstone of our nation's conscience.

How can America make reparations for over 135 million years lost to slavery and the centuries we allowed white supremacy to go unchecked? How is America to make reparations for its complicity in Black torture, rape, and family dismemberment? How are we to repay failing to hold the Confederacy and our nation's white supremacy to account following the Civil War? These are the questions we must wrestle with. America's racial crimes against flesh and spirit are not reducible to commodities to be purchased. Reparations for such crimes must be as thoroughly political, psychological, and spiritual as white supremacy itself.

As we continue on the stony road to reparations, we move from the days of slavery to those of Reconstruction. In many ways, America's second revolution began at Ford's Theatre with Booth's bullet. Americans North and South knew the end of the Civil War did not equal the beginning of peace. The war-torn nation now faced the precarious challenge of piecing life back together without either the cornerstone of slavery in the South or the leader who led the North through the nation's darkest hours. In his final speeches, Lincoln's vision for Reconstruction continued to evolve. He continued to champion a politics of mercy toward the Confederates and a politics of inclusion toward the freed people. Economically, he envisioned free labor replacing the slave economy and breathing life into the South's dry bones. Yet, this too represented a fundamentally insufficient framework.

From a flawed framework and the ashes of war, modern America was born. After the shackles shattered, the question that faced America was what to do with the opportunity for freedom and democracy that she sacrificed so much to achieve. Would America follow Lincoln and learn to repent? What would become of the racialized architecture of white supremacy that shaped both the Northern and Southern way of life? The answers to these questions were crafted in the roughly one hundred years between the Civil War and the struggle for civil rights.

Lynchings

The Mythology of Black Pathology from Reconstruction to Civil Rights

The race question involves the saving of black America's body and white America's soul.

—James Weldon Johnson, director of the NAACP,
"The Burning of Ell Persons at Memphis"

Our country's national crime is lynching. It is not the creature of an hour, the sudden outburst of uncontrolled fury, or the unspeakable brutality of an insane mob. It represents the cool, calculating deliberation of intelligent people who openly avow that there is an "unwritten law" that justifies them in putting human beings to death . . . without opportunity to make defense, and without right of appeal.

—Ida B. Wells, "Lynch Law in America," 1900

5

Slavery without Paternalism

From Shackles to Lynchings

> In slave times the Negro was kept subservient and submissive by
> the frequency and severity of the scourging, but, with freedom,
> a new system of intimidation came into vogue; the Negro was not
> only whipped and scourged; he was killed.
>
> —Ida B. Wells, "A Red Record," 1895

As the smoke over the Civil War's battlefields dissipated and Lincoln's eulogies were penned, the struggle to piece our nation back together was just beginning. The racist ideas woven into our founding documents and the racial compromises those ideas facilitated failed and left a bloodbath in their wake. That failure forced America's racial imagination to evolve, and that evolution would be dictated not by innate differences that Mother Nature provided to divide races but by intentional decisions and depraved public policies that the American people supported.

As America's racial imagination evolved, so too did America's racial symbols. In the days of slavery, the racial symbol was the shackle. During slavery, particular aspects of white supremacy's savagery often occurred under the public's consenting gaze through public lashings, advertisements of enslaved people for sale, and the auction block itself. Yet, as public as white supremacy's violence was during slavery, a significant portion of the brutality and sadism—the torture and the rape—occurred behind the closed curtains of domestic life. The full extent of slavery's violence needed to be hidden from the public eye for enslavers to pose as benefactors and to portray the enslaved as harmless but wild children who needed the parental discipline of the enslaver's lash for domestication.

With the South's surrender, the shackles of chattel slavery were forever shattered and a new racial symbol was needed for the South's new world order. Following the Civil War, the ritualistic lynching of Black people provided that symbol. Black people were no longer portrayed as harmless children needing domestication but as beasts to be broken and hardened criminals to be ruthlessly controlled. The privatized violence of enslavers and overseers was no longer sufficient for enforcing such a racial order. In this new nation without slavery, reforging a white republic demanded a contagion of fear, demanded fomenting white people into a frenzied mob and for racial violence to become a more transparent public spectacle.

The lynch necessitated sharpening America's racial lies and logic to root racist fears in white hearts and minds. From every sector of American life—from popular culture and communities of faith, to the most prestigious universities and sacred halls of power—white American minds would be bombarded with racist ideas to ensure racial brutality continued as the nation's cultural common sense. No longer posing primarily as paternalists, white supremacists masqueraded as vigilante knights protecting society itself, and white women in particular. Ritualistic lynchings became popular communal events of terrorism explicitly designed to traumatize Black people and trap entire Black communities at the bottom of America's social hierarchy.

For white supremacists, the greatest crimes in the era of lynching were interracial intimacy and proud Black people thriving. Black Americans who dared to express their equality became the targets of lynch mobs that sought to ensure Black subservience. As America's racial imagination evolved, lynchings replaced slavery as white America's vehicle for Black oppression, extending the case for reparations into the twentieth century.

Following the Civil War, it was not clear how to piece the world back together again. In the South, these were dire times. "The poor blacks have a multitude of miseries," General Robert E. Lee wrote to his wife prior to the war. "I hope death that must come sooner or later will end them all."[1] Defeat at the hands of the enslaved—whom Southern leaders would rather exterminate than emancipate—turned the Southern world upside down. Without the enslaved, what was the South? Without supremacy, who were white people? The North felt equally bewildered by the emerging world order. "Slavery is dead," read the *Cincinnati Enquirer*, "the negro is not, [and] there is the misfortune."[2]

Despite the anxiety of the war-torn nation, an undeniable electricity existed within the ranks of a radical faction of the Republican Party and the newly emancipated as they pursued reconstruction. In the earliest years of Reconstruction, Radical Republicans and newly freed Black people fought tirelessly to harness the energy generated by emancipation and the South's surrender to bring freedom and equality to Southern soil for the first time. The Constitution was reborn as the Thirteenth Amendment ended slavery, the Fourteenth Amendment granted freed Black people citizenship and equality under the law, and the Fifteenth Amendment provided Black men the right to vote. As Black men's participation in the political process soared, democracy came alive in ways previously unknown in American history. Expanding the electoral franchise inspired interracial democracy, public education emerged in educational wastelands, and Black public service ranged from the halls of power to jury boxes and law enforcement.

Instead of vengeance, Black America set its own priorities during Reconstruction and began the work of creating and strengthening communal institutions. Black people's first priority was often to reunite families torn apart during the days of slavery.[3] The death of slavery also led to the unveiling of the Black church, which had secretly nurtured Black people by providing a haven for the community's ambitions for generations. No longer shrouded in secrecy, the Black church acted as an incubator for Black communities' activism and educational efforts. Under the umbrella of the Black church, politics and education became all-consuming passions in Black life. From the North, both white and Black teachers swarmed to the South to establish schools in every conceivable space ranging from churches to abandoned railroad cars.[4] Through family, church, politics, and education, Black America provided freedom and citizenship the richest meanings imaginable.

The seeds of a radical vision for Black liberty and independence were sown well before the end of the Civil War, perhaps most famously during a gathering between Secretary of War Edwin Stanton, General William T. Sherman, and a Black delegation led by the Rev. Garrison Frazier on January 12, 1865. "The best way we can take care of ourselves," Frazier counseled, "is to have land. . . . We want to be placed on land until we are able to buy it and make it our own." Four days later, General Sherman issued Special Field Order No. 15, temporarily providing Black people forty acres and a mule on the Sea Islands of South Carolina and the low country south of Charleston. Special

Order No. 15 led to Congress's creating the Freedmen's Bureau in March 1865 to assist both poor whites and the newly freed.[5] Yet, year after year, from its inception to its demise, the Freedmen's Bureau received insufficient resources from Congress. Justifying such stinginess was the racist fear that providing resources to the Black community would foster dependence, not liberty.[6]

Despite such challenges, those through whom the electricity flowed believed they were just beginning. A more thoroughgoing economic revolution was envisioned by Radical Republican Thaddeus Stevens to provide reparations in real time that went well beyond Sherman's forty acres and a mule. Stevens's proposal made millions more acres available through the seizure of the lands of the South's wealthiest 10 percent of landowners. In one move, Stevens envisioned striking the death blow to white supremacy that Lincoln had refused to deliver—ending both the minority reign of the South's landed aristocracy and the powerlessness of the landless majority.

Justice even came to Black people through America's judicial system. In April 1878, Henrietta Wood, a freedwoman who had been kidnapped and reenslaved for fifteen years, won her case for reparations against her abductor, Zebulon Ward. Such crimes against African Americans were common, and the case set a powerful precedent.[7] With such visions and miraculous moments, Blacks in America believed the times of Pharaoh and Egypt land had passed. The time the biblical prophets and the apostle Paul foresaw, in which "justice roll[s] on like a river" and there is "neither Jew nor Greek, neither slave nor free" (Gal. 3:28), had arrived.[8]

If we place the American experiment in a global context, we can better appreciate its revolutionary nature. The United States came to the work of emancipation relatively late.[9] Yet, despite America's late entrance into freedom's dance, it was only in America in the nineteenth century that a nation that emancipated the enslaved began to enfranchise them as well. No utopia was born in the wake of the Civil War, but the dazzle of new political possibilities proved more than pixie dust.

Every step forward was earned at great cost and in the face of vengeance from those whose power was slipping away. If America's second revolution proved to be one of the most radical of the nineteenth-century world, it also inspired some of the most violent counterrevolutions in both the North and the South. Following the Civil War, the economic revolution never matched the nation's political revolution. The Freedmen's Bureau would be shuttered only a few years after its inception, and America even reneged on its meager commitment of forty acres and a mule in South Carolina's lowlands.

Compounding our racial crimes, after refusing freed people modest tracts of land, we distributed huge tracts to white people through the Homestead Acts while constructing land-grant colleges to empower them to develop the land they received free of charge. Between 1866 and 1934, a full 10 percent of our nation's land—246 million acres—would be dispersed to 1.5 million white people.[10] Despite these generous public benefits for white Americans, Black people were left to scratch out freedom amid poverty and landlessness.

Enemy number one for Reconstruction was Andrew Johnson, Lincoln's vice president from Tennessee, who ascended to the presidency following Lincoln's assassination. "This is a country for White men," declared President Johnson, "and by God, as long as I am President, it shall be a government for White men."[11] Through presidential appointment, every governor President Johnson installed in Southern states adamantly opposed Black suffrage. Through presidential pardon, every Confederate leader received amnesty and restoration without repentance. Despite early hopes for his presidency, President Johnson made clear that his commitment was to the restoration of white supremacy, not Lincoln's new birth of freedom.[12]

As Black people attempted to breathe life into new democratic possibilities, former Confederate soldiers created terrorist organizations like the Ku Klux Klan to extinguish any vestige of Black power or participation in politics and reestablish white dominance in every facet of American life.[13] In Alabama, Louisiana, Mississippi, North Carolina, and South Carolina, white supremacists murdered elected officials and overthrew duly elected governments. These acts of violence are the foundations upon which state governments throughout the South now stand.

Convict leasing schemes that once aimed to control the labor of the South's poor whites shifted to focus on the newly freed, Slave Codes resurrected, and the Black Laws of the North moved south as the classist and racist laws of the prewar South and North combined into Black Codes. Black Codes foisted a rope around the necks of Southern Black communities by robbing Black people of every political right.[14] For the newly emancipated, the right to control one's labor, the right to own land, the freedom to choose where to live, the right to bear arms—all quickly evaporated as Black people were left with neither legal nor physical protection from a society determined to exact vengeance.

The violence of the Klan proved so pervasive that Congress was moved to pass the Ku Klux Klan Act of April 1871, making offenses against constitutional rights a federal crime. From South Carolina to Texas, every time the federal government intervened, the Klan fled and the violence ended. Public hearings were held, culminating in a 632-page report that detailed the widespread torture, rape, and sadism Black America endured following the fall of the Confederacy. The report revealed that the leniency of Southern amnesty led to the brutal reentrenchment of the South's racial hierarchy, not repentance or the rewriting of Southern life. Without repentance, only two paths to national reconciliation existed: the nation could invest more deeply in the struggle to realize racial justice through Reconstruction, or the nation could retreat from Reconstruction, ignore the new Constitution and Southern atrocities, and reconcile on the grounds of white supremacy.

At both economic and emotional levels, white America thirsted for national reconciliation—even if that reconciliation rendered the sacrifices made for Black emancipation meaningless. At an economic level, the North was poised to return to the business of getting wealthy from Southern agriculture. To discerning eyes in the North, Reconstruction in the South was providing interracial political and economic alliances capable of recalibrating every aspect of America's infrastructure. This was as terrifying and unacceptable to the economic elites of the North as it was to the former plantation owners in the South.

On an emotional level, the Civil War left psychic and social wounds with few equals in American history. America longed to heal those wounds, and reconciliation between white people—North and South—provided a quicker and less costly path to healing than Reconstruction's struggle to realize an interracial democracy. With each passing year, America's will to realize racial justice waned as its appetite for white reconciliation waxed. Horace Greeley captured the mood of the moment in the nation's felt need "to clasp hands across the bloody chasm which has too long divided."[15]

With an appetite whetted for white reconciliation, the Ku Klux Klan Report was dismissed by many in white America as inaccurate or irrelevant. Though the report led federal forces to dismember the Klan, it failed to revive the nation's experiment with interracial democracy in the South. In fact, perhaps the most meaningful result of the report was the adding of fuel for a counterrevolution via an organized national misinformation campaign that sought to justify the Klan's violence and the eradication of interracial democracy. The misinformation campaign began nearly as soon as the war ended. In 1866, Edward Alfred Pollard released *The Lost Cause: A New Southern History of the Civil War*, arguing for the South's superiority and a bright future for white supremacy despite the fall of slavery. Slavery's death would lead to resurrection and a new life for white supremacy through a racial hierarchy better tailored to the modern age. With each passing year, the misinformation campaign intensified. As America retreated from Reconstruction, misinformation gained traction across America by reenergizing Jefferson's racial mythologies about Black sexuality, sloth, and intellectual inferiority. Reconstruction was framed as the realization of white America's racial nightmare and the preeminent threat to the purity of American democracy.

The misinformation campaign intentionally aimed to use racial propaganda to misshape the nation's memory regarding the origins of the Civil War and the realities of Reconstruction. The work to misremember was vast and wide-ranging. Memorials honoring the Confederates arose across the South, and white-only Blue and Gray reunions for Civil War veterans were inaugurated to foster a national aura of a "harmonious forgetfulness."[16] Misinformation traveled through popular anti-Black novelists and memoirists as well as academic and amateur historians who invented a pristine prewar South void of racial conflict. While national celebrations and histories were reduced to racist fantasies and racial propaganda, America's racial scientists entered a determined pursuit to quantify Black inferiority. The nationwide misinformation campaign sanctified the South's racial violence and created a context that painted Southern horrors as essential to the protection of the United States' national identity.

The campaigns of historians and scientists cleared the way for reconciliation to take place on the grounds of white supremacy and Southern self-understanding. Issues of racial justice and the causes and consequences of the war moved to the periphery of America's political imagination, while white reconciliation increasingly took center stage. Since the cost of this reconciliation required nothing less than a national embrace of Southern atrocities, the lyncher's noose became the cord to rebind a nation torn asunder.

As a network of activists, intellectuals, and politicians fought to return the nation to its commitment to white supremacy, the US Supreme Court and legal system breathed new life into racist hopes. The courts crafted a new interpretive lens for the Constitution to accommodate the laws of the land to the mood of the moment. During slavery, the Supreme Court's decisions harmonized with the proslavery *intentions* of the writers of the Constitution. However, after Southern surrender, the Supreme Court narrowed its vision, ignored the egalitarian intentions of the Thirteenth, Fourteenth, and

Fifteenth Amendments, and interpreted the Constitution in ways distinctly at odds with the aims of the amenders.

Consistent with its history and foreshadowing future racist decisions, Supreme Court justices such as Samuel Miller and Morrison R. Waite began interpreting every constitutional amendment and piece of progressive legislation through the lens of states' rights. As the Supreme Court's rulings moved the issues of voting and political violence from federal to local jurisdiction, governmental protections themselves pivoted from protecting democratically inspired Black Americans to protecting racially inspired white terrorists. In just ten years, from 1873 to 1883, the Supreme Court's decisions unwrote interracial democracy in America.[17]

As damning as the Supreme Court decisions were for Black life, at lower levels within the legal system, a loophole within the Thirteenth Amendment was discovered with equally disastrous consequences. The Thirteenth Amendment read: "Neither slavery nor involuntary servitude, except as a punishment for crime whereof the party shall have been duly *convicted*, shall exist within the United States." The amendment's exception for convicted criminals opened an opportunity to reintroduce slavery by other means.

To reenslave Black Americans, all white Southerners needed to do was invent crimes that allowed for convicting masses of freed people. Black Codes arose. Vagrancy laws were created along with bans on communal gatherings and restrictions on housing, hunting, marriage, and gun ownership. These codes allowed Black people to be imprisoned at whim. With this racialized twisting of the law, convict leasing schemes that once extracted labor out of poor white people were redesigned to wring white profit from the mere allegation of Black criminality. Between the Civil War and the 1940s, millions of Black Americans found themselves in chains once more as Black chain gangs replaced slave labor throughout the South.

Unsurprisingly, new racial myths arose to justify America's new expressions of white supremacy. After the passage of the Thirteenth Amendment, Black people's alleged inferiority was no longer limited to sexual depravity, a poor work ethic, and mental deficiencies. Now, Black people also began to be caricatured as inherently criminal. Caricaturing Black people as criminal made reenslaving so many of them appear to be in harmony with the laws of nature in an emancipated and multiracial society. As the nineteenth century closed and the twentieth century opened, such thinking passed as racial progress.

The logic that dominated American courts in this period was voiced in the majority opinion in the Civil Rights Cases of 1883. "When a man has emerged from slavery," wrote Justice Joseph P. Bradley to justify the removal of federal protection for Black Americans, "there must be some stage in the progress of his elevation when he takes the rank of a mere citizen, and ceases to be the special favorite of the laws."[18] As Black Codes, convict leasing schemes, and voter suppression strategies eroded every gain of the Emancipation Proclamation and Union victory, the Supreme Court decided that the opportunity to remove the last vestiges of protection for Black America had arrived. Frederick Douglass moaned: "O, for a supreme court of the United States which shall be as true to the claims of humanity as the Court formerly was to the demands of slavery!"[19]

The tragedy of the United States' retreat from Reconstruction was never that protecting Black people or interracial democracy was impossible. The tragedy is how very possible such an interracial reality was and how little help from the federal government was needed to realize it. As American apartheid displaced the interracial democracy of Reconstruction, the age of the shackle evolved into the age of lynching. "The slave went free; stood a brief moment in the sun, then moved back again toward slavery," wrote W. E. B. Du Bois, capturing the essence of the moment. "The whole weight of America was thrown to color caste. . . . A new slavery arose."[20]

To experience Reconstruction and its aftermath was to live in an era of whiplash. The political drama ricocheted from the highest hopes of interracial democracy down to some of the most depraved scenes of racial violence our nation has ever witnessed. And it was within these violent ricochets that America's commitment to white supremacy was secured and that her racial mythologies took on new and profound powers.

As we continue to construct a framework for understanding reparations by tracing the evolution of white supremacy from the shackle to ritualistic lynchings, we reenter the fray at the turn of the twentieth century by opening the caskets of two pivotal but often forgotten molders of America's racial imagination: Thomas Dixon Jr. and Madison Grant. By the beginning of the twentieth century, the fight over America's memory was consolidating into a unified consensus that Reconstruction and the pursuit of an interracial democracy was a tragic mistake. In this context, Thomas Dixon played a preeminent role in shaping an emerging literary genre committed to cementing white supremacy by heralding the heroics of the Klan, dramatizing Black criminality, and misremembering Reconstruction. Dixon hailed from South

Carolina's aristocracy. His father was a preacher and his uncle was the grand dragon of the Ku Klux Klan. Dixon became a state-level politician who later found greater power in the pulpit. His preaching ministry took him to Boston and New York, where he became one of the nation's most famous and liberal preachers in the Social Gospel movement. His Southern roots and Northern pedigree provided a perfect platform for uniting the North and the South after decades of division. And that platform was put to use when Dixon turned to writing novels, plays, and movie scripts that spread a gospel of racist fears to solidify and perpetuate a new era of racial brutality.

Madison Grant was not a Southern saint. Grant was from New York and part of a more secular aristocracy. Rather than claiming piety or religious sophistication, Grant rooted his racism within the scientific guild and larger circles of the intelligentsia. Through his masterpiece, *The Passing of the Great Race*, Grant became the preeminent spokesperson for the racial sciences. Grant's biographer Jonathan Spiro dubbed the book "the bible of scientific racism," as it pioneered the path from scientific racism to the sinister politics of the eugenics movement.

As we shall see, the influence of Dixon and Grant extended beyond America, as they helped shape the racial project of early twentieth-century Germany as well. One of the costly challenges of examining the impact of Dixon's and Grant's writings is navigating the deep interconnections between how America's anti-Black ideologies and public policies inspired Nazi Germany to weaponize anti-Semitic sentiment. The United States and Germany participated in a long relationship of mutual learning in how to sharpen racist ideas into laws and how to use racial propaganda to transform those laws into a national identity. And Dixon and Grant are among the United States' most important players at this intersection.

While America and Germany were never mirror images, they were ideological colleagues in crafting the racial politics that defined each nation. Isabel Wilkerson's remarkable work in *Caste* and James Q. Whitman's *Hitler's American Model* demonstrate that no foreign political movement provides greater clarity about the nature of America's racial program for Black people in the early twentieth century than what transpired in Nazi Germany. Understanding these interconnections is critical for conceptualizing the anti-Black character of twentieth-century America and how that character demands twenty-first-century reparations.

Today, popular preachers and elite secular intellectuals seem strange bedfellows. But it is a testament to the nature of both white Christianity and Northern progressivism at the turn of the twentieth century that neither they nor their followers saw any conflict between the brutality of their racist vision and their sacred and scientific worldviews. With a remarkable degree of overlap in their social circles, both Dixon and Grant rose with the most important leaders of America's Progressive Era. They rubbed elbows with presidents and titans of industry. Their political influence ran deep and wide, touching Presidents Theodore Roosevelt, William Howard Taft, Woodrow Wilson, Warren G. Harding, Calvin Coolidge, Herbert Hoover, and Franklin Delano Roosevelt. When presidents fought Dixon or Grant, presidents were known to lose. When Dixon and Grant spoke, people in power learned to listen. Thanks to Dixon's sermonics and Grant's nature conservation and eugenics efforts, their connections to industry often came from the support they received from the philanthropic community. This equally impressive list included the likes of John D. Rockefeller, J. P. Morgan, Andrew Carnegie, and Cornelius Vanderbilt. The adulation of the most influential Americans was the atmosphere that surrounded both of their careers and literary accomplishments.

As the mythologies of the age of the shackle evolved into the age of the lynch, Dixon and Grant acted as the moral, historical, and scientific compasses for navigating the emerging world order. Thanks to Dixon and Grant, Jefferson's and Lincoln's racist ideas would lose none of their power. In important ways, the racist ideas that justified slavery gained even more power after slavery's fall.

6

Thomas Dixon

Burning Down Uncle Tom's Cabin

> I am writing you this letter to express the attitude and feeling of
> ten million of your fellow citizens toward the evil propagandism
> of race animosity to which you have lent your great literary pow-
> ers. Through the wide-spread influence of your writings you have
> become the chief priest of those who worship at the shrine of race
> hatred and wrath.
>
> —Kelly Miller, *As to* The Leopard's Spots*: An Open Letter
> to Thomas Dixon Jr.*, September 1905

IF MONTICELLO PROVIDED AN ENTRANCE into the mind that helped inspire America's first revolution, Thomas Dixon's novels, *The Leopard's Spots*
and *The Clansman*, provide an entrance into the mind of the white South
following Reconstruction.[1] Though Dixon's style was radically different from
Jefferson's, like Jefferson, he was one of the preeminent "ideas" men of his era.
Whether in biology, sociology, theology, or history, Jefferson's racial mythologies provided *the* lens for any intellectual work in America that intersected
with race, politics, or religion in nineteenth-century America. Dixon was
intimately familiar with a wide range of these academic disciplines, particularly theology, history, and the racial sciences.

He graduated from Wake Forest College with more honors than any student had ever received. Dixon then attended graduate school at Johns Hopkins University. Established in 1876, Johns Hopkins University was founded
for the express purpose of institutionalizing German-style research in the
United States. Dixon studied under Herbert Baxter Adams, from whom
he received the cutting-edge research methods and racial assumptions of
Germany.[2] Gifted and remarkably ambitious, Dixon would take the ideas

he learned inside the ivory tower and reformat them for mass consumption by everyday Americans. Through the vivid images in Dixon's stories and the new technology of motion pictures, tens of millions of Americans would experience the power released when the racist ideas of Germany and America collided.

Dixon enjoyed a long, varied, and illustrious career in communicating his ideas to large audiences. His professional life moved him from politics to law to Christian ministry and then the lecture circuit. But these venues failed to provide a large enough platform for his national ambitions. After his brief but remarkably successful career as a Social Gospel preacher and traveling lecturer, the thirty-seven-year-old Thomas Dixon exchanged the pulpit and podium for a pen. And he proved a one-of-a-kind writer.

As part of the nationwide misinformation campaign, new novels emerged that romanticized the Southern way of life to reinvigorate Southern identity and self-confidence. Writers like Thomas Nelson Page and Joel Chandler Harris blazed new literary paths for reconciliation by inviting readers from across the nation to reimagine the South as a place of pastoral peace and virtue. In this land, the enslaved were happy in bondage, the South was the embodiment of Christian civilization, and all the turmoil of the present moment was forgotten. These novels acted as the tip of the spear in the fight to redeem white supremacy, and in this fight, Thomas Dixon was the fiercest of warriors.

Though Dixon's life took many twists and turns, he never wavered in his commitment to act as an apologist for the South and the racial ideas upon which America had been founded and through which he believed her future must be built. Dixon never aimed to be a world-class novelist. His aim was more pragmatic. He desired to communicate history on Southern terms and to pass forward the racial convictions of Thomas Jefferson and Abraham Lincoln by tailoring them for the new century. Novels became his chosen vehicle, because they allowed him to employ the most striking images he could imagine to sear racist caricatures onto the hearts and minds of the American people. "A novel," he wrote in a letter to the readers of his final work of fiction, "is the most vivid and accurate form in which history can be written."[3]

Jefferson's racial convictions concerning Black sex, sloth, and inferior intelligence were ever present in Dixon's stories. Like Jefferson, Dixon was obsessed with defending America against the threat of miscegenation. Like both Jefferson and Lincoln, he heralded the need for colonization to avoid the direct confrontation of a racial war that aimed to exterminate Black people. And though the extermination of Black people would become an explicit aim in the American racial imagination, a direct confrontation would cost much wealth and many white lives. Another path into the future was needed, and Dixon worked diligently to promote the alternative of the South's racial ways.

Lincoln was one of Dixon's favorite characters to write into his novels, and it seems Dixon had at the tip of his fingers every racist utterance Lincoln ever made. Unsatisfied with Lincoln playing a minor role, Dixon wrote an entire novel with Lincoln as the lead. Published in 1913, the novel is titled *The Southerner* in honor of Lincoln's Virginian roots and racist ideas.

Though Dixon's style was uniquely his own, much of the content of his writings possesses little originality. Where Dixon broke new ground was in being one of the first American writers to perceive socialism as a threat to America's *racial* order. Like other progressives, Dixon was not a fan of laissez-faire capitalism due to the ways industrialism devastated poor white workers. But he understood that any economic order that pursued equality would eventually destroy the concentration of wealth and intergenerational privileges that secured white supremacy. Dixon would not live to see the full fruit of his efforts to center the nation on the fear of socialism, but in time, the fear of socialism would mature into one of the greatest protectors of white supremacy in the twentieth century.

If Jefferson and Lincoln provided Dixon his inspiration, abolitionist Harriet Beecher Stowe's *Uncle Tom's Cabin* provided the fuel for his rage.[4] *Uncle Tom's Cabin* was never a masterpiece of antiracist writing: it is thoroughly paternalistic and mired in the white supremacy of its day. However, its aim was Black liberation. Stowe's political goals were to elicit public sympathy for the work of abolition and the plight of the enslaved in the wake of the Fugitive Slave Act's passage. Ida B. Wells believed *Uncle Tom's Cabin* was the "indirect cause of the abolition of slavery," and Frederick Douglass referred to it as "the master book of the nineteenth century."[5] When Abraham Lincoln met Stowe, he allegedly greeted her by asking, "Is this the little woman who made the great war?"

Thomas Dixon wrote his novels to set a torch to *Uncle Tom's Cabin* as part of his effort to redirect the nation's sympathy from the plight of the enslaved to the propaganda of the Ku Klux Klan. "It may shock the prejudice of those who have idealized or worshipped the negro as canonized in 'Uncle Tom,'" Dixon said in 1903, following the release of his first novel, *The Leopard's Spots*. "Is it not time they heard the whole truth?"[6]

Dixon's stories both narrated the white violence of the South and reinvigorated that violence in the new century. Both the violence Dixon narrated and the violence he inspired testify to the reality that any serious consideration of reparations must include the white terrorism that defined slavery's afterlife.

The Leopard's Spots: A Romance of the White Man's Burden—1865–1900 and *The Clansman: An Historical Romance of the Ku Klux Klan* are the first two installments of Dixon's trilogy on Reconstruction. This trilogy attempted to enable the nation to see the post–Civil War world through Southern eyes and to create a national solidarity behind white Christianity, chivalry, and civilization. Buttressed by both academic histories and the racial sciences, the repeated theme of the trilogy is that without the positive influence and beneficent care of slave masters, Black Americans started to degenerate following emancipation. As freed people devolved, they came to pose an existential threat to America's democracy and racial purity, forcing the pious South to arise and protect their way of life through virtuous acts of violence.

As political propaganda, Dixon's novels operated on multiple levels. At the level of national reconciliation, they attempted to hasten the longing for reconciliation by turning the nation's remembrances of the Civil War from the issues of slavery and treason toward empathy for Southern suffering and respect for Southern sincerity. By persistently eroding the memories of how slavery and treason combined to ignite the Civil War and fostering empathy and respect for the South, Dixon labored to position national reconciliation to take place on Southern terms.

At the level of securing white supremacy, Dixon's propaganda provided the apologetics for the South's emerging twin customs: segregation and lynching. In terms of the former, his novels framed segregation in the South as a necessary protection from the depraved behavior of Black people during Reconstruction rather than a perpetuation of slavery's rabid racism. In terms of the latter, according to Dixon's own words, his trilogy aimed to provide "the best apology for lynching," to instill "a feeling of abhorrence in white people, especially white women,"[7] and to make the fear of miscegenation a national obsession.

Just as Jefferson's *Notes on the State of Virginia* decisively shaped America's racial imagination following the Revolutionary War, Dixon's fiction—and the movies it inspired—became the preeminent shaper of America's racial imagination at the turn of the century and for the next sixty years. In his writings, lynchings transform into a symbol of a heroic counterrevolution aimed at redeeming civilization from the realization of one of America's deepest fears: an interracial democracy.

In the first installment of his trilogy, *The Leopard's Spots,* Dixon weaves together common tales of his era regarding a mystical, magical South victimized by the nightmare of unleashed slaves and an overreaching and militaristic federal government. "Over all the earth hung the shadow of the freed Negro," wrote Dixon, setting the mood, "transformed by the exigency of war from Chattel to be bought and sold into a possible Beast to be feared and guarded. Around this dusky figure every white man's soul was keeping its grim vigil."[8]

The Leopard's Spots begins following the surrender of the South as Confederate veterans migrate back to warm embraces in their war-torn homeland to reunite with family and loved ones. Following family reunions, the veterans prove eager to reconnect with their preacher, the Rev. Dr. John Durham. Through the character of Durham, Dixon begins one of his central missions: using white Christianity to baptize the vision of a racist South in the fear of God and white piety. "The church was the centre of gravity of the life of the people," Dixon writes. He continues:

> Society was torn from the foundations of centuries, but you would never have known it from the lips of the Rev. John Durham. These things were but passing events. When he ascended the pulpit he was the messenger of Eternity. He spoke of God, of Truth, of Righteousness. . . . The wise received it. The fools rejected it and were damned. That was all there was to it.[9]

What becomes obvious as *The Leopard's Spots* progresses is that the role of the Rev. John Durham and Southern Christianity will be to lead the community not in repentance but in *redemption*—reclaiming as much of the Southern way of life as possible.

It is no coincidence that white ministers play a central role in Dixon's novels. From America's inception through the early twentieth century, white Christianity provided the dominant moral and intellectual force in the country, and white ministers often acted as the community's intellectual and moral anchors. When Dixon was writing, this influence was at its zenith. Both Thomas Dixon and Black radicals understood that religion often acted as the heartbeat of America's racial project. While Black Christian leaders consistently employed the Christian tradition to break the grip of white supremacy, most white Christian leaders—from Northern progressives to Southern fundamentalists—worked continually to reinforce America's racial hierarchy. Well-known radical Christian abolitionists like William Lloyd Garrison and Wendell Phillips and lesser-known influencers like Elizabeth Margaret Chandler and Lucretia Mott were among the numerous exceptions to the rule during slavery. At the turn of the century, however, the exceptions were hard to find. White supremacy's demonic nature desired a spiritual host, and white Christianity willingly volunteered.[10]

Of all the aspects of America's racial project, none earned deeper scorn from Black America than white Christians and their ministers. When faced with the violence of white supremacy, with rare but notable exceptions, white ministers like the Rev. Durham supported the project through either their full-throated endorsements or their silent acquiescence. From experience, Frederick Douglass believed the main effect of white Christianity was to increase the violence of enslavers. "Of all forms of negro hate in this world," Douglass later lamented, "save me from that one which clothes itself with the name of loving Jesus."[11] For Du Bois, white Christianity was a "failure" rooted in an "utter denial of the first principles of the ethics of Jesus Christ." The basic nature of Southern Christianity, wrote Du Bois, "is its heathenism."[12] In the works of both Black radicals and Thomas Dixon, the first step in national reconciliation "across the bloody chasm" was to position white supremacy at the foot of Jesus's cross. Such racist reconciliation became part and parcel of the work of Christianizing American society.[13]

If the confidence in Southern morality continued to find its roots in white Christianity, confidence in Black depravity continued to find its roots in the myths about Black sexuality. As we saw in *Notes on the State of Virginia*, the myths of Black sexuality during slavery often focused on female promiscuity. After slavery, the mythologies of Black sexuality became a double-edged sword as the accent shifted from hypersexual females to the new caricature of Black men as predatory beasts.

In Dixon's novels, when Black women and white men engage in interracial liaisons, the crime is the seductive nature of Black women.[14] When Black men and white women are intimate, the encounter is always understood as the crime of a Black rapist. Of course, Dixon's framing is self-serving, but it accurately captures how the nation consistently framed interracial intimacy.

By inventing the predatory Black man and placing him at center stage in America's racial-sexual imagination, white supremacists attempted to hide the reality of interracial intimacies between, as Black editor Jesse Duke coined, "Black Romeos" and "white Juliets."[15] As racialized sexual mythology criminalized interracial intimacy, it also sought to justify the random acts of mob violence designed to instill white supremacy's terror in Black psyches and trap Black people at the bottom of America's racial caste system.

The Leopard's Spots was Dixon's first attempt to sell these Southern sexual fantasies as national facts. As the story unfolds, the honorable Tim Shelby becomes a focal point of its racist mythologies. *The Leopard's Spots* describes Shelby as a "full blooded Negro" who escaped slavery in Kentucky, organized armed militias of freedmen, and fought in the Union army. Using the power of oratory as a political tool to climb the ladder of success, Shelby becomes one of the primary political power brokers in South Carolina. Unsurprisingly, Shelby becomes Dixon's caricature of the overly ambitious and thoroughly corrupt Black legislator who threatens the Southern order.

The Rev. Durham's inner monologue provides a succinct summary of Southern views concerning Black leadership in the postwar South: "He thought of . . . Haley, Perkins, and Tim Shelby robbing widows and orphans and sweeping the poverty-stricken Southland with riot, murder, and brigandage." For the Rev. Durham, things go from bad to worse as federal authorities and Shelby collaborate to confiscate the property of vulnerable people of the South and pass an order that "commanded intermarriage, and ordered the military to enforce the command at the point of the bayonet."[16] From Dixon's pen, a racial rationality is reinforced—against all available facts—that paints Black statesmen as unjustly profiteering from the suffering of their Southern constituents. For Dixon, Shelby symbolizes more than one corrupt politician among a body of duly elected officials. Shelby symbolizes the "era of a corrupt and degraded ballot in the South" that began when freedmen gained the ballot and "intelligence, culture, wealth, social prestige, brains, conscience and the historic institutions of a great state had been thrust under the hoof of ignorance and vice."[17]

Such sentiments failed to harmonize with reality, but they provided a telling picture of the virulent backlash that every step of Black progress on American soil would produce. Time and again throughout Reconstruction, Black Americans defied the racist caricatures that white Americans crafted of them. And it was precisely the failure of Black people to be inferior and the threat of Black equality that fueled the most violent white backlash. "If there was one thing that South Carolina feared more than bad Negro Government," wrote W. E. B. Du Bois after laying out mountains of evidence regarding the political accomplishments during Reconstruction, "it was good Negro government."[18]

As Dixon spins his tale, he moves from Black politicians corrupting democratic government to Black politicians polluting white people's racial purity.[19] Dixon weaves together the fear of miscegenation with horrendous acts of sexual violence and retaliation throughout his novel. Perhaps his favorite refrain in *The Leopard's Spots*—repeated five times in five different settings—is focused on his central fear of racial impurity: "One drop of Negro blood makes a Negro." Dixon ties national disaster to that one drop: "It kinks the hair, flattens the nose, thickens the lip. . . . The Anglo-Saxon can not do this [intermarry with Black people] without suicide. . . . One drop of [Black] blood in my family could push it backward three thousand years in history."[20]

Earlier in the novel, at a white wedding the young bride is kidnapped by Black federal troops. As the kidnappers seek escape, the father of the bride insists that those with guns fire on them as they flee. Both the Black soldiers and the bride are killed. The next day, the father seeks solace in his pastor and confesses that despite his heartbreak, he knows there are things worse than death. "Preacher, I'd a killed her with my own hand if I couldn't a saved her no other way. I'd do it over again a thousand times if I had to."[21] Later still, a young girl named Flora is raped, and the brutality of the crime leads to her death. The Black culprit is caught and burned alive.

Yet, even amid this violence, Dixon goes to great lengths to portray Southern people as a peace-loving and patient people who wanted no racial war despite all the sins perpetrated against them. But under such burdens, even a straw can break a camel's back. In *The Leopard's Spots*, that straw is Tim Shelby's last and most ghastly deed. Shelby attempts to kiss a white teacher who came to him in the hope of securing a job at the school. After all they witnessed, Southern Christians would not wait idly by for Shelby's next move. In gruesome detail, Dixon narrates the morning after the attempted kiss:

> Tim Shelby was dangling from a rope tied to the iron rail of the balcony of the courthouse. His neck was broken and his body was hanging low. . . . His thick lips had been split open with a sharp knife and from his teeth hung this placard: The answer of the Anglo-Saxon race to Negro lips that dare pollute with words the womanhood of the South.—K.K.K.

Under the lifeless body, Dixon evokes language that continues to justify racial violence today and anoints the Klan as the "Law and Order League," which simply "sprang up like magic in a night."[22]

"Mob violence and eventually lynching were so deeply embedded in black folk memory," writes historian David Blight, "that virtually every major African American writer since emancipation had made these subjects central to his or her work in poetry and prose."[23] Perhaps no one in American history engaged in more thorough investigative work on lynching than Ida B. Wells.

Her journalism examined the surrounding circumstances and detailed the grotesque violence of lynching. Her research took her to the crime scenes. She diligently combed the white press to corroborate her accounts with the those of white writers. She wrote that what she witnessed possessed "all the horrors of the Spanish Inquisition and all the barbarism of the Middle Ages."[24] Her writings were as knowledgeable of the statistics as they were of the stories. She told and retold the stories of Tom Moss, Calvin McDowell, and Will (Henry) Stewart, who were lynched in Memphis for protecting their grocery store. She told and retold the story of Henry Smith, who was lynched and burned alive in Texas for taking a white lover. She told and retold the story of Eliza Woods, who was lynched under false suspicions after a husband had poisoned his wife in the home where she worked.

Through her writings, Wells excoriated America for its readiness to believe every racist lie that justified mob violence and its refusal to face the facts. Over and over, Wells's writings highlighted "the fact that only one-third of the . . . victims to mobs have been charged with rape, to say nothing of those of that one-third who were innocent of the charge."[25] Wells's research revealed that the genesis of lynchings rarely resided in rape, but instead often resided in the economic and social ascendency of Black people, the attempt to cover up white crimes, and the ever present reality of interracial intimacy.

Like Douglass and Du Bois, Wells excoriated the white press and pulpit alike. But she believed pulpits provided the most essential machinery in the South's misinformation campaign, for they acted as the community's conscience. "Should not all the white preachers . . . ," demanded Wells, "charge themselves with the thousands of lynchings by white men?"[26] When Wells preached, not many white Christians said, "Amen." When it came to racial justice, too often the cowardice of white preachers reduced them to either moral monsters or moral mutes. For Ida B. Wells, there was no difference between the two. "Cowards who fear to open their mouths before this great outrage," Wells charged, "do not see that by their tacit encouragement, their silent acquiescence, the black shadow of lawlessness in the form of lynch law is spreading its wings over the whole country."[27] Despite Wells's rigorous research and relentless determination, America encased itself in its racial worldview and ritualistic lynchings continued unabated.

In his writing, Dixon moves quickly from one grotesque image to the next. After imagining explicit sexual justifications for the Klan's violence, *The Leop-*

ard's Spots moves to the Klan's war on interracial democracy and the violent campaign to return the ballot box to white hands. Following the murder of Shelby, "every troop of the Klan" is summoned "in full force the night before the election." Orders are issued: "You are to visit every negro in the country and warn every one as he values his life not to approach the polls at this election." Rather than staging this violence as a war against democracy itself, Dixon frames it as a test of manhood for democracy's purification. "Those who come, will be allowed to vote without molestation," promises the Klan leader. But "all cowards will stay at home. Any man, black or white, who can be scared out of his ballot is not fit to have one. . . . This is simply a test of manhood."[28]

White supremacy's war against democracy that Dixon narrates squelched the Black vote for the next one hundred years. Unsurprisingly, it was again Ida B. Wells who cut to the heart of the matter. "No Negro domination," Wells wrote, "became the new legend on the sanguinary banner of the sunny South and under it rode the Ku Klux Klan." For Wells, nothing embodied the character of white America's politics and religion more poignantly than the Klan. A devout Christian committed to realizing interracial democracy in America, Wells confessed that "the blood chills and the heart almost loses faith in Christianity when one thinks of Yazoo, Hamburg, Edgefield, Copiah, and the countless massacres of defenseless Negroes, whose only crime was the attempt to exercise their right to vote."[29] For Wells, the society that most clearly rejected Christian teaching and the spirit of democracy was spelled U-S-A.

The Leopard's Spots stands in a long line of American white supremacist writings. The caricature of the criminal beast broke no new ground. Ever since the loophole in the Thirteenth Amendment opened the door to the proliferation of convict leasing schemes throughout the South, such caricatures were commonplace in racist thinking from everyday citizens to social elites like Charles R. Carroll, who published *The Negro a Beast* in 1900.[30] Yet, for as much as Dixon looked to the past for racial guidance, *The Leopard's Spots* was more than a recycler of racial stereotypes of slavery. Dixon sought to bring to life the new and emerging racial caricature that painted Black men as criminal beasts driven by a perpetual desire to rape white women. And the vivid and vicious nature of his caricature broke the mold.

For all its failures with historical facts, Dixon's writing certainly succeeds in introducing its readers to the state of white Southern self-understanding.

Of course, the deeper impact was not in simply revealing the Southern state of mind but in fostering the terroristic racial practices and racist public policies that aligned with Southern insanity. The defeat of antilynching laws, the radicalization of antimiscegenation laws, and the achievement of voter suppression are all interlinked with legacies of Dixon and *The Leopard's Spots*. In addition to these crimes, when we consider reparations in light of Dixon's work, one of the most difficult questions we must wrestle with is how to make reparations for weaponizing Christianity in the cause of white supremacy.

The evolution of racial lies and language from the age of the shackle to the demands of the modern world was well underway. *The Leopard's Spots* spread like wildfire. One of the most revolting romances ever written sold nearly a million copies, making Dixon a very wealthy man. Perhaps Dixon's initial success failed to lift him to Harriet Beecher Stowe's status, but he was already gaining ground.[31]

With his words in demand, Dixon quickly put together more novels. *One Woman* appeared in 1903, the year following *The Leopard's Spots*. It outsold Dixon's first novel and landed on the bestsellers list. Written well before the Red Scare stymied the work of racial justice and workers' rights, *One Woman* was Dixon's first novel in a trilogy that focuses on the threats of socialism and communism to America's economic and racial order. Since the days of slavery, Southern pulpits had long tied together abolitionism, atheism, socialism, and communism. Through Dixon, Southern pulpits were given a national stage.[32]

In 1905, Dixon provided the sequel to *The Leopard's Spots* with the release of *The Clansman*. Though he worked expeditiously, Dixon enhanced his persuasive powers by studying literary techniques from his fellow Southern novelists. What he learned was the patience to tell his story in a way that would create a greater common bond between the North and South without losing his unique edge. For the entire first two books of *The Clansman*, Dixon focuses on leading his readers to sympathize with the suffering of the South and crafting a more sentimental form of white supremacy.

He could not have chosen a better place to begin his novel. Rather than setting its opening scene in Dixie, *The Clansman* begins in a military hospital in Washington, DC, shortly after the war's final shots. In the hospital, Dixon introduces his novel's hero, Ben Cameron, a young, wounded veteran of South Carolina and the future grand dragon of the Klan. Nursing Ben back to health is Elsie Stoneman of Pennsylvania, whose father is the leading Radical Republican in Congress who is seeking to destroy the Southern way of life. As Dixon's tale unfurls, the wounded Southern soldier and Northern nurse fall in love. "She had entered on her work among the hospitals a bitter partisan of her father's school, with the simple idea that all Southerners were savage brutes," reveals the narrator. "Yet as she had seen the wounded boys from the South among the men in blue, more and more she had forgotten the difference between them."[33] From such a setting, *The Clansman* becomes a love story between the North and the South, and through Ben and Elsie's romance, the reader learns to see Reconstruction through Southern eyes and empathize with the South's suffering.

Before the romance takes off, the work of reconciliation begins with Lincoln himself as Ben's mother pursues a presidential pardon for her son. Despite his claims otherwise, Dixon's writing aimed at neither subtlety nor historical accuracy. Facts proved very flexible in Dixon's hands; however, despite the hopes of Black intellectuals, his recklessness with the truth rarely led his readers to question his judgment.[34] In real time, Southern papers characterized Lincoln as "an illiterate partisan . . . the beau ideal of a relentless, dogged, free-soil border-ruffian" and asked "after him what decent white man would want to be President?" Immediately following Lincoln's election, the convention of Dixon's home state of South Carolina unanimously voted to secede from the Union, and Charleston held a parade with an effigy of Lincoln. Members of the enslaved community were forced to place the figure of Lincoln on a scaffold to be set ablaze amid "the cheers of the multitude."[35]

Yet, in *The Clansman*, Dixon began rewriting Southern sentiments, and Ben's mother christens Lincoln a "Christian Father . . . and a Southern man." Lincoln makes only a brief appearance in *The Leopard's Spots*, but in *The Clansman*, Dixon takes his time to repaint Lincoln as the embodiment of a Southern gentleman. When the character Mrs. Cameron is granted an audience with the president, she approvingly notes his Southern style: "your looks, your manner of speech, your easy, kindly ways, your tenderness and humour, your firmness in the right as you see it, and, above all, the way you rose and bowed to a woman."[36]

If in real time Lincoln's election was less than popular in the South, the popularity of his Proclamation proved even more anathema. In the words of Richmond's *Enquirer*, the Emancipation Proclamation was the "last extremity of wickedness . . . at which even demons should suffer." The Proclamation revealed Lincoln "as black of soul as the vilest of the train whose behests he is obeying. So far as he can do so, he has devoted the Southern Confederacy to the

Direst destruction that can befall a people."[37] Yet Dixon, in *The Leopard's Spots* and again in *The Clansman*, portrays the South as celebrating the end of slavery. A typical passage from Dixon reads: "Every man in South Carolina to-day is glad that slavery is dead. The war was not too great a price for us to pay for the lifting of its curse."[38] The issue for Dixon and the South was no longer slavery, but the racial, political, and economic orders that would rise in slavery's wake. And it is to address those issues that Dixon begins to move his story south.

As the story heads to Dixie, Dixon resows the seeds of the old racial mythologies to justify aligning the South's new racist ways with her old world order. Among the first seeds Dixon chooses is the ever ironic mythology of Black sloth and dependence. During slavery, the racist imagination believed both that the enslaved were inherently lazy *and* that only the enslaved could perform the grueling work of the plantation. Yet, if any segment of society was slothful and dependent in slaveholding America, it was surely the enslavers, not the enslaved. As Alexis de Tocqueville recounts in his 1835 classic, *Democracy in America*: "The southerner loves grandeur, luxury, reputation, excitement, pleasure, and, above all, idleness; nothing constrains him to work hard for his livelihood, as he has no work which he has to do, he sleeps his time away, not even attempting anything useful."[39] Nonetheless, in works like *The Clansman*, old myths of Black sloth continue to justify new forms of oppression. In the evolving racist imagination, rather than slothful slaves depending on slave masters, these same slaves now depended on the federal government. And Dixon began exploiting that racist idea for all it is worth.

Though America's response to Black needs following the Civil War was meager, the mythology of dependence and sloth acted as a contagion that burrowed deeply into the American psyche. Dixon committed himself to accelerating that entrenchment. As Ben and Elsie move to the South, Dixon relentlessly portrays freed people as living off government rations from the Freedmen's Bureau without working. Though the Freedman's Bureau lent much of its assistance to impoverished whites, typical of the tropes Dixon employs is the lament that Ben's father, Dr. Cameron, expresses in a letter to his son: "No crop was planted this summer. The negroes are all drawing rations at the Freedman's Bureau."[40] Cottonseeds never cared whose hands planted them, yet Dr. Cameron seems unable to imagine white hands preforming the tasks Black hands had conducted so successfully for centuries.

The way the myth of Black sloth empowered the concentration of white power and profit is as simple as it is traumatizing. From the very beginning of America's racial project, creating maximum wealth with minimal time and effort became a primary goal of white supremacy. What was needed were institutions and ideas that provided working people the least amount of leverage, and nothing created that leverage better than the institution of slavery and the racist ideas that divided labor into racial factions. Black writers such as Frederick Douglass and W. E. B. Du Bois warned how white elites manipulated white workers to identify with their race rather than their class in order to shatter potentially transformative interracial worker alliances that would be capable of demanding living wages and a greater share of the profits their labor produced.

As attested by the abundance of Mississippi millionaires and the concentration of wealth throughout the South, the lower the wages for workers, the higher the profits for the wealthy. The better the system worked, the more it empowered the sloth of those who reaped the profits. "The masters could not bring water to boil, harness a horse, nor strap their own drawers without us," narrates Ta-Nehisi Coates in his novel *The Water Dancer*. "Sloth was literal death for us, while for them it was the whole ambition of their life."[41] Despite propaganda, in America, wealth and work were never tied at the hip. In a profitable land abundant with cotton fields, both slavery and radical economic inequality testify to how regularly the wealthiest whites refused either to work or pay a fair wage for the labor that undergirded their wealth.

After slavery ended, the mythology of Black sloth continued to justify the coldhearted readiness to leave Black people in deprivation and inspired racist public policies that strangled access to the basic necessities needed to achieve freedom, liberty, and life.[42] Without governmental assistance and protection, freed people possessed no leverage in their struggle for economic independence from those who once enslaved them and new forms of oppression arose to take the place of the slavery of old.

As Frederick Douglass looked back at the ways racism had reinvented itself to destroy Reconstruction, there seemed little to celebrate. The indifference to Black destitution demonstrated that though the institution of slavery had been slain, the moral depravity behind slavery—the depravity of white supremacists like Robert E. Lee—continued to thrive. "The world has never seen any people turned loose to such destitution as were the four million slaves of the South," Frederick Douglass said in 1875. Douglass mocked:

> They were free! free to hunger . . . free to the pitiless wrath of enraged masters, who . . . were willing to see them starve. They were free, without roofs to cover them, or bread to eat, or land to cultivate, and as a consequence died in such numbers as to awaken the hope of their enemies that they would soon disappear. We gave them freedom and famine at the same time.[43]

In Black America, the differences between slavery and the freedom to starve were often difficult to discern.

Besides failing to secure for Blacks the basic resources life demanded, America also frequently failed to provide them military protection or the firearms necessary for self-protection. Following Reconstruction, the fury at the modest military presence in the South led the region to paint itself as being ruled, as one of Dixon's chapter titles in *The Clansman* indicates, "At the Point of the Bayonet." The myth of government overreach and vast military presence following the Civil War again replaced facts with fiction. If anything, the most remarkable aspect of the military in the post–Civil War South was how quickly it disbanded and removed Black troops, and how often it *refused* to intervene to protect the lives of citizens within the freed community.

Within only a few months following Lee's surrender, General Grant and President Andrew Johnson quickly ensured the removal of Black soldiers to ensure that the South and its economy continued under white control. "The good of the country, and economy, require that . . . where there are many freedmen . . . there should all be white troops," recommended Grant to Johnson in his *Report on Conditions in the South*. "The reasons for this," Grant wrote, "are obvious."[44]

Nonetheless, in Books I and II of *The Clansman*, Black troops and bayonets seem ever present, even as mob violence is mysteriously absent. By the end of Book II, one wonders if Dixon lost his verve or forgot the name of his novel. But in Book III, the tide turns, as a Black Union soldier named August[45]—whom Ben Cameron's family had formerly enslaved—embodies the Southern myths of Black sloth, sexuality, and bayonet rule. In the chapter bearing the soldier's name—"August Caesar"—Southern fears and racist mythologies provide the prelude to Southern violence.

As Ben returns to his home, he runs into August, who "had the short heavy-set neck of the lower order of animals. His skin was coal black, his lips so thick they curled both up and down . . . his nose was flat. . . . Sinister bead eyes . . . gleamed ape-like under his scant brows." Ben hurries to confront him. "Didn't I tell you, Gus, not to let me catch you around this house again?" Ben leans back against the fence and places his hands on a loose picket as August musters the courage to claim his rights, saying, "I reckon de streets is free." But there would be neither conversation nor debate. "Quick as a flash of lightning the paling suddenly left the fence and broke three times in such bewildering rapidity on the negro's head."[46] Though August manages to escape, the confrontation with Ben Cameron and the Piedmont community is just beginning.

After the assault, August begins a precipitous rise in the Union army's ranks and becomes a captain overseeing eighty thousand Black men.[47] Unsurprisingly, as the story progresses, Dixon transforms the aspiring soldier into a violent rapist. The shift between a leader on the rise and an animal on the prowl is not subtle. After leading his troops through drills, August next appears at the cabin door of Mrs. Lenoir and her daughter, Marion. Lacking the protection of a Southern man, the women find themselves unprotected from August's lust. August kicks the door in with pistols in hand. His troops tie the mother up. August lets Marion know, "We ain't atter money!" Dixon brings the nightmare of sexual violence to a crescendo with "a single tiger-spring, and the black claws of the beast sank into the soft white throat and she was still."[48]

The sun rises the next morning with the mother and daughter alive but with the family's racial and sexual purity stained. Unable to bear their shame, Mrs. Lenoir and Marion choose to jump off a cliff together. The suicide leaves the Piedmont community to pursue justice without any evidence as to the crime or the identity of the criminal—precisely the type of case that demanded the extralegal intervention of the Klan, who freely pursued justice with their own standards of evidence.

In *The Clansman*'s chapter "The Hunt for the Animal," Dixon labors to show how cases of Black ravenousness demanded unauthorized proceedings to secure a truer justice than courtrooms allow. To do so, Dixon reveals how unique evidence arose in the South against criminals like August. "I believe," says Dr. Cameron to his Carolina colleagues, "that a microscope of sufficient power will reveal on the retina of these dead eyes the image of this devil as if etched there by fire. . . . Impressions remain in the brain like words written on paper in invisible ink. . . . If we can trace them early enough . . . , I believe the fire-etched record of this crime can yet be traced."

Dr. Cameron peers deeply into Marion's lifeless eyes with a microscope but sees nothing. Then he moves to Mrs. Lenoir. His body shivers with excitement as he sees in the fire of Mrs. Lenoir's lifeless eyes "the bestial figure of a negro—his huge black hand . . . The massive jaws and lips are clear—merciful God!—yes!—it's Gus!"[49] Science revealed to Dr. Cameron the sinister deed of his former slave, and "the hunt for the animal" was on.

With military efficiency, the Klan captures August as he attempts to escape Piedmont by train. They bind him and bring him to a cave lit by candles, "which had been the rendezvous of the Piedmont Den of the Klan since its formation. The meeting-place was a grand hall eighty feet deep, fifty feet wide, and more than forty feet in height." Dixon details the beauty of the Klan's uniforms and begins the trial with a prayer by the Chaplain, who requests God's favor as they "wrestle with the powers of darkness now strangling our life" and God's mercy as they face "Black death."[50]

The trial proceeds. The Scribe opens the Book of Record and solemnly greets the knightly circle as "the lovers of law and order, peace and justice." Dr. Cameron is summoned to produce his evidence against his former slave. Fearing a lack of credibility from the method that revealed the fire-etched truth of Augustus's guilt, he proposes to produce something better than evidence. He proposes to place Augustus under the power of his hypnosis and let him reenact his deeds on the night in question. The hypnosis takes. August relives his violent passions for all to see. The Klansmen are broken by what they witness, and "strong men began to cry like children."[51]

Fiery crosses lit the hills that evening. In the morning, Augustus Caesar's body lay lifeless and broken on the front lawn of the lieutenant governor with a note from the Klan. "Under their clan-leadership the Southern people had suddenly developed the courage of the lion, the cunning of the fox, and the deathless faith of religious enthusiasts," writes Dixon as the novel nears its end. "Civilisation has been saved . . . and the South redeemed from shame."[52] With such visions, *The Clansman* comes to its romantic close.

The Clansman went on to sell millions of copies as it became, in the words of journalist Douglas Blackmon, "the first true blockbuster in modern U.S. publishing." The popularity of the novel was bolstered by the endorsement of Abraham Lincoln's son. For Robert Lincoln, *The Clansman* was a "work that cannot be laid down."[53]

Though Dixon's novels operate on multiple levels, their significance was never their sophistication. Instead, according to the Black preacher and novelist Sutton Griggs, it was in how their violent images could "grasp upon the emotions of men, . . . [could] arouse and sway their feelings." Griggs was well positioned to understand Dixon's power. "In the long line of men of letters of the Anglo-Saxon race," Griggs reflected, "we find no counterpart of Mr. Dixon."[54] Through simple stories communicated in poignant but uncomplicated prose, Dixon repurposed the myths of white supremacy and the racialized research of his own era and positioned them to thrive for commercial audiences. In works like Dixon's, no longer were Black people harmless children needing white paternalism. Without the shackles of slavery, harmless children had degenerated into dangerous beasts.

Highbrowed literary critics berated Dixon's simplistic style. "His pile of wood," wrote one such reviewer, "is cut often with a dull axe and never sawed with a sharp sword."[55] But Black writers and activists understood that Dixon's simplicity was never a liability in his mission to replace Harriet Beecher Stowe as the molder of America's racial imagination. Rather, it proved his strongest asset, for it made the racist ideas germinating across the American landscape available for mass consumption.[56]

But the novels were only the beginning of Dixon's commercial success and influence, as they led Dixon to seek new media for his ideas. In 1906, following the release of *The Clansman*, Dixon combined and adapted *The Leopard's Spots* and *The Clansman* into a touring stage play that was wildly popular across the nation. But this, too, provided only a foretaste of what was to come. In 1915, film director D. W. Griffith brought *The Clansman* to life on the silver screen. Dixon, who worked closely with Griffith on the film's production, was so moved by his first viewing that he insisted the title be changed to *The Birth of a Nation*. America knew no shame concerning her fascination with Dixon's work. Dixon's Johns Hopkins classmate Woodrow Wilson used the release of the film to make history. For the very first time, the White House would host a movie screening, and *The Birth of a Nation* received the honored viewing. "It's like writing history with lightning," President Wilson remembered after viewing it with his cabinet and their families. "My only regret is that it is all so terribly true." Soon, special viewings would be provided for members of Congress and justices of the US Supreme Court.[57]

In time, the movie acted as a Hollywood pep rally for the Klan, and Americans crammed theaters to join the celebration. Since the film resonated so completely with the convictions of white audiences, few reviews felt the need to question the film's historical accuracy. In New York, the film attracted over three million viewers. The celebration would be long-lived. By 1930, approximately 90 percent of white Southerners had viewed the film, and *The Birth of a Nation* remained the best-selling movie for two decades. The official box office take topped $18 million, though in 1960, *Vanity Fair* estimated that a more accurate number was closer to $50 million, making it the highest-grossing film in history.[58]

Dixon the idea man had found his medium. "The motion picture is the finest vehicle of historical exposition ever devised," he exclaimed. "I can teach more history in fifteen minutes of motion pictures than in six months of the library or the classroom."[59] Dixon's lesson in history had power in the present. With the overwhelming popularity of the film, the Klan, which had been dormant for decades, resurrected, sinking its claws into Northern and Southern communities. Following *The Birth of a Nation*, the Klan's membership grew nationwide, inhabiting every state of the Union. The Klan would be dubbed "the Invisible Empire," whose two to six million members provided not only a nationwide presence but also national power. Its membership included governors, Supreme Court justices, senators, scores of congressional members, and titans of industry. Not to be completely outdone, the Women of the Ku Klux Klan (WKKK) reawakened, and their membership grew to 1.5 million white women. Auxiliaries arose like Junior Ku Klux Klan, the Tri-K Klub, and the Ku Klux Kiddies to train children in the way they should go.[60]

"There was fed to the youth of the nation and to the unthinking masses," W. E. B. Du Bois lamented, "a story which twisted emancipation and enfranchisement of the slave in a great effort toward universal democracy, into an orgy of theft and degradation and wide rape of white women."[61] And as Du Bois repeatedly pointed out, the mythology of Black pathology never segregated itself along either class or regional lines. No segment of white society was immune to the contagion. Decades later, Du Bois's preeminent biographer and Pulitzer Prize–winning Black historian David Levering Lewis would write that *The Birth of a Nation* "was uniquely responsible for encoding the white South's version of Reconstruction on the DNA of several generations of Americans."[62] And through that accomplishment, it became clear that Harriet Beecher Stowe's *Uncle Tom's Cabin* no longer held sway over the nation's racial sympathies. Dixon had burned her cabin to the ground.

As with Jefferson and Lincoln, it is hard to fully comprehend the impact of Thomas Dixon on America's racial imagination. His racial propaganda infected every facet of American life, and the Black rapist claimed center stage. Even physicians got involved, warning that the rapist within Black men was being released by a popular new drug: cocaine. In 1910, President Theodore Roosevelt nominated Dr. Hamilton Wright as the United States opium commissioner. Dr. Wright reported that "it has been authoritatively stated that cocaine is often the direct incentive to the crime of rape by the Negroes of the South and other sections of the country." In 1914, Dr. Christopher Koch declared: "Most of the attacks upon the white women of the South are the direct result of a cocaine-crazed Negro brain." In the same year, New York physician Edward Huntington Williams titled his article in the *New York Times* "Negro Cocaine 'Fiends' Are a New Southern Menace."[63]

But perhaps Dixon's impact is best measured by the wrath he elicited from Black American writers. Similar to Benjamin Banneker in the eighteenth century, Kelly Miller was a Black renaissance man who used his remarkable giftedness for the uplift of Black America. Miller was the first African American to attend Johns Hopkins University and worked as a mathematician to debunk the racial sciences and as a writer to lambast white supremacists.[64] In an open letter to Dixon from Howard University, Miller felt no need for nuance:

> You preside at every crossroad lynching of a helpless victim; . . . wherever the cries of the crucified victim go up to God from the crackling flame, behold, you are there; when women and children, drunk with ghoulish glee, dance . . . and mock the death groans of their fellow-man . . . , you have part in the inspiration of it all.[65]

Sutton Griggs proved even more direct as he imagined a tombstone to encapsulate Dixon's legacy: "This misguided soul . . . did all things which he deemed necessary to leave behind him the greatest heritage of hatred the world has ever known. Humanity claims him not as one of her children."[66]

The scorn Dixon earned from Black Americans came from the simple fact that more than any person writing at the turn of the twentieth century, he was the one who secured white supremacy's future by enshrining lynching as a sacred American ritual. Dixon not only helped cement Black depravity into America's racial imagination, but in so doing, he also perpetuated some of our nation's most racist public policy failures. In 1918, the Dyer Anti-Lynching Bill was introduced to make lynching a federal crime in the wake of the lynchings *The Birth of a Nation* had inspired. It eventually passed the House of Representatives in 1922, but afterward, the bill was killed in the Senate through a Southern filibuster. In total, Congress proposed over two hundred anti-lynching bills, but it would take until 2022 for antilynching legislation to be signed into law through the Emmett Till Antilynching Act. In making a case for reparations from the era of lynching, perhaps no better evidence exists than the federal government's support of the ritual that murdered thousands of Black Americans and entrapped entire communities in terror.

But it was not only the protection of lynching that Dixon's legacy helped secure. Both antimiscegenation laws and laws that disenfranchised Black voters were ubiquitous in states across America. And Dixon and the work of Southern redemption sharpened these laws. In 1910, Tennessee passed the "one-drop rule" regarding racial identity, and other states quickly followed suit as white supremacy became entrenched in twentieth-century America. Antimiscegenation laws were not banned until 1967, when the Supreme Court reversed its 1883 ruling in *Loving v. Virginia*. It was not until 2000 that the State of Alabama officially recognized interracial marriages.

As far as voting laws, it was the passage of the Voting Rights Act of 1965 that officially protected Black America's voting rights from white vigilantes, but even many of those provisions would be overturned in the coming decades. The devastation the war against democracy wrought in American politics is still difficult to fathom. The loss of the Black vote was never simply a devastating strike against the Black community. Inherent in the loss of the Black vote was the loss of the Black community's wisdom and imagination for the uplift of the entire nation. The loss of the Black vote was the loss of the most redemptive political and moral tradition America has ever known. Without Black wisdom, America's entire democracy was placed in the hands of those incapable of thinking beyond the barriers of white supremacy. When the Black South was robbed of the vote, a Southern bloc of senators formed that acted as the auction block of old by making American democracy subservient to those most committed to white supremacy. From the Three-Fifths Compromise to today's voter suppression, the more leverage Black voters lost, the more power racist legislators gained.

Black America eventually won meaningful victories in the struggle for interracial democracy, but as the attempted coup by white supremacists on January 6, 2021, and the voter suppression that followed testify to, the fight for democracy never ended. It is a sad testament to the intimate intertwining of race and American politics that every victory of interracial democracy has inspired the racist attempt to "purify" our nation's democracy by protecting the ballot from Black and Brown hands. Dixon's writings reveal the roots and rationality of voter suppression in the twenty-first century.

According to documentation by the Equal Justice Initiative, over 4,084 Black American lives ended at the end of a rope between the end of Reconstruction and 1950.[67] Yet, the victims of lynching were never limited to individual people brutalized under Southern magnolias. The purpose of the ritual was not to create the highest body count but to etch terror into the entire Black community. As Richard Wright wrote of so hauntingly in *Black Boy*:

The things that influenced my conduct as a Negro did not have to happen to me directly; I needed but to hear of them to feel their full effects in the deepest layers of my consciousness. Indeed, the white brutality that I had not seen was a more effective control of my behavior than that which I knew. . . . As long as it remained something terrible and yet remote, something whose horror and blood might descend upon me at any moment, I was compelled to give my entire imagination over to it, an act which blocked the springs of thought and feeling in me, creating a sense of distance between me and the world in which I lived.[68]

With the help of Thomas Dixon and his colleagues, the lynch became the crucible of America's racial consciousness. Black people became criminals without trials. White people epitomized innocence no matter how many Black people they murdered. When we read Dixon, we are not simply reading the mind of a fringe or regional racist. We are entering into the racial imagination of every echelon of white American society at the turn of the twentieth century. From presidents to preachers, from the Supreme Court to the mobs, Dixon helped etch the racial logic of lynching into the mental landscape of America.

Dixon died on April 3, 1946. In a tragically productive literary career that began at age thirty-seven, Dixon wrote close to thirty novels and over ten plays and was involved in nearly twenty film productions.[69] Dixon considered his last novel, *The Flaming Sword*, "the most important thing I have ever done."[70] In it, Dixon unleashes his fury as he combines his ideas on Reconstruction with his warnings against the threats of socialism and communism. In *The Flaming Sword*, the novel's villain is closely modeled after Black intellectual W. E. B. Du Bois. In the words of one reviewer, Dixon "gathers up the loose threads of the race problem . . . and weaves them into the pattern of a new national menace, Communism."[71]

After *The Birth of a Nation*, Dixon's finger lost its ability to find the American pulse, and his popularity entered a precipitous decline. But the significance of *The Flaming Sword* did not reside in its popularity. It pointed to a near future in which the fears of socialism and communism would begin to replace the lynch as the protector of America's racial imagination. More than twenty years after Dixon began viewing socialism and communism as "signs of racial degeneracy," Red Scare hysteria would sweep across America during the 1920s and be revived in the '40s and '50s to upend Black Americans' pursuit of equality.

Through it all—from Reconstruction through the Red Scare—the aim of Thomas Dixon's work never changed its mark. "I have simply tried in all my writing," he told a fellow minister in the last year of his life, "to develop Lincoln's and Jefferson's views through the characters I have created, showing separation is the only sane solution."[72] Through Dixon, America saw its racial myths in motion like never before. And never since.

Madison Grant

Eugenics and Purifying the Republic

> Two problems have much in common—Berlin and Birmingham.
> The Jewish people and the Negro people both know the terror of
> Nordic Supremacy. We have both looked into the eyes of terror.
> Klansmen and Storm Troopers are brothers under the skin.
>
> —Langston Hughes, "Nazi and Dixie Nordics," *Chicago
> Defender*, March 10, 1945

As freedom for Black Americans became restricted and white dominion and violence spread throughout the South following the death of Reconstruction, a trickle of Black migrants began heading north and west.[1] The exodus that had begun as a rivulet in the 1890s was by 1916 a rushing river. As Isabel Wilkerson describes in *The Warmth of Other Suns*, during the Great Migration, the Underground Railroad was replaced by overground railroads as Black Americans seeking freedom purchased one-way tickets heading out of the South. When Black migrants disembarked onto the railway platforms in cities across the North and West, they were ready to be done with the nation's racist mythologies that the South had valorized from the times of Thomas Jefferson to Jefferson Davis to Thomas Dixon. But America's racial mythologies were not done with them. In fact, cities like New York were ready and waiting for the Black migrants with mythologies that had been sharpened with a scientific edge.

One year after the release of *The Birth of a Nation* and the same year the *Chicago Defender* started to notice the Great Migration, a book was published that played a pivotal role in setting the world ablaze.[2] *The Passing of the Great Race* had been written by an aristocratic New Yorker named Madison

Grant. If Thomas Dixon had provided the entry point into the racial imagination of the sacred South, it was Madison Grant who revealed the racial work taking place in the minds of the North's most privileged elite.

Grant descended from a long and wealthy line of New York's leading families, and his life and thinking had taken shape within a context of the most exclusive echelons of progressive thinking in both America and Germany. Many American reformers of his era went to college or graduate school in Germany. But Grant's relationship began even earlier when, at the age of sixteen, he moved to Dresden to learn for four years under Europe's leading tutors. Likely, it was in Dresden that Grant first immersed himself in the racial sciences that worked to move white supremacy from the abstract realms of the philosophers to the surer sciences of statistics, biology, ethnology, anthropology, sociology, and economics. Grant took what he learned from Germany and headed to Yale, where he excelled in tests of prose but floundered in his class on logic.

From Yale, Grant headed to Columbia University's School of Law. After graduating, he displayed little interest in legal practice. Grant's inherited wealth provided him with a life of luxury without the need for a day job. This enabled him to hobnob with New York's most powerful and influential men through social clubs that kept their members up-to-date on the worlds of politics and science. Driven by deep ambitions, Grant committed himself to leveraging his networks and using the racial sciences as a whetstone to sharpen the racial laws of the land in order to protect the privileges of his people and class.

In his work, Grant proved indefatigable, throwing himself wholeheartedly into the two social causes he championed. His rich man's hobby of exotic hunting led Grant to give significant portions of his life and energies to conserving the nation's land and wildlife. The conviction of early conservationists like Grant and Theodore Roosevelt was that their virile Anglo-Saxon forebears conquered America's wilderness and that this wilderness must be preserved to promote the pleasure and masculinity of the Anglo-Saxon line. In today's vernacular, the conservationist cause was inseparable from a potent mix of white privilege and toxic masculinity.

But it was another white supremacist cause that led to Grant's international fame. That cause was the eugenics movement, which attempted to shape public policies in harmony with the revelations of the racial sciences. As the world matured, proponents of racism desired a surer foundation for their worldview and racist public policies, and nothing provided a firmer foundation than science. Throughout the 1800s and well into the 1900s, the racial sciences labored to transform the myths of the age of slavery and the more modern racist fictions of the Ku Klux Klan into scientifically certified facts. Rather than scientific fields providing a haven from racist propaganda, they often acted as the primary incubator for monstrous racial ideas.

Grant's early exposure to the racial sciences developed into a fascination that shaped his entire life, positioning him for a place of preeminence in the evolution of America's racial imagination and public policies. He was well versed in the long history of the racial sciences as well as in the cutting-edge research taking place in America and throughout Europe. Grant's writings not only tied the racial thinking of New Orleans to New York but also connected the racial policies of Birmingham to the future of Berlin. If anyone exemplified the sickening racial work happening in the North, it was Grant. In penning *The Passing of the Great Race*, Grant lit a stick of dynamite and placed it on a nation and world that were already a racial powder keg.

When *The Passing of the Great Race* hit New York's presses in 1916, white supremacy was nearing its zenith in American history. Anti-Black racism was so well established that there was little left to do. Nonetheless, white supremacists like Grant were not done in their attempts to perfect the nation. In fact, they believed themselves to be entering a new era in which their work was just beginning. And in important ways, they were right.

To fully appreciate the impact of *The Passing of the Great Race* requires recovering some of the history of the racial sciences that once played a significant role in American life but that was later essentially erased from America's common consciousness. The racial sciences tied together racist ideas, history, and the scientific method to conceptualize a human hierarchy and shape racist public policies accordingly. The human hierarchies not only were anti-Black but also pitted Europeans against one another to lay a groundwork for a society more thoroughly formed by both racism and classism. It was the United States' and Germany's infatuation with the racial sciences that intimately tied together their racial projects. Today, the wild racism of Grant's writings appears exotic and eccentric. In truth, it was anything but—Grant's writing was the fruition of the most refined Western research, and it represented what was becoming America's mainstream *progressive* thinking.

During the Revolutionary era, the racial sciences were in an embryonic state, and the emerging racial hierarchies deeply influenced America's founders. At the bottom of Europe's hierarchy were the wily Irish, and at the top were Anglo-Saxons, who had migrated from Germany's woods to England. Our founders viewed England as the height of the world's political genius, and it was through such Anglo-Saxons that the Founding Fathers traced their family lines. Naturally, Thomas Jefferson owned the largest collection of Anglo-Saxon documents and learned to read them in their original language. He rooted America's demand for freedom from Britain in their shared Anglo-Saxonism that endowed the colonies with the God-given right to self-government. Jefferson institutionalized his fascination with Anglo-Saxonism through the University of Virginia and employed a German scholar to teach Anglo-Saxon ideologies to the South's aristocracy.[3]

The fiercest debates among the legislators of the Constitutional Convention were often not over the *exclusiveness* of limiting citizenship to white people but over the *inclusiveness* of encompassing all people of European heritage.[4] Wouldn't American democracy and republican values go to hell if the Irish had the ballot? However, the racial reality of America at the time of the Revolution was that some 95 percent of white Americans were Anglo-Saxon, and what modest immigration was occurring only strengthened that dominance. A white hierarchy became a politically moot point and the Convention granted citizenship to "all free white men," even the Irish.

But what was politically moot proved intellectually stimulating. Racial scientists delved into the work of refining the world's racial hierarchy by providing a "scientific" rating system that distinguished between European nations at the top and the world's other peoples at the bottom.[5] Unsurprisingly, the scientists consistently found ways to keep Africans as the mudsills of the various pyramids they created. Differing histories and interrelationships emerged for European nations, and the terms "Anglo-Saxon," "Aryan," "Caucasian," "Teutonic," and "Nordic" each enjoyed their day in the sun. As can be imagined, these different hierarchies and histories did not always offer consistency, but the through line "again and again," as Nell Irvin Painter writes, was that "racial hierarchies set the poor and powerless at the bottom and the rich and powerful at the top."[6] The upshot of the argument was that *both* racial *and* class divides reflected superior and inferior genes. From methods to measurements to the interpretation of datasets, every step in the process of the racial sciences was prone to be twisted by white supremacist commitments, as the very mission of the sciences was to prove every racist and classist assumption.

As the racial sciences gained traction and credibility despite their inconsistencies, changing immigration patterns were transforming America's racial landscape to position the racial sciences to assume new and profound powers. Beginning in the latter half of the nineteenth century, wave upon wave of immigrants began landing on American shores, and these immigrants represented white folks of a "different" type.[7] Before 1870, eastern and southern Europeans accounted for about 1 percent of America's immigrant population. By 1910, they accounted for nearly 70 percent and often consisted of Jews, Catholics, and Orthodox Christians. The Founders' fears about inferior white people were no longer merely theoretical. They now carried practical impact on the most pressing political questions.[8]

What became clear during America's racial transformation that the waves of immigrants inaugurated was that anti-European immigrant racism was not nearly as ingrained in society at large as it was becoming in the racial sciences. Under the leadership of Francis Amasa Walker, new statistics within US census reports became available as early as 1870, making the census the thermostat of America's racial atmosphere. Like many of America's most ambitious reformers, Walker received his graduate school training in Germany, and the census reports he created enabled new demographic studies to track both people newly freed from slavery and those newly arrived from Europe. What the reports revealed was a deeper poverty and a heightened "criminality" within both populations.

However, since anti-Black racism was more deeply embedded in the American psyche than anti-immigrant racism was, the criminality that both impoverished communities held in common elicited two strikingly different responses. As Khalil Gibran Muhammad details in *The Condemnation of Blackness*, due to the presupposition of Black inferiority, no systemic solutions would be pursued to alleviate Black suffering. "White social workers and white philanthropists failed to invest," Muhammad notes, "advising these communities to 'work out their own salvation' before others could help them."[9]

Yet, when philanthropists and public policymakers viewed the same data on European immigrants, immigrant poverty and criminality were interpreted sympathetically through a social and environmental lens. This interpretation inspired the helping hands of philanthropy and generous public policies to provide immigrant communities with the resources needed to relieve some of their suffering. Criminality was seen as a very logical consequence of broken social and economic conditions. If you can't buy food, you steal food. Seeing both need and opportunity in the immigrant community, local public policymakers and philanthropic communities responded by advocating for resources to provide immigrant communities with social, economic, and political stability. And as public policy and philanthropy went to work, European immigrants received the white privilege to assimilate into American life and find a productive place within America's melting pot.

For Madison Grant, the melting pot threatened the exceptionalism of the United States and its Anglo-Saxon identity. Inspired by hordes of "inferior" European immigrants and the anti-white racism within the racial sciences, Grant placed pen to paper to author a new chapter in the evolution of America's racial imagination. With it, he aimed to accomplish nothing less than turning the tide of America's racial trajectory by developing a more precise calculus for dealing with *all* of America's vulnerable and marginalized people—from the poor and disabled to Irish and Jewish immigrants. But in the United States, it was Black people who paid the highest price for Grant's brilliance.

To turn the tide of America's racial trajectory, Grant wrote *The Passing of the Great Race* with moxie, stating precisely and transparently what the actions of white supremacists had long revealed but what hardly anyone had risked putting into such explicit terms. Grant believed the waves of inferior immigrants threatened to derail Anglo-Saxon republicanism and positioned democracy itself to destroy America by leading it toward socialism and an equality at odds with the laws of nature. Immigrants were bringing with them not only Europe's most degraded racial stock but also their degrading ideas. Immigrants began organizing for workers' rights and weakening American capitalists' control of the labor market. The corrupting actions and ideas of immigrants extended into interventionist social politics that sought to weave social equality into America's fabric and called into question Anglo-Saxon superiority. For Grant, the time to attack "democracy and its illegitimate offspring, socialism" had arrived.[10]

As with Dixon, Grant's brutal worldview harmonized with the racial convictions of America's highest social echelons. "This book is a capital book; in purpose, in vision"—so said Theodore Roosevelt in a laudatory letter to his friend, Grant. According to Roosevelt, *The Passing of the Great Race* was "the work of an American scholar, and gentleman; and all Americans should be sincerely grateful to you for writing it."[11] Roosevelt had long feared that the best of America's racial stock failed to reproduce as quickly as America's lower classes and that the imbalance was leading to a "War of the Cradle" that ate away at America's racial superiority. In *The Passing of the Great Race*,

Roosevelt saw a battle plan to win this war and avoid what sociologists referred to as "race suicide."[12]

Grant also received a similar letter from Adolf Hitler, who had studied
The Passing of the Great Race while working on *Mein Kampf* from Landsberg
Prison.[13] Hitler had held a long and abiding admiration for America, particularly for its genocide of the Indians, Andrew Jackson's Trail of Tears, and its
treatment of Black Americans. Grant's work only deepened Hitler's admiration. "The book," Hitler wrote to Grant after assuming the role of führer,
"is my bible." And in time, Grant's *The Passing of the Great Race* would be
widely received, in Jonathan Spiro's words, as "the bible of scientific racism,"[14]
providing a sharp two-edged sword in the struggle to aim public policy at the
pursuit of racial purity. That Grant's work received endorsements from the
führer and a president displayed just how fertile the soil of both Germany and
America was for the racial sciences and eugenics movement.[15]

What made Madison Grant's masterpiece "the bible of scientific racism"
was not new ideas but its bringing together of a wide range of inconsistent
and conflicting racist myths to provide a clearer portrait of racist lore.[16] Of
all the work the racial sciences produced, none proved more formative for
Grant than that of the racial theorists in Europe writing in the wake of Darwin's *On the Origin of Species*. As Ibram X. Kendi reveals in *Stamped from
the Beginning*, Darwin's original title was *On the Origin of Species by Means
of Natural Selection, or the Preservation of Favoured Races in the Struggle for
Life*. Over time, people learned to overlook the racial bent of Darwin's theory
until eventually the Western world forgot that the connection between white
supremacy and the theory of evolution had ever existed. But the first generation on which *Origin* landed saw in Darwin's convictions concerning "the
preservation of favoured races in the struggle for life" the scientific lynchpins
that validated the racial mythologies that shaped the racist worldviews of the
Western world.[17]

Darwin's disciples often disagreed about how to interpret his work and
their theories often led in contradictory directions, but they agreed that
Darwin and the racial sciences must begin shaping society through public
policies and economic systems. Critical to *The Passing of the Great Race* was
the ecosystem of thinking Darwin created through those he inspired. Perhaps
his two leading disciples were fellow Englishmen Herbert Spencer and Sir
Francis Galton, whose works ensured the racial sciences would always carry
an English accent.

Spencer coined the term "survival of the fittest" and would later be dubbed
the father of social Darwinism. Spencer's "survival of the fittest" and Darwin's

natural selection would be considered interchangeable by both authors, and Darwin himself would include Spencer's term in his sixth edition of *Origin*. Galton, Darwin's cousin, framed debates about racial inequality through the rubric of "nature versus nurture" and rose to fame as the father of eugenics. In the common vernacular, the racial edges of "nature versus nurture" often gets lost in translation—but questions about race acted as the debate's heartbeat, and Galton wrote to inspire a eugenical "Jehad," or holy war, against inferior races.[18]

The war America's racial scientists waged was centered on two main questions: Why are immigrants and Black people more likely to be in poverty, poorly educated, unemployed, and incarcerated? Are struggling immigrants and Black people the problem to be eliminated or the oppressed needing empowerment? Since eugenicists believed that only certain races could benefit from government benevolence, with rare but notable exceptions, the response of the intellectual guild was, in Grant's words, that "the lesson is always the same, namely, that race is everything."[19]

The line between social Darwinist and eugenicist was thin and permeable.[20] Both believed destiny is predetermined by race and heredity, and that the most pressing political question was how to handle the racial misfits of the day in order to get to the promised land of racial purity as efficiently as possible. Racial scientists were interdisciplinary practitioners who actively comingled their ideas with the work of economists, demographers, and sociologists to provide scientific justifications for any atrocity a racist mind might imagine. Imagining history as a biologically shaped, "winner takes all" struggle between the races for supremacy, they regarded empathetic public policies that benefitted inferior races as not only wasted resources but also potentially suicidal for "the master race."

Inspired by such a vision, eugenicists and social Darwinists demanded policymakers act to hasten nature's work via oppressive policies that actively destroyed inferior people, families, and communities and prevent all humanitarian interventions. As the racial sciences gained increasing traction, the more severe and dehumanizing racial public policies began to be considered the most enlightened course to take. Social Darwinism's racist ideas about the superiority and inferiority of racial groups shaped intellectual leaders and institutions throughout the United States and Germany from the late nineteenth through the early twentieth centuries and beyond. If reparations are demanded for weaponizing Christianity to serve white supremacy, so too reparations are demanded for the ways the racial sciences intentionally supplied ammunition for racist public policies. Together, white Christianity and the racial sciences during the age of lynching show why, in addition to financial remediation, reparations must recraft the inner workings of white people's minds and morality.

⁓

For all the brilliance of the racial scientists, the challenge of keeping their work alive was simply that its foundations were racist commitments without empirical validity. Not all racial scientists were alike. Many allowed their racial commitments to shape the very designs of their experiments and bias their measurements to produce data that easily fit their racist presuppositions. The methods and measurements of other racial scientists proved precise. But from precise datasets, remarkably nimble interpretations arose to harmonize with a priori racial commitments. From within the ecosystem of the racial sciences, theorists made highly flawed predictions about the future disappearance of Black Americans from the nation's demographic landscape and insidious claims about the limits of the giftedness of Black and poor people. When history refused to align with the racial theories, more nimble interpretations were needed so that the science's undergirding convictions could remain unmoved.

In an increasingly science-obsessed world, keeping myths alive in the face of countervailing facts is difficult work. And Madison Grant worked very hard. Not only had the racial sciences of craniology and recapitulation fallen on hard times; the very histories and hierarchies of the Anglo-Saxon, Teuton, and Aryan collided and conflicted.[21] So when the puzzle pieces of the racial histories and sciences failed to connect, which was not rare, Grant got creative and crafted new pieces of racial lore to bring the picture together. These pieces often lacked historical or empirical validity. His work was insane, yet the detailed maps he designed, his wide reading, and his confident writing style provided the illusion of intellect that allowed for ludicrous racial fictions to be received as scientific fact.

In 1927, Edward Franklin Frazier dissected the nature of America's more modern racism in his article "The Pathology of Race Prejudice." For Frazier, "the behavior motivated by race prejudice shows precisely the same characteristics as that ascribed to insanity."[22] From presidents to the people, white America was insane. What made America's racism pathological was not a lack of rationality. As the racial sciences had proved, no one rationalizes more than the insane do. Just as Thomas Jefferson proved immune to every evidence of Black equality, Frazier argued that the heart of the problem was that the rationality of the insane is deeply rooted in delusions and that "the delusions of the insane . . . show a greater imperviousness to objective fact." Deepening the crisis was that even though the insanely racist proved immune to facts, they also proved highly susceptible to racist propaganda. "Just as the lunatic seizes upon every fact to support his delusional system, the white man seizes myths and unfounded rumors to support his delusion about the Negro," warned Frazier. Accordingly, any fact that fails to fit the racist system is twisted and tortured "to preserve the inner consistency of his delusions."[23]

Frazier's description of rational racists provides an accurate assessment of Grant's state of mind as he undertook writing *The Passing of the Great Race*. Grant dedicated his book to the "attempt to elucidate the meaning of history in terms of race," as he sought to open American minds to think beyond anti-Black racism and expand its racial persecution to include inferior European immigrants too. Grant wanted America to realize that European immigration threatened the racial stock of modern America in similar ways that slavery had once threatened the racial purity of the colonial plantations. The challenge for twentieth-century America was to learn how to manage her white immigrants with the rigor and cruelty with which the nation always managed her Black people.

For Grant, by investing in creating an environment conducive to integrating European immigrants into America's melting pot, America's policymakers had driven the nation down a path dictated by sentimentalism, not science or history. In Grant's mind, America's melting pot led the nation toward what sociologists had long feared: race suicide. "We Americans must realize that the altruistic ideals . . . and . . . sentimentalism that has made America 'an asylum for the oppressed' are sweeping the nation toward a racial abyss," Grant warned. "If the Melting Pot is allowed to boil without control, and we continue to . . . blind ourselves to all 'distinctions of race, creed, or color,' the type of native American of Colonial descent will become . . . extinct."[24] Grant wrote *The Passing of the Great Race* and other works to avoid this racial apocalypse.

In *The Passing of the Great Race*, Grant begins the fight for America's future by looking backward into history to highlight the ascendence of the Nordic race among its European counterparts. Through craniological studies that examine the differences among skulls found throughout Europe, Grant asserts that "three distinct subspecies of man" originated in Europe: the Nordic, the Mediterranean, and the Alpine. These races were distinguished by the color of their eyes, their hair, their stature, and their noses. Despite European similarities, "the Nordic race in its purity has an absolutely fair skin, and is consequently the *Homo albus*, the white man par excellence," or the "*master race*."[25] Grant was an outdoorsman, and when he imagined the Nordic race, he did so through the lens of toxic masculinity and illusions of self-grandeur. Nordics were virile and violent warriors, first into battle and the last ones standing. They were the most brilliant scholars and statesmen and produced the most beautiful people.

In Grant's reading, all American founders originated from the Nordics, and those founders designed our nation for the Nordics and no one else. Through Nordic myths, Grant sought to teach America a larger lesson. Not only were white Americans superior to nonwhite people, but they proved exceptional even among their European counterparts. Zeroing in on the threat of undesirable immigrants from Europe, Grant believed America's future hinged on expanding the nation's racist imagination. With European nations sending their "most undesirable races and classes . . . desirous of unloading on us their social discards,"[26] America's anti-Black racism was simply not racist enough. For Grant, it was urgent for the nation's public policies to align to keep "America for Americans."

Rarely before in America's history had white supremacy's dehumanization of poor and working-class European people been as explicit as in the writings of Madison Grant.[27] Yet Grant seemed to worry little about his explicit antiwhiteness. He did, however, work diligently to clarify that underneath his anti-immigrant racism, just like underneath the Nazis' anti-Semitism, was an even more deeply abiding disdain for Black people.[28]

Grant understood how easy it was for the scientifically uninitiated to get confused by the intricacies of his racial rhetoric and his focus on the threats of people of European origin. To not lose anti-Black racism in his efforts to heighten anti-immigrant racism, Grant decided he needed to delineate *Homo sapiens* from *Negroes*. "The main European races are the subject of this book . . . which, taken together, we may call the Caucasian for lack of a better name." If the Enlightenment sought to call into question African humanity, the racial sciences sought to answer that question. Those Grant refers to as "Negroes and Negroids"[29] represent not simply a different human race but an altogether different type of humanity unrelated to Caucasians in any meaningful way. He would further clarify in *The Conquest of a Continent* that not all humans are part of the family of *Homo sapiens*. Such thinking was "old-fashioned. . . . A new system must be formulated [because] the physical differences between the Nordics and the Negroes . . . would be much more than sufficient to constitute not only separate species" but a separate animal family.[30] For Grant, Nordics and Negroes share no more in common than a lion and a mouse. Both species are mammals. Yet only one species produces kings.

For W. E. B. Du Bois, there was nothing new in such arrogant absurdity. Grant's project of Americanization through the rhetoric of "America for Americans" was simply the newest expression of aristocratic hate for both humanity and democracy. No one mastered the art of race hate quite like Madison Grant and his aristocratic friends. "The ignorant and poor may lynch and discriminate," Du Bois jeered, "but the real deep and the basic race hatred in the United States is a matter of the educated and distinguished leaders of white civilization."[31]

For Du Bois, Americanization was an antidemocratic mission to privilege the aristocracy and disenfranchise anyone who threatened their concentration of power. "What we think we mean by Americanization is the making of this country one great homogenous whole working for the same ideals, defending its integrity, preserving its hard found liberty," wrote Du Bois in the NAACP's *Crisis* magazine in 1922. But, "as a matter of fact what the powerful and the privileged mean by Americanization is . . . but a renewal of the Anglo-Saxon cult; the worship of the Nordic Totem, the disfranchisement of Negro, Jew, Irishman . . . the world rule of Nordic white through brute force."[32] For Du Bois, Americanization placed the South and North into the same army in a war against both human rights and democratic ideals. Years later, in *Darkwater*, Du Bois scathingly pointed to the irony that a society that felt free to brutalize her own citizens thought of itself as a democracy at all: "We push below this mudsill the derelicts and half-men, whom we hate and despise, and seek to build above it—Democracy!"[33]

But white America was not listening to Du Bois or Frazier, for Madison Grant and his fellow white supremacists continued to strengthen white supremacy's hold on the national imagination. For Grant, the future must be shaped by the demands of racial sciences, not the ideologies of democracy. And from the crucible of the immigration crisis and white supremacy's pinnacle in US history, the racial sciences demanded erasing democratic convictions. It is this demand that Madison Grant seared on the soul of America and the world.

America's flaws were deeply rooted. And the deepest flaw in America's racial imagination was neither the Three-Fifths Compromise within the Constitution nor her overall compromises with the institution of slavery. For Grant, like the young Lincoln, the Constitution prior to the Civil War was an "amazing document" with no need to alter or amend.[34] The flaw within America's racial imagination, he believed, traced back to the Declaration of

Independence and the false equivalency among *Europeans*. That error made the American republic susceptible to the unscientific "democratic theories of government . . . based on dogmas of equality formulated some hundred and fifty years ago. These dogmas rest upon the assumption that *environment* and not *heredity* is the controlling factor in human development."[35] America needed to remember "our form of government is based on the Constitution of the United States and *not* on the Declaration of Independence."[36] When America leaned toward the Declaration of Independence, democracy itself threatened the aristocratic nature that had made the American republic exceptional.

If Grant proved less than sympathetic with the author of the Declaration of Independence's prose, he was nonetheless in solidarity with Jefferson's deepest fears of interracial intimacy that might destroy the republic. In Grant's mind, when white America consisted of the Nordic race, democracy was not a particular threat to the American experiment. The Nordic race naturally and rightly relied upon the aristocracy for political representation and leadership. But with the racial transformation of America, the tried-and-true dependence on aristocracy was beginning to wane, and political rights were extending into places where America's founders never intended them to go. Reading the mythical threat of miscegenation onto America's racial landscape, Grant deduced that mixing Mediterranean, Alpine, and Black blood into the nation's body politic denigrated our democracy. Grant argued that as races mix, mediocrity replaces aristocracy in political positions and "a diminution of the influence of genius" occurs that dumbs down our nation and her leadership. "Where we have a mixture of races," Grant laments, "some of the most important elements of freedom for which our ancestors fought have to be abandoned."[37]

The United States, so it seemed to Grant, simply refused to progress with time by learning the lessons her racial history clearly taught. Linking America's past with the nature versus nurture debate, Grant writes: "There exists to-day a widespread and fatuous belief in the power of environment." But that fiction simply repeats the mistakes of the "sentimentalists of the Civil War period. . . . It has taken us fifty years to learn that speaking English, wearing good clothes, and going to school and to church, does not transform a negro into a white man." Rather than the recent European immigrants providing the exception to the rule, "we shall have a similar experience with the Polish Jew" and Europe's other racial refuse.[38] Despite America's sentimental tendencies, Grant attempts to finalize the lessons of science—"the limits of . . . development are fixed for it by heredity and not by environment."[39] Funneling limited resources to feed, educate, and uplift society's outcast groups was like placing a mound of ice cream on a mound of manure. Ice cream cannot improve manure, but manure can sure mess up ice cream.[40]

For Grant, the hard lesson America learned from its "failure" to lift the freed people to civilized status through Reconstruction, it needed to heed with its immigrant population. That lesson is this: rather than seeking to construct "an asylum for the oppressed," America needed to abandon her poor and disinherited and allow nature to perform the work she desired to accomplish with ruthless efficiency. On such points, Grant writes with nothing less than the zeal of a prophet:

> Where altruism, philanthropy, or sentimentalism intervene with the noblest purpose, and forbid nature to penalize the unfortunate victims of *reckless breeding*, the multiplication of inferior types is encouraged and fostered. . . . Mistaken regard for what are believed to be divine laws and a sentimental belief in the sanctity of human life, tend to prevent both the elimination of defective infants and the sterilization of such adults as are themselves no value to the community. *The laws of nature require the obliteration of the unfit, and human life is valuable only when it is of use to the community or race.*[41]

With such stark sentences, the racial edges of scientific racism and American-made fascism begin setting the stage to set the world ablaze. But Grant was not finished.

In eugenic thought, the preeminent example of creating a productive environment for America's inferior races was slavery—for slavery was the only time in American history when Black Americans neared the full realization of their God-given potential. "Negroes have demonstrated throughout recorded time that they are a stationary species, and that they do not possess the potentiality of progress or initiative from within," notes Grant. Black progress came "by the slavers' lash." With slavery's overseers as inspiration, Grant paints a picture of what type of nurture he thinks the lower races needed.[42] As with nearly everything Grant wrote, he did not stand alone in making such arguments. These were mainstream views of scholars such as those associated with the American Economic Association led by Walter Wilcox of Cornell University.[43]

For a better world, the lower races needed neither higher culture nor Christianity, neither higher education nor industrial training, neither arts nor sciences. What the world needed was Nordic wrath unsheathed upon inferior people. The cruel insanity of eugenicists like Madison Grant helped cement the conviction that only by resurrecting public practices like that of slavery could the modern world provide environments that either eliminated inferior races or motivated them to reach the maximum of their minimal potential. The idea that only deprivation and "tough love" empowered Black self-improvement was not new to conservatives at the end of the twentieth century. Such racist convictions come directly from the founding fathers of the eugenics movement and shaped racist public policies throughout the twentieth century. In passages such as those quoted above, the influence of the racial sciences is fully felt.

Eugenics, like slavery, represented far more than racial violence against Black people. It represented an all-encompassing crime that corrupted the entire nation's humanity. This is why when we speak of reparations, in addition to paying our financial debt, we must deal with the ways in which our nation must be reborn by reforging our conscience and consciousness around antiracist practices and policies. It is only through a holistic process of reparations that we can be released from the eugenical fiction that it is only through punitive paths that progress is made. It is only through a holistic process of reparations that we can reclaim aspects of the shared humanity we lost when we placed our nation's mind, body, and spirit into white supremacy's genocidal hands.

In Madison Grant's writing, he often comes across as an aristocratic whiner. But the reason Grant writes is not to whine about America's political reality but to fight for tomorrow by warring against America's mediocre elements and setting the stage for a more aristocratic and Nordic future. Grant writes to pit the power of science against sentimentalism. "Man has the choice of two methods of race improvement," Grant asserts. "He can breed from the best, or he can eliminate the worst by segregation or sterilization."[44] The hope for America's future resided in a full investment in both positive eugenics— breeding brilliant and beautiful people like bunnies—and negative eugenics—segregating and sterilizing those on the lower end of the bell curve.

Admittedly, Grant viewed positive eugenics as a utopian vision rather than a practical political solution. It would prove "extremely difficult . . . to determine which were the most desirable types, . . . [and] it would be, in a democracy, a virtual impossibility to limit by law the right to breed to a privileged few." Thus, what was needed was "a rigid system of selection through the elimination of those who are weak or unfit." Negative eugenics harmonized not only with the sharpest insights of science but also with practical politics. Or in Grant's words: "Under existing conditions the most practical and *hopeful* method of race improvement is through the *elimination* of the least desirable elements in the nation *by depriving them of the power to contribute to future generations*."[45] In that simple sentence, Grant reveals one of the explicit aims of segregation and Black deprivation in postslavery America: the elimination of Black people and communities.

To avoid missing the implications of Grant's statement, we must view segregation through the hopes and convictions of the culture that implemented it. Following the Civil War, segregation coincided with the rise of the "Black extinction hypothesis." The theory was anchored in the subterranean racist hope in white America—and that hope was that rather than the Emancipation Proclamation leading to an interracial democracy, it would hasten nature's work of eradicating Black Americans.

Such hopes were seen not only in the writings of Robert E. Lee but also in the North's leading and most influential intellectuals, including Ralph Waldo Emerson. "If the black man is feeble, & not important to the existing races, not on a par with the best race," Emerson wrote in his journal in 1844, "the black man must serve & be sold & exterminated."[46] Walt Whitman concurred. "The nigger, like the Injun, will be eliminated," Whitman wrote. "It is the law of races, history, what not."[47] Both Northern and Southern intellectuals often believed following emancipation that history itself would fulfill the dream of Black extermination, as Black people's inherent "inferiority" and the racist public policies of segregation coupled to hasten the annihilation of the formerly enslaved.

This was all very scientific stuff, as such hopes closely followed in the footsteps of the Western world's foremost scientific intellectuals. "At some future period, not very distant as measured in centuries," Charles Darwin mused in *The Descent of Man*, "the civilized races of man will almost certainly exterminate and replace the savage races throughout the world."[48] Herbert Spencer, however, thought that nature might not be so patient. In his final edition of *First Principles*, Spencer dedicated a chapter titled "Segregation" to articulating a particular process of "natural selection" that allowed for the "continual purification of each species from those individuals which depart from the common type in ways that unfit them for the conditions of their existence." Through such a process, the "unfit" could efficiently be "killed off."[49]

Under the spell of the Black extinction hypothesis, nineteenth-century segregation never aspired to America's later rhetoric of "separate but equal," but rather was all about lynching entire communities. The hope for extermination via deprivation was a motivating driver for progressive segregationists.[50] In 1919, Grant's colleague Prescott Hall framed the logic like this: "Just as we isolate bacterial invasions and starve out the bacteria by limiting the area and amount of their food-supply, so we can compel an inferior race."[51]

As the nineteenth century transitioned into the twentieth, Black extinction theory and the rhetoric of racial sciences evolved into the eugenics movement, keeping the hope of elimination alive and well. It is not a coincidence that Jim Crow laws in the South strengthened even as overflowing urban ghettos of Northern cities grew more dire. The ideologies of social Darwinism provided scientific blueprints for dealing with America's racial outcasts that would soon inspire Germany to begin designing ghettos for their own racial outcasts. This is the historical background of today's marginalized minority communities. Without this historical vantage point, our understanding of segregation is not merely superficial; it is inaccurate.

That segregation also alleviated Madison Grant's and other white supremacists' fears of miscegenation in the short run was a bonus. As Grant wrote in one of the most famously racist passages of *The Passing of the Great Race*: "Whether we like to admit it or not, the result of the mixture of two races, in the long run, gives us a race reverting to the more ancient, generalized and lower type." Grant then puts the scientific point in more explicitly racial language: "The cross between a white man and an Indian is an Indian; the cross between a white man and a negro is a negro; the cross between a white man and a Hindu is a Hindu; and the cross between any of the three European races and a Jew is a Jew."[52] Leaning fully into the theories of denigration that stretched back to ancient times, Grant gives ancient anxieties modern life. In the United States, racial mythologies proved so powerful in the early twentieth century and the new scientific age that only the most stringent and absurd levels of segregation provided peace to scientifically disciplined minds.

These theories transformed into policy throughout the United States and attained infamy through Grant's most infamous pupil. Admittedly, the prose of Hitler's *Mein Kampf* is a bit tamer than Grant's—but Grant's influence on Hitler's racial imagination is fully felt. Moderating Grant, Hitler writes in his chapter "Nation and Race":

Any crossing of two beings not at exactly the same level produces a medium between the level of the two parents. This means: the offspring will probably stand higher than the racially lower parent, but not as high as the higher one. . . . Such mating is contrary to the will of Nature for a higher breeding of all life.[53]

"Nation and Race" would be the only chapter from *Mein Kampf* to be turned into a pamphlet for mass consumption as Grant's ideas helped set Germany on the path to racial purity.[54] That many white Americans could be enraged about Hitler's crimes while embracing racial practices so deeply aligned with Nazi ideologies testifies to the power of segregation's war against self-awareness.

As we consider reparations in a nation haunted by racial inequalities, inequalities made all the more dire in segregated communities, we must remember that the pervasive poverty within America's minority communities was never an American accident. It was and is destruction by design. Grant's work reminds us that segregation was not only the sign of the deeply rooted bigotry of Southern Christians, but also a reflection of the racial edges of the Northern intelligentsia's scientific, philanthropic, and progressive politics. In Jonathan Spiro's remarkable biography about Grant, *Defending the Master Race*, Spiro notes the tragedy that "eugenics was the *ultimate* progressive idea."[55] That is the kicker. The hope for the elimination of Black Americans was not a fringe element within America's racial imagination; it was the essence of Southern Christians' and Northern progressives' vision of utopia.

The racial scientists tracked census data seeking to confirm their hopes and theories that Black Americans would die off and that the realization of a racially pure, white America was drawing closer with each passing year. But the weight of history would soon overthrow the hopes of the "Black extinction" theorists. Against great odds, Black Americans refused to give up their struggle to thrive.

Twenty years after *The Passing of the Great Race*, Grant himself wrote that the high hope that nature would eliminate Black America was dead. "In view of the present vital statistics of the two races," Grant wrote in his attempt to face reality, "natural selection . . . can no longer be relied upon to solve the problem by a gradual elimination." Per usual with Grant, however, he was not content to just face reality. He strove to shape it and postulated about resurrecting the colonization schemes of the nineteenth century or making segregation more radical still by restricting Black Americans to land along the Gulf of Mexico. "Whatever the final outcome, the Negro problem must be taken vigorously in hand by the whites."[56] It was a testament to the depth of Grant's racial convictions that even after the very theories of scientific racism he based his worldview on failed on the national stage, his fight to bring our world in line with his racist worldview never wavered.

It requires little time reading Madison Grant to realize that nearly nothing he says is based on anything resembling empirical analysis or evidence-based research. Grant, like Thomas Jefferson and Enlightenment philosophers, intentionally sought to provide racial propaganda a veneer of intellectual credibility. Such propaganda intentionally buried the truth and proved as dangerous as any policy it sought to justify. As Du Bois would lament:

> Indeed, the greatest and most immediate danger of white culture, perhaps least sensed, is its fear of Truth. Its childish belief in the efficacy of lies as a method of human uplift. . . . We deliberately and continuously deceive not simply others, but ourselves as to the truth about them, us and the world. We have raised Propaganda to capital "P" and elaborated an art, almost a science of how one may make the world believe what is not true, provided the untruth is a widely wished-for thing like the probable extermination of the Negros.[57]

Du Bois understood that what made Grant's propaganda so persuasive was that the very ideologies of racial science simply confirmed America's preconceived convictions about racial differences that traced back to the nation's founders. It takes little rigor or evidence to convince people of what they believe they already know.

Yet, the upshot of Grant's ability to write the dogmas of racial science without the need to analyze the evidence was his ability to write with a confidence that provided the illusion of authority. Grant often wrote from his imagination without any footnotes. And though Grant's lack of footnotes and tendency to craft theories free of supporting evidence proved troubling for some of his supporters, many leading academics looked past such foibles to support Grant as the nation's leading intellectual light.

Grant's writing rested on the assumption that the scientific guild had established that nature and heredity proved more determinative for humanity's potential to flourish than nurture and environment. And though it was true at the time that the supremacy of nature over nurture was presumed throughout much of the scientific world, there is a difference between presumption and proof. And *no* studies proved capable of providing evidence that nature was more determinative than environment.[58]

It was only after writing *The Passing of the Great Race* that Grant entered into any meaningful relationship with evidence-based research. That entrance was through IQ tests. As seen in the work of Thomas Dixon, following the Civil War, so much of white America's racist focus was on Black criminality, depraved sexuality, and ingrained sloth that little focus on Black intellectual capacity was needed. But the racial sciences were still diligently at work in the background, seeking to quantify white people's supposedly superior intelligence. One of the earliest quantifications of intelligence came through the discipline of craniology, which argued that bigger brains equated to greater brainpower. Craniology's attempt to quantify the superiority of white skulls displayed significant staying power, only to eventually crash into the rocky shoreline of its own inconsistencies.[59]

Instead of craniology's failures leading scientists to question the presuppositions of the racial sciences, however, they instead simply quickened the thirst to find better ways to reduce human brilliance to a single measurement. Enter IQ tests. Created in 1904 by Alfred Binet in France, IQ tests were designed to identify French students in need of special educational help to perform at grade level. In his research, Binet explicitly repudiated the claims of the racial sciences, rejecting the notion that intelligence could be reduced to a single number or to inborn traits unrelated to one's history, background, and socioeconomic factors. When it came to his test, Binet rejected any claim that the results were predictive of a person's potential or useful in comparing different people groups. His singular hope was to help France's vulnerable students get the assistance they needed to thrive. His singular fear was that the results of his tests might create a self-fulfilling prophecy by falsely framing vulnerable students as people with limited potential. Such fears proved prescient.[60]

Not long after the creation of France's intelligence test, the eugenicist Henry Herbert Goddard imported it to America and repurposed it to serve the exact assumptions Binet rejected. Against its very design, eugenicists implemented Binet's test in the US in a manner that suggested intelligence could be simplified down to a single number without considering either cultural or socioeconomic variables. Fueled by fears of immigrants and the dehumanization of mentally disabled people and impoverished families, eugenicists weaponized IQ tests at places like Ellis Island, psychiatric facilities, and poorhouses to weed out the "unworthy" and eliminate their bloodline

through deportation or sterilization. From Ellis Island, Goddard would declare 84 percent of immigrants were feebleminded. Though Goddard's test
was primitive and was administered to only 141 subjects, his work made
headlines, sending shock waves across the nation. In communities across
America, Binet's worst fears took on flesh as his test was weaponized to
dehumanize the already vulnerable.[61]

And then his nightmare grew. In World War I, the eugenicist Robert
Yerkes convinced the US Army that the IQ tests could help win the war and
received permission to test 1.75 million men. The administration of the test
ran into multiple challenges, as it proved impossible to administer it on so
many men with precision. Yet, what the military test lacked in quality, it made
up for in quantity, producing a dataset whose size was without equal. The
vastness of the data endowed the test with unparalleled authority, or at least
that was how it was promoted.[62]

The potential to use the new IQ datasets to promote a racial hierarchy
occurred to Charles W. Gould, an ardent Grant disciple and wealthy philan-
thropist. In collaboration with Madison Grant, Robert Yerkes, and Carl C.
Brigham, eugenic enthusiasts set a plan in motion with the explicit goal of
both engineering and interpreting intelligence tests in a way that displayed
different levels of intelligence in harmony with Grant's imagined human hierarchy. The plan proved a smashing success, producing the precise results
its authors intended.

All that was now needed was the stamp of approval from a leading intellectual institution. And Princeton University proved to be a natural partner.[63]
Published by Princeton University Press, *A Study of American Intelligence*
was released in 1923 to wide acclaim, with Brigham receiving full credit for its
authorship. The study concluded that on average, Black Americans possessed
the intelligence of a ten-year-old, and that immigrants were consistently intellectually inferior to Anglo-Saxon Americans.[64]

In the United States, intelligence tests represented the gold standard for
measuring human potential throughout the twentieth century and played
an indispensable role in driving racial inequality by justifying the disinvestment in Black education. In 1981, Stephen Gould released his groundbreaking
book, *The Mismeasure of Man*. In it, Gould provides a deep dive into the
racial sciences of the 1800s and early 1900s, robbing the scientific guild of
its illusions of intellectual innocence. From methods to measurements to
interpretations, Gould details how the work of the racial sciences—and intelligence tests in particular—had twisted and tortured the scientific process
to rationalize draconian public policies. Gould's argument that the sciences

and our reliance on intelligence tests often served as politically driven racial propaganda scandalized the scientific community.

Perhaps unsurprisingly, what Gould wrote in 1981 was what Black America had been writing all along. In 1908, Kelly Miller used his skills as a mathematician to debunk the Black extinction theory of the racial sciences. In 1924, Horace Mann Bond took aim at intelligence tests. "It has ever been the bane of any development in science," Bond wrote, "that its results, in the hands of partial and biased observers, may be twisted and interpreted in such a manner as to provide traps for the unwary and weapons for the prejudiced."[65] For Bond, what passed as scientific rigor in white communities was too often little more than racial hate wrapped in scientific rhetoric.

Bond's case in point was "such perverted thinkers as Madison Grant, . . . who have advocated long and fatuously the predominance of the super-man of Nordic blood." Bond lamented that the excitement around IQ tests that the eugenicists had ignited "amount to a furor," especially in American universities. For Bond, America's ecstatic embrace of intelligence tests posed as grave a threat to Black America as the racist misinformation campaign following Reconstruction. "They have ceased to be scientific attempts to gain accurate information and have denigrated into funds for propaganda and encouragement of prejudice." Bond moves from this to blast how military intelligence tests administered through racially biased methods "serve[d] as reservoirs of information . . . for the use of showing the intellectual inferiority of some of the races who gave without stint of their lives for the maintenance of their country!" He goes on to denounce *A Study of American Intelligence* and how it was weaponized to ingrain the perception of inferiority into Black students and justify the wider public's disinvestment from their education. Bond's fear that intelligence tests would provide a significant barrier to the pursuit of equality was prophetic. After all, it was Carl Brigham, the eugenic author of *A Study of American Intelligence*, who later pioneered the SATs and promoted the test's results as a race-neutral proof regarding the superior intelligence of white students.

Bond's insights failed to inform many white imaginations, and the nation's confidence in the eugenicists' intelligence tests went unquestioned. Thanks to the eugenicists, colonial myths about Black intelligence were now quantified and endowed with scientific validity. Intelligence tests gave eugenicists, segregationists, and advocates for rigorous immigration restrictions a remarkable amount of ammunition. *A Study of American Intelligence* could not have been timelier. Thanks to the collaboration of his disciples, Grant now possessed all the firepower he needed to end the flow of immigrants to

America. In 1924, the new datasets positioned Grant and his colleagues to successfully lobby for the Immigration Restriction Act. In supporting the Grant-backed legislation, President Harding declared: "I chose quality over quantity in future immigration."[66] America was no longer a haven for the world's outcasts.

Fatefully, when Jews began to flee Germany, they simply failed to meet American standards. In 1936, when a *Fortune* magazine survey asked, "Do you believe that in the long run Germany will be better or worse off if it drives out the Jews?," only a slim majority answered "worse off." By 1939, such sentiments led Congress to reject the Wagner-Rogers Bill to provide haven for twenty thousand Jewish children. Later that year, the *St. Louis*, a ship carrying nearly one thousand Jews from Hamburg, was refused entry into the US. Thanks to voices like Madison Grant, America learned to listen to "race science" rather than sentimentalism. The children would be left to the Nazis following the invasion of Poland, and the *St. Louis* would return to Europe, where its passengers were transported to concentration camps.[67]

Reich Minister of Propaganda Joseph Goebbels once remarked, "If there is any country that believes it has not enough Jews, I shall gladly turn over to it all our Jews." Yet, as historian Arthur Morse laments: "There were no takers." Nonetheless, after rejecting Jewish children, the US quickly passed legislation to welcome British children. With stark clarity, this action demonstrated that America's complicity with Nazi Germany was never merely theoretical. Racial ideologies were—everywhere and always—about realpolitik, about justifying national violence against vulnerable people.[68]

If Madison Grant's writings reached rare mountaintops of influence, they also experienced some of the most radical reversals of fortune. In the context of a world again at war, the popularity of Grant's work began to evaporate. The tragedy was that as America learned to see how the ideas and instincts of racial scientists touched ground in racial crime scenes throughout Germany, they too often refused to see how those same ideas and instincts created racial crime scenes throughout America. Rather than owning our complicity in the Nazi project, we wiped Grant and his fellow intellectuals clean from America's memory. Desiring distance from Nazi ideologies, we began erasing the racial descriptor "Nordic" from our vocabulary as quickly as Grant had helped the term dominate racial debates on both American and German soils.

To defeat Nazi Germany, the United States committed to a common cause, and millions upon millions of Americans risked their lives. Over four hundred thousand Americans paid the ultimate price. After such sacrifices, it is unsurprising—perhaps even understandable—that we desired to forget how America's ideas had acted as significant bookends to Nuremberg's role in the Nazi experiment. When the 1934 Nuremberg Laws were designed in the effort to embed racist ideologies in Germany's national order, German public policymakers looked for guidance from the greatest racist success in translating racist convictions into national public policies. That guidance came from the United States. When the Nazi project came to its end in the Nuremberg trials in 1947, the defense team for Major General Karl Brandt of the Waffen-SS presented *The Passing of the Great Race* as evidence that Nazis were on trial for American ideas.[69]

Some people in white America were troubled by the similarities of America's racial violence to that of Nazi Germany. Yet, by and large, World War II's victors proved unable or unwilling to meaningfully acknowledge their kinship with the villains. Despite a quarter of a millennium of white supremacist public policies and racial practices, the majority of white America refused to recognize how Nazi ideologies were reflections of America's own racial commitments. The United States preferred to see their contributions to the history of racial sciences, racial public policies, and racial practices as nothing more than an insignificant aberration in a purer history defined by the democratic ideals of liberty, equality, and justice.

But precisely because of America's racist history, Black Americans simply could not unsee the tragic interconnectivity between Germany, America, and the colonial project. For Black Americans, Nazism was never a foreign threat. It was a domestic reality. Since World War I, Black writers consistently compared America to Germany. "It is curious to see America, the United States, looking on herself, first, as a sort of natural peacemaker, then as a moral protagonist in this terrible time," Du Bois wrote in 1920. He continued:

> How could America condemn in Germany that which she commits, just as brutally, within her own borders? . . . No nation is less fitted for this role. For two or more centuries, America has marched proudly in the van of human hatred,—making bonfires of human flesh and laughing at them hideously.[70]

As World War II approached, Du Bois's words had lost none of their power.

It is not that Black America was against fighting Germany; indeed, most Black Americans valiantly supported the war effort. It was that Black America believed, in the words of Langston Hughes, that "democracy, like charity, begins at home. With a mote in one's own eye, it is hard to remove the beam from another's." As Hughes reflected on the intimacy between Germany and America, he pleaded that "the whole English-speaking Caucasian world, from Australia to Jim Crow South Africa, needs its eyes opened. They are all full of the dust of race prejudice." The whole Western world had gone blind through the insanity of white supremacy. "Where," asks Hughes, "can we find a specialist to treat eyes clouded by Nordic 'superiority'? We intend to lead Germany, but it is not easy for the near-blind to lead the blind. We must do something about our own bigots and soon."[71] Hughes understood that if the Allies failed to fully reckon with their own racist ways, the world's ceasefire would fail to save our nation's domestic victims from the racial violence of the victors.

Indeed, Black suffering following World War II only increased. Returning Black veterans became targets of lynch mobs, and conflicts between Black workers and returning white soldiers intensified the nation's racial unrest. Unable to find justice in American courts, Black Americans attempted to enlist the newly formed United Nations as an ally in protecting human rights. However, to safeguard its own racial hierarchy, the United States, and the progressive Eleanor Roosevelt in particular, continued to undermine any attempt to make the protection of human rights a meaningful part of the UN's work. "We have conquered Germany, but not their ideas," Du Bois lamented. "We still believe in white supremacy, keeping the negroes in their place and lying about democracy."[72]

Few people have ever shaped the mind of our nation as thoroughly as Madison Grant. His writings and ideas molded an entire generation of power brokers by becoming an integral part of college curricula across America. Academics from schools such as Harvard, Princeton, and Yale endorsed Grant's vision and began incorporating his work into their own writings and courses. Prior to *The Passing of the Great Race*, less than 10 percent of colleges included eugenics in their course offerings. Yet, within a little more than ten years following the publication of "the bible of scientific racism," nearly 75 percent of universities opened the minds of their students to the genius of eugenics. Biographer Jonathan Spiro provides a succinct summary: "Grant was able to change history by convincing a small but well-connected group of influential figures of the rectitude of his ideas. His book may have only been read by thousands, but the works of his disciples were read and seen by millions. And as a result, race consciousness among America's Nordics was revived to the level of antebellum days."[73]

In his own day, Grant proved integral in shaping the US's white supremacist policies on immigration, Black deprivation, sterilization, antimiscegenation laws, and the larger work of segregation. His dominance in these arenas lasted nearly fifty years. Thanks in large part to Grant's influence, America pursued an anti-immigrant course from 1924 to 1965, setting quotas so low that America essentially cut itself off from receiving the world's immigrants. In this era, the US explicitly rejected its role as a haven for the world's refugees and immigrants.[74]

As eugenicists successfully transformed immigration policy, they also helped ensure that underneath the anti-immigrant racism they fostered lurked an even more insidious anti-Blackness that aimed to eliminate Black America through the politics of deprivation. From Reconstruction through the first decades of the twentieth century, Black people lived in dire poverty, with unemployment rates often 80 percent higher than those of white Americans.[75]

As he did with the earlier president Roosevelt, Grant enjoyed a close connection with Franklin Delano Roosevelt. FDR admired Grant's "mighty mind." The warmth of the relationship between the two men led to an exchange of letters addressed respectively to "My dear Madison" and "My dear Frank." Nonetheless, Grant referred to the New Deal as the "Jew Deal" and viewed the interventionist approach to the failures of capitalism with disdain.[76]

Though Grant despised the New Deal's provisions for poor white people, he could certainly find comfort in the New Deal's treatment of poor Black people. Despite the fact that the rate of Black unemployment was nearly double the rate of white unemployment during the 1930s, Black people were often excluded from the New Deal's benefits. Rather than the New Deal protecting Black Americans, it often intensified their economic suffering. The situation grew so dire that Black Americans dubbed the National Recovery Agency "the Negro Removal Act" and "Negroes Robbed Again."[77] The New Deal provided some of the most racist public policies ever crafted, segregating public benefits that provided jobs, housing loans, educational funding, and social security along racial lines. It intensified the racial wealth gaps that continued to grow increasingly dire by the day. If this was not Grant's explicit aim, it is nonetheless an integral part of his legacy and why the racial crimes of his age demand reparations.

Given the history of the US Supreme Court, we should not be surprised that Grant won over both the most conservative and the most liberal justices to his cause. Perhaps no case crystallized the influence of racial science more than *Buck v. Bell* in 1927. Carrie Buck was a young white woman from Virginia. Though never accused of a crime, Ms. Buck was pregnant out of wedlock, and eugenicists believed she embodied the nightmare of reckless breeding and should be sterilized so that her genetic line would no longer pose a threat to society. The Supreme Court agreed. Looking at Ms. Buck's family history through a progressive lens, Justice Oliver Wendell Holmes wrote the majority opinion's verdict: "Better for all the world, if instead of waiting to execute degenerate offspring for their crime or let them starve for their imbecility, society can prevent those who are manifestly unfit from continuing their kind. . . . Three generations of imbeciles are enough." That Carrie Buck was the victim of rape at the hands of a foster family was beside the point. An IQ test—that later proved highly flawed—had determined the traumatized young woman was an "imbecile." And who can argue with science? With the backing of both science and law, eugenicists hoped to sterilize up to 10 percent of America's population. Eugenicists never eliminated as many American citizens as they hoped. Yet, their legislation passed in thirty states and led to the sterilization of over thirty thousand people in Grant's lifetime and sixty-five thousand by 1970.

If the sterilization of Carrie Buck became a preeminent example of the price an individual could pay when IQ tests are weaponized to support white supremacist policies, Black America embodied the price an entire community would pay. When Black people underperformed in IQ tests, low scores became one way to justify white America's refusal to invest in the education of Black America. After quantifying the racist belief in Black people's inferior intelligence, our nation continued to view investing in Black education as pouring money down a drain. By the mid-twentieth century, 85 percent of Black elementary students went to school for only half the day, and the price to erase educational discrepancies between white students and Black students exceeded $1 trillion. This disinvestment perpetuated poverty, affecting every aspect of Black people's standard of living, from wealth to health to housing. Despite *Brown v. Board of Education*, these wrongs were never righted. Following *Brown*, educational inequality for poor Black Americans often grew worse even as access to quality education grew more essential with each passing year.[78]

In addition to promoting a politics of deprivation, Grant's leadership proved critical in Virginia's passing of the Racial Integrity Act of 1924, which formally outlawed the marriage between white people and a person possessing "one drop" of African blood. That act provided blueprints for other states following in their footsteps. Grant's fear of communism and socialism swept the nation from 1917 to 1920, and a second wave of this fear flooded America in the 1940s and '50s to drown promising economic and racial legislation aimed at equity. By the second wave of the Red Scare, Grant was dead and gone. But that his fear of socialism continued to dominate the American imagination through the rest of the century displays how powerfully his eugenical influence is still with us.

By the time of Grant's death on May 30, 1937, the tenets of scientific racism had entered an intellectual and political wasteland. After Grant's passing, his family and many of his friends destroyed virtually all his personal papers and correspondence in a collaborative attempt to blow out one of our nation's leading lights from America's collective memory.[79] Despite attempts to bury his legacy, when we look at Grant's work in the context of the evolution of America's racial mythologies, it is clear that even if scientific racism died, it still managed to keep the mythologies of white supremacy and Black pathology alive.

As Grant's influence moved from explicit to implicit, it proved no less remarkable than when his celebrity had been in its heyday. Grant's myth about "reckless breeding" had provided a paradigm for policymakers for decades to come. When poor Black people bear children, America continues to fear the corruption of the nation's social fabric, seeing poor families as society's burden, unworthy of the public's investment and beyond the reach of equality. The instinct to demonize the procreation of poor people, and of Black people in particular, as "reckless breeding" perfectly aligns with Madison Grant's eugenic principles. Those principles continued to decisively shape political rhetoric and inspire scientific attempts to link racial inequalities with sloth, criminality, and intelligence long after the era of lynching.

When it comes to the nature versus nurture debate, Grant may have lost the intellectual battles within his last days, but he certainly did not lose the war. Indeed, the American mind continues to question the roots of racial inequalities and often traces them to factors other than racism. And it is common to trace inequalities to an inherent inferiority of poor Black people. Why do Black inner-city schools fail? Maybe those kids and teachers are not as smart or don't work as hard. Why are Black Americans more likely to go to prison? Maybe they are more criminal. Such radical inequalities come to be seen as a reflection of the natural world order, and pursuing a democracy rooted in racial equity is denigrated as nothing more than a utopian dream. Like Madison Grant, Thomas Dixon, Abraham Lincoln, and Thomas Jefferson, we too often see the pursuit of such equality as a fanciful sprint that runs against the laws of nature itself.

In the age of lynching and segregation, white America turned to slavery's racial lies once more as if they were our most cherished and timeless hymns. And when the age of lynching came to an end following the Civil Rights Movement, another racial age emerged that heralded itself as a "colorblind" age. In the Colorblind Age, the mythologies of Black pathology would resurrect once more. Race-specific rhetoric disappeared from political speech. But white Americans proved well trained and learned to dance as the racial dog whistles of "law and order" and "welfare queens" continued to push the work of white supremacy forward. If Madison Grant would reject the "Colorblind" Age's race-neutral rhetoric, he certainly would celebrate its race-specific results.

8

The Lasting Legacy of Lynchings

Racial Terrorism, Scientific Racism, and the American Way

> Until the killing of . . . black mothers' sons, becomes as important
> to the rest of the country as the killing of a white mother's sons,
> we who believe in freedom cannot rest until this happens.
>
> —Ella Baker, August 6, 1964, following the murders of
> James Chaney, Andrew Goodman, and Michael Schwerner

The era of segregation was not about Colored Only signs. Behind
the signage stood the ritual of lynching, the racial sciences, and brutal public
policies that destroyed Black people and communities. The history of the
lynching era, a history eerily similar to that of Nazi Germany, is not the history most white Americans desire to share with their children. It is, however,
the history we inherited and must own. From America's antimiscegenation
and anti-immigration laws to its burning people alive and incarcerating entire communities in ghettos, the Germans perceived in America that their
student in the racial sciences had become their teacher in public policymak-
ing.[1] If we refuse to find the courage to name the common racist ideas and
violent practices that tie together the history of America's anti-Black racism
with the anti-Semitic ideologies of Nazi Germany, we will fail not only to
understand our racial crisis but also to develop the strength to fight for a
reparative future. Germany and America were never identical twins. But
German Jews and Black Americans were lynched on the same family tree.
And the patriarch of that family is white supremacy.

In the age of lynching, America warred against Black people, families,
and communities. It warred against democracy and the well-being of vulnerable people across the nation's racial spectrum. Through popular novels
and movies that were undergirded by the racial sciences, the age of lynching

warred against hope itself by breathing new life into slavery's racial myths of Black people's innate inferiority. And America once again threw her Black citizens to white wolves—not simply based on political expediency, but as living sacrifices on the altar of racist convictions. Understanding the era of the lynch reveals why the mission of reparations must include addressing slavery's afterlife.

In meaningful ways, white supremacy had yet to reach its pinnacle on American soil during the age of slavery. In the era of lynching, its aims evolved from enslavement to extermination. Of this reality, the works of Thomas Dixon and Madison Grant offer ample evidence. Dixon and Grant clearly worked to radicalize white supremacy in the white American psyche, but such influence would have been impossible unless it was inextricably tied to how well their writings and work reflected America's deeply rooted racial and political common sense.

When we look at Thomas Dixon and Madison Grant, we must recognize that they were *not* conservative reactionaries. They were integral players in white America's progressive politics, and those politics provided the seeds for America's twentieth century liberal tradition. Their close friends Woodrow Wilson and Theodore Roosevelt were *the* most progressive politicians of the early twentieth century. They were also the two presidents who were most influential on Franklin Delano Roosevelt, imagining in original ways an interventionist federal government duty-bound to serve the common good.[2] Despite important differences, Dixon, Grant, Wilson, and both Roosevelts agreed that the government must serve the common good—and they defined this as serving white America. That commitment provided the racial edges of the New Deal and the New Deal's afterlife in twentieth-century American liberalism.

The most salient difference between Dixon and Grant and the progressive tradition in which they participated centered on socialism. Neither Wilson nor Theodore Roosevelt feared socialism. Both presidents believed the fight for economic equality was essential to a healthy democracy. In helping to plant the fear of socialism, communism, and equality in America's psyche, Dixon and Grant proved far more influential than either of their presidential pals. The American mind proved fertile soil for Dixon and Grant's seed, and the fears of socialism, communism, and equality grew into a tree on which racial and economic justice are lynched today.

For Thomas Dixon, perhaps his largest legacy was as a brilliant propagandist. Dixon, a Social Gospel liberal, understood the power and importance of employing white Christianity as a lynchpin in the United States' racial propaganda machine. To help white supremacy thrive, it was critical to foster an illusion of moral and religious superiority in white people. Such illusions hid a deeply depraved worldview under the mask of religious piety and family values. No one used such masks more brazenly than Thomas Dixon.

Yet, in employing religion to secure white supremacy, Dixon showed little originality. What made Dixon's work exceptional was his ability to exploit new media to make racist ideas more visible and available for mass consumption. Dixon understood that the more alive and vivid racist ideas became in the minds of white Americans, the more power they possessed to sway the nation's future. Through the explicitness of his novels and films, white supremacy came alive in the American imagination in new and profound ways as Dixon seared white supremacy more deeply into white America's soul.

If America provided lessons to Nazi Germany on racialized public policies, it also provided pivotal lessons in racial propaganda. "The most brilliant propagandist technique will yield no success," wrote Adolf Hitler in *Mein Kampf*, "unless . . . it confines itself to a few bare essentials and those must be expressed as far as possible in stereotyped formulas. These slogans should be persistently repeated. . . . In this world, persistence is the first and most important requirement for success."[3] Nothing has been more repetitive or persistent than America's racial propaganda. Blacks are sexually depraved. Blacks are lazy. Blacks lack brilliance. Blacks are criminal. Blacks are inherently inferior. Hit repeat for four hundred years and counting. American influence runs thick throughout *Mein Kampf*, but Dixon's influence was never clearer than in 1935 when the Nazis released their propaganda film *The Triumph of the Will*. In a real sense, *The Birth of a Nation* was Germanized.

When we turn our gaze toward Grant, we must wrestle with the fact that we buried the racial realities of the era of lynching as deeply—if not more deeply—than the racial realities of slavery. By refusing to confront our complicity in the Nazis' racial crimes, white supremacy and Jim Crow were allowed to go essentially unchecked, embedding themselves ever more deeply into American public policies and psyches for the next three decades.

In erasing Grant and our ties to Germany from our common memory, we also lost significant knowledge of how our nation's racial imagination evolved in the early twentieth century and how that evolution shapes us today. We lost the knowledge of how white supremacy sought to annihilate Black people after slavery as well as of white supremacy's war on all defenseless people.

One of the significant differences between German Nazism and white supremacy in America was the embrace of social Darwinism by United States intellectuals and public policymakers. Grant and the American eugenicists' rejection of government assistance to poor white people struck the Nazis as absurdly cruel. Indeed, it was only after Franklin Delano Roosevelt passed the New Deal legislation that provided government assistance to white America and excluded Black America that he earned Hitler's praise for fully embracing a more enlightened form of white supremacy.[4] By failing to remember these racial crimes, we are empowered to repeat them.

What also becomes clear by remembering Madison Grant is that though white Christians played an indispensable role in creating and perpetuating white supremacist culture, so too did white secular scientists. Throughout American history, ideologically opposed white people—liberals and conservatives, in today's parlance—generally held more in common with each other than they did with the more radical egalitarian commitments prevalent in Black America. That is often as true today as it was then. If Thomas Dixon helps us understand why white Christianity never saved America's soul, Madison Grant helps us understand why white liberal intellectuals never saved America's mind.

As white supremacy burrowed more deeply into American society following Dixon and Grant in the 1940s through 1960s, it often took "softer" forms. Yet, the softer forms continued to war against racial justice. "The Negro's great stumbling block in the stride toward freedom," lamented Martin Luther King Jr., "is not the White Citizen's Counciler or the Ku Klux Klanner, but the white moderate who is more devoted to 'order' than to justice."[5] Good intentions never made white supremacy nonviolent. For King, the racism of the white moderate and liberal was more deeply buried and so thoroughly wrapped in self-delusion that it proved nearly impossible to confront or hold accountable.

After America refused to pursue a Nuremberg trial following the Civil War, it also failed to create a Truth and Reconciliation Commission to confront our sins in the era of lynching. We passed civil rights legislation. But we never adequately entered a process of public accountability or repentance to exorcise our racial demons. And that failure continues to haunt our life together.

As we look into the caskets of Dixon, Grant, and the era of lynching in America, a reckoning is demanded if American democracy is ever to be healed from its inhumanity. How do we make reparations for creating the caricature of Black criminality and resurrecting the mythologies that paint Black sex and families as pathological, Black workers as lazy, and Black brilliance as below average? These caricatures not only continued to devastate Black people and communities but damned the very soul of the United States and white Americans in particular.

How can America make reparations for the racist policies that intentionally attempted to annihilate Black America through lynch mobs and ghettos? How do we answer for the tens of millions of Black lives consumed by the convict leasing programs that proliferated in the South following slavery?[6] How do we make reparations for interpreting the Constitution in a manner that sanctioned the lynching of over four thousand Black people? How can we atone for the profound damage these policies and that ritual did to the minds, bodies, and spirits of Black people across our nation? This says nothing of Jim Crow's discrepancies in education, employment, housing, and health care that cost Black Americans trillions of dollars. Monetary measurements fail to tell the full extent of the destruction. In 1951, Black radical William L. Patterson demonstrated how racist policies had killed an estimated thirty-two thousand Black Americans per year and reduced the average Black life expectancy by nearly a decade.[7] While public policies killed Black people, white people often argued that Black America was dying from self-inflicted wounds. In truth, Black people were dying from white America's moral diseases. How do we make reparations for that?

To engage this history, we must seek to understand our nation from the perspective of the Black struggle. From the end of the Civil War through the end of the Civil Rights Movement, Black Americans fought against the racial insanity of a nation that desired to annihilate her own citizens. For Ida B. Wells, one of the most infuriating aspects of lynching was our nation's refusal to confess her sins or make reparations for the families and communities of Black victims. Yet, when lynch mobs tortured and murdered immigrants from foreign countries, the United States confessed its sins and repented to foreign governments. "This confession, while humiliating in the extreme, was not satisfactory," Wells writes. "And, while the United States cannot protect, she can pay. This she has done." Wells then produces a bullet point accounting for the nearly $500,000 that the United States paid in reparations to China, Italy, and Great Britain for the crime of lynching their citizens.[8]

Historically, it is not that America generally refused the notion of reparations. We were, after all, ready to pay reparations to enslavers. It is that we specifically rejected the notion of reparations for our sins against Black people. And that is the wrong that must be righted.

As difficult as it is to respond to what actually happened, we must also wrestle with the roads not taken and the Black leaders we refused to follow. What would happen if America allowed Black people into the machinery of democracy and protected Black legislators and voters from being hunted down, slain, and silenced? That was a road dramatically not taken. Callie House was a Black leader we refused to follow. While Dixon wrote *The Leopard's Spots* and *The Clansman*, House was brilliantly leading the National Ex-Slave Mutual Relief, Bounty and Pension Association, which assisted Black people while spearheading the fight for reparations. House labored for nearly twenty years. For her diligent efforts and steadfast commitment to Black justice, she was placed in prison. We must remember that Callie House and the National Ex-Slave Association provided an antiracist alternative to Dixon and the Klan. That alternative provided an opportunity to alter not only America but also the world.[9]

In 1922, at white supremacy's high tide, W. E. B. Du Bois defiantly refused to believe that white supremacy possessed the power to indefinitely determine the future of Black America. He wrote that "the attempt of some parts of the Nordic race to own and dominate the earth is a well-known program." But despite white supremacy's long history and present power, "it is a program that is fighting against the stars in their courses." Of that, he was sure, because "democracy is going to develop." It was going to be a long and bloody struggle, and "great and grimmer battles" lay on the horizon. Yet, "in that battle the triumph of Democracy for the darker races, for the segregated groups, and for the disadvantaged is written in the everlasting stars."[10]

When we think of reparations, we must wrestle with how to make amends for excluding the Black brilliance, vision, and wisdom of Ida B. Wells, Callie House, and W. E. B. Du Bois. As a nation, we must reckon with the price we paid when white people stood in solidarity with organizations like the Ku Klux Klan, the American Eugenics Society, and the American Economic Association instead of standing with organizations like the National Ex-Slave Mutual Relief, Bounty and Pension Association and the NAACP. At a more profound level, we must wonder what America would look like today if Black brilliance, wisdom, and political vision was allowed a role in shaping the souls of *all* America's children.

When world war broke out for a second time, the Double V campaign rippled through the nation as Black Americans committed themselves to "victory over fascism abroad and victory over racism at home." In many ways, it proved prophetic sloganeering. Black leaders like A. Philip Randolph, Pauli Murray, Walter White, William Patterson, Paul Robeson, and Audley Moore kept Black America's fight against white supremacy alive throughout the war. After the Black veterans who helped defeat Nazism abroad returned home, they often turned their energies toward defeating domestic terrorism. Veteran Medgar Evers survived Normandy and yet lost his life in the domestic struggle against white supremacy in Jackson, Mississippi.

It was the fight against American white supremacists North and South following World War II that lay the foundation for the struggle of the Civil Rights era. Ella Baker, Diane Nash, Fannie Lou Hamer, Martin Luther King Jr., Malcolm X, and Stokely Carmichael's struggle was not simply against segregation's signage but against the vicious violence America employed to protect her dehumanizing social order. Like the Black writers and activists who shattered the shackle, those who fought against the racial order of the lynch would know victory and progress—and become intimate with defeat and backlash. For all the heartache and despair of their journey, a context was created that provided our nation with an opportunity for a second Reconstruction through the Civil Rights Movement that committed itself to both racial inclusion and economic equity.

If the era of lynching began to emerge after John Wilkes Booth assassinated Abraham Lincoln, it would come to an end 103 years later when James Earl Ray's bullet slayed Martin Luther King Jr. on the balcony of the Lorraine Motel in Memphis, Tennessee. King's death was the nail in the casket of the Civil Rights era *and* the era of lynching. And once again, the question was, What would America do with the opportunity that Black Americans had sacrificed so much to achieve?

Black Americans were still all in on the revolution. Following King's assassination, the vision of the Black people still committed to the struggle deepened and grew more radical. "The system under which we now exist has to be radically changed," declared Ella Baker in 1969. "This means that we are going to have to learn to think in radical terms."[11] How would America respond to Black demands for power and freedom? Would a new age bring about a more radical racial revolution in our nation, or would white supremacy and racial mythologies resurrect once again? America had choices to make after King's funeral. And those choices paved the path to a "colorblind" age. Perhaps many in America truly desired to be done with shackles and lynches, but the myths of those eras were not done with us.

PRISONS AND POVERTY

The Mythology of Black Pathology
in the Colorblind Age

The world does not become raceless or will not become unracialized by assertion. The act of enforcing racelessness . . . is itself a racial act. Pouring rhetorical acid on the fingers of a black hand may indeed destroy the prints, but not the hand. Besides, what happens in that violent, self-serving act of erasure to the hands, the fingers, the fingerprints of the one who does the pouring? Do they remain acid-free?

—Toni Morrison, *Playing in the Dark*

The widespread and mistaken belief that racial animus is necessary for the creation and maintenance of radicalized systems of social control is the most important reason that we, as a nation, have remained in deep denial.

—Michelle Alexander, *The New Jim Crow*

9

Two Roads Diverge

Pathological Black Families or White Racism

> What I am trying to suggest to you is that it was not an accident, it
> was not an act of God, it was not done by well-meaning people. . . .
> It was a deliberate policy hammered into place in order to make
> money from black flesh. And now, in 1963, because we have never
> faced this fact, we are in intolerable trouble.
>
> —James Baldwin, "A Talk to Teachers," 1963

DISMAY. DESPERATION. DESPAIR. Across the ideological spectrum, the
assassination of Martin Luther King Jr. was traumatic and knocked the hope
out of many Black Americans. If the nation refused to protect the prince
of nonviolent protest from a senseless and gruesome end, what hope was
there for Black people, for Black justice, for racial redemption in such a sick
nation? For many, King's assassination elicited an apocalyptic foreboding.
"The atmosphere was black," James Baldwin later wrote, "with a tension in-
describable—as though something, perhaps the heavens, perhaps the earth,
might crack."[1] For others, like King's close companion Stokely Carmichael,
the assassination represented a declaration of war on Black America.

By 1968, assassinations had become a central component of America's
politics and racial struggle. Medgar Evers, June 12, 1963. John F. Kennedy,
November 22, 1963. Malcolm X, February 21, 1965. Bobby Kennedy would be
assassinated only sixty-three days after King. Fewer than four years separated
the mountaintop moments of the passage of the Civil Rights Act of 1964 and
the Voting Rights Act of 1965 from the valley of the shadow of death when
over one hundred million people in our nation stopped for King's funeral.

In 1964 and 1965, the nation appeared to be on the precipice of unprecedented change. The president in this moment of transformation was Lyn-

don B. Johnson, who, like President Andrew Johnson, was a southern vice president who ascended to the presidency following a presidential assassination. Both Johnsons attained power during a time of racial transition, but the skill sets and aims of the two Johnson presidents were as different as night and day. Lyndon Johnson's initial aim was not to reforge a white republic but to finish the racial revolution Reconstruction had begun. He was, admittedly, one of the least likely leaders to spearhead either a politically empowered racial revolution or the fight for economic equality. Throughout his career, Johnson played a leading role in the southern bloc of senators fully committed to enforcing white supremacy's reign. From 1937 to 1956, Johnson amassed, in the words of Robert Caro, "a perfect 100 percent record of voting against every civil rights bill that had ever made it to the floor, even bills aiming at lynching." On economic matters, labor union leaders referred to Johnson as their "arch foe."[2]

Yet, as time revealed, LBJ was a man rife with contradictions. In the wake of the Kennedy assassination, an unexpected side of LBJ was unveiled when he committed his administration to realizing two primary domestic tasks: securing civil rights and inaugurating a War on Poverty. Upon assuming the presidency, Johnson phoned Martin Luther King Jr.: "I want to tell you," the president confided in King, "how worthy I am going to try to be of all your hopes."[3] LBJ referred to his vision for America as the "Great Society." After declaring his War on Poverty and passing the 1964 Civil Rights Act that ended segregation, LBJ won the 1964 election against Barry Goldwater in a landslide. It seemed the nation was entering a time for healing and that the day for the nation to give life to its creed, "that all people are created equal," had finally dawned. Following the 1964 election, a constituency with enough strength emerged to make progress despite entrenched opposition to racial justice and economic equity. The first full congressional session President Johnson oversaw was the eighty-ninth, and it passed more progressive legislation across color lines than all the previous sessions of Congress combined. In addition to a second civil rights bill, critical instruments in the War on Poverty were instituted, including Medicare and Medicaid, Head Start, federal funding for education, and environmental protections. The Immigration and Nationality Act of 1965 that reversed the policies white supremacists inspired was also signed into law. Building on a strong economy and new initiatives, the War on Poverty cut poverty in America in half.

But the dawning of a new day also brought ominous clouds, and a storm descended that tore the traumatized nation asunder as historical accomplishments gave way to deepening factions, inaugurating a culture war that continues to divide our nation today. On the white right, racial progress was met with a backlash whose intensity was reminiscent of the days of Reconstruction. On the white left, it was not the domestic agenda but the international agenda that fueled their fury. As LBJ readied to fight a War on Poverty in America, he also employed deception to radicalize America's commitment to a war in Vietnam. This decimated his credibility in liberal circles across the nation.

In Black America, an altogether different crisis arose in the streets. Revolts swept the nation, often on the heels of police brutality. But the causes of the uprisings went much deeper than Black people's problems with police. A significant portion of the anger resided in the gap between the nation's intense rhetoric concerning a War on Poverty and her refusal to fund the radical transformations that justice demanded in inner-city communities.

Despite meaningful progress on poverty initiatives in other demographics, the suffering of Black inner cities remained largely untouched. By the mid-1960s, Black America's rage was passing its boiling point. Beginning in 1964, insurrections in Black communities were becoming commonplace. In 1966, 43 uprisings ripped through Black neighborhoods across America, followed by over 163 in 1967. White America was shell-shocked that these communities exploded despite the passage of the Civil Rights Acts of 1964 and 1965. What more could Black communities demand from our nation? When it came to Black uprisings, 1966 and 1967 were only preludes to the fury unleashed following King's assassination in 1968. Within days, the embers of racial rage exploded into revolts, rampaging through 110 American cities.[4]

Driven by the desire to secure domestic control, Johnson responded to Black uprisings by expanding his War on Poverty to include a War on Crime. If the War on Poverty failed to provide the funding to address inner-city misery, the War on Crime only poured fuel on communities already in flames. For many white Americans, hoses and police dogs unleashed on children and peaceful citizens provided lasting images that legitimized the demand for civil rights. Yet from 1966 to 1968, the images of American cities ablaze seemingly legitimized white backlash and the necessity of bringing the work of racial progress to an immediate end. If the age of the lynch was gone following the passage of the Civil Rights Acts, so too was the sense of moral clarity that underwrote the progress and the conviction that a deeper revolution was still demanded.

As chaos replaced clarity, dreams for racial equity were deferred, and the nation's emphasis pivoted from the pursuit of racial justice and economic equity to new forms of control. In the post–Civil Rights age, both white supremacy and the struggle for Black justice were forced to evolve. For those who opposed racial justice, it became increasingly difficult to speak of Black segregation and suffering as a *positive* good in and of itself. In time, what transformed was not our nation's racist ideas about Black people but our ability to translate those racist ideas into racist laws without mentioning race at all. During slavery and segregation, explicitly racist ideas shaped explicitly racist public policies. In the Colorblind Age, the explicit became implicit—while remaining just as racialized and just as lethal. As overt racism became covert, the work of protecting white power shifted from public lynchings to public policies perfectly designed to keep Black people in poverty and place millions of Black people in prison.

The latter half of the 1960s was an era of social transformation and unrest, of white backlash, Vietnam protests, and uprisings in Black communities across the nation. This unrest acted as the birthing pains of the Colorblind Age and foreshadowed the struggles to come. To understand how hopes for racial equality devolved into an era that systematically perpetuated Black poverty and placed Black people in prison, we must revisit America's renewed attempts to understand the intersection of race, public policy, poverty, and crime during this time. To guide us through the racial ideas during the birthing pains of the Colorblind Age are two landmark but contradictory reports released during the Johnson administration: *The Negro Family* and the Kerner Report. In hindsight, choosing which ideas from these reports our nation would follow into the Colorblind Age represented the proverbial diverging paths in the woods. The choices we made shaped America's current racial crisis and demand reparations.

When Johnson declared his War on Poverty, no consensus on either the origins of poverty or how to end it existed. And yet in the high tide of liberal confidence, public policymakers began believing they could defeat poverty within a decade. In the context of urban unrest, confidence soon transformed into concern as the Johnson administration worked to understand the revolution they were witnessing and attempting to guide in real time. The first attempt of the Johnson administration to provide a framework for understanding America's racial crisis and how to balance the War on Poverty with rising crime was released in the summer of 1965. The report was titled *The Negro Family: The Call for National Action*. It was penned by Assistant Secretary of Labor Daniel Patrick Moynihan. Moynihan considered himself a committed liberal, and throughout his career, he positioned himself as an intellectual activist and displayed a strong penchant for political opportunism.

Moynihan possessed a remarkable gift with words and vivid turns of phrase. Almost immediately, *The Negro Family* became known as the Moynihan Report. But like most white experts who address matters of racialized poverty, Moynihan was not informed by a firsthand knowledge of Black communities or people. "Moynihan," an enraged Fannie Lou Hamer insisted after the report was released, "knows as much about a black family as a horse knows about New Years."[5] And she was right. Instead of firsthand knowledge, Moynihan's expertise centered on the leading research and intellectual debates about the intersection of culture, poverty, racism, and crime. In this debate, leading research was riddled with racial assumptions and poignant tensions were rising as many white progressives came to view poor Black people themselves as the preeminent obstacle to realizing the aims of equitable public policies.

After the fall of eugenics, the idea of tying racial inequality to the biological inferiority of Black people fell out of favor in understanding and justifying America's racial realities. New theories were needed to fill the void. Soon, explanations of Black poverty shifted from a biological to sociological and psychological frameworks. Building upon emerging perspectives from writers like Oscar Lewis, theorists and public policy experts suggested that a pathological psychology led to a "culture of poverty" that pervaded impoverished communities, fostering intergenerational poverty and leading to crime. Though this formulation was precisely the opposite of Lewis's research and conclusions, the new cause-and-effect understanding became that a pathological psychology leads to pathological cultures, which leads to poverty and crime.[6] Unsurprisingly, Black communities became the prime example. In the emerging Colorblind Age, the problem for Black people was not inferior genetics but that racial oppression produced a pathological psychology, creating a culture of poverty that threatened to perpetuate Black impoverishment and criminality even after the United States offered more equal racial opportunities.

This newer psychological/sociological framework fit most of America's racial mythologies concerning Black families as effortlessly as the biological framework it replaced. Yet what was striking about the new generation of liberal theorists was that their shared aim was exactly opposite of the aim of their progressive forebears like Thomas Dixon and Madison Grant. Instead of seeking Black America's extermination, they sought to raise support for policies that would empower our nation to realize racial equality.

The challenge for the emerging liberal policymakers became that the Black mythologies that influenced their theories were antithetical to the egalitarian ideals they heralded. These theories and that contradiction were woven into the intellectual framework of Johnson's Great Society in general and the tensions between the War on Poverty and the War on Crime in particular. These theories and that contradiction proved pervasive in Moynihan's report and ensured that its political impact would be precisely the opposite of his expressed purposes.

In keeping with the mainstream liberal thought at the time, Moynihan expressed the necessity of interlocking public policies and federal programs to attack racial inequality. But Moynihan was never content with simply regurgitating liberal thought. His report's very title, *The Negro Family*, provided a not-so-subtle hint as to which aspect of America's racial crisis he believed needed fixing. In one sense, by moving the liberal accent for Black people's pathological psychology to reside wholly within the family, Moynihan was moving liberalism's argument into a new terrain. Yet in a more deeply troubling pattern, Moynihan was simply using fresh statistics and different racial theories to revive the well-worn racist ideas regarding Black people's pathological sexual and slothful behaviors. Moynihan's work showed just how easily the racial ideas of the Colorblind Age could harmonize with the deep-seated racist instincts from the ages of slavery and segregation.

Moynihan begins his report by quoting the 1965 State of the Union address in which President Johnson declared that our nation's struggle to realize equality "has often brought pain and violence." He continues in his own words: "The racist virus in the American blood stream still afflicts us. . . . The circumstances of the Negro American community in recent years has probably been getting worse, not better." Yet for Moynihan, the typical measurements of "income, standards of living, years of education deceive." Lurking underneath these inequalities was the true challenge for Black equality: "At the heart of the deterioration of the fabric of Negro society is the deterioration of the Negro family. . . . Unless this damage is repaired, all the effort to end discrimination and poverty and injustice will come to little."[7]

In his chapters "The Negro Family" and "The Roots of the Problem," Moynihan writes passionately about the crisis facing Black families. He cites a ticker tape of statistics to provide "an index of family pathology." The index ranges from IQ tests to illegitimacy rates, to the increasing rates of separation and divorce, to the persistent and pervasive unemployment and underemployment of Black men. Perhaps most troubling of all for Moynihan was "a startling increase in welfare dependance."[8] No longer did unemployment lead to welfare. Now, Moynihan suggested, welfare led to unemployment, because pathological Black people had grown addicted to the dole.

Moynihan traces the origins of this dysfunction directly to slavery. If slavery got the problems of the Black family rolling, what kept them going? Answering that question leads to chapter 4, "The Tangle of Pathology," where Moynihan roots Black suffering in the distinctives of the Black family. The phrase "tangle of pathology" was not original to Moynihan, but he employed the concept in unique ways by centering it on the Black family structure.[9] "In essence," Moynihan writes, "the Negro community has been forced into a matriarchal structure . . . which seriously retards the progress of the group as a whole." Moynihan argues that the matriarchy of the Black family precludes Black Americans from flourishing in a patriarchal society. "Due to the broken foundations of family, most Negro youth are in danger of being caught up *in the tangle of pathology* that affects their world, and probably a majority are so entrapped. . . ."[10] Yet again, Black families—rather than racist public policies—found themselves in the crosshairs of white America's explanations of Black America's plight. Black people had to overcome not only a racist society but also families that endowed them with a pathological psychology that fostered sexual deviance, sloth, and crime.[11]

With a title page dated March 1965, the Moynihan Report began to circulate internally within the Johnson administration that spring, but it would not be made public until August. A week after the report surfaced, the uprising in the Watts community of Los Angeles began. Moynihan's report became the primary interpretative lens through which many in the nation sought to understand what they were witnessing in the streets of Los Angeles.

Though most of Moynihan's conclusions would be upended by evidence-based research within five years, neither well-informed politicians nor the media were immune to the contagion of his ideas. The Moynihan Report shaped the headlines and media coverage of Watts across the nation. The *Wall Street Journal*'s headline read: "Behind the Riots: Family Life Breakdown in Negro Slums Sows Seeds of Race Violence; Husbandless Homes Spawn Young Hoodlums." The journal's coverage proved equally poignant, speaking of an "orgy of violence" and asserting that "a growing army of such youth is being bred in the Negro sections of cities across the country by broken homes." The report was interpreted as revealing that what America was witnessing was not a political revolt against systemic injustice but pathological Black people produced by "broken homes, illegitimacy, and female oriented homes."[12]

Filtered through the racist ideas of the Moynihan Report and the drama of the moment, most coverage of Watts left unexplored the systemic issues of economic destitution, under-resourced education systems, and police brutality that was devastating the neighborhood. The coverage empowered white audiences to reduce Watts to the epitome of the dangerous tangle of pathologies Black inner cities bred without understanding at all what made Watts a tinderbox for Black revolt.[13] For much of white America, if Black pathology caused the revolt, costly progressive public policies need not be part of the solution.

Quickly, white backlash transformed into racist public policies. Under the sway of the Moynihan Report, media coverage, and public demands for "law and order," the Senate and House responded to Watts by unanimously passing the Law Enforcement Assistance Act, which helped militarize local police to "control" urban unrest. On September 22, 1965, President Johnson signed the bill into law. This marked, in the historian Elizabeth Hinton's words, "the official start of the War on Crime." At the time, President Johnson was still committed to the War on Poverty. But the demand of the day was domestic control—and meeting the demand of the day marked a decisive turning point away from the pursuit of racial justice and toward punitive policies.[14]

Unsurprisingly, militarizing local police failed to still the unrest that often followed on the heels of incidents of police brutality. The shift in policy antagonized already volatile impoverished Black communities and cities exploded across America in the long, hot summer of 1967, losing the administration whatever amount of credibility the civil rights legislation had achieved. After the heavy-handed law-and-order approach failed to bring peace from the chaos, President Johnson established a bipartisan and interdisciplinary eleven-member committee later known as the Kerner Commission.[15] The Kerner Commission was named in honor of its chair, Governor Otto Kerner, and was overwhelming white, with only two Black members.[16] Johnson hoped to confirm that a nationwide conspiracy was afoot involving Black radicals, communists, or both. Too confident in his interpretation, the president tasked the commission with answering three basic questions about the proliferation of Black uprisings in communities across the nation: What happened? Why did it happen? What can be done to prevent it from happening again and again?

While Moynihan, in his report, took an ivory tower approach that relied entirely on his well of academic knowledge, the Kerner Commission took the opposite approach. The commissioners, commission staff, and a team of field researchers conducted a seven-month period of exhaustive and detailed examination of the 1967 uprisings. During these months, the communities themselves became the classroom as the commissioners and their teams visited the sites of revolts in twenty-three cities to understand what had happened.

Though the commissioners and team members came from different backgrounds and ideological perspectives, few proved ready to see what they saw. Each site told its own story, but common themes proved impossible to ignore. Nearly all uprisings took place following incidents of police brutality. Employment opportunities were rare to nonexistent. Housing was both expensive and completely inadequate. Educational institutions were woefully underfunded. The War on Poverty had focused largely on rural communities and had proven severely insufficient in Black urban areas due largely to President Johnson's refusal to invest in inner-city job creation.[17] In this context of pervasive systemic failures, Black people were left to scratch out their existence in squalor.[18]

Again and again, instead of uprisings originating in the irrational rage of Black people, research revealed Black people's concrete political aims after nonviolent attempts at redress had failed. A hundred years after Black abolitionists traded prayers for pistols, the Black struggle moved from nonviolent truths spoken in love to torches of righteous rage. The immersive experience proved transformative for even the most conservative of the commissioners. "I'll be a son-of-a-gun," Tex Thornton told the *Cincinnati Enquirer*. What he witnessed "brought me 99 miles to the left than I thought I would be."[19]

As significant as what the commissioners found is what they did not find in either community or FBI interviews. No conspiracy among Black radicals. No conspiracy with communist sympathizers. And no evidence that those who revolted were disproportionately the communities' least educated or most impoverished residents. That is, there was no evidence that Johnson's instincts or the emphasis on the Negro family in Moynihan's report were accurate at all.

To a nation anticipating another report on Black pathology or communist plots, the commissioners wrote about what they had learned via their bottom-up approach:

> This is our basic conclusion: Our nation is moving toward two societies, one black, one white—separate and unequal. Reaction to last summer's disorders has quickened the movement and deepened the division. Discrimination and segregation have long permeated much of American life; they now threaten the future of every American.[20]

Yet according to the report, a racial apocalypse was not inevitable. America's future depended on facing the truths of America's racial pasts and the depths of the present crisis. "What white Americans have never fully understood—but what the Negro can never forget—is that white society is deeply implicated in the ghetto," declared the Kerner Commission. "White institutions created it, white institutions maintain it, and white society condones it."[21] Rather than following the media's lead and casting Black people as instigating senseless rebellions, the Kerner Report was clear that the issue was "white racism" and "white terrorism." Fulfilling its commission, the report provided a blueprint for how to begin to address America's racial crisis through massive investments in urban communities and a rewriting of America's racial attitudes, understanding, and political will.

It would be hard to imagine a report that better encapsulated Martin Luther King Jr.'s concerns during his final and most radical years of work. King heralded the Kerner Report as a "physician's warning of approaching death, with a prescription for life." The report also sparked public interest, selling nearly a million copies within two weeks of its release. Nonetheless, rather than engaging Johnson's curiosity, it enraged him—damning the hope of the administration implementing its recommendations. Its recommendations would cost billions of dollars to implement, and by 1968, those billions were being used to escalate the Vietnam War and militarize police across America.[22]

Exactly five weeks after the Kerner Commission released its 426-page report, King was slain. Following the racial unrest after King's assassination, Johnson ignored the holistic nature of the Kerner Report and settled on passing the Fair Housing Act, which aimed to honor King by integrating housing. The gesture would be well remembered, but the law proved largely symbolic, as the mechanisms to enforce it proved toothless and unequal to the challenges of America's segregated landscape. But other legislation was lurking in the background that had not only teeth but fangs. This legislation had a much longer-lasting impact and was eerily predictive of the direction American public policies would take in the decades to come. The bill was called the Omnibus Crime Control and Safe Streets Act of 1968. By signing it into law in June 1968, President Johnson doubled down on his War on Crime, foreshadowing the War on Poverty's descent into a war on the poor. As would become clear, by 1968, the nation felt more thoroughly committed to law and order than to democracy and human dignity.

In an era of upheaval, the Kerner Report and the Moynihan Report provided two very different understandings of America's racial crisis. In those understandings resided two very different sets of priorities to create a path into the future. By the end of the Johnson presidency, the progressive consensus of 1964 had disintegrated. Would America prioritize policies and investments that confronted white racism and police brutality, and seek to eradicate racial disparities, or would it deploy its resources and political will in community controls to instill law and order amid economic and social despair?

In the presidential contest of 1968, only four months after Johnson intensified the War on Crime, Richard M. Nixon rose to power on a law-and-order platform in one of the closest presidential elections in history. What propelled Nixon to the Oval Office was his ability to harness the white backlash of those he referred to as the "silent majority." While national attention had been fixated on protests for civil rights and against the Vietnam War, Nixon was listening to those who were saying nothing at all. And he heard in their silence a resentment simmering beneath the surface of society concerning the changes that civil disobedience over race and war had wrought on American norms. In that resentment resided a power with the potential to transform American politics once again. Through Thomas Dixon, "law and order" became the apologetic for the Ku Klux Klan. After Nixon, law and order would be the mantle sought by both political parties for the rest of the century.

The narrow margin of Nixon's victory displayed the lack of unity in the American mind about the best path into the Colorblind Age. But Nixon proved to be in tune with white America's mood and intentionally went about the work of strengthening broad support for his program. As Nixon moved the nation further from its commitment to the fight against poverty and discrimination, he deepened and further racialized her commitment to the War on Crime. In conversations with aides in 1969, Nixon advised: "You have to face the fact that the whole problem is really the blacks. The key is to devise a system that recognizes this while not appearing to."[23]

In the age of the shackle and lynching, white America believed racial differences *required* racist public policies to explicitly enforce America's racial caste system. Yet, following the eras of the shackle and lynching, America's racial hierarchy was firmly established to such an extent that explicitly racist public policies were no longer needed. In hindsight, Daniel Patrick Moynihan's chillingly apocalyptic words carried a prophetic warning. "At this point," Moynihan predicted, "the present tangle of pathology is capable of perpetuating itself without assistance from the white world."[24]

On a surface level, not a word or idea in Moynihan's sentence was true. But the sentence did point to a deeper truth beneath Moynihan's intentions, which is that the public policies America had adopted throughout the ages of slavery and segregation cemented a racial hierarchy into our nation's very infrastructure. And that infrastructure was positioned to perpetuate racial inequality in our nation's housing, education, and wealth without mentioning race at all. Now all that was needed to perpetuate Black poverty was merely white indifference and allowing the system to perform the racial work it was designed to do.

Under the Nixon administration, Daniel Patrick Moynihan returned to the White House as the assistant to the president for domestic policy. To protect what little racial progress had occurred, Moynihan urged the president in a 1970 memo to adopt a policy of "benign neglect" toward Black America. On top of the memo Nixon scribbled, "I agree."[25] In the following year, Nixon further racialized the War on Crime by transforming it into a War on Drugs that focused on Black communities. Though neither "benign neglect" nor the War on Drugs reached its full potential under Nixon's watch, the seeds of America's new racial era had been planted, and the work to reap a long harvest was underway.

By painting the struggle against racism as "mission accomplished" and suggesting that any remaining racial inequality resulted from Black pathologies rather than racist public policies and the unfinished work of the War on Poverty and the Civil Rights Movement, white Americans calloused their conscience to Black suffering once again. As the American conscience calloused, myths about pathological Black families, Black dependence, and Black criminality flourished. Nothing soothed white anxieties more than knowing Black people were the nation's real problem.

In the election of 1972, Nixon secured 60 percent of the popular vote and 520 votes in the Electoral College. It was the largest Electoral College tally in history. That within an eight-year span, from 1964 to 1972, American consensus ricocheted from supporting LBJ's Great Society with the highest popular vote total in American history to supporting Richard Nixon's vision of "law and order" with the highest Electoral College tally showed how powerful white backlash against civil rights and the War on Poverty became during the first years of the Colorblind Age.

Yet nothing about America's future was set in stone by America's right turn or Nixon's popularity. Watergate hit. The newly created consensus around law and order shattered for a time, and white America was forced to search for a new molder of the nation's political identity. Re-creating consensus in a deeply fractured nation required one of the most unique leaders our nation has ever known. To understand both how a longstanding consensus in white America was constructed and how racial crimes were committed in the Colorblind Age, we must open the casket of one of the most influential racial ideologues in American history and one of the most beloved leaders of the era: President Ronald Reagan.

Reagan's first national success came as an actor, followed by a role as a national salesman for General Electric. But it was politics that provided a platform for Reagan to fully unveil his remarkable skill set on the world stage. His political convictions were forged on the heels of the Second World War within the furnace of the second Red Scare. With impeccable timing and an uncanny gift for one-liners, Reagan constructed his arguments about politics, economics, and race with a simplicity that gave his rhetoric the feel of a finely honed common sense that resonated with white America's deepest instincts and self-understanding.

Through his own brand of politics, Reagan was able to help craft a long and abiding national consensus concerning how to face the crises of race, economics, poverty, and crime. He proved nearly as popular with America's white working class as he was with the corporate executives whose interests he lobbied for and lionized. The face of America's racist ideas was no longer the vitriolic images of segregationists but Reagan with his welcoming warmth. The warm innocence Reagan learned to exude made it not only difficult to demonize the man but also nearly impossible to hold him accountable for the results his policies produced. He provided white America with confidence in the purity of the nation's intentions, and at the height of his power, only "out of touch" liberals and "impossible to please" Black people failed to fall in love.

In time, Reagan's warmth established the ethos of the Colorblind Age. Explicitly advocating for race-based laws proved too divisive. What would be required to resecure white supremacy would, in fact, be insisting on racial innocence while lobbying to roll back civil rights protections and designing policies that consistently benefitted the wealthiest white enclaves and destroyed poor Black communities. What would be required to resecure white supremacy would be shifting the public's understanding of racism itself from public policies to inner feelings. In so doing, Americans found wider freedom to support anti-Black and antipoor policies while claiming themselves to be neither racist nor cruel.

Reagan's primary contribution to the Colorblind Age was finalizing the turn in the nation's moral compass from the pursuit of civil rights and the common good to a rugged individualism rooted in unregulated capitalism and unfettered by any concern for the common good. Reagan believed the pursuit of a Great Society through the logics of liberalism had failed. However, if America wished to regain her swagger, all she needed was a deeper trust in her founding principles—a deeper trust in God, in the free market, and in the power of every individual to carve out their dreams in the land of opportunity.

In his first famous political speech in 1964, Reagan asked the nation to choose between the current revolution centered on racial and economic justice and a counterrevolution to recenter the nation on traditional American values. And over the course of the coming decades, most white Americans would choose to reject the wisdom of those fighting for civil rights and Black power and instead embrace the conservative counterrevolution. White America spelled their revolution R-E-A-G-A-N.

10

Fighting a King

Ronald Reagan and Rejecting Civil Rights

> Don't discount Reagan as the next threat to [the] Negro.
>
> —Jackie Robinson, 1968

When we envision the adversaries of the Civil Rights Movement in general and Martin Luther King Jr. in particular, the common cast of characters is often limited to the segregationists on the southern side of the Mason-Dixon line. The lineup generally includes the likes of George Wallace, Bull Connor, and fiendish white mobs attacking dignified and disciplined Black children and adults. That is, the lineup is limited to stock characters who prove as easy to demonize as they are for most white Americans to disassociate themselves from. This lineup reflects the nature of the training we received to understand racism itself—training that outlaws obvious expressions of racism while protecting the deeper and more systemic aspects of white people's power.

Much of that training came from a Hollywood actor turned politician who fully committed himself to upending the pursuit of Black socioeconomic justice. His name was Ronald Reagan, and his racial politics proved more influential and destructive than the entire pantheon of racist stock characters in the twentieth century. If racial crimes during the ages of slavery and lynching demand reparations, so too do the racial crimes of the Colorblind Age that placed millions of Black people in prison and kept even more in poverty.

From 1953 to 1989, Ronald Reagan became one of the most beloved Americans in United States history. And from 1953 to 1989, Ronald Reagan used his public life and remarkable gifts to adamantly oppose the Civil Rights Movement and roll back its every gain. Reagan possessed very few of the hallmarks we learned to look for in those who fought against the Civil Rights

Movement. As leading journalists of the time noted, "The star of so many 'all-American boy' movies just did not look right for the part of kook."[1] His rhetoric and style differed drastically from those of George Wallace and Bull Connor. Where Wallace and Connor had stoked the flames of racial animosity, Reagan focused on comforting the conscience of a nation rife with racial injustice with surety in its own moral superiority. In the Colorblind Age, Reagan shifted the presentation of racist ideas from the cinematics of Dixon's *Birth of a Nation* to the all-American warmth more akin to *The Andy Griffith Show*. For the victims of America's racial injustices, the racism of the Colorblind Age proved nearly as lethal as the racial violence in the age of the lynch. But for white audiences, the nation's new racial cinematics felt like a whole new show, a show that helped convince them they were no longer racists.

If on the surface Reagan shared little in common with the likes of George Wallace and Bull Connor, he nonetheless shared much with the white supremacists of generations past. Like Jefferson, Reagan deftly deflected accountability for his own dehumanizing racism while explicitly working to callous white America's consciousness to the suffering of Black America. Like that of the young Lincoln, Reagan's racism resided in the racial assumptions of his age. Unlike Lincoln and others within the "Greatest Generation," Reagan refused to grow or question his racial wisdom. Thomas Dixon understood that power was in popular propaganda and in striking images that rooted racist caricatures deeply in the American psyche. So too did Ronald Reagan. Madison Grant believed America's future depended on public policies that privileged American Nordics and pillaged Black and poor people. Substitute "wealthy white people" for "Nordics," and you get the policies and politics of Ronald Reagan. Dixon and Grant had planted the seeds of weaponizing the fears of socialism and communism to upend the struggle for racial justice and economic equality. Throughout his career, Reagan nurtured those seeds until they were ready for harvest. Reagan was no one's mirror image, but he proved just as influential—if not more so—than any white supremacist that the ages of slavery and lynching had produced.

America has produced more brilliant intellectuals than Ronald Reagan, but rarely, if ever, have we produced a more gifted communicator. When it comes to translating the gift of persuasion into political power, the Founding Fathers and Franklin Delano Roosevelt are the only Americans in Reagan's league. Reagan's particular talent was his ability to help white America see the world through his eyes. Reagan was a master of political theater and placed words and ideas together in ways that shined new light on America's basic racial instincts and self-understanding. He possessed the power to get white Americans to feel what he wanted them to feel and think what he wanted them to think—about our complex world and the very nature of politics, economics, religion, and national identity. Perhaps Reagan's most meaningful contribution to America's political imagination was the freedom he provided white Americans to support antipoor and anti-Black public policies while genuinely considering themselves compassionate, inclusive, and "colorblind."

Reagan's most important political formation happened during the second wave of the Red Scare. His first major national stage in politics came during the 1964 presidential campaign when he left behind his lifelong commitment to the Democratic Party to campaign for the segregationist and right-wing radical Barry Goldwater. Reagan's allies in the struggle against communism and civil rights consisted of the angriest and most racist politicians, from the Red Scare's Joseph McCarthy to Richard Nixon, George Wallace, and Strom Thurmond. Yet Reagan was his own man. He did not impersonate. He improvised and improved upon the persuasive powers of his forebears while staying faithful to their aims. Reagan guided white supremacy's evolution by moving the accent of white resistance from the fury generated by Black people's pursuit of equality to a calm indifference toward Black people's suffering. Reagan's version of white supremacy came not from the realms of biology or psychology but from a moral compass oriented by economic ideologies of free-market individualism and personal responsibility. Reagan imagined wealthy white people as society's most worthy and the nation's poor and Black people as society's preeminent problems.

As we navigate white supremacy's evolution from lynchings to the Colorblind Age, we begin with Reagan's political conversion as the conservative gospel of unregulated capitalism replaced his commitment to the liberal gospel of government for the common good. In time, Reagan's revolution led to an end to America's political consensus that began with the New Deal. If the best of the Greatest Generation left a legacy of racial and economic progress that aimed to perfect our nation, the generations who followed in Reagan's footsteps displayed the devastation that occurs when the ideas of freedom and liberty are divorced from a determined pursuit of racial and economic justice.

Admittedly, Ronald Reagan was not the most likely spokesperson of America's emerging racial order shaped by the wealthiest white Americans. Reagan was born in Illinois in 1911. Like many at the time, his parents were poor. He was shaped by his Irish Catholic father Jack's experience of America's anti-Catholic animosity and their family's commitment to the Democratic Party in the heyday of Republicanism. Jack was a hardscrabble salesman, a wonderful storyteller, and a man who struggled with alcoholism. When it came to America's racism and anti-Semitism, Jack Reagan made sure to let his sons know where he stood. When *The Birth of a Nation* came out, his father refused to allow Ronald or his brother, Neil, to watch the film. "It deals with the Ku Klux Klan against the colored folk, and I'm damned if anyone in this family will go see it," his father said. "The Klan's the Klan, and a sheet's a sheet, and any man who wears one over his head is a bum."[2] Ironically enough, the Reagan family was living in an Illinois town named Dixon at the time. Reagan remembered his father as "a handsome man—tall, swarthy and muscular, filled with contradictions of character. A sentimental Democrat, who believed fervently in the rights of the workingman."[3] After FDR became president, both Jack and Nelle, Reagan's mother, put their politics into practice by working for the federal Works Progress Administration.

In high school, Reagan would be class president, and after graduation, he left to attend Eureka College, where he majored in sociology and economics. However, academics was not Reagan's passion. His energies were more deeply invested in the extracurriculars of football, drama, and student government. America first met Ronald Reagan as an announcer for the Chicago Cubs in 1932 before he headed to Hollywood in 1937. Adversaries later denigrated Reagan as a "B-list actor." Though it was true he was never Hollywood's leading man, Reagan had earned a star on Hollywood's coveted Walk of Fame. His work before the camera, both in movies and television, made Reagan very wealthy and much more successful than most of his critics. In typical Reagan fashion, he displayed the confidence and wisdom to welcome opponents to underestimate him by mismeasuring his abilities.

Jack and Nelle's politics rubbed off on Ronald. Throughout the 1940s, Reagan held the greed and recklessness of Republicans during the Roaring Twenties accountable for the suffering of families across the nation, including his own. He viewed FDR as a national savior protecting the American people from greedy corporate titans. Reagan voted for FDR four times and carried his commitment to fight racism with him to Hollywood. In Hollywood, Reagan leaned left in an industry in which it was profitable to lean right on racial questions. He partnered with organizations fighting against racism, lobbied for films that provided Black actors opportunities for dignified roles, and joined efforts to highlight the threat of the KKK. In 1946, neofascism was on the rise and Reagan participated in a radio series titled *It's Happening Here*. Reagan compared the Klan to the Reich's führer. "I have to stand and speak, to lift my face and shout that this must end," Reagan declared. "Stop the terror, stop the murder!"[4] Reagan was not a radical for social causes, but neither was he a silent bystander.

In 1948, Reagan campaigned for Truman and supported the future senator Hubert Humphrey, who fought to include a proposal to end racial segregation in the Democratic platform. When Truman wrote that there was "disturbing evidence of intolerance and prejudice" in the United States that was "similar in kind" to that of Nazi Germany, the president reflected a readiness in segments of white America to confront racism and deepen self-awareness.[5] Likely, such convictions played a role in Truman receiving Reagan's endorsement. During these years, Reagan described himself as "a near-hopeless hemophilic liberal. I bled for 'causes.'"[6]

Following World War II, neither politics nor the fight against fascism were side shows for Reagan; they were central to his identity—and his aspirations were remarkably ambitious. "I would work with the tools I had," he wrote in his 1965 autobiography. "My thoughts, my speaking abilities, my reputation as an actor. I would bring about the regeneration of the world I believed should have automatically appeared. . . . Thus my first evangelism came in the form of being hell-bent on saving the world from Neo-fascism."[7] By 1948, Reagan was a middle-aged man who positioned himself as an adversary of the Klan in Hollywood and an advocate for equity between corporate profits and workers' wages on the Democratic campaign trial.

This, of course, raises the question of what happened that converted Reagan to the extent that he was ready to partner with the imperial wizard of the Ku Klux Klan by endorsing segregationist Barry Goldwater in 1964.[8] From the late 1940s through the early 1960s, three powerful forces—personal tragedies, the Red Scare, and new relationships—coalesced to transform Ronald Reagan from a supporter of liberal ideas to the most persuasive conservative provocateur our nation ever produced.

Nothing prepares the ground for a personal transformation more than a season of personal crisis. Behind the scenes of the campaign season, between 1947 and 1949, Ronald Reagan found himself in a time of storms that threatened to blow his life asunder. In early June 1947, a case of viral pneumonia sent Reagan to the hospital and nearly proved fatal. Then things got worse. On June 26, 1947, Reagan's wife, the actress Jane Wyman, went into labor three months early. Their daughter, Christine, never made it out of the hospital. Instead of taking home their newborn, Reagan and Wyman took home a death certificate. Reagan's marriage with Wyman had been rocky for quite some time. Like many men, Reagan desired a wife who not only instilled confidence in him but who also excitedly played the subordinate role of supportive admirer. But Wyman's star power far exceeded Reagan's. She could play many difficult roles, but not that one. Reagan wanted to work things out. Wyman, who often felt demeaned by her husband and distant from his political ambitions, felt little compulsion toward reconciliation. In 1948, the marriage officially ran ashore when Wyman filed for divorce, devastating Reagan.[9]

Reagan's personal difficulties involved more than his dissolving family life. They were professional as well. "The year 1949 was a terrible year for dad," his son, Michael, wrote later. "He had already lost his wife and his children. That year he also broke his leg in an amateur baseball game. . . . He stopped making movies [and was going through] the worst dry spell of his career."[10] Life had knocked Reagan down and kept on kicking him.

In addition to his personal and professional losses, paranoia in the political arena reached a hysterical pitch and continued to climb even further. The second wave of the Red Scare engulfed the nation in 1947 as fears of communism began replacing the fears of fascism through the help of political opportunists such as Senator Joseph McCarthy. It is little wonder that hysteria was in the air. From Mussolini to Hitler to Stalin, totalitarianism ravaged the world and filled its cemeteries with armies of soldiers and even more unarmed citizens. These crimes were recent events, and the fact that it was now a nuclear age placed the whole world on edge. With Nazism soundly defeated in Germany, the lone remaining totalitarian threat to world peace was perceived to be communism. And at the height of the Red Scare hysterics, Americans saw potential communists everywhere—even where they weren't.

Reagan's entrance into the Red Scare came through his unexpected ascendency to the presidency of the Screen Actors Guild in 1947. By the end of the twentieth century, thanks in significant part to Reagan's leadership, the defeat of communism felt so well established that the original fears of communism and many aspects of its social impact disappeared from American memory. In the minds of most Americans, communism was understood as a discredited, totalitarian, atheistic alternative to American democracy, capitalism, and religiosity. In this understanding, which Reagan shared, communism promised economic equity only to deliver destitution, whereas American democracy and capitalism provided political power and economic prosperity for anyone ready to embrace the freedom of personal responsibility.

Unsurprisingly, this picture of neither communism nor America was wholly accurate. As seen in the works of Thomas Dixon and Madison Grant, in the early to mid-twentieth century, issues of race and civil rights were continually at the center of America's conversations about communism. In the international court of public opinion, Russia hammered America's racial politics for its similarities to fascism and its hypocrisy in preaching human equality while perpetuating some of the world's greatest racial violence and most radical economic inequalities. Unable to deny the charges, throughout the 1920s and '30s, America promoted anticommunist propaganda through anti-Black racism. The Communist Party would often be referred to as "the nigger party," and Red Scare propaganda warned of communism's threat to white supremacy due to its commitment to interracial solidarity and social equality among citizens. Throughout the first wave of the Red Scare, communism was decried as the path to miscegenation with the same fervor that once justified slavery and lynching.

In the shadow of World War II, however, international public opinion forced America's fight against communism to evolve from explicitly racial fears to a more "colorblind" rhetoric. America's anticommunism propaganda pivoted to excoriate communism as the vehicle for a totalitarianism that would end democracy and reverse the incredible economic recovery the New Deal and World War II had inaugurated. However—and this is critical—if much of the explicit racism disappeared from the Red Scare's political rhetoric, the Red Scare's ability to undermine both workers and Black progress never waned. The driving force behind the Red Scare often had little to do with actual communists and much more to do with political opportunists seeking to protect America's racial and economic hierarchy. In the future, those looking to protect white supremacy without explicit appeals to race could look to the second wave of the Red Scare as a test case in the type of politics that could get that job done. It was in just such a context that Ronald Reagan began to learn political chess. He would, in time, become a grand master.

Black America's relationship to communism was complex and conflicting—but, by and large, it was not hysterical.[11] Throughout American history, most Black people's commitments to interracial democracy and economic equity always ran deeper than their commitment to capitalism. Just as most Black Americans refused to equate the politics of democracy with the economics of inequality, so too the vast majority of Black America refused to equate the organized pursuit of economic equality with the totalitarian politics of Soviet dictatorship. What most Black Americans held in common throughout the Red Scare was the conviction that white America's hysterics over communism merely masked America's deeper fears of racial and economic justice. Very few Black Americans considered communism public enemy number one, because it wasn't. For most Black people, America's public enemy number one was, always and everywhere, white supremacy.[12]

In 1949, Langston Hughes voiced the concern of many Black people that our nation was once again revealing fascist reflexes by fearing all the wrong things. "This is exactly what happened in Germany," Hughes wrote. "First Hitler locked up the Communists. The Jews were No. 2 on Hitler's list. In America, the Negroes are No. 2 on bigotry's list. Hitler began with the Reichstag Fire Trial of the Communists. He ended by burning the Jews alive in the ovens of Buchenwald." Knowing racism, not communism, was the greatest threat to the American experiment, Hughes noted that "the voices who cry 'red' the loudest have never been known to be raised against segregation or the color line" but "are the very persons and organizations known to be the most anti-Negro, anti-Jewish and anti-labor."

Instead of following in the Nazis' footsteps by responding hysterically to communism, Hughes wrote that "America can learn some good things about race relations, democratic education and health programs, and insurance against poverty from the Soviet people." After writing a series supporting some of the Soviet programs, Hughes stated precisely what America was not ready to understand. "I am not now, nor have I ever been a member of the Communist Party," he wrote, "but I believe in equality."[13]

During the Red Scare, the distinctions between democracy, socialism, and communism blurred. Red Scare backlash often erased the lines between progressive taxation; a commitment to political compassion for hungry children, needy mothers, the sick, and the elderly; and totalitarianism. Within the fire of the hysterics, the very fight for equality—for racial minorities and workers—within a capitalistic system became an increasingly dangerous enterprise.

And it is in this context of political crisis that falsely pitted American democracy and capitalism against civil and workers' rights that Ronald Reagan's political imagination began to be reforged. America had underestimated the threat of Nazi Germany. Reagan was committed to not repeating that mistake with Russia. But in refusing to repeat the errors of the past, Reagan rushed headlong into new mistakes. Gone forever in Reagan's imagination was fear of the Klan, white terrorism, and the kinship between white supremacy and fascism. In Reagan's reforged imagination, liberalism, socialism, and communism represented the new totalitarian threat. And under the sway of that fear, Reagan labored to extinguish all progress regarding racial and economic justice.

The private transformation from a bleeding-heart liberal and "New Dealer to the core" to a Cold War capitalist had begun. "Light was dawning in some obscure region in my head," he wrote years later as he publicly processed his conversion from liberalism to conservatism. "I was beginning to see the seamy side of liberalism. Too many patches on the progressive coat were of a color I didn't personally care for."[14] The era of the Red Scare was Reagan's refiner's fire, forcing him to reexamine everything and begin a serious rewriting of his personal priorities and political perspectives. A new Reagan was emerging.

As his thirst to provide serious leadership quickened, Reagan, who was a lifelong reader, became even more avid. "I determined to do my own research, find out my own facts," he wrote of this season in his life. "A series of hardnose happenings began changing my whole view on American dangers."[15] Both during the Red Scare and in the years to come, the tragedy of Reagan's thirst for knowledge was his lack of curiosity in the thinking beyond the most conservative and reactionary writers white America had to offer. Disillusioned with liberalism, Reagan ignored both white progressives and Black America's most incisive advocates. The writings of Du Bois, Hughes, and Baldwin never leavened Ronald Reagan's thinking about the challenges confronting our nation, because he never meaningfully engaged with anything they wrote. As with most American presidents, Black wisdom played no role in Reagan's political convictions.

For a public figure like Ronald Reagan, private transformations can stay private for only so long before people begin to take note. Hedda Hopper, *Los Angeles Times'* Hollywood gossip columnist and a collaborator in Red Scare hysterics, was one of the first to take note of the new Reagan. He had moved from "being quiet and unassuming" to being "the spokesman for all movie actors," who "walks around the studio with a portable radio . . . [and] reads every book he believes he should read . . . [and] most political columns. . . . He is not only an actor, but a politician."[16]

Reagan's transformation involved much more than his personal crises and the Red Scare. Perhaps the most transformative catalysts of Reagan's transformation were two new relationships that reoriented his personal and professional worlds. One relationship was rooted in romance and opened the doors to a network of the nation's most connected right-wing conservatives. The second relationship was with a mentor uniquely positioned to shape Reagan's thinking and prepare him to provide transformational national leadership.

As Ronald Reagan began navigating single life, a new actress had moved to town. Her name was Nancy Davis. Nancy was the daughter of Chicago surgeon Loyal Davis, an influential conservative who held economic and "political views to the right of Herbert Hoover."[17] Nancy was very ambitious and she was serious about finding a husband. Her list of candidates was rumored to be divided by industry. And at the top of her list of actors was the newly minted bachelor Ronald Reagan.

When Ronald and Nancy met in 1949, Reagan still sported a cane as his broken leg continued to heal. In many ways, Reagan was on the mend both physically and personally. As he healed, Reagan was more interested in playing the field than finding a spouse. "I tried to go to bed with every starlet in Hollywood," was how Reagan described it, "and damn near succeeded."[18] But between Nancy's determination and the reality that she was already carrying Ronald's unborn child, by 1953, Nancy Davis became Nancy Reagan. When Reagan married Nancy, their ambitions merged in the singularity of Reagan's career. In Nancy, Reagan found not only a wife ready to play the role of his most adoring fan, but also an aggressive and well-connected socialite completely committed to his meteoric rise. Nancy's family brought Reagan into the highest echelons of conservative power and helped him network with people like the Davises' next-door neighbor, Barry Goldwater.[19]

In 1954, another relationship came into Reagan's life that was likely via Nancy and her parents.[20] This relationship would be lesser known but no less influential. Before Jack Welch, General Electric (GE) had the pioneering genius of Vice President of Labor and Community Relations Lemuel Boulware. Working in the aftermath of the Great Depression, Boulware dedicated himself to understanding the psychology of America's working class and the ways in which the working class could be persuaded to support the political and economic interests of America's largest corporations.

It was a mammoth task. Ever since the Great Depression, government and union power had been painted on the wall of the American mind as democracy's defense and the people's protector against the threats of unregulated capitalism. Boulware was committed to transforming these hieroglyphics into a new picture that painted corporations as America's shepherds and government regulations and unions as wolves in sheep's clothing.[21] Boulware formed what would become known as focus groups to test out corporate messaging as he sought to restore corporate America's image. Through his research, two themes continually struck a chord: personal liberty and individual responsibility.

In time, Boulware would be heralded as the corporate executive with the deepest understanding of what drove the minds of America's working class and perhaps the most effective corporate labor negotiator in American history. He meticulously engineered a propaganda machine that saturated GE communities with ideological rifts by equating corporate and individualistic self-interest with freedom itself. Ultimately, Boulware's accents and themes became Ronald Reagan's political gospel.[22]

The project that brought the two men together was the launching of a weekly TV show, *General Electric Theater*. The show needed a wholesome host who would double as GE's spokesperson to preach its corporate gospel and write the company's principles on the minds and hearts of the American people. GE was already one of America's most innovative and imaginative companies, and *General Electric Theater* proved to be one of the most ambitious projects in corporate America's history.

With Reagan as host, *General Electric Theater* quickly garnered top ratings and went on to host over fifty Academy Award winners.[23] Despite the show's remarkable success, it was only the tip of the iceberg of Boulware's work and Reagan's responsibility as a company spokesman. GE executives wanted their audiences and employees to see the world through the executives' eyes, to believe that by fighting against governmental regulations and union control, GE was in fact fighting for the heart of the American experiment. With Boulware's help, GE provided select writings for reading groups and rigorous trainings for their employees in free-market economics. It is not clear whether a distinction existed between indoctrination and education for GE employees, for the company needed not simply employees but acolytes.

One of the primary aims of Boulware's program was manufacturing a "great communicator."[24] And Boulware had an eye for talent. In identifying Reagan, Boulware unleashed the greatest evangelist corporate America ever created. No longer seeking to bring down fascism, Reagan received intensive training in how to harmonize democratic ideals with the principles of free markets and the priorities of America's corporations. He became Boulware's most important student. If Reagan had proved a lackluster scholar without a deep yearning for academic knowledge during his undergraduate years at Eureka College, at GE, Reagan's thirst proved ravenous.

What the well Boulware dug for Reagan to water the life of the mind lacked in diversity, it made up for in fervency. Like Reagan's personal reading list, Boulware's included many of the most conservative apologists. The readings consisted of writers who specialized in simplifying, shining, and sharpening free-market ideologies for mass appeal in ways similar to how Thomas Dixon had dramatized academic histories. Typical of Reagan's reading list were works like *The Road Ahead: America's Creeping Revolution* by John T. Flynn, *The Road to Serfdom* by Friedrich A. Hayek, and *Economics in One Lesson* by Henry Hazlitt. Some of these writers were Nobel Prize winners and some were laymen, but what they held in common was a commitment to communicating conservative ideologies in a way that allowed for mass consumption and tailoring their ideas for publications such as the *Reader's Digest* and the *National Review*. These writers provided to Reagan what Enlightenment writers had provided to Jefferson: a philosophical framework capable of harmonizing radical racial and economic inequality with America's commitment to democracy and human equality.

Reagan often traveled between speaking events at GE plants and communities by luxury train car, and those cars became his classroom. "Those GE tours became almost a postgraduate course in political science for me," he later wrote in his 1990 autobiography. "I was seeing how government really operated and affected people in America, not how it was taught in school."[25] And for Reagan and GE, the only antidote to the way government actually operated was to turn the nation from its liberal New Deal ideologies and return it to free-market principles.

Reagan later spoke of his capitalistic convictions as trusting in the "magic of the marketplace."[26] Yet, GE provided training in a very particular version of capitalism, a corporate capitalism that would, in time, distinguish our nation from the socially conscious capitalism of other industrialized countries around the world. Lest we forget, Adam Smith, the father of capitalism, instilled in his economic vision a social conscience committed to a living wage and that measured the health of a nation's economy by the living standards of its poorest workers. Smith wrote that "profit is . . . always highest in the countries which are going fastest to ruin" and that only economic equity—and explicitly not law and order—provided the path to a thriving society.[27] Smith also warned that the greatest threat to a truly wealthy nation is allowing business interests to shape a nation's political priorities.[28] All these lessons of capitalism were expunged from GE's corporate evangelism. Perhaps no project, product, or politician in history better embodied Adam Smith's greatest fears about the commingling of business interests and politics better than the liaisons between GE and Ronald Reagan.

Rather than a socially conscious capitalism, the writers Reagan read equated political remedies to social concerns with totalitarian communism.

Reagan read these writers as if they preached the gospel truth. The journalist John T. Flynn provides a typical example of the wisdom Reagan's readings provided, a wisdom that wiped out racial justice in the name of corporate capitalism. Flynn writes:

> The Negro question does not stand before us alone. . . . Here he must make a choice. Is he going to put his weight on the side of a revolutionary Red drive to recruit the Negro in order to swell the ranks of the army of Socialist voters who will be used to complete the destruction of our political and economic system? Or will he say that this Negro question must be subordinate to the greater one of preserving our political and economic civilization? Will we hurry the Negro to the polls to set us upon a path which will end in destroying liberties of us all—white and black alike?[29]

Nothing in that paragraph represents mental or moral clarity, but we cannot underestimate the significance of this educational experience for either Reagan or the nation. Reagan took right-wing radicals like Flynn and polished their ideas with his remarkable rhetorical gifting until the depravity of their arguments sounded like common sense. Due to Reagan's remarkable gifts, it would be hard to identify any more important classrooms in America than the ones that moved Reagan over the train lines during his years working for GE.

When it comes to reparations and America's evolving racial imagination, the era of the Red Scare marked a significant shift in America's racial rhetoric. Outside Black America, the shift was subtle enough to go largely unnoticed. Apart from Southern segregationists, racial division was no longer easily spoken of as a positive good that protected civilization itself. Instead, at a national level in the context of the Red Scare, a racialized society was increasingly positioned as the lesser of two evils. Writers Reagan consumed imagined America at the proverbial fork in the road that allowed for but two alternatives: trusting the free market to provide the path of true liberty and freedom, or heading toward a totalitarian and communistic state. As the "Negro question" became "subordinate to . . . preserving our political and economic civilization," a rhetoric emerged that manipulated the fears of communism to make America immune to the call for economic and racial justice. Rather than perfecting the nation, intentional pursuits of justice were framed as the preeminent threat to American democracy.

There was one final aspect of Reagan's experience as GE's spokesman that readied him for revolutionary political power. The greatest downside to political hopefuls' pursuit of wealth, fame, and power is that it leaves them isolated from everyday Americans—out of touch with the national vibe and unable to connect to the hearts of the American people. GE devised a remedy for that isolation. On their tours, GE placed Reagan on the plant floors and allowed for abundant interaction with people of America's working class. Reagan learned to work a room and, like Boulware, became intimate with not only the thoughts and ways of executive elites but also the thoughts, feelings, and frustrations of everyday Americans. If Boulware was the corporate executive with his finger on the pulse of America's white working class, through his tutelage, Reagan became his political equal. In the twentieth century, no politician, either through natural gifting or education, was better placed to build a common set of convictions between corporate elites and everyday working Americans than Ronald Reagan—and that proved the linchpin for creating national consensus in white America's racial imagination that stood the test of time.

GE discipled Reagan in its political and economic gospel for eight years, and he emerged as one of the most powerful and polished products corporate America ever produced. Through GE's program of discipleship, Reagan sharpened his powers of persuasion to draw a clear line in the sand between right and wrong. On the right side of history stood corporate executives, entrepreneurs, and racial conservatives protecting Americans from the Russian way. On the wrong side were civil rights workers, white liberals, and government bureaucrats who attempted to replace rugged individualism rooted in American democracy with a soft-minded collectivism rooted in communism. To this gospel, Reagan gave his heart, soul, and mind. A perfect marriage was born between corporate interests and the corporate dramatist with the ability to move his audiences any way he pleased. "I wasn't just making speeches," Reagan recalled. "I was preaching a sermon."[30]

And preach he did. The more political Reagan's sermons grew, the more his speaking circuit expanded—reaching well beyond the confines of GE and into community organizations across America. By the late 1950s and early '60s, he had developed a coherent, polished ideology that railed against federal investment in education, Social Security, and the Veterans Administration. "We can lose our freedom at once by succumbing to Russia or we can lose it gradually by installments," Reagan prophesied in 1961. Either way, "the end result is slavery."[31]

Though Thomas Jefferson championed progressive taxation before Karl Marx was born, Reagan equated progressive tax structures with class warfare, and class warfare with communism.[32] "There can be no justification of the progressive tax—an idea hatched in the Communist revolution," Reagan thundered as the Red Scare evolved into the Cold War. Like a preacher fearing the fate of the souls of his flock, Reagan begged for white America to wake up before it was too late. "The inescapable truth is that we are at war, and we are losing that war simply because we don't or won't realize we are in it. We have ten years." The clock was ticking, and it was "not ten years to make up our mind, but ten years to win or lose—by 1970 the world will be all slave or all free."[33]

On the lips of lesser preachers, equating the education of children, care for the elderly, taxation of the rich, and provision for veterans with Soviet dictatorship and slavery would be the theater of the absurd. But Reagan was entirely sincere. And sincerity sells. With the help of his artistic touch, Reagan landed right-wing logic on listening ears in a manner that opened many of white America's hearts and minds to his message. Admittedly, Reagan was not yet at his best. But he was damn good and getting better.

For Reagan, times of crisis had left scars that rewrote his worldview and left him deeply cynical about the government's ability to produce positive change. But the season also served as a crucible, endowing him with strength, resolve, and clear convictions—and refining his already remarkable God-given gifts of persuasion. If crisis functioned as Reagan's crucible, his relationships with Nancy Davis and Lemuel Boulware cemented his conversion to conservatism while giving his newfound powers a national platform. Reagan was now on a new path, and he was determined to change the trajectory of the entire nation. After a decade of training, he was ready for the biggest stage of all: presidential politics.

In 1964, the stage was set for Reagan's political coming-out party. It was a tension-filled moment for Republicans. In 1964, the Republicans were fighting against LBJ's push for civil rights and the War on Poverty. To lead the charge as their presidential nominee, they selected the right-wing segregationist Barry Goldwater, whose eerie slogan was "In your hearts you know he's right."[34] For socially conscious Republicans, like Black baseball Hall of Famer Jackie Robinson, Goldwater was nothing short of a nightmare. "If we have a bigot running for the president of the United States," Robinson warned, "it will set back the course of the country."[35] Republicans refused to heed Robinson's warnings. Nonetheless, Robinson attended the 1964 Republican National Convention. "I now believe I know," he wrote afterward, "how it felt to be a Jew in Hitler's Germany."[36]

But Reagan was undeterred by Robinson. Two months later, Reagan gave a nationally televised speech titled "A Time for Choosing." After years of perfecting the speech, Reagan unveiled his brilliance on a national stage. Using facts, figures, and fictions, and personal stories and experiences, Reagan sought entrance into his audience's heads and hearts. He quickly jabbed his audience with facts that enraged him. And then he hit them with a joke to relieve the tension his rage had produced. In one moment, government was wasting its money on welfare. Reagan claimed one proposal to relieve unemployment would "spend just on room and board for each young person $4,700 a year." He was outraged. And then he was funny. "We can send them to Harvard for $2,700 a year." Slight pause. "Of course, don't get me wrong," Reagan mused, "I'm not suggesting Harvard is the answer for juvenile delinquency."

Reagan was one of the funniest politicians in American history, and he knew how to use his humor to relax the room and provide the space to introduce his vision of revolution.[37] Self-deprecation fueled much of his humor. Yet when he wasn't the butt of his own joke, it was the liberal elite in the crosshairs. And on this night, his aim was lethal. "The trouble with our liberal friends is not that they're ignorant," Reagan quipped. "It's just that they know so much that isn't so." For Reagan, it was time to admit that American liberalism had failed. "For three decades, we've sought to solve the problems of unemployment through government planning, and the more the plans fail, the more the planners plan."

As Reagan moved between personal stories and cosmic visions, from sincerity to sarcasm, he held the audience in the palm of his hand. He effortlessly moved them from rage, to empathy, to laughing at liberal failures to keep from crying. By the end, it was clear Reagan was deadly serious—this fight was for the future of our children. Reagan closed with his favorite phrase from FDR: "You and I have a rendezvous with destiny," he said, nearing his close. "We'll preserve for our children, this, the last best hope of man on earth, or we'll sentence them to take the step into a thousand years of darkness."[38]

After championing a segregationist fighting against civil rights and economic equity, Reagan exited stage right to a thunderous ovation, and the future of conservatism moved with him. In a foreshadowing of things to come, the spellbound audience that night had been the orchestra, he the conductor, and the performance was perfect. Pulitzer Prize–winning commentator David Broder heralded "A Time for Choosing" as "the most successful political debut since William Jennings Bryan's Cross of Gold Speech in 1816."[39] It would become known simply as "The Speech."

The Speech was not designed to withstand scrutiny. It was designed to work on the heart and mind in ways much deeper than what mere facts and accuracy allowed. Oliver Wendell Holmes once said: "Most people reason dramatically, not quantitatively."[40] Ronald Reagan understood this insight and utilized it for political gain more effectively than any other politician in the final half of the twentieth century. It was not that Reagan avoided statistics; it was that he was gifted in injecting facts and figures with dramatic flair. In The Speech, as throughout his career, Reagan rarely felt the need to align his political rhetoric with reality. If the facts failed to make the right point, Reagan usually felt free to make up his own.[41]

Reagan was convincing, not to the fact-checkers, but to those in his audience most weary of the changes inherent in the pursuit of civil rights and Lyndon Johnson's Great Society. His simplified logic and rhetorical genius enabled his audience to see old issues in a new light. He had deftly supported segregationists without mentioning race and had supported free market capitalism without mentioning the suffering of America's poor. By submerging these political realities underneath the fear of communism, Reagan had effectively erased these issues from the conscience of the conservative cause. And that was his brilliance.

Despite the lavish praise The Speech generated, most Americans underestimated what they had witnessed in the fifty-three-year-old Hollywood actor who seemed past the prime of his career. The Speech was not the momentary brilliance of a shooting star. It was an opening act. Indeed, despite his age, Reagan's star was on the rise, and a new trajectory had just been established. The Speech not only launched Reagan into a new orbit; it also provided a preview of a new way for conservatives to win the struggle for America's heart, soul, and mind. If white America liked the actor Ronald Reagan, they *loved* Reagan as the folksy, conservative truth-teller.[42]

"A Time for Choosing" raked in somewhere between $250,000 to $2 million for Barry Goldwater's campaign. But even Reagan's heroics could not save the Republican nominee.[43] When Reagan entered headlong into the conservative cause, conservatives were losing and losing badly. The New Deal marked the birth of American liberalism, and the idea that it was the federal government's calling to protect and promote the well-being of its citizens provided a bipartisan consensus for America's mainstream politics from the early 1930s until Reagan's presidency in 1980. Following LBJ's landslide victory in 1964, American liberalism was at its crest, and everyone believed the strength of the wave would only increase. Following the election, the opinion of the experts was that the conservative cause of reactionaries like Reagan and Goldwater was on its deathbed, and the obituaries should be prepared for print.

If this was what the pundits and those in the know knew, it was certainly not what Ronald Reagan learned from his travels to communities across America. Following The Speech, Reagan was positioned to be a leading man for the conservative cause. For Reagan, more training was needed before claiming the title of Republicanism's favorite son, but it was clear he was ready to fight for his place in the national spotlight. His first contest would be for the governorship of California, where he unveiled his strategy that weaponized the backlash against civil rights and the War on Poverty to empower a conservative counterrevolution.

Shortly before announcing his bid for governor, Reagan delivered his speech "The Myth of the Great Society."[44] He spoke of the election and the Democrats' commitment to the liberal status quo. "Status quo," Reagan smirked. "That's Latin for the mess we're in." He lamented that the limited government the Founders envisioned had "given way to planners, and they've laid an increasingly heavy hand in every facet of our lives." His empathy was with neither America's poor nor her marginalized, but "the businessman eaten out of our substance." Reagan mourned the way that providing housing for the poor warred against property rights through the power of eminent domain. He lamented the way that *Brown v. Board of Education* placed the federal government between local communities, parents, and the education of their children. "Textbooks devote a chapter to public welfare," Reagan grieved, "and not one line to Patrick Henry."

Reagan believed the threat of communism meant it was time to get tough:

> Every lesson of history tells us that as a nation has grown in culture and refinement and advanced, it has softened, and when confronted by the barbarian, the less cultured, the barbarians have triumphed. . . . You and I have come to our moment of truth.

America, his speech suggested, needed to shift her focus and realize that the true threat to American democracy was neither racism nor economic inequality. Such concerns only made the nation soft and vulnerable to the threat from the Russian barbarians at her gate.

Despite this threat, Reagan closed his speech with his trademark confidence and optimism. Only eighteen months earlier, Lyndon Johnson signed the Civil Rights Act of 1964, only to lament that he had lost the white South to the Republican Party for an entire generation. Reagan believed Johnson underestimated the backlash that was brewing. It was not just the white South that Johnson's pursuit of racial justice would cost the Democratic Party but white people across the nation. After the passage of not one but two civil rights bills, Reagan told dis-eased white Democrats to "have no feeling of disloyalty if you have decided you can no longer follow the leadership of that party. . . . The leadership of that party has long abandoned you."

Reagan had a clear vision for the Republican Party. "Today, the Republican Party is the vehicle we must use as the party of opposition. . . . It's an awesome responsibility, and you and I who are Republicans cannot meet it with a splintered party." He noted how experts predicted Republican demise, but the experts had missed what he had learned in his travels across America. "I'd like to suggest there is a bloc we can appeal to. It's a voter bloc of millions and millions of people. It crosses party lines . . . economic lines. . . . I say to you that bloc . . . that bloc of voters can be ours."

In time, political commentators with any balance were forced to admit that Reagan possessed an "almost flawless political instinct."[45] But as Reagan ran for California governor, not everyone was so sure. Issues of race were considered Reagan's Achilles' heel, and rather than race relations existing at the periphery of the 1966 election, issues of race were essential—especially in California. In California, the Rumford Act sought to end segregated housing, but the California Supreme Court overturned it, protecting the legality of racial restrictions throughout the state.[46] Prior to the Rumford Act, segregated housing had been the norm in California, and Los Angeles was a prime example. By 1940, a full 80 percent of Los Angeles homes contained a restrictive covenant prohibiting Black ownership.[47]

Unsurprisingly, Reagan made it known he fully supported the court's verdict—not because he himself was racist but because he felt property owners possessed the right to be if they so desired. Due to such stances, the two-term incumbent governor Pat Brown felt the actor was so extreme and "beatable" that he helped fund a smear campaign against Reagan's primary opponent.[48]

Only two years had passed since Republicans ignored Jackie Robinson's fears about nominating a racist. California Republicans knew Black voters played nearly no role in Republican primaries, but how could the party compete without embracing the need for racial change in America? Reagan's reasons for rejecting civil rights legislation included believing it was poorly written and that it trampled on private property rights. As late as 1980, Reagan rejected civil rights simply because he felt they were "humiliating to the South."[49] Some California Republicans feared that racists of Reagan's ilk were simply too much for the party to bear.

This fear was on display March 6, 1966, as Reagan campaigned at the Convention of National Negro Republicans in Santa Monica. A delegate shared her concern about Reagan's candidacy: "It grieves me when a leading Republican candidate says the Civil Rights Act is a bad piece of legislation." The comment jolted Reagan, and, for a rare moment, the candidate lost his composure. "I resent the implication that there is any bigotry in my nature," he fumed, slamming his fist on the table. "Don't anyone ever imply I lack integrity. I will not stand silent and let anyone imply that—in this or any other group." With that, he exited the convention floor. Reagan's outburst was revelatory because it was unrehearsed, providing a rare glimpse into the inner workings of a disciplined actor. Remarkably, despite supporting segregation and candidates endorsed by the Ku Klux Klan, Reagan sincerely believed he was not racist.

Following his blowup, Reagan recovered his composure and reentered the room. He refused to repent of either his opposition to the civil rights legislation or his support of Barry Goldwater. "If I did not know that Barry Goldwater was the opposite of a racist," Reagan said to set the record straight, "I could not have supported him."[50]

The moment revealed a new racial consciousness emerging in those fighting against civil rights and Black justice. As racist public policies came more and more in the crosshairs, those like Reagan who defended racist public policies refused to correlate their politics with racism at all.[51] In this new world, it became increasingly possible to be *personally* against segregation *and* to support white people's freedom to perpetuate segregation. For Reagan and his followers, racism revolved around interpersonal relationships and in no way involved public policy. To bolster his "not a racist" credentials, Reagan routinely recalled his relationship with Black teammates from his college football days whose mistreatment opened his eyes for the first time to the realities Black America faced. After a hotel denied his teammates shelter, Reagan and his parents had personally hosted them in their home. How could people of such personal warmth and hospitality be called racists?

In the emerging consciousness that dominated the Colorblind Age, the charge of racism became a white emotional trigger. If pulled, the trigger released an avalanche of rage. The charge of racism infuriated Reagan for the rest of his career. By raising the emotions in the room to a fever pitch, he closed the possibility of critically addressing the implications of his thinking and public policies.

For white people, responses heavy on emotions and light on understanding the interconnections between public policies and racial impact proved remarkably effective in avoiding rigorous accountability. As this tactic became mainstream, critical conversations concerning politics and race became impossible, and—for those most committed to the status quo—silence became synonymous with progress.

This lack of sufficient accountability created a context for white people to vote for politicians who supported anti-Black and antipoor legislation while feeling innocent of the racial and economic injustices their political power perpetuated. In the ages of the shackle and lynching, racist public policies were fueled by explicitly racist ideas to perform explicitly racist work. In the new racial era, a determined denialism concerning the role of race replaced explicitly racist justifications for the nation's racial public policies. The determined denialism often proved no less violent than America's previous, explicitly racist policies. And the crimes that denialism inspired are no less worthy of reparations.

Though Reagan had effectively used his fury in Santa Monica, rage was not his usual calling card. As he ran for governor and beyond and addressed issues such as the Rumford Act, Reagan was much more effective at weaponizing his trademark warmth. His typical approach was on display in his interview on the nationally televised show *Meet the Press*:

> Well, I agree with you he [a Black man] has a right to live where he wants to live. The unfortunate thing in my mind with regard to those people who are entrenched with the sickness of prejudice and discrimination is that they have certain constitutional rights. . . . Even though we disagree with them and even though we disapprove of their use of discrimination and bigotry, I believe the greater danger in violating any individual's constitutional right is the precedent it establishes.

That his political calculus provided white people the constitutional right to extinguish the constitutional rights of Black people either failed to occur to Reagan or failed to bother him. Yet, he wanted to get his stance on racism on the record: "I myself, I will tell you now, I do not subscribe to it."[52] In what would become a repetitive formula, when Reagan stated his support for policies to brutalize Black people and those in poverty, he began by denouncing racism and insisting on the need for empathy and compassion for those in need. Reagan was, in the words of one economist, "a warmly ruthless man."[53]

Later in the 1960s, Reagan let the press in on the formula that distinguished him from his ideological colleagues. When it came to America's cold reception of Goldwater and its warm reception of him, Reagan confessed: "The funny thing is . . . I said some of the same things." Yet, Reagan understood that brutal public policies demanded a humanitarian touch. So the formula he employed when he advocated for heartless policies always began with a meaningless but seemingly compassionate qualifier. Reagan explained: "I've always believed you say the qualifier first." If you fight to defund Social Security, to remove benefits for the poorest families in America, or to support segregation, you start with a qualifier. On Social Security, "you say, 'Now, let's make it plain: The first priority must be that no one who is depending on it should have it taken away from him, or have it endangered.'" On welfare, you say: "Now, I am not suggesting that we stop welfare tomorrow. *So, having qualified with that. . .*"[54] The humanitarian touch of Reagan's rhetorical qualifiers proved marvelously effective and positioned him to support antipoor and anti-Black policies without coming across as antipoor or anti-Black to white audiences.

And that was Reagan's magic: introduce proposals to end Social Security by emphasizing the intention to provide for the elderly, call for an end to welfare by declaring the intention to serve the poorest Americans, justify segregation in the context of a commitment to the rights of Black America, and argue to upend civil rights gains by asserting that racial justice was already "mission accomplished." What sold Reagan's responses was not their rationality but his sincerity and confidence. Reagan truly believed what he was selling.

And the man could sell. When it came to understanding the American electorate, he was almost always right, while the experts were regularly wrong. Reagan promoted his campaign for California governor with a racially loaded warning that played up the caricature of Black criminality. "Our city streets," Reagan declared as he prepared to use one of his favorite metaphors, "have become jungle paths after dark."[55] Due to the overwhelming consensus among white Californians that Reagan helped craft, one of his top aides spied a new path to power without the need for interracial appeal. "We'll settle for the white voters," the aide stated flatly. "And that," journalists noted, "is what he got."[56] With the emerging white consensus of the Colorblind Age, Black voters became nearly as powerless as in the days of disenfranchisement.

Despite winning only 5 percent of the Black vote, Reagan won the governorship in a landslide in a state dominated by Democrats, flipping the loyalty of California's white working-class voters from the Democratic to the Republican Party. Reagan knew his first landslide victory had been generated by white resentment to the Civil Rights Movement, and when the press asked him about the connection, Reagan refused to dodge. "The people," Reagan remarked, "seem to have shown that we have moved too fast" on civil rights.[57] The defeated Pat Brown concurred: "Whether we like it or not," Brown lamented after his election night thumping, "the people want separation of the races."[58]

What is more, in keeping with Reagan's predictions concerning national politics, after the rise of Black Power activists, conservatives began dominating only two years after LBJ's landslide. In 1966, the postelection headlines read: "Stokely Carmichael and the New Left helped elect a number of 'white backlash' governors, Congressmen, and sheriffs." Conservatives became so dominant in Congress that President Johnson, who had once moved mountains, failed to win approval for even the Rat Extermination Act to protect children from infestations in impoverished communities. In addition to Reagan, the Republican Party swapped seven other governorships in their favor.[59] The reversal that Reagan predicted would not be short-lived. When it came to presidential politics, Republicans went on to win five of the next six elections. These elections were not close. Republicans took 2,501 electoral votes to the Democrats' 628. And that includes Jimmy Carter's narrow win following Watergate.

In fighting to build a consensus among the white electorate, white conservatives were sometimes pitted against white liberals. But the deeper battle of white counterrevolutionaries was not primarily with white liberals but with the vision of Martin Luther King Jr. and the Civil Rights Movement. The significance of the white consensus that Reagan and his Republican colleagues began crafting for the white resistance in the mid-1960s and throughout the Colorblind Age is perhaps best seen in light of the vision they rejected. Between Reagan and King, the conflict was certainly personal—very personal. But the conflict was much more than that. It represented warring traditions

and worldviews. The Reagan Revolution was the product of an American tradition that harmonized racism, corporate capitalism, and the political power
of white Christianity. King's work and worldview were inseparable from the
Black church and the Black Freedom Movement's continuous fight for interracial democracy and economic equality. It was the unique gifts of each man
that set the nation on fire, inspiring both transformation and backlash.

Though Reagan was nearly twenty years older than King when Reagan
rose to political prominence, the trajectory of his career and King's ministry
were headed in opposite directions at blazing speeds. After the victories of
1964 and 1965 were etched in stone, King's vision grew increasingly radical
as his influence increasingly dwindled. With bipartisan support, America's
war in Vietnam and War on Crime intensified, and it bled the funding coffers for the Great Society. King watched as the doors to a more egalitarian
and interracial democracy that the Civil Rights Movement had kicked open
were slammed shut. "Unemployment rages at a major depression level in the
black ghettos," King grieved, "but the bipartisan response is an anti-riot bill
rather than a serious poverty program. It seems that our legislative assem-
blies have adopted Nero as their patron saint and are bent on fiddling while
our cities burn."[60]

Despair hung thick in the air as King's dream descended into a nightmare.
Yet his final writings and speeches reveal that in his darkest days, his understanding of America's racial trauma and the path forward only grew more
incisive and compelling. In King's last book, *Where Do We Go from Here:
Chaos or Community?*, he wrote that the election of white backlash leaders
displayed the moral bankruptcy of America. Following the passage of the civil
rights bills, King made it explicit that Reagan epitomized the insanity of white
backlash, writing that "white backlash had become an emotional electoral
issue in California . . . and elsewhere . . . as political clowns had become governors . . . , their magic achieved with a witches' brew of bigotry, prejudice,
half-truths and whole lies." The electoral betrayal was salt in Black America's
wounds as Nazi flags began to dot the American landscape and civil rights
workers continued to be martyred. Through tearstained eyes, King wrote,
"many of us wept at the funeral services for the dead and for democracy."[61]

As Reagan barnstormed the nation denigrating civil rights, promoting
unbridled capitalism, and demanding a more violent approach to the Vietnam War, King's message focused on denouncing the "triple evils" of "racism,
materialism, and militarism." For King, the triple evils are interrelated and
have been "lurking within our body politic from its very beginning." King
began repeatedly dissecting America's economic choices and insisting that

"truth is found neither in traditional capitalism nor in classical communism. Each represents a partial truth. . . . A socially conscious democracy . . . [must] reconcile the truths of individualism and collectivism."[62] For King, America's approach to race, economics, and the military threatened our nation's soul and placed the United States on a path to self-destruction.

Amid the poverty following Jim Crow's demise in the South and the urban poverty in the North, King called for a national agency to ensure full employment in a manner similar to what the New Deal accomplished for white people during the Great Depression. "It is barbarous to condemn people desiring work to soul-sapping inactivity and poverty," King declared. "I am convinced that even this one, massive act of concern [to provide jobs] will do more than all the state police and armies of the nation to quell riots and still hatreds." He lamented our nation's budgets: $35 billion for Vietnam, $20 billion for spaceships, but only crumbs "to put God's children on their own two feet right here on earth."[63] King stared into the nation's abyss to articulate the depth of radical revolution required to save the nation from catastrophe. In a way only a preacher could, King imagined America in the shoes of Nicodemus and aimed Jesus's words at the American people: "America, you must be born again!"

As the night closed in on King, his message to America moved from "love to justice." In "A Testament of Hope," one of his final essays, King contended that "the black revolution is much more than a struggle for the rights of Negroes. . . . It is exposing evils that are rooted deeply in the whole structure of our society. It reveals systemic rather than superficial flaws and suggests that radical reconstruction of society itself is the real issue to be faced."[64] Continuing a theme from early in his ministry, reparations were essential in that restructuring. "A society that has done something special against the Negro for hundreds of years," wrote King in his final year, "must now do something special for him." The closer King came to his last days as he worked on the Poor People's Campaign, the more reparations were on his mind. "When we come to Washington in this campaign," he declared, "we are coming to get our check."[65]

The radical nature of King's arguments led the FBI to brand him as "the most dangerous Negro of the future in this Nation from the standpoint of communism, the Negro, and national security."[66] By 1966, white America was ready to turn the page on King. A Gallup poll revealed that 72 percent of white America held an unfavorable view of him. On the day of King's funeral, as Black America convulsed in rage and sorrow, Reagan lacked even a touch of empathy. The "great tragedy," then Governor Reagan asserted, "began when we started compromising with law and order, and people started choosing which laws they'd break."[67] If Reagan mourned at all, it was for King's refusal to bow Black lives before the altar of Jim Crow's laws. According to polls, Reagan was not alone in his callousness. A full 31 percent of America believed King brought his demise upon himself.[68]

As the nation rejected King's vision to increasingly embrace Reagan's racial rationality, the memory of King and the radical transformation that was possible faded. Though it is impossible to fully grasp the significance of rejecting King's wisdom, when we think of reparations today, we must do so in light of that rejection. What would America look like if she had repented of the triple evils of racism, materialism, and militarism? If she had fought for domestic equality with the same intensity with which she raced to the moon and warred against the Vietnamese? Where would we be as a nation if she had learned to think about economic possibilities through a socially conscious capitalism? If instead of militarizing our police forces and expanding our prison system, she had invested in job creation and Black education? All these options were on the table. Each represented redemptive yet practical politics. And all of them were rejected. In time, we forgot both how thoroughly we rejected King's vision and the truth that rather than our nation's radical racial and economic inequality being inevitable, they were and are the byproduct of white supremacy molding our public policies. "It is an aspect of their sense of superiority," King lamented, "that the white people of America believe they have so little to learn."[69]

After two years as governor, it became clear that that role provided too small a stage for Reagan's political ambitions. The presidential contest of 1968 gave him his first shot at the Oval Office. The unrest across the nation raised his hopes that the nation was ready for his message. Reagan promised that, if nominated, "I will run like hell." In the wake of his dominance of California in 1966, Reagan's appeal spread from the right wing of the Republican Party to the person who embodied Republican moderation. After visiting with Reagan in 1967, President Dwight D. Eisenhower let it be known that though "there are a number of men who would make fine Presidents in our party, Governor Reagan is one of the men I admire most in this world."[70] Reagan's growing appeal to moderates, however, was not because he moderated. It was because, slowly but surely, moderates proved ready to align with Reagan's radical vision.

The election of 1968 took place during some of the deepest unrest in our nation's history. Black communities were in flames. The war raged on in Vietnam. Protests poured into the streets, where military technologies developed to combat foreign enemies were now unleashed against American citizens. Yet, these troubling times changed Ronald Reagan not at all. Despite the assassination of Martin Luther King Jr. and the Kerner Commission's findings, Reagan rejected any connection between nationwide revolts and either the evil of Vietnam or the failure to address urban poverty.

For Reagan, the responsibility for the revolts rested on the shoulders of those who pushed too hard for racial and economic justice. "Our nation is out of control," Reagan fumed. Cities were burning because Black activists and white allies had raised Black people's expectations too high, opposed the Vietnam War, and advocated for "huge make-work programs in the city slums with the money diverted from Vietnam. . . . It is a grand design for the apocalypse."[71] On *Face the Nation* only two months after King's assassination, Reagan attempted to delegitimize King's entire philosophy of peaceful civil disobedience as well:

> It is well and good to say they are staging civil disobedience with the idea that they are paying the price by being arrested. . . . How do you repay the person whose house burned down because the fire department could not get through the thousands of people? . . . In taking the law into your own hands, you rarely, if at all, can do this without interfering with the basic rights of someone else, and this we have no right to do.[72]

For Reagan, the concrete injustices Black Americans protested in no way legitimized the hypothetical inconveniences their demonstrations forced on white Americans.

What about King's Poor People's March? Reagan was clearly incensed. "I am in disagreement with this particular march and . . . with the government's acceptance of it. . . . There is grave disillusionment coming to many people. First of all, that they can persuade the Congress to pass some law that can eliminate or even alleviate poverty is a falsehood."[73] Yet, as Reagan preached a gospel of despair and deprivation to extinguish Black hope, he also actively sought to reinstill confidence and optimism in the breasts of the people most disturbed by civil rights' progress. And what became clear by witnessing the electricity conservative candidates generated in 1968 was that the white power structure the Civil Rights Movement threatened might now be reforged.

As he pursued the presidency, Reagan strategically drew himself close to fellow presidential candidate George Wallace. Offered the opportunity to differentiate himself from Wallace on issues of race, Reagan demurred. Well, the press wanted to know, "What views of George Wallace do you disagree with?" "That would be kind of hard to pin down," Reagan responded. "He's dwelling mainly on law and order, patriotism, and so forth, and these are attractive subjects, and I'm sure that there are very few people in disagreement."[74] But Reagan did want to take issue with Wallace's economic record. For Reagan, Wallace's cardinal sin was *not* his support for the Klan or segregation. For Reagan, Wallace's sin was supporting governmental interventions to relieve poverty. Wallace, for Reagan, was simply too soft for the demands of the day.

In the end, Richard M. Nixon outmaneuvered Reagan to place his name on the ballot and win the presidency. Yet Reagan performed well. When he returned to California, the hopes of a presidency in his future still shone brightly.

Reagan served as governor of California from 1967 to 1975. Throughout his tenure, he battled a strong legislature. Rather than governing as a purist, he was frequently forced to play the role of a political pragmatist. In his first year, California's state budget was the largest in history and he presided over the largest tax increase in history. By the end of his terms, California's budget had ballooned from $4.6 billion to $10.2 billion as the tax burden on the average individual nearly doubled.[75]

Nonetheless, the anti-Black, antipoor, and anticommunist themes consistently marked his rhetoric, public policies, and budget proposals. Following his inauguration in 1967, Reagan shuttered eight of thirteen service centers in deeply impoverished areas, eliminated $210 million in Medi-Cal services to 1.5 million eligible poor Californians, and ended services to five thousand children with serious health conditions. By 1969, Reagan's cuts went from disabled children to hungry children by reducing a school lunch bill approved by the legislature by 90 percent. By 1970, Reagan aimed a $25 million budget cut at the elderly, blind, and disabled.[76]

Campaigning for a second term, Reagan envisioned a more radical restructuring of welfare. In an internal memo, he demanded a study to "place heavy emphasis on the tax-payer as opposed to the tax-taker; on the truly needy as opposed to the lazy unemployable. . . . I am determined to reduce these programs to essential services." For Reagan, it was time for "all-out war on the tax-taker. This is our NUMBER ONE priority."[77] Since able-bodied men made less than 1 percent of the caseload, 99 percent of those impacted by Reagan's proposed cuts were the aged, disabled, and dependent children and their mothers. When Reagan's budgets failed to pass, funds serving at-risk Californians were repeatedly subjected to line-item vetoes. The cuts became so severe that they broke federal laws and placed his administration in legal jeopardy. Reviewing the funds Reagan vetoed, three Republican-appointed judges determined that Reagan's vetoes proved "totally irresponsible and without foundation."[78]

If it was not a good time to be poor in California, it often felt dangerous to be Black. California's police brutality led directly to the founding of the Black Panthers, who organized armed patrols to protect community residents from trigger-happy police. Asked about Governor Reagan's years in California, Oakland pastor, community advocate, and Black Panther ally J. Alfred Smith refused to mince words:

> Reagan was pushing a white supremacy agenda by stigmatizing Black women as welfare cheats, by closing down mental health programs for the disabled, and being anti-free speech on college campuses, and demonizing the Black Panthers. . . . My memory buried many of the details because they were painful and unpleasant.[79]

Instead of holding police accountable for systemic brutality, in 1967, Reagan signed the Mulford Act to disarm the Black Panthers, compromising their Second Amendment rights and undermining their ability to protect Black communities. Black radical professor Angela Davis, who partnered with the Panthers and was publicly tied to the Communist Party, fell into Reagan's crosshairs as well, and the governor revived Red Scare legislation from the 1940s to instigate her firing.

As governor, Reagan proved as antiprotester as he was anti-Black. Reagan considered the entire Berkeley campus "a haven for communist sympathizers, protesters, and sex deviants."[80] May 15, 1969, would become known as "Bloody Thursday" through the People's Park protest at Berkeley. The Reagan administration issued a directive to quell the protest by any means necessary against a body of six thousand protesters. Over one hundred protesters and bystanders were seriously injured and hospitalized along with twenty-five law enforcement officials. Sheriffs fired buckshot into the backs of fleeing protesters. James Rector was sitting on a roof when he was lethally shot. Hundreds of others were tear-gassed, and thirteen protesters lost at least one eye due to the gassing. Though Reagan's tactics only exacerbated protests around the state, Reagan simply replied, "If there is to be a bloodbath, let it be now."[81]

In California, Reagan's brutal brand of politics only grew his popular appeal even as he failed to find the governmental leverage to remake the system to reflect his ideologies. Nonetheless, if Reagan sometimes governed as a pragmatist, he was still free to preach as a radical with national ambitions. And in both public and private, as governor and after, preach he did. Following eight years as governor, Ronald Reagan was positioned to make a second run at president in 1976.

When the presidential campaigns got underway, the Watergate and Vietnam scandals left the 1976 presidential candidates seeking the support of a vastly different country than those who had fought for the presidency in 1968. The challenges of the 1970s were nearly impossible to anticipate from the apex of the Civil Rights Movement and the War on Poverty. A briefly united nation was now deeply divided. On top of the scandals was the reality that the strongest economy the world had ever created began to sputter. The crises of economic stagnation and monetary inflation were thought to be mutually exclusive—that is, until the 1970s, when both hammered the American economy simultaneously. Deindustrialization hit, and jobs that provided living wages to blue-collar workers began to evaporate. Black Americans were hit hardest as the unemployment rate doubled from 7 to 14 percent.[82]

As the nation was confronted with complex issues, Reagan preached a simple gospel. All America needed were tax cuts for the wealthy and welfare cuts for the poor. If the nation had drastically changed since 1964, Reagan had not. But there was a discernable difference between Reagan's public sermons during the 1960s and those of the 1970s. Racial caricatures of Black people had taken an increasingly central role in his political rhetoric. Rationally, both taxes and welfare exist more in the realm of economics than in racial matters. But such rationality was not reality. Through what became known as the Southern Strategy, such issues carried ever increasing racial weight. As Lee Atwater, one of Reagan's future advisers, explained, instead of using the N-word, which backfired, "Now, you're talking about cutting taxes, and all these things you're talking about are totally economic things, and a by-product of them is blacks get hurt worse than whites."[83] Though the majority of welfare recipients were white, Reagan employed the Southern Strategy to demonize welfare and then consistently place the imagined failures of welfare on the backs of Black America. In Florida, the caricature took the form of "a strapping young buck" who used food stamps to purchase a T-bone steak, while working (i.e., white) folks were waiting in line to purchase hard-earned hamburger meat. "If there's a Southern Strategy," Reagan declared to a crowd in Mississippi in his 1976 campaign, "I'm part of it."[84]

Reagan knew how to tick white people off, and his best storytelling centered on a mythical "welfare queen." "She used 80 names, 30 addresses, 15 telephone numbers to collect food stamps, Social Security, veterans' benefits for four nonexistent deceased veteran husbands, as well as welfare. Her tax-free cash income alone has been running $150,000 a year."[85] His story was, admittedly, much better than his sources. "Welfare queen" was first coined by George Bliss of the *Chicago Tribune* to describe Linda Taylor, whose $8,000 of welfare fraud was neither typical nor quite as salacious as $150,000 a year. Despite flagrant inaccuracies, the more Reagan repeated stories of welfare abuse, the more persuasive his caricatures became.

The irony was, when it came to fraud and the public coffers, a real crisis was brewing in the 1970s that threatened our nation's financial sustainability. The crisis was not welfare queens but tax evasion kings who worked with tax experts to protect personal wealth from public accountability. By 1980, tax experts had created over eighteen thousand different forms of tax shelters that robbed the public treasury of billions of dollars in lost revenue while crippling the IRS's ability to ensure America's wealthiest families paid their fair share. Reagan knew all about the tax evasion kings. He was one. He paid no taxes in 1970 and, like other wealthy Americans, successfully dodged significant portions of tax responsibility year after year without consequence.[86] In a nation claiming insufficient funds for the pursuit of economic and racial justice, tax evasion was never a victimless crime. It was a crime against vulnerable people and impoverished communities. No one paid a higher price for tax shelters than Black America.

Such flexibility with the facts was typical of Reagan. When it came to welfare and race, most of Reagan's public sermons flew in the face of everything the nation learned through the evidence-based research the War on Poverty had inaugurated. Research had provided abundant evidence that recipients' use of welfare was almost always temporary and rarely impeded their motivation to work. The entire "culture of poverty" thesis would be continually discredited until, like the racial sciences of old, it had to be abandoned. Moynihan's report provided the preeminent example of how, according to one researcher, "we social scientists misled the architects of the War on Poverty by putting forth notions which turned out to be spurious"[87]—and racist. Nonetheless, Reagan's sermons reveal how far he was ready to go to divorce public policy and public opinion from anything related to evidence-based research. If the best research validated the findings in the Kerner Report, Reagan's rhetoric helped ensure public policies would still be shaped by Moynihan's misinformation.

In 1976, Reagan failed to find the strength to unseat the incumbent Gerald Ford, and Ford lacked the strength to retain the presidency. Despite losing the battle of the moment, Reagan strategically positioned himself to win the war. Following his time as governor, Reagan turned down an invitation to appear weekly on the *CBS Evening News*. Instead, he dove headlong into talk radio. The decision drove his advisers batty, but Reagan bet on his own wisdom. "People will tire of me on television," he explained. "They won't tire of me on the radio."[88]

In his radio shows, Reagan taught through parables on all things related to public life—from sex education and voter fraud, to taxes and welfare abuse, to glorifying the noble venture in Vietnam. Reagan buttressed his parables with facts and figures that made his stories all the more persuasive. Neither the parables nor the facts were consistently rooted in reality. But they were dramatic, repetitive, and remarkably persuasive.

Each show started with a tantalizing hook prior to the commercial break and ended with "This is Ronald Reagan. Thanks for listening." And from the hook to the curtain call, Reaganesque wisdom prevailed. "I've had a report from one district that the venereal disease rate among young people in that district went up 800 percent in the first few years after sex-ed became a part of the curriculum. Why don't we find out if what we are doing is part of the problem?" "Labor leaders were conducting a kind of class warfare using some very questionable economic theory." "It is time for Washington to hear from the people about the 'instant voter registration plan' now sailing through Congress with the wind at its back and only voter fraud ahead." "The suppressed study reveals that 80 percent of air pollution comes not from chimneys and auto exhaust pipes, but from plants and trees."[89]

His commentary made clear his consistent disdain for elite research and poor people. "The American people are the most generous people on earth," Reagan emphatically declared. And then in a more ominous tone, he warned that "they can also be the most angry people on earth when they feel they are being cheated. I'll be right back." And back he was, again and again, with story after story of "leeches who drink up the resources." "The food stamp caper . . . For a monthly investment of 59 cents [in food stamps], his take each month was $15 in cash plus $73.59 worth of food." "Welfare is a dangerous drug destroying the spirit of people once proudly independent. Our mission should be to help people kick that particular drug habit." "We aren't salvaging people; we are making them permanent clients of a professional group of welfarists whose careers depend on the preservation of poverty." "It can be straightened out if Washington will close down its welfare shop."[90]

Great storytellers don't simply tell stories. They repeat them and improve upon them with each telling. Again and again, Reagan brought his folksy fury to his audience. If anyone wanted to be enraged, no DJ in America provided more ammo. And in the difficult decade of the 1970s, many people thirsted for Reagan's rage. "At the end . . . we were speaking to 50 million Americans per day," said Michael Deaver, who later served as White House deputy chief of staff under Reagan. "Ronald Reagan wrote every radio show himself."[91]

By 1980, it was time to shut down the radio shop and cash in on a candidate who had been preparing to save the nation from its good intentions for over three decades. Year by year, it seemed, the nation was becoming more fertile soil for ideologies and public policies that harmonized with Ronald Reagan's worldview. A difficult decade was coming to an end, and difficult decisions had to be made. Could America still govern for the common good? Would white America understand the persistent racial inequalities as evidence that Moynihan was right about pathological Black families, or would white America remember Kerner's dire warnings? By 1980, all that was clear was that America had lost its way, and a revolution was brewing.

11

The Reagan Revolution

Fighting the Dream, 1980–1988

> We do not admire their president.
> We know why the White House is white.
>
> —Alice Walker, "Each One, Pull One," 1985

In 1980, Ronald Reagan faced off against incumbent president Jimmy Carter. In 1976, hope was on the rise in Black America as they overwhelmingly voted for change by voting for Carter. Writing in light of Black suffering under the Nixon administration, James Baldwin penned an open letter to the new president to warn of the dangers of allowing white America to retain its grip on her Black citizens. Line by line, Baldwin laid out his lament: "Too many of us are in jail, my friend; too many of us are starving, too many of us can find no door open." It was a time for repentance and reflection. It was time a president humble himself and listen and learn from Black America. "Consider that we may all have learned, by now, all that we can learn from you and may not want to become like you. At this hour of the world's history," Baldwin declared, "it may be that you, now, have something to learn from us."[1]

As the 1980 election approached, Martin Luther King Jr.'s verdict that "it is a difficult thing to teach a President"[2] had proven as true with President Jimmy Carter as it had with President John F. Kennedy. Despite Carter's initial overtures to Black America, time and again, Black people seemed to be Carter's last priority. Within only a year of his election, the title of intellectual provocateur Chuck Stone's article in the *Black Scholar*, "Carter's Paternalistic Racism and the Inept Presidency," reflected the mood of many Black Americans. Black leaders feared the "benign neglect" of the Nixon years had evolved into a "callous neglect" under Carter's watch.[3]

If Black America was disenchanted by Carter, so too was white America. Polling data showed what the Carter team dubbed "a crisis of confidence." Polls had the presidential approval ratings bouncing between 19 percent and 25 percent. A full 50 percent of Americans considered themselves "long-term pessimists." And for the first time, the American people believed America's past was brighter than her future.[4]

Yet, the pinch for America—and Black America in particular—was that the 1980 alternative to Carter was Reagan. Though Reagan was the leading man for the nomination as soon as he tossed his hat into the ring, victory was anything but foreordained. In fact, in 1979, Reagan's own campaign research indicated his potential ascendancy to the presidency as far-fetched. On a personal level, internal polling proved disconcerting. Only 22 percent of respondents saw Reagan as a politician who cared about people; a mere 23 percent believed he was trustworthy; an unflattering 19 percent believed he possessed "high moral character"; and, to add insult to injury, only 27 percent considered him knowledgeable about domestic and international affairs.

At a policy level, the markers in campaign research were horrendous. Reagan's top priority of cutting government spending was supported by only 2.8 percent of Americans, only 1 percent feared the governmental overreach he repeatedly lambasted, and less than 1 percent were worried about the state of America's military might. "The nation," wrote Rick Perlstein, "shared his opinions hardly at all."[5] But Reagan was no political dunce. And in 1980, he leveraged the American mood of malaise and white backlash to get white America to see the world through his convictions and confidence and readily follow his lead into the future. And it would be a future that realized Black America's worst fears.

For many Black voters, a vote for Reagan represented racial suicide. In March 1980, Reagan's welfare queen story evolved once again. "In some inner cities," Reagan said to paint his picture Black, "there are . . . young girls, underage, who deliberately go out to have a baby so that they can get what they call 'a pad.'" After collecting her welfare check, "she then goes and gets rid of the baby, and the government pays for it with tax dollars, and the government is bound by law to protect her privacy and not let her own parents know."[6] Alleging that Black women's pursuit of welfare checks led to bearing disposable children was less philosophical than Jefferson's racial myths in *Notes on the State of Virginia*. On the campaign trail, however, it proved no less powerful in framing Black suffering as a byproduct of the innate flaws of Black people.

Highlighting America's economic plight, racial tensions, and the failures of Democratic leadership, Republicans chose Detroit as the place to hold their convention. On July 17, 1980, Reagan accepted the Republican nomination. The conservative, common-sense truth-teller had never been better. He sought to "build a new consensus with all those across the land who share a community of values embodied in these words: family, work, neighborhood, peace and freedom." He leaned into his rhetorical formula with full force. He demanded we care for the poor. And that we cut welfare. He demanded we prioritize preserving the environment. And that we expand coal production to "reaffirm that the economic prosperity of our people is a fundamental part of our environment." He promised to unleash the forces of the free market to revitalize America's inner cities and introduced his campaign theme as "a great national crusade to make America great again!"[7]

By 1980, Reagan's rhetoric was decades in the making, and what the convention showed was how—at least for white audiences—it had only improved with age. With warmth, self-assurance, and experience, Reagan hypnotized people who had lost their confidence and longed for a guiding light. As he came to a close, he asked his audience to "begin our campaign together in a moment of silent prayer." Roughly thirty seconds later, rather than "Amen," it was "God bless America." With that, the revolution began in earnest. If Reagan's speech had failed to convince Black America to vote for him, it had surely started many Black alarm bells ringing.

Less than a week later, Reagan visited New York's Urban League. There had been a racially motivated assassination attempt on Urban League president and civil rights advocate Vernon Jordan. Reagan visited him in the hospital. "We weren't expecting to pick up any black votes in New York," an adviser explained. "We just wanted to show moderates and liberals that Reagan wasn't antiblack." At the Urban League, Reagan pled to not be viewed as "a caricature conservative who is 'antipoor, antiblack, anti-disadvantaged.'"[8] It was, of course, an impossible ask of anyone in Black America who had watched and listened to Reagan for the last twenty years.

The day before his trip to New York, Reagan began his campaign at the Neshoba County Fair in Philadelphia, Mississippi. For Martin Luther King Jr., Philadelphia, Mississippi, was "a terrible town, the worst I've ever seen."[9] In 1964—the same year Reagan campaigned for Barry Goldwater—Philadelphia gained international notoriety for the murders of civil rights workers James Chaney, Andrew Goodman, and Michael Schwerner. Nonetheless, in 1980, with Klan violence and white terrorism on the rise throughout the nation, Reagan took to the podium, seemingly at home among the Confederate flags surrounding him on the fairgrounds stage. Then, Reagan made the promise the audience of fifteen thousand had gathered to hear as he committed to "restore to states and local governments the powers that properly belong to them."[10]

Martin Luther King Jr.'s companion and former lieutenant Andrew Young responded to Reagan's campaign speech in an article published in the *Washington Post* titled "Chilling Words in Neshoba County." "The thought of Philadelphia, Miss., always sends chills up my spine," Young confessed. After detailing his own visits with King under the threat of death, Young emphasized the significance of the Klan's recent enthusiastic embrace of Ronald Reagan. "Bill Wilkinson, imperial wizard . . . [of] the largest Klan organization in the country—wrote in his group's newspaper that they endorsed Reagan and that the Republican platform 'reads as if it were written by a Klansman.'" As fewer and fewer white Americans partnered with the Klan by parading in white robes, Young sensed a far more sinister threat germinating. Young feared Reagan's coded rhetoric had opened the door to evolve white supremacy from the realms of public spectacle to sinister and subtle public policies designed to ensure white power and Black suffering.[11]

Young's fears were well founded. Yet, while Andrew Young saw the threat of Klan resurrection, white evangelicals saw in Reagan a potential savior. Reagan seemed a peculiar candidate for those proclaiming the need to return to a family values agenda. Reagan's children considered him a horrendous father. In his first marriage, Reagan was Jane Wyman's third husband. In choosing his second wife, Reagan chose someone committed more to astrology than to Christianity.[12] Reagan was deeply shaped by Christian piety, but his religious practices rarely included churchgoing, and his theological convictions were neither orthodox nor evangelical. When it came to public policy, as governor, Reagan had signed the Therapeutic Abortion Act. California's abortion rate went up from 518 the year prior to the legislation to averaging over 100,000 per year between the bill's passage and the time Reagan ran for president.[13] Reagan's governorship also opened the floodgates to divorces in America by his signing the first "no fault" divorce law in the United States. Other states followed suit, and the divorce rate doubled in America in a span of less than two decades.[14] In addition to the clear differences between the evangelical community and Reagan's personal life and public policies was the fact that Jimmy Carter was perhaps the most deeply committed and consistently evangelical candidate in American history.[15]

So what accounted for Reagan's chemistry with the Religious Right? Well, as it turns out, their connections ran deep. While the Civil Rights Acts and the War on Poverty represented the political longings of the Black church, Reagan's promotion of free-market economics, fear of communism, and small government and his stances on race made Reaganism fit white evangelicalism like a customized glove.[16] Moral Majority leader Jerry Falwell declared that the struggle for racial and economic justice "is a terrible violation of human and private property rights. . . . It should be considered civil wrongs rather than civil rights."[17] Billy Graham confessed: "My own theory about Communism is that it is masterminded by Satan."[18] Such political ideologies continued white Christianity's consistent complicity in perpetuating our nation's racial crimes and exhibit why evangelicals and Reagan were a match made in white heaven.

The preview of the partnership between Reagan and white evangelicals occurred at the Religious Roundtable National Affairs Briefing in August 1980. Reagan was introduced by evangelist James Robison, who provided Politics 101 for the gathered flock. "The unbridled and uncontrollable federal government is a confiscator! And a consumer! And a disperser of your wealth," Robison raged. "It produces nothing! And it functions best when it functions least."[19] After thanking God for a savior from California, Robison introduced Reagan, who played the white evangelical audience like a fiddle. "I know you can't endorse me," Reagan drawled, "but I want you to know that I endorse you."[20] On Reagan's lips, the endorsement rang with the beauty of a wedding vow.

Fearing the unholy matrimony between Reagan and the Religious Right, James Baldwin joined Andrew Young in the attempt to warn the nation of the inherent risk in a Reagan presidency. Caught between Carter's failures and Reagan's risk, Baldwin wrote "Notes on the House of Bondage." As he worked, his thoughts were surrounded by his nieces' and nephews' interrogation: "Who are you voting for, Uncle Jimmy?" While Reagan made Young feel chills up and down his spine, Baldwin saw in Reagan's politics a revival of America's genocidal instincts toward those she formerly enslaved. "Who are you voting for, Uncle Jimmy?" the children demanded. "John Brown," Uncle Jimmy answered. Baldwin brings his family's children into Black America's agonizing political choices and the cold calculus of choosing the lesser of two evils at the ballot box. "And since I am not the only black man to think this way," he tells the children, "if Carter is re-elected, it will be by means of the black vote, and it will not be a vote for Carter. It will be a coldly calculated risk, a means of buying time."[21]

It is easy to imagine Baldwin lighting a cigarette as he continued to put his conversation with his nieces and nephews on paper. "In a couple of days, blacks may be using the vote to outwit the Final Solution." He exhales a lung full of smoke. Pauses. "Yes. The Final Solution. No black person can afford to forget that the history of this country is genocidal." White supremacy and backlash again returned the nation to the precipice of catastrophe, and Baldwin feared the groundwork was being laid to destroy the next generation of Black people. The conversation continued. "Why are you voting for Carter, Uncle Jimmy?" Baldwin shifts in his seat, adjusting his posture from that of a writer to that of an earnest witness. "Well, don't, first of all, take this as an endorsement. It's meant to be a hard look at the options. . . . I lived in California when Ronald Reagan was governor, and that was a very ugly time." Baldwin recounts Reagan's persecution of Black America and her leaders in California, "but what I really found unspeakable about the man, was his contempt, his brutal contempt, for the poor."[22] For Baldwin, 1980 was "the charged, the dangerous, moment, when everything must be re-examined, must be made new; when nothing at all can be taken for granted."[23]

The election proved far worse than either Young or Baldwin could have predicted. Despite Black America voting against Reagan at an 80 percent clip, his popularity with white voters, including the young boomer generation, provided a decisive victory. In a three-way race, Reagan took 51 percent of the total votes, outperforming Carter within the white electorate by 20 percentage points while taking home 489 electoral votes to Carter's 48. Reagan's campaign for presidency was now a mission accomplished, but his "great national crusade to make America great again" was just beginning.

In white America, there was much to love with Reagan's first inaugural address. The *New York Times* dubbed it "Reagan's Dramatic Success." "Mr. Reagan was not only generous but wise and even compassionate. . . . These were things right out of Franklin Roosevelt's oratory," James Reston wrote. Perhaps the White House polish would remove Reagan's edges. Gone was the Goldwater and talk radio radical. "We see Reagan now in Washington, with his easy smile and cheery wave, not mad at anybody. . . . He is the 'nice guy.' . . . So far, like the fireworks, he has been spectacular."[24] And indeed he was.

Yet tucked tightly into the heart of the speech, there was one line that proved most prophetic for what would occur in Washington over the course of Reagan's presidency. "In this present crisis," Reagan declared, "government is not the solution to our problem; government is the problem."[25]

When Reagan began presiding over the White House, he was no longer a political or administrative novice. He was there to inaugurate a revolution in public priorities and policies. And he got to work. The Reagan Revolution was fought on multiple fronts simultaneously in an attempt to defeat communism abroad and reverse the domestic gains achieved through the New Deal, the Civil Rights Movement, and the War on Poverty. For Reagan, these threats were interlaced and called for total warfare.

The first and most efficient front in Reagan's revolution was the internal workings of his administration. Following the Civil War, President Andrew Johnson had weaponized the power of presidential appointment to thwart Reconstruction throughout the South. From governmental agencies to the judicial branch, Reagan followed in Johnson's footsteps by intentionally choosing leaders ready to bring disaster to Black America.

In governmental agencies, Reagan frequently chose leaders ideologically opposed to the very agencies they were tasked to oversee, as he did with "Silent Sam" Pierce of the Department of Housing and Urban Development.[26] At one time, the budget of Housing and Urban Development was second only to that of the Department of Defense. Reagan cut it by almost 70 percent.[27]

At other times, Reagan selected loyalists like Richard S. Schweiker to run the Department of Health and Human Services.[28] Often, Reagan got both loyalty and ideologues. In his Education Department, whose explicit function was to provide funding for schools in America's most impoverished communities, poor students heading to college, and students with special needs, Reagan played the long game. The department was woefully underfunded, and his administration considered it a "great bureaucratic joke."[29] For their punchline, they selected T. H. Bell as the department's secretary with the explicit agreement that he would work to eliminate the Department of Education entirely. Though Bell managed to protect the Department of Education from elimination, the drastic budget cuts under his tenure devastated the nation's poorest schools.[30]

In his second term, Reagan nominated William Bennett to the Department of Education's top leadership post. Bennett cut the budget by another 33 percent and referred to poor college students as "beach bums" who needed to "give up their stereos to pay tuition instead of expecting government aid."[31] Bennett would later serve in George H. W. Bush's White House, to strategize prison and police expansion. Tellingly, he limited drug treatment and prevention to approximately 4 percent of his budget.[32] Secretary Bennett's views on Black children became transparent in his later job as a talk show host. If you wanted to fight crime, Bennett said, "you could abort every black baby in this country, and your crime rate would go down."[33]

In his book *Savage Inequalities*, education expert Jonathan Kozol wrote that after taking the reins of power, Reagan was able to turn back the clock on social services by decades. However, "this assertion . . . is not adequate to speak about the present-day reality in public education. In public schooling, social policy has been turned back almost one hundred years."[34] If white America desired to protect white supremacy by academically shutting minorities out of avenues for social advancement, Reagan's education efforts provided a perfect blueprint. Reagan's cuts were not simply draconian, but lethal. By 2000, it is estimated that low education levels were a factor in over two hundred thousand deaths per year in the wealthiest nation on earth.[35]

In the Department of Justice, affirmative action critic William Bradford was appointed to head the Civil Rights Division, while committed Black justice advocate Mary Frances Berry was fired without cause. Rising star and Black conservative Clarence Thomas was selected to lead the Equal Opportunity Employment Commission. Under the new leadership, statistically verifiable inequalities were no longer sufficient for proving discrimination. The new standard of racial bias was raised to the often unscalable height of proving intentional and conscious discrimination. Discrimination cases plummeted as employers who left no paper trail were no longer liable for racially rigged hiring practices.[36] As readiness to enforce discrimination cases disappeared, Black unemployment and poverty continued to climb, with unemployment reaching nearly 20 percent in 1983 and never dropping below 11 percent at any point in the 1980s.[37]

Perhaps the perfect embodiment of the perversions of Reagan's appointments and inner circle was Edwin Meese III, who served first as counselor to the president then as attorney general. As Christmas approached in 1983, Presidential Counselor Meese denied "any authoritative figures that there are hungry children" and claimed the high demand for food pantries came from the simple fact that "the food is free and . . . that's easier than paying for it."[38] As always, Black America paid the highest prices for the administration's callousness toward needy citizens. During a speech at Dickson College in 1985, then Attorney General Edwin Meese laid out the administration's racial logic: "A new version of the Separate but Equal doctrine is being pushed upon us. I speak, of course, of the debate over Affirmative Action." Not content with equating affirmative action with segregation, Meese deepened his analysis. "You should not forget that an earlier generation of Americans heard from some that slavery was good not only for the slaves but for society." For Black leaders, such "ludicrous" logic as equating affirmative action with segregation and slavery became "typical" in Reagan's Department of Justice.[39]

Not to be outdone on the international front, Reagan's Department of State under the leadership of Alexander Haig and George Shultz consistently harmonized international diplomacy with white supremacy. The preeminent example of the Reagan administration's support for international white supremacy was its embrace of South Africa's apartheid regime.[40] Reagan had long admired South Africa's white leaders. "They must be the ally with whom we line up in any world strategy," he wrote to a friend during the 1980 campaign.[41] And line up with South Africa, America did. The administration dubbed their alliance with South Africa as "constructive engagement" and authorized the building of three new honorary consulates on American soil. In 1984, Bishop Desmond Tutu dubbed the Reagan administration's alliance with South Africa's apartheid regime "immoral, evil and totally un-Christian."[42] And following the bishop's meeting with Reagan, Tutu declared Reagan "a racist, pure and simple."[43] Unmoved, in 1986 Reagan vetoed the Comprehensive Anti-Apartheid Act that placed economic sanctions on the racist regime.

These executive actions represent only the tip of the iceberg. The tip of the *spear* was the judicial branch. Reagan made 372 federal judge appointments, choosing judges much wealthier and whiter than either his predecessors or successors had. The Supreme Court was ideologically divided on civil rights when Reagan took over.[44] It would not be when he left. The changing of the guard in the Supreme Court shifted the court from the institution whose decisions protected civil rights and progressive government to the institution whose decisions ensured the demise of both. Reagan's new judges committed themselves to an "originalist" interpretation of the Constitution. In the eyes of many Black Americans, Reagan's originalist judges were about as concerned with protecting the human dignity of the descendants of the enslaved as Justice Roger B. Taney had been with the human rights of Dred Scott.[45]

In his first year in office, Reagan nominated Sandra Day O'Connor, who voted against minorities in thirty-nine of forty-one cases by 1998.[46] When Chief Justice Warren Earl Burger retired as chief justice in 1985, Reagan did not flinch in nominating William Rehnquist. Rehnquist's personal history included affirming separate but equal as well as the intimidation and suppression of Black voters. As Supreme Court justice, he voted against the rights of women, the elderly, the disabled, and racial minorities in eighty-two of eighty-three opportunities, providing a foretaste of the court's bitter direction under his watch.[47]

Not only did Burger's retirement provide room for Rehnquist's promotion, but it also provided the space to add the conservative Antonin Scalia, which secured an anti–civil rights majority in the Supreme Court. In his prior career as an academic at the University of Virginia, Scalia had written that "the racist concept of restorative justice is fundamentally contrary to the principles that govern, and should govern, our society." On the court, Scalia argued that affirmative action was bad for both Black students and elite schools, encouraging minority students to attend a "less advanced school, a slower-track school where they do well." In time, Scalia became the intellectual anchorman of the originalists and was dubbed the most influential Supreme Court justice of the last quarter of the twentieth century.[48]

In 1989, Justice Thurgood Marshall took measure of the damage Reagan wrought on the Supreme Court. "For many years, no institution in American government has been as close a friend to civil rights as the United States Supreme Court." Yet the tide had turned, and the hallowed court had "come full circle" from the closest friend of civil rights to one of her most dangerous adversaries.[49]

As Reagan used the power of appointment to undercut the federal government's attempt to mitigate racism and poverty, he simultaneously and successfully pursued budgetary and tax cuts that crippled the nation's ability to serve millions of her citizens. The budget battle began in the first weeks of Reagan's administration and proved bruising. In one of history's twists, the most significant name in this battle other than Reagan himself was that of would-be assassin John Hinckley Jr., whose bullets provided a decisive early turning point in the Reagan Revolution.

Only sixty-nine days into his first term, Monday, March 30, 1981, was a rainy afternoon in Washington. As Reagan made his way to his limousine following a speaking engagement, multiple gunshots rang out. It was Hinkley's sixth bullet that ricocheted off the limousine's armor and burrowed into Reagan's chest within an inch of his aortic valve. His life hung in the balance as he was rushed to George Washington University Hospital.

While on the hospital gurney, Reagan was amazingly calm—and funny. As the doctors prepared him for emergency surgery, Reagan joked: "Please tell me you're Republicans." The doctor tasked to save Reagan's life was actually a Democrat. But he was magnanimous. "Today, Mr. President, we are all Republicans," he replied.[50]

News outlets noted Reagan's confidence and humor in the heat of the battle—and his performance paid dividends in spades. "Today, Mr. President, we are all Republicans" proved a pervasive mood in Washington and across the nation. His already strong approval rating jumped to 73 percent. The *Washington Post* dubbed Reagan's popularity spike "as sharp as any yet recorded" for a president.[51]

During the weeks spent recuperating from surgery, Reagan fought for his tax cuts from his hospital bed.[52] To fully leverage his newfound popularity after his hospital stay, Reagan called for a joint session of Congress to appeal to the nation to support his budget. Somewhat gaunt, Reagan was received by Congress with the adoration of a wounded but victorious warrior returned home from war. Across our nation, over fifty million people watched on TV. He took out a get-well letter from an eight-year-old and read: "Dear Mr. President, I hope you get well quick—or you might have to make a speech in your pajamas." Reagan's delivery brought the house down. Just as seamlessly as Reagan had started, he shifted to the seriousness of the business at hand. He confessed our nation faced challenges that lacked an overnight remedy. The cure for America's woes was Reagan's budget, which would "get America back to work." The problem of poverty and unemployment resided in the fact that "our government is too big, and it spends too much." Standing ovation. Reagan was succinct and powerful. The speech that began by thanking the nation for its compassion ended in the call for a budget to end or reduce America's assistance to its most vulnerable citizens. His speech continued to strike chords on both sides of the aisle and ended to thunderous applause. With the final ovation, the Reagan Revolution was officially embraced in Washington as the national consensus that began in the New Deal era came to a euphoric and bipartisan end.[53]

"Only the Lord Himself could save this one," said Democratic Speaker Tip O'Neill as Reagan leveraged his newfound strength to transform the nation's budgetary priorities. But no divine intervention came.[54] The official dawning of a new age in America arrived Thursday, August 13, 1981, at Reagan's California ranch, Rancho del Cielo. It was an overcast day. For dramatics, Reagan was attired in boots, blue jeans, and a denim jacket. He was a simple man doing the work of the people. Before placing pen to paper, Reagan provided brief remarks for the press that had gathered. "These bills that I'm about to sign . . . the budget bill, and . . . the tax program . . . represent a turnaround of almost a half a century of a course this country's been on and marks an end to the excessive growth in government bureaucracy, government spending, government taxing."[55]

By the time the ink dried, 400,000 families of America's working poor had lost all benefits, while another 300,000 had lost significant provisions that protected them from the ravages of poverty. One million people lost food stamps. School districts serving America's poorest communities needed radical increases in federal funding. Instead, the budget reduced education funding by $200 million. Cuts were aimed directly at students needing food subsidies, and 26 million students began receiving smaller meals. Rather than these cuts getting America back to work, the greatest recession since the Great Depression engulfed the nation, making already difficult times dire. The number of poor Americans increased by 2.2 million and raised the percentage of Black Americans living in poverty to a staggering 34.2 percent.[56]

Yet, if impoverished mothers wept for hungry children in American communities struggling to survive, those furthest removed from the realities of poverty were provided a reason to party. The top income tax rate fell from 70 to 50 percent, and capital gains taxes fell from 28 to 20 percent. In the coming years, the bottom would continue to fall out of the highest income tax brackets, finally settling as low as 28 percent in Reagan's second term. This marked a startling tax burden decrease of 60 percent for the highest earners.

By Reagan's second term, Don Regan, who served as the Treasury secretary and chief of staff, had seen enough. The tax shelters from the 1970s had transformed into bunkers protecting people making over $1 million a year from the need to pay taxes at all while increasing the tax burdens on the poorest Americans. Regan tried to get Reagan to see the injustice of the situation. "The tax system we have now is designed to make the avoidance of tax easy for the rich and has the effect of making it almost impossible for people who work for wages and salaries to do the same," Regan pleaded to the president. "As your secretary of the Treasury, I'm telling you that it ain't fair and that it is undermining the morale of taxpayers and crippling the economy."[57] Like many of the president's supporters, Don Regan had underestimated the president by thinking that he failed to grasp the very nature of the tax code his administration had crafted. What Regan interpreted as a reckless presidential oversight was by contrast the end game of a well-executed presidential plan.

As tax burdens for the wealthiest Americans decreased, their wealth was intensified as corporations' effective tax rates plummeted 85 percent. Before Reagan's bill, corporate tax rates were 33 percent. After the bill, they stood at a meager 5 percent.[58] That was before the loopholes. From 1981 to 1983, multibillion-dollar corporations such as General Electric, Lockheed, Boeing, and Dow Chemical paid no taxes. A study investigated 129 companies whose collective profits totaled $45 billion. What the study revealed was an effective tax rate of 0.4 percent for these companies. Reagan promised his cuts would lead to corporate investments in industrial infrastructure to provide higher-quality jobs. Instead, the report showed that corporate investment dwindled and instead the trend of shutting up shop and exporting high-paying blue-collar jobs continued unabated.[59]

During the 1981 tax cuts, the only thing better than being rich was having rich parents. As Reagan removed food stamps from the poorest families and reduced-price school lunches from the poorest students, Reagan's signature provided changes in estate tax exemptions that increased rich kids' tax-free access to their parents' wealth over 300 percent. Over the forty years following Reagan's first year in office, the estate tax exemption rose nearly 7,000 percent, from $161,000 in 1980 to $11,180,000 in 2020.[60] Reflecting this shift, from 1983 to 2021, the wealth of America's richest families increased by an incredible 1,007 percent.[61]

"Trickle-down economics" was perhaps the cleverest designation for an economic doctrine that intentionally and explicitly concentrates wealth in the fewest hands while ensuring that wealth never makes its way to those living and working on the ladder's lowest rungs. The tax code represented the heart of the Reagan Revolution and his conviction that in America, corporations and wealthy families were the worthy, while the welfare system and poor families were the problem. For too long, the system privileged tax takers. Under Reagan, privileges and profits returned to the moneymakers. Talking taxes is one of the least enticing topics of conversation. Yet, at the heart of how our nation's economic racial inequalities were radicalized are these shifting tax structures that sheltered wealth for the richest white families while intentionally intensifying the suffering of America's most marginalized families and communities.

The budget and tax cuts represented the new spirit Reagan helped usher into American politics. After the New Deal, the Civil Rights Movement, and the War on Poverty had injected the wisdom of the Good Samaritan into American politics, the Reagan Revolution looked for inspiration elsewhere. Exemplifying the new ethos of the era, after food allowances for the nation's children were cut, the First Lady used public dollars to purchase $200,000 worth of exclusive dinnerware. During Reagan's administration, the White House would undergo $44 million in luxurious renovations on the taxpayers' dime. Richard Cowen wrote for the *Washington Post* that "the spirit of Marie Antoinette infuses the administration of Ronald Reagan."[62] And by intentional and explicit design, it was Black America that paid the highest price for the new spirit of American politics.

In 1981, Reagan's revolution and the devastation wrought on Black America by his budgets were only beginning. No president in history removed the safety nets of more marginalized Americans than Ronald Reagan. Despite his easygoing veneer, he undertook his work with religious zeal. As in his days at GE, Reagan continued to preach his political gospel of rugged individualism, the magic of the free market, and the threats inherent in government intervention, affirmative action, and welfare. Only now, rather than evangelizing from behind a podium with a GE logo, Reagan evangelized from behind podiums bearing the presidential seal.

From the budget cuts of 1981 to the budget cuts yet to be realized, time and again the sacrificial lambs of America's new civic religion were poor children. Reminiscent of the Roaring Twenties, as the Reagan Revolution gained momentum, the focal point of America's cultural consciousness rarely centered on the realities confronting the working poor. But it was precisely poor children and their families to whom Marian Wright Edelman had dedicated her life. Five years after Reagan's budget cuts began, Edelman issued a report on their devastating impact through her book, *Families in Peril*.

Throughout *Families in Peril*, Edelman alternates between the poetics of a seasoned advocate and the cold calculations of a public policy analyst as she dissects how America's budgets revealed a morally bankrupt nation. Edelman demonstrates how the combination of a worsening economy, restrictions on workers' rights, and America's "benign neglect" made the lives of poor children worse in 1979 than they had been in 1969. But when Reagan took over, "the bottom fell out," and over a million children a year fell into poverty in 1981 and 1982. America now faced the reality that "over a five-year period, more American children die from poverty than the total number of American battle deaths during the Vietnam War."[63]

Why were so many children impoverished in such a wealthy nation? For Edelman, the problems were complex, but their roots were clear. "Children are poor," Edelman writes flatly, "because our nation has lost its moral bearings." Edelman continues:

> Recent federal government policy has spawned a new set of beatitudes which measure success . . . not by how many hungry infants can be nourished, but by how many federal nutrition dollars can be held back as the waiting list of hungry babies grows. Not by how many poor homeless families are provided adequate shelter and minimum food, but by how many MX missiles we can [hide].[64]

The malnutrition of America's poorest children reflected the poverty of the nation's democratic ideals. For Edelman, Reagan's budgets turned "this nation's plowshares into swords . . . bringing good news to the rich at the expense of the poor."[65]

Working with both passion and nuance, she wrote, "Our welfare system is far from ideal, but it is even further from being a vast engine of social destruction." Due to the War on Poverty and a strong economy, poverty was cut in half during the 1960s. Despite the deepening economic struggles of the 1970s, the vast majority of those whom the War on Poverty had raised out of poverty stayed out of poverty. Through the 1960s and 1970s, marked gains occurred in health care via Medicaid and Medicare programs. Head Start proved remarkably successful in serving poor students and positioning them for academic success. Food stamps significantly reduced malnutrition. And by 1977, the rates of Black and white high school graduates entering college were equal. Rather than a record of abysmal failure, "we transformed the lives of millions of children from despair to hope, from sickness to health, from ignorance to learning. Instead of being defensive, we should be proud."

"Welfare," Edelman concludes, "is not a vast engine of social destruction. It is, however, a vast engine of social mythology."[66] Edelman took aim at the implicit racism of welfare's most vocal critics. Instead of seeking to intimately understand and implement welfare improvements, too many critics rooted every welfare shortcoming in the logics of America's oldest racial mythologies concerning pathological Black sex, Black sloth, and Black criminality. Under the sway of racial mythologies, these critics argued that the pursuit of economic and racial justice was impossible and that welfare should be dismembered rather than perfected.

As in the previous eras of white supremacy, the logic of the Reagan Revolution proved nearly immune to facts. Yet Edelman wanted her questions answered. If welfare incentivized teen pregnancy, why did states with the highest benefits consistently experience low rates of teen pregnancy and states with the lowest benefits consistently experience the highest rates of teen pregnancy? If generous public benefits led to an exodus from the workforce, why did the nations with the highest worker protections and best family benefits also experience the most robust workforce participation? "President Reagan likes to quip that we waged war on poverty and poverty won," Edelman noted. However, Edelman rejected Reagan's myth that poverty was an undefeatable foe. It was simply that in the War on Poverty, America failed to fully commit her resources. Poverty, in Edelman's words, was not a foe defeated by "one-third an army, one-fifth a navy, and no air force." The War on Poverty deserved the nation's complete commitment.

Though Edelman continually opposed Reagan's policies, she granted common ground on both the essential dignity of work and the need for the welfare system to integrate that dignity into its mission. The difference between Edelman and Reagan was that she was intimate with both the poor and the realities poor people faced. Edelman understood that weak wages, not a weak work ethic, was the main driver of poverty. While Reagan proclaimed to businesspeople that "a job at $4 an hour is priceless in terms of the self-respect it can buy,"[67] Edelman let her audience know that "millions of children remain locked in poverty because hard-working parents cannot make enough income to provide for their basic needs. . . . This includes more than half of all poor households and fully 80% of men who head poor households."[68]

Rejecting both simple answers and nihilism, Edelman wrote, "Democracy is not a spectator sport." For Edelman, the gravest threat to our future did not reside in a failure to realize our hopes and dreams in the here and now. The gravest threat, instead, was giving up on the pursuit of interracial and egalitarian democracy by making peace with Reagan's revolution and its afterlife. Despite trauma and disappointment, Black America refused to surrender. Marian Wright Edelman joined a chorus of other Black leaders, writers, and activists, like bell hooks, Cornel West, Mary Frances Berry, and Randall Robinson, who continued to shine their lights. And the fight for an interracial and egalitarian democracy raged on.

As Reagan's first term neared its end, his administration was operating on all cylinders. To translate ideologies into public policies takes a remarkable amount of intentionality and discipline. Greatly underestimated by both his admirers and critics, Reagan harmonized the vast powers of the executive office with an efficiency few presidents ever achieved. However, as transformative as his appointments and budgets had proved in rewriting American life, what solidified those changes was the battle Reagan waged on a third front—the battle for America's heart and mind through a racial propaganda campaign. Nothing displayed Reagan's ability to strategically reframe issues better than how he transformed issues of race from the systemic issues of power and economics to mere interpersonal relationships. And in this transformation, nothing proved more pivotal than Reagan's ability to rewrite the legacy of Martin Luther King Jr. for white consumption.

Following his assassination, King's legacy became a focal point for America's evolving racial imagination and consciousness. In 1968, John Conyers began introducing legislation for the creation of a federal holiday celebrating King's birthday on a yearly basis. Year by year, more states across the nation began celebrating King's birthday, and more people began joining the coalition to make the celebration a federal holiday. Unsurprisingly, Reagan fought long and hard against the holiday, publicly denouncing it from 1968 through January 1983.[69]

As can be imagined, the relationship between Reagan, the King family, and the leading advocates for civil rights was ice-cold. "I am scared that if Ronald Reagan gets into office," Coretta Scott King confessed during the 1980 presidential campaign, "we are going to see more of the Ku Klux Klan and a resurgence of the Nazi Party." Nothing in Reagan's presidency alleviated these fears. So on August 27, 1983, Coretta Scott King and a radical coalition of organizers brought together 250,000 people for a second March on Washington not only to remember Martin Luther King Jr. but also to push the Civil Rights Movement forward.[70] Throughout the day, the speeches at the march placed King and the call for civil rights in the spotlight and Ronald Reagan in the crosshairs. Reagan's face was plastered on wanted signs for the criminality of his policies. When John Lewis spoke, the fire in his bones still burned with the same fury it had in 1963. They had come, Lewis declared, because "it is sad and tragic . . . that the president of the United States is woefully out of step and out of tune with [the] human spirit. . . . The Reagan administration, from his pious pronouncements to the disaster of his public program, has demonstrated an insensitivity beyond belief." In the upcoming election, Lewis called voters to put "the Reagan administration . . . out to political pasture [and] cast those who are indifferent to human needs into political exile."[71]

Despite Lewis's call, Reagan never needed Black votes. But in 1984, America's racial landscape was shifting as Reagan's policies made select white people much wealthier and Black America's poverty more pervasive and dire. This made the need to convince white voters that the Reagan Revolution was "not racist" even more poignant in 1984 than in it had been in 1980. Nothing embodied this need more than the swelling support to make Martin Luther King Jr.'s birthday a federal holiday. From 1968 to 1983, honoring King with a federal holiday moved from anathema to receiving bipartisan consensus. Even Georgia conservative and future power broker Newt Gingrich signed on to the idea, as did two-thirds of Republican senators. On July 29, the House approved the federal holiday in a veto-proof vote of 338–90.

Though King's popularity was growing, Reagan's convictions about the man had not changed since he publicly lambasted King in the very shadow of his assassination.[72] Yet, Reagan was always more strategic than his adversaries or advisers acknowledged. He knew that sometimes generals must be willing to lose a battle to win a war. As he reconsidered honoring King through a federal holiday, it seems his political perspective on the event evolved from viewing it as a grave threat to a remarkable opportunity. By selecting limited and specific quotes, the politicians most opposed to King and his movement could weaponize the holiday to misremember his legacy and, in doing so, align his popularity with those working to restore white supremacy through more subtle means.

Admittedly, Reagan's first performances on Martin Luther King Jr. Day were not his best. Reagan rarely came across as icy in public, but at the 1983 signing ceremony to finalize honoring King with a federal holiday, Reagan came across as a man sentenced to eat cold crow. However, the 1984 election proved that every bite was worth it and provided a foretaste of the ironic racial work Martin Luther King Jr. Day would accomplish as the political gap between white and Black America grew even wider. Reagan grew white consensus affirming his revolution to an overwhelming 66 percent of white voters while losing significantly more ground with Black America. And the revolution rolled on.

On January 20, 1986, the United States celebrated Martin Luther King Jr. Day for the first time. In his radio address before the celebration, Reagan took advantage of the opportunity to portray King's vision of equality as antithetical to affirmative action and to praise his own administration for protecting Black people's civil rights and economic progress. According to Reagan, all that was needed to finish realizing King's vision was to "cut tax rates, stop penalizing initiative, and sit back and watch the fireworks go off."[73] As Reagan drew to a close, he asserted this bottom line for Black America:

> The answer to the question "How are blacks doing in America?" is "Better than ever before" . . . if we continue to allow the economy to expand and continue to work for a more perfect society, then people of all colors will prosper. And isn't that what Dr. King's dream and the American dream are all about?[74]

In a remarkable accomplishment in the history of political rhetoric, nearly twenty years after his death, King was reborn as an advocate of deregulation and an opponent of public policies that protected Black people and provided for the poor. Likely, the celebration proved persuasive only to people more familiar with *The Cosby Show* than with King's brilliance or the state of Black America. But that, after all, was Reagan's intent.

However, not everyone was impressed. "The facts are clear, Mr. President," Representative William Gray of the Congressional Black Caucus told the Associated Press in response to the president's address. "Thirty-two percent of black families lived in poverty in 1980. Today, 42 percent of black families live in poverty."[75] Recent polls revealed that over half of Black America believed Reagan was racist, and only one in four approved of his job performance.[76] Civil rights activist Roger Wilkins seethed as he responded to Reagan's celebration. "Two American men who lived in the same century could have hardly agreed less," Wilkins wrote. "King's concern for the poor and the powerless is matched by Reagan's concern—as indicated by his tax, domestic and budgetary policies—for the wealthy and the powerful." Rather than the "never better" Black American reality that Reagan imagined, Wilkins believed that "the black poor are more hopeless and isolated than they have ever been."[77] For Wilkins, Reagan's intentional warping of King's memory and legacy on MLK Day twisted the knife into fresh wounds. That twisting became a bipartisan ritual in the years to come, and some Black leaders began to refer to the tradition of misremembering King as his "second assassination."[78]

Over time, Reagan's performances improved as he learned to leverage MLK Day to strengthen cross-racial alliances with Black leaders who readily supported conservative racial logic. Alliances with conservative Black people like Arthur Fletcher and Thomas Sowell provided politically useful illusions of racial consensus among the reasonably minded.[79] As conservatives co-opted King's legacy, he was intentionally distanced from Black radicals like Malcolm X and Stokely Carmichael, as well as America's fiercest Black critics in the years to come. No one's critique of our nation was more scathing and holistic than King's, and yet through Reagan's editing, King's message was efficiently reduced to provide the nation easy listening concerning our nation's racial progress. With the president's warm embrace of King as the backdrop, the more truthfully that Black people spoke, the more angry, unreasonable, and out of touch with reality and King's "true message" they sounded. So it was that rather than leading white America to rethink issues of racial justice through the lens of King's fiery brilliance, the celebration that inaugurated Martin Luther King Jr. Day cleansed our nation's conscience as we received training to think about racial issues through the racial logic of Ronald Reagan.

And what we cannot forget is that Black America paid a very tangible price for the superficial wisdom of America's emerging racial thinking. The upshot of Reagan's strengthening grip on America's racial imagination was the nation's inability to actually hear King's call to confront the crisis facing Black America. By embracing Ronald Reagan, mainstream America rejected Martin Luther King Jr. and continued its crimes against Black and Brown people with a clean conscience. That rejection helped create the context of today's racial injustices. That rejection demands reparations and continuing the work of the radical King.

As Reagan moved into his second term, the influence of his appointees, budgets, and racial propaganda was seeping into all corners of American life. For as incisive as the critiques of Black America proved in Reagan's first term, in a very real way, the situation facing America's Black communities was likely much more dire—and sinister—than Marian Wright Edelman, John Lewis, and other Black radicals dared to imagine. A new form of racial war was in the offing. That war was Reagan's War on Drugs, which devastated Black families and communities in ways eerily reminiscent of the auction block and lynching tree.

Reagan's War on Drugs traced its roots to LBJ's War on Crime in the 1960s and Nixon's more racialized War on Drugs in the early 1970s. In the face of a heroin epidemic and growing urban violence, Nixon had spied a political gold mine. Rather than treating narcotics as a medical emergency or addressing the underlying causes of crime, Nixon's War on Drugs intentionally sharpened the racial edges of the War on Crime. "You want to know what this was really all about?" Nixon's domestic adviser, John Ehrlichman, recalled. Nixon's administration "had two enemies: the antiwar left and black people." Though "we couldn't make it illegal to be either against the war or black," Ehrlichman continued, they could shape public opinion by "getting the public to associate the hippies with marijuana and blacks with heroin, and then criminalizing both heavily." Once hippies and Blacks were caricatured as criminals, "we could arrest their leaders, raid their homes, break up their meetings, and vilify them night after night on the evening news. Did we know we were lying about the drugs? Of course we did."[80] Nixon's team explicitly crafted "a subliminal appeal to the antiblack voter" and made that appeal ever "present in Nixon's statements and speeches."[81]

On October 14, 1982, Reagan made his intentions to revive America's War on Drugs public knowledge. The announcement's timing seemed odd.

In 1982, few Americans considered drugs a serious problem. Overall, illegal drug use was declining, and heroin use was stagnant. Surveys on marijuana showed modest declines in use coupled with a rising disapproval rate among teens. Only 2 percent of Americans believed that drugs were America's primary problem. It seemed that no longer could drugs be sold as public enemy number one. Unless, of course, that salesman was Ronald Reagan.

In his "Remarks Announcing Federal Initiatives Against Drug Trafficking and Organized Crime," Reagan began with his trademark humor to place his audience in his pocket before shifting attention to the purpose of their gathering. Gravity replaced levity as Reagan began laying out a plan for dealing with America's "drug and crime crisis." He got rolling quoting a few crime stats—over twenty thousand homicides and $8.8 billion in financial losses. "These stats," said the president, "suggest that our criminal justice system has broken down."

What precisely was the problem? For the rest of his speech, Reagan shifted his weight from statistics to lean heavily into his philosophy. Though poverty killed nearly 400 percent more Americans than homicides, Reagan began by separating America's economic crisis—the worst economic conditions since the Great Depression—from her crime crisis.[82] Instead of fighting poverty, Reagan warred on poor people, or, in his words, a "new privileged class in America, a class of repeat offenders and career criminals." The new privileged class no longer consisted of society's wealthiest people. The new privileged class was composed of impoverished people from the working class who were led to a life of crime by the welfare system. In words reminiscent of Madison Grant, Reagan continued: "This rise in crime, this growth of a hardened criminal class," was tied to "a misguided social philosophy" with "utopian presumptions about human nature." That philosophy saw "individual wrongdoing . . . as the result of poor socioeconomic conditions or an underprivileged background" and believed that "by changing this environment through expensive social programs, . . . government can permanently change man and usher in an era of prosperity and virtue." Reagan believed such sentimentalism threatened America's very existence.

By now, Reagan was in rhythm as he repeated well-rehearsed punchlines of his philosophy concerning welfare, crime, and drugs. In Reagan's world, there existed a clear cause-and-effect relationship between welfare and economic dependency and a life of crime and drugs. Reagan's ideas about welfare, dependency, and crime that culminated in the War on Drugs rejected nearly all evidence-based research. Reagan's War on Drugs rested not in the details of empirical data but in the drama of Reagan's racialized ideologies. In

1998, additional research was released by Lance Hannon and James DeFronzo showing unequivocally that Reagan was right to link welfare to crime. But the empirical research showed that the relationship was opposite of what Reagan repeatedly insisted. Welfare proved a significant tool *for* fighting the entire spectrum of street crimes. When welfare was reduced, crime increased.[83]

Again, against all evidence, Reagan claimed that under his watch, the tides had already turned and "a new political consensus among the American people" demanded that "retribution must be swift and sure." Reagan stood ready to spend millions upon millions—which would soon become billions upon billions—to realize his vision to punish "every street punk or two-bit criminal" and to keep the new "privileged class" in their place. For the first time in American history, the resources of the "the FBI, the DEA, the IRS, the ATF, Immigration and Naturalization Services, the US Customs Service and the Coast Guard" as well as "the Department of Defense" would collaborate with local law enforcement to war against America's criminal class.

As always with Reagan, the nation once again found itself at a historic crossroads. The question President Reagan seared on America's soul was this: "Can we honestly say that America is a land with justice for all if we do not now exert every effort to eliminate this confederation of professional criminals?" Reagan's call to intensify the War on Drugs was communicated with religious fervor as he sought to save America "from the dark, evil enemy within."[84]

When Reagan was behind the dais, it was easy to believe that he sincerely reiterated the prevailing wisdom of the day. But that was in no way the case. Reagan was playing the part of "the Great Communicator," transforming cultural common sense and creating a new—and remarkably more vindictive—consensus. From 1974 to 1982, between 0 and 2 percent of Americans believed drugs were America's primary problem, and far more people believed economic solutions provided a better way forward than draconian public policies. Nonetheless, Reagan believed he was positioned to utilize the rhetoric of law and order to place radically more of America's new "privileged class"—America's "street punks," "vermin," and "parasites"—in prison cells. And he was right.

Soon, Reagan's power of political persuasion sparked an extraordinary turn in public opinion. Legislative transformations rewrote America's racial landscape and political principles in a direly more predatory direction. The first legislation to insert Reagan's philosophy into bipartisan public policy was the Comprehensive Crime Control Act of 1984. Following the joint conference committee, the legislation garnered deep bipartisan approval, passing the House 252–60 and the Senate 78–11.

The Comprehensive Crime Control Act of 1984 possessed numerous interlocking gears. Prison sentences drastically increased. Police were provided military weapons and training. The bill allowed the corrupting practice of confiscating the property of suspects without the need of a trial to retain the seizure. This, in turn, incentivized transforming innocent citizens into criminal suspects. Perhaps the most ironic twist was how the legislation positioned drug kingpins to use their wealth to craft plea deals that routinely bought their way out of hard time. Small-time dealers, addicts, and the innocent either got hard time in prison or returned to their communities with little more than the clothes on their backs. And those backs were overwhelmingly Black, despite the fact that the majority of dealers and users were white. Black people accounted for a full 99 percent of drug-trafficking defendants nationwide between 1985 and 1987.[85]

Looking back at the first years of the War on Crime, a curious word was missing from Reagan's initial speech and the 383 pages of the Comprehensive Drug Act of 1984. And that word is "crack." The word was nowhere to be found, because Reagan's War on Drugs began before America's crack epidemic. Despite the War on Drugs, between 1982 and 1984, the importation of cocaine increased a remarkable 50 percent and began to find its way into inner-city communities in the hardened and more affordable form of crack. This reality was largely not on the national radar. That changed in 1986, when the famous University of Maryland basketball player Len Bias died from what was reported as a crack overdose. Seemingly overnight, crack became the new American nightmare.

That the autopsy corroborated witnesses' testimony that Bias had died of cocaine, not crack, did little to soothe national hysteria. Crack became public enemy number one, and both political parties began equating political virility with vengeance on Black people who peddled or were addicted to drugs. A toxic struggle between Republicans and Democrats ensued to see which party could provide the toughest sentences. Machismo has never produced nuanced public policy, and the Anti-Drug Abuse Act of 1986 was no exception. Stiffer penalties were instituted across the board, but the kicker was the legislation's racial ratio. Five grams of crack—the drug with the most perceived Black users—received the same penalty as five hundred grams of cocaine. On Friday, October 17, 1986, the legislation and its logics received a unanimous vote in the House, and the Senate passed it through on a voice vote alone.

If politicians proved ready to partner with the White House to wage a war on crack, so too were the physicians, psychologists, and the press. No physician proved more instrumental than neonatal expert Ira Chasnoff, who published his 1985 research in the *New England Journal of Medicine* about the impact of crack on infants. Perhaps the fact that Chasnoff's article was limited to a study of only twenty-three infants should have called into question the certainty of his findings. But it didn't. Tom Brokaw caught wind of the story, and soon Peter Jennings and Dan Rather were addressing the threat of crack babies as well. The story about what Black mothers were doing to their babies went viral.

As crack babies became the hottest topic in the nation, no one wanted to miss out. Like the eugenicist of old, researchers and writers went to work to create the strongest propaganda by making their fears sound like scientifically reasoned facts. *Time* magazine labeled crack "the issue of the year," while *Newsweek* would compare it to Vietnam and Watergate. Research psychologist Coryl Jones reported evidence of crack corrupting "the central core of what it is to be human." A *Washington Post* columnist reported that "the inner-city crack epidemic is now giving birth to the newest horror: a bio-underclass, a generation of physically damaged cocaine babies whose biological inferiority is stamped at birth." Between Len Bias and the stories about babies, America had the story it needed about the threat of poor Black mothers to the nation's promise. Danger was at the door, and it was time to protect the country by punishing the predators.[86]

So it was with Nancy Reagan standing by his side that Ronald Reagan came before the cameras for the presidential signing ceremony of the Anti-Drug Abuse Act of 1986. Reagan said the legislation represented a "vaccine" for an American epidemic. With his soothing voice, he was uniquely gifted at wrapping America's punitive wisdom in pure intentions. "We must be intolerant of drugs not because we want to punish drug users," he patiently intoned, looking away from his notes and into his audience's eyes, "but because we care about them and want to help them." He reiterated the compassion at the heart of the draconian legislation. "This legislation is not intended as a means of filling our jails with drug users," Reagan continued. "What we must do as a society is identify those who use drugs, reach out to them, help them quit, and give them the support they need to live right." He thanked Nancy for the simplicity of her "Just Say No" campaign. Nancy's brilliance was, apparently, the only help and support addicts needed, for it was just about the only help and support the administration extended. Despite promises of meaningful drug education and prevention, that priority received only a dime on the dollar in the final budget.[87]

As the War on Drugs rolled on, the vaccine the punitive legislation had engineered failed to protect America from its crime or drug epidemics. The president and Congress got together again and produced another bill that garnered *overwhelming* bipartisan support. Reagan's compassion for addicts was on display once more as he signed yet a stronger measure providing stiffer penalties and resurrecting federal capital punishment. In the Anti-Drug Abuse Act of 1988, desperate times called for desperate measures, and lethal injection became a uniquely American vaccine to fight the contagion of drugs.

While public policies quickly responded to the recent and terrifying scientific discoveries, Ira Chasnoff realized his research was misleading. In his two-year follow-up study, it turned out that crack's impact was very similar to that of malnutrition, and additional research confirmed that the response to crack babies was rooted more in fear than in sound scientific research. Needless to say, the more meticulous follow-up research failed to amend the public policies the original scientific research inspired.[88]

After Reagan launched his War on Drugs, money poured into the war chest. The budget for the FBI's antidrug work increased from $8 million to $95 million. Within ten years, the Department of Defense would see its antidrug appropriations budget that began at $33 million increase to over $1 billion. What modest money existed for drug treatment shrank by similar proportions. And that only got the ball rolling. In less than ten years, spending on Reagan's policies more than doubled state corrections' budgets, increasing them from $15 billion in 1982 to $32.5 billion in 1991.[89] Like other ill-conceived American wars, the War on Drugs created its own economy, producing financial incentives to perpetuate a fight long after the war itself has proved as disastrous as it was misguided. Today, the prison industrial complex represents a roughly $87 billion per year industry that fails to ensure either justice, safety, or our nation's healing.[90]

Ironically, in the long run, capital punishment ended up being one of the least lethal aspects of the legislation the War on Drugs inspired. Capital punishment ended the lives of dozens. Mass incarceration wrecked the lives of millions. Between 1970 and 1980, America's prison population ballooned from 357,292 people to 513,900—an incredible 41 percent increase in only ten years. In the 1980s, that balloon transformed into a blimp, more than doubling to 1,117,200 by 1990. Across America, the incarceration rates of Black men skyrocketed. In some cities today, nearly 80 percent of young

Black males now possess criminal records.[91] "Nixon coined the term 'a war on drugs,'" Michelle Alexander stated in the documentary *13th*, "but President Reagan turned that rhetorical war into a literal one."

Through the power of presidential appointment, budgets, racial propaganda, and legislative transformations, Reagan organized an onslaught of political power that reduced many Black communities to rubble. Despite the Black suffering the Reagan administration caused, many of their maneuvers were perfectly legal. Yet, what became clear toward the end of his presidency was that Reagan was never bound by the rules of engagement that might have kept lesser presidents in check. War crimes are commonplace, and Reagan's fight in the War on Drugs was not the exception to but the epitome of that rule.

The question raging in many Black communities was how crack became ever present in Black neighborhoods *after* the War on Drugs was declared and the money began flowing into the antidrug war chest. "From the outset," reports Michelle Alexander in *The New Jim Crow*, "stories circulated on the street that crack and other drugs were being brought into black neighborhoods by the CIA."[92] Despite denials from the Reagan administration, the rumors never died. The National Urban League's 1990 State of Black America report looked at the War on Drugs as Baldwin's fears of a "Final Solution" coming to pass on America soil: "There is at least one concept that must be recognized if one is to see the pervasive and insidious nature of the drug problem for the African American community," the report read. "Though difficult to accept, that is the concept of genocide."[93]

For many, the very idea of charging the CIA with complicity in drug trafficking and the executive wing with designs to engineer the suffering and elimination of Black people sounded preposterous. There was, however, a troubling precedent. In 1972, *The Politics of Heroin in Southeast Asia* was released by Yale PhD student Alfred William McCoy, detailing the CIA's complicity and collaboration with the mafia and heroin traffickers from World War II through the Vietnam War era. Often, the target communities for those drugs had been Black America. Yet, surely the CIA had learned its lesson.[94] Or had it?

In 1985, investigative journalism and mounting evidence combined to transform what had once been merely street rumors and outrageous conspiracy theories to a nationally published account on the complicity of the US government with drug cartels. The coverage of the conspiracy centered on the fight against communists in South America. In Nicaragua, a regime open to US corporations and backed by the American government had fallen to left-wing revolutionaries known as the Sandinista National Liberation Front. After their successful coup, the Sandinista were challenged for control of Nicaragua by a terrorist organization known as the Contras, who were seen as more friendly to America's economic and political interests.

Though evidence mounted on Contra atrocities that included rape, murder, and pillaging, what mattered most to Reagan was that the Contras were adamantly anticommunist. For Reagan, that was enough to characterize the Contras as the pulsating heart of the fight against communism in Latin America, and he heralded their violent insurrectionists as a "moral equal of our Founding Fathers." In 1982, Congress showed a strength and independence that was rare in the Reagan era, rejecting the president's priorities and voting unanimously to halt funding to the Contras.

Reagan was forced to sign the veto-proof bill, but his devotion to the modern "Founding Fathers" and their "fight against communism" never wavered. If anything, the lengths to which the Reagan administration immediately went to fund the Contras only intensified. Under the direction of the White House, John Poindexter and Oliver North spearheaded an operation to sell weapons to Iran and illegally funnel funds of the sale to the Contras. When the story broke as the Iran-Contra Affair in November 1986, it made front-page news and threatened to take down the Reagan presidency.

Yet, Iran-Contra was only half the story of the United States' illegal collaboration with the terrorist organization. The other half could be dubbed "Cartel-Contra-Coke," for it was not only money from guns but also money from cocaine that provided fuel for the Contras' war machine. To make their drug smuggling networks as profitable as possible, the Contras recruited the help of Oliver North, the Reagan administration, and the CIA. Predating the revelation of Iran-Contra by almost an entire year, on December 20, 1985, investigative journalists Brian Barger and Robert Parry of the Associated Press penned a damning article. Though the title of the initial article that ran was typically bland—"Reports Link Nicaraguan Rebels to Cocaine Trafficking"—the initial investigation made the line between reality and the absurd more difficult to decipher. According to the AP, as the Contras grew desperate for cash, they fostered networks with drug cartels to fund their war. Some shipments were as large as one hundred tons.[95]

White House officials attempted to drown the story before it could run. When that failed, they were ready with a cascade of denials and well-orchestrated charges of shoddy journalism.[96] But one reader was intrigued as much by the article as by the denials and believed an investigation was warranted. He was a first-term senator named John Kerry. In 1986, Kerry launched an in-depth commission that lasted nearly three years.

The commission's report, *Drugs, Law Enforcement and Foreign Policy*, later dubbed the Kerry Report, landed in December 1988, only weeks before Reagan's final day in office. The concise, 169-page report was written with a cold hand, thoroughly footnoted, and limited exclusively to documented facts and policy recommendations. Those facts, however, were firebombs, and the report was one of the most damning publicly released congressional investigations in US history.

What the commission found was that not only had the AP article been based on solid evidence but also the AP had only scratched the surface of the corruption. The corrupt connections among US governmental officials, the Contras, and narcotic traffickers were not limited to a few bad apples—they were a well-managed orchard, or, in the words of the CIA chief: "It was not a couple of people. It was a lot of people. . . . We knew that everyone around [the Contra leader] was involved in cocaine. His staff and friends . . . were drug smugglers."[97]

Under the Reagan administration, the conspiracy tied together CIA initiatives in seven Latin American nations to provide cover and assistance for the distribution of the largest cartels in the world—including the infamous Medellín Cartel. Rather than connections with the CIA being inconsequential to the rise of the Medellín Cartel, evidence suggests it could have been central. The beginning of the Reagan administration's covert war coincided almost exactly with the cartel's rise in power. Further, as Alfred McCoy wrote in an updated edition of *The Politics of Heroin*, "all major U.S. agencies have gone on the record stating . . . that the Medellín cartel used Contra forces to smuggle cocaine into the United States."[98] As impressive as the organizations listed in the report were the people named: Manuel Noriega, Pablo Escobar, Oliver North, Attorney General Edwin Meese, and Vice President George H. W. Bush.

The report did not reveal an unbroken line connecting the federal government to the cartels to the user on the street. Instead, the report revealed that the US played an indispensable role in ensuring that each link in the cocaine chain possessed the strength to move the drugs through the jungles of Latin America to the streets of the United States. In his updated book, McCoy details how the Contras' alliance with the CIA ensured the cartels' protection and a minimum of interference by creating "enforcement-free zones." All that was needed from the cartels was a little kickback to the Contras, and the Reagan administration would provide the grease to make the engine hum.[99]

The Kerry Report was careful to ensure the sensationalism of the conspiracy did not override its domestic impact and laid out the discovered facts in bullet points. Almost all the crime in the nation was associated with drugs. After the War on Drugs was declared and the congressional funding for the Contras terminated, drugs poured into communities across America in unprecedented quantities. Perhaps no figure better encapsulated the surge in cocaine than its price. "The street price for a kilo of cocaine in the United States," the Kerry Report bullet-pointed, "has plummeted from $60,000 in 1980 to approximately $9,000 a kilo today."[100] The quality of the cheaper cocaine had significantly increased as well. The report was impossible to read without concluding that the spike in drug use and violence that followed the War on Drugs was not coincidental but involved the coordination of the Reagan administration, the Contras, and the cartels.

As the Kerry committee worked, Reagan's administration orchestrated a coordinated attempt to cover their tracks by obstructing the investigation and actively attempting to discredit the report upon its release. The media buried its coverage of the Kerry Report, and the little attention it received often aimed to belittle the investigation rather than take seriously the evidence and testimony it gathered. Though "crack babies" made front-page news, major news organizations like the *New York Times*, the *Los Angeles Times*, and the *Washington Post* buried news of the Kerry Report with only brief mentions on pages 8, 11, and 20.[101] Yet, over the next decade, from the work of investigative journalists to congressional hearings, many of the damning details of the Kerry Report would be confirmed by deeper investigations and further admissions from the CIA itself. Like the Ku Klux Klan Report in 1870, the mind-numbing crimes revealed in the Kerry Report show why the work of reparations must take into account the crimes of slavery's afterlife. Despite the report's revelations, the damage it wrought on the Reagan administration amounted to no more than light rain on a windshield.

Yet, what the Kerry Report revealed was that the Reagan administration was integral in unleashing an altogether different kind of downpour on Black communities across America. After devastating Black schools, families, and employment opportunities through draconian policies, the Reagan administration either directly helped flood Black communities with cocaine or knowingly refused to prevent it. After the flood, drowning communities were then fed into the prison system. Ironically, it was only after placing Black Americans in handcuffs and behind prison bars that the Reagan administration proved willing to pay for food, housing, and utilities for poor Black people.

When we look at US presidents through the lens of reparations, President Reagan provides one of the strongest cases for reparations. Due to Reagan's War on Drugs and its aftermath, the prison system alone robbed one in four Black children of a parent. The number of children orphaned through the combination of Reagan's public policies and War on Drugs was not in the thousands but in the millions.[102] Reagan never went to war on foreign soils, but the body count that his public policies produced in lost and maimed American lives through the increase of prisons and intensification of poverty rivals that of *any* wartime president.

Writing for those seeking to survive the wreckage wrought by our public policies, James Forman Jr. penned *Locking Up Our Own* in an attempt to understand why America—including many Black Americans—originally embraced the War on Drugs. Forman sums up his findings this way: "One of this book's central arguments [is]: Mass incarceration is the result of small, distinct steps, each of whose significance becomes more apparent over time."[103] Forman characterizes the support from Black, white progressive, and some conservative lawmakers for the broader War on Drugs as more in keeping with Greek tragedy than an intricate blueprint to eradicate Black America. As inner cities went into dire decline, conservatives and liberals, Black and white, both believed tougher law enforcement was necessary to quell the chaos. In time, that bipartisan consensus proved a deadly cocktail that was made all the more lethal by the rejection of Black America and their white allies' insistence on progressive policies to curb poverty and treat drugs as a health crisis instead of a crime crisis.

Looking at how the struggle against communism and the War on Drugs interweaved in the context of Reagan's revolution, however, provides a different angle with far more disturbing implications. There is a difference between Black leaders and white progressive and conservative politicians who supported the War on Drugs out of fear of the violence taking place in Black communities, and an executive wing whose twisted fight against communism led them to protect drug cartels as they flooded poor Black communities with lethal narcotics. For the Reagan administration, the War on Drugs was an integral component of an overall blueprint with disastrous racial ramifications. In 1980, if anyone desired to design a plot to destroy Black America, it is hard to think of a more destructive blueprint than what Ronald Reagan began to implement as soon as he arrived in Washington. The only way to address the blueprint of Reagan's intentional devastation of Black communities is with an equally intentional blueprint for reparations that, in addition to making payments to Black families, also aims to reconstruct the communities that our War on Drugs decimated.

In 1988, any progress on racial justice seemed unlikely. On March 16, 1988, Ronald Reagan vetoed the Civil Rights Restoration Act, making him the first president since Andrew Johnson to veto civil rights legislation.[104] Three months later, George H. W. Bush followed the direction of Reagan adviser Lee Atwater and launched his stumbling election campaign by rolling out the Willie Horton ad that played into the mythology of the Black rapist.[105] However, in the background of these anti-Black maneuvers was a bill representing fifteen years of determined Japanese American advocacy titled the Civil Liberties Act of 1988. Focused on the criminal internment of Japanese Americans during World War II, the legislation provided $20,000 in reparations to internment survivors, established an Office of Redress Administration, and issued a presidential apology. With Reagan's dogmatic ideologies, it seemed unlikely he would support such legislation. An internal memo in the Reagan White House detailed concerns warranting a veto. Among the points highlighted by hand was "The bill could establish a bad precedent for other groups who feel that they have suffered injustices."[106]

Despite this concern, Reagan considered the treatment of Japanese Americans during World War II as "one of the few black marks on American history,"[107] and so he gave his full support to reparations' cause. The $1.25 billion reparations package received strong bipartisan support and included repentance for "race prejudice, war hysteria, and a failure of political leadership."[108]

At the signing ceremony, Reagan confessed: "No payment can make up for those lost years. What is most important in this bill has less to do with property than with honor. For here we admit wrong."[109] The ceremony honoring Japanese Americans wrongfully imprisoned through the World War II internment camps would be hosted by the Bush administration in the Great Hall of Justice in 1990. "By finally admitting a wrong, a nation does not destroy its integrity, but rather reinforces the sincerity of its commitment to the Constitution, and hence to its people," declared Attorney General Dick Thornburgh during an emotional ceremony. Along with a check of $20,000 each, the honored attendees received a formal letter from President George H. W. Bush reading, "We can never fully right the wrongs of the past. But we can take a clear stand for justice."

It was a remarkable moment in American history. A national injustice was named. Repentance occurred. Reparations were paid. And a precedent was established that atoning for racial sins represents the most practical of political practices. Yet, for all the glory of the moment, the bipartisan reparations package also provided a painful remainder of the lines of demarcation in America's racial imagination. Japanese Americans represented "model minorities" worthy of the justice the nation provided, while Black America continued on as the demonized minority who seemingly earned the suffering they endured. From wrongfully providing reparations to enslavers to rightfully paying reparations for violence against immigrants, Native Americans, and Japanese Americans, our nation has repeatedly proved ready to make reparations—just not reparations to the formerly enslaved or their descendants.

By the close of Reagan's final term, the Reagan Revolution had secured its place in American history. If the greatest challenges Reagan desired to face as president were runaway inflation rates, the Russian menace, and white America's sagging confidence and lack of unity, he could rightly claim to have overcome them all. A transformative presidency is predicated on harmonizing the vast powers of presidential office to achieve concrete aims and objectives while getting the American people to play along. When we look at the Reagan presidency in the longer arc of American history, there are few that proved more transformative—or more disastrous for Black Americans. These disasters, which were designed in the lifetime of boomers and Generation X, demand reparations.

As Reagan readied for his postpresidential life, it was in many ways a new day. The Reagan presidency ushered in, to use his phrase, "morning in America." White America had regained its swagger. In his final address, Reagan referred to our nation's economic turnaround as "the American miracle." America's reforged confidence represented "the new patriotism." He looked into the camera to communicate his sense of the significance of his revolution. "Once you begin a great movement, there's no telling where it will end. We meant to change a nation, and instead, we changed the world. . . ." Considering their accomplishments, the commander in chief delivered "a final word to the men and women of the Reagan Revolution, [who] brought

America back. My friends: We did it. We weren't just marking time. We made a difference. . . . All in all, not bad, not bad at all. And so, goodbye, God bless you, and God bless the United States of America."[110]

As usual, Reagan's rhetoric displayed a magical ability to resonate with most of white America's deepest hopes and desires. And, as was often the case, Reagan's rhetoric hardly matched reality at all. Take, for instance, America's economic turnaround. A turnaround had happened, but it had been a bit less miraculous than Reagan indicated. It had included the worst recession since the Great Depression. The growth rate of the GDP during the administration had averaged a modest 3.5 percent. Despite this modest economic growth, the wealthiest Americans had become remarkably wealthier. The income of the top 1 percent increased nearly 50 percent, the number of millionaires increased by 225 percent, and the number of billionaires increased 400 percent—from thirteen in 1982 to fifty-two in 1988. As the nation largely adhered to Reagan's economic blueprint in the following decades, the concentration of wealth that began in the 1980s only intensified.[111] Despite modest economic and employment growth, poverty became both more dire and more far-reaching.[112] Jobs had continued to trickle back into the American economy following deindustrialization, but in the 1980s a full 75 percent of the new jobs created were for minimum wage, and a full-time job no longer protected people from poverty.[113] As poverty increased across the board, even white men were much more likely to be poor after Reagan than they had been before his taking office.[114] After Reagan cut federal housing funding by 70 percent, homelessness in the 1980s exploded. In 1980, the best estimates for homelessness ranged from 200,000 to 400,000 Americans. By 1987, that estimate was 2 to 3 million. Homelessness hit Black America the hardest, and children accounted for more than 500,000 of the victims. By 2018, the number of homeless children in the nation reached 1.3 million—nearly five times the total homeless population when Reagan's punitive polices began.[115]

For everything Reagan accomplished during his presidency, there was an incredibly high price that was paid, and Black America bore too much of that burden. As much as any president in US history, Reagan's worldview was warped by the racial mythologies concerning Black sex and families, Black sloth, and Black criminality. And his coordinated attack on Black America demands reparations. What separated Reagan from his modern presidential forebears was his ability to transform federal agencies, budgets, and public

policies in targeted ways to cripple Black education, health, and job opportunities while winning overwhelming public support from white America.
On Reagan's watch, infant mortality in Black America doubled that in white
America, and the life expectancy of males born in Harlem fell below that of
males born in Bangladesh.[116] Reagan's racialized War on Drugs and public
school disinvestment not only decimated Black America in the 1980s but
also continues to dim the future of Black children born today. Under Reagan,
the phrase "school-to-prison pipeline" entered the American vernacular as
students at underfunded minority schools throughout the nation often began
to be more likely to go to prison than to graduate from college.

Just as a racial misinformation campaign about Black people and welfare
had been integral in Ronald Reagan's pursuit of power, so too a racial misinformation campaign played a critical role in his presidency. The Reagan
Revolution's misinformation campaign aimed to foster plausible deniabil-
ity for the devastation our nation's public policies and covert conspiracies
wrought in the lives of Black people and communities. Throughout it all,
Black Americans cried out for the nation to come to its senses and confront
the nation's racial crimes. Instead of heeding their cries, white America ques-
tioned Black sanity. From slavery through Reconstruction, lynchings, and the
ages of prisons and poverty, many in white America seemingly craved racial
misinformation, and that craving created complicity.

As in previous racial ages, Reagan's misinformation campaign bred ignorance, and that ignorance promoted indifference to Black America's suffering.
As Black destitution compounded, so too did the popularity of blaming Black
people for America's racial inequalities. Our tendency to deny our responsibility for reparations in the face of the apocalyptic nature of racial injustice
is inseparable from the success of Ronald Reagan and his intentional work
to intensify Black suffering *and* white hardheartedness. Writing forty years
after the Reagan Revolution, noted Black historian Ibram X. Kendi wrote
succinctly: "Denial is the heartbeat of racism."[117]

On January 20, 1989, the blades of Marine One swirled on the East Lawn
as the presidential helicopter awaited Ronald and Nancy Reagan. Nancy
had tears in her eyes, as did many of Reagan's normally stoic associates and
supporters who learned to deeply admire the actor they had once belittled.
Perhaps there were tears in the eyes of many Black Americans as well, for
the racial politics of the Reagan Revolution and the Colorblind Age were

only gaining deeper traction. Reagan had crafted a white consensus that would long outlive his administration. That consensus laid the train tracks into our nation's future, leading us to the troubling crossroads where we find ourselves today.

It is the gift of the actor to pull their audience into an imagined world and to move that audience's thoughts, feelings, and instincts in a way that they experience the actor's created reality as their own. Ronald Reagan was a gifted actor, and politics provided him witth the perfect platform. He wrapped white audiences in the American dream, comforting his crowds with the dream's warmth, hope, and confidence during an uncertain time in our nation's history. But throughout the Colorblind Age, white dreams continued to produce Black nightmares. And now, forty years after the Reagan Revolution began, the question is how white people will respond once they awake.

12

The Lasting Legacy of "Colorblindness"

Deepening America's Divides

Reagan is the Pres, but I voted for Shirley Chisholm.

—Biz Markie, "Nobody Beats the Biz," 1988

WHEN THOMAS JEFFERSON TOOK HIS FINAL BREATH in July 1826, Harriet Tubman was an enslaved four-year-old in Maryland. When Harriet Tubman left this life as a freedwoman in March 1913, Ronald Reagan was a two-year-old in Illinois. That a single lifetime touches the times of both Presidents Thomas Jefferson and Ronald Reagan displays the condensed nature of both American history and the evolution of white supremacy. As Reagan entered his second term as president, *Notes on the State of Virginia* celebrated its two hundredth anniversary, and under his leadership, the racial caricatures within *Notes* continued to prove more powerful than the declaration of equality in the Declaration of Independence.

For all Reagan accomplished to upend racial justice, the white supremacy of the Colorblind Age would not reach its intellectual zenith until the presidency of Bill Clinton with the publication of *The Bell Curve*. Written by Richard Herrnstein and Charles Murray, the book sought to scientifically validate the age-old racial myth about the inferiority of Black intelligence. By the time *The Bell Curve* hit the presses, both authors were already quite famous for their focused writings on the problems of Black people and communities. As Richard Nixon launched the War on Drugs and worked to end the War on Poverty, Richard Herrnstein achieved notoriety with a September 1971 article in the *Atlantic* titled "IQ" that leaned heavily on the work of Francis Galton, the father of eugenics. With even less evidence-based research than the racial scientists at the century's beginning, Herrnstein concluded that America was a meritocracy whose social divides accurately reflected an individual's

222   PRISONS AND POVERTY

IQ. "A cautious conclusion," Herrnstein wrote, "is that the upper-class scores about thirty points above the lower class."[1] Herrnstein essentially denied that centuries of racist public policies played a meaningful role in racial inequalities. For Herrnstein, white America's average IQ score and socioeconomic privileges were higher for the simple reason that on average, white people are smarter than Black people.

Herrnstein's coauthor Charles Murray's previous groundbreaking book was *Losing Ground*.[2] Published in 1984, it presents imaginative thought experiments to argue that welfare should be eradicated, as welfare, it claims, provides perverse incentives that trap people in poverty, harming those it intends to help. The book proved so popular in the Reagan White House and harmonized so smoothly with the administration's political ideologies that the *New York Times* referred to the book as the administration's "bible."[3] Though Murray made important and valid points, his true brilliance was displayed by his ability to forget landmark accomplishments that came from the War on Poverty and any data that conflicted with his interpretation.[4]

Repeating the authors' strategy of releasing their work in a politically charged moment, *The Bell Curve* went to print in 1994 amid the fight to make the wars against drugs and welfare more draconian during the Clinton years. Spanning nearly seven hundred pages, Murray and Herrnstein drown readers in carefully selected and interpreted statistics, ignore studies replete with conflicting evidence, and, after framing Black people as intellectually inferior, blame their readers if they see anything racist in their writing.

For Murray and Herrnstein, the greatest threat to effective public policies is treating different classes of people as if they were intellectual and genetic equals. The key to effective public policy, they argue, is in not overestimating or overinvesting in the potential of the poor. With sophisticated prose and eugenical rationality, they write: "Much public policy towards the disadvantaged starts from the premise that interventions can make up for genetic or environmental disadvantages, and that premise is overly optimistic." That is a well-written sentence that suggests that public policies that aim to positively impact the lives of the poor people are too reliant on faulty notions of equality. For Herrnstein and Murray, it was time America's public policies matured past such convictions and embraced the truth, "desperately denied for so long," of "group differences in cognitive ability."[5]

Despite its many shortcomings, *The Bell Curve* is a rhetorical masterpiece that represents the high point of white supremacy's intellectual evolution in America. Herrnstein and Murray's writing lacks many things but never confidence. It is a long road between the simplicity of the racial prose in *The*

Clansman and *The Passing of the Great Race* and the sophisticated racial rationality presented in *The Bell Curve*. And that sophistication proved persuasive to many who longed for evidence that the growing racial inequalities of the Colorblind Age were rooted in anything but racism. After *The Bell Curve*, Black inferiority was once again quantifiable, and the idea that racial inequality resulted from a combination of Black people's intellectual inferiority and self-inflicted wounds was well positioned to continue shaping public policy well into the new millennium. In *The Bell Curve*, the Colorblind Age completed the circle of racial mythologies of the nation's previous ages, leaving no racist idea crafted during the eras of slavery or lynchings underutilized.

From Moynihan to Herrnstein and Murray, racial theorists of the Colorblind Age chose to rely on repetition rather than novel ideas. For all its publicity, *The Bell Curve*'s central argument for slashing social services is rooted in the conviction that poor people are so inherently inferior that they cannot be helped. And there is nothing new in that argument. But our nation's infatuation with their work said something very meaningful about our nation: that for all its claims concerning racial progress, our nation continued to act as fertile soil for the world's most racist and classist ideas.

***

As we take one final look inside the casket of Ronald Reagan's legacy, we must not lose sight of the big picture. More than any election, nomination, budget, or public policy, Reagan's most meaningful contribution to America was his unique worldview that in time became nearly synonymous with white America's racial, economic, and political common sense. And that common sense rewrote America's racial and economic landscape.

When it comes to reparations and the years that predate Reagan's presidency, we must examine the price Black America and our nation paid throughout the twentieth century for prioritizing the fears of communism over the everyday suffering of poor and Black people. When the Red Scare successfully quelled racial progress without the need to mention race at all, Black America was given an omen of what awaited on the other side of their struggle against lynching and segregation. Concerning the 1960s and '70s, we must consider the cost we paid for rejecting all evidence-based research, reembracing the racial mythologies of slavery and lynching, and pivoting from seeking to end poverty to seeking to end welfare. The nation's embrace of Moynihan showed that myths of Black pathology were not only the theoretical framework of bygone eras but also the lens through which we continued to contemplate national priorities as Black lives hung in the balance. That embrace demands reparations.

Nothing displayed our misplaced priorities more than the wrong wars we fully invested in and the right war we ended too soon. We *chose* the Vietnam War and the War on Crime over the practical politics of the War on Poverty. By the end of the 1970s, Vietnam had ended in defeat. Prison populations increased 43 percent and turned from majority white to majority Black and Brown in the process. Due to embracing all the wrong wars, America's poor children were worse off in 1979 than they had been in 1969. Despite claiming the need for realistic politics to justify brutal policies domestically and internationally, the War on Poverty helped cut poverty in half and was the only war that showed progress in achieving its aims. And we abandoned it nonetheless. How do we make reparations for that?

The repetitive nature of America's racial history is ghastly. In the mid-1800s, the North won the Civil War, while the South won the struggle for America's heart, soul, and mind. In the 1960s, the Civil Rights Movement defeated lynching and segregation, while the segregationists—and Reagan in particular—successfully rooted white supremacy in the heart and mind of the Colorblind Age.

In 1980, with white America's self-confidence on the brink and malaise gripping the nation, Reagan began to build a long-lasting white consensus in America. In following Reagan, the nation renounced the pursuit of economic equity and racial justice that the Greatest Generation had inaugurated. Reagan's appeal in white America proved so pervasive that many in the white working class shifted their loyalty to the Republican fold. Democrats such as Bill Clinton, Joe Biden, Nancy Pelosi, and Chuck Schumer dubbed themselves "New Democrats," representing their readiness to continue the nation's business on Reagan's terms. And as both parties moved forward on Reagan's terms, America's modest commitment to economic and racial equity evaporated.

The racial crimes of the Colorblind Age were a thoroughly bipartisan affair. No legislator proved more committed to incarcerating Black people than Senator Joe Biden. In 1994, President Bill Clinton displayed the deep alignment between America's racist ideas and its public policies as he doubled down on the War on Drugs by signing the 1994 Crime Bill. The Crime Bill deepened the crisis of mass incarceration and its racial injustices and made Clinton the greatest incarcerator in chief in American history. Thanks to Clinton, thirteen-year-olds could be tried as adults while inmates seeking to better themselves would lose all access to Second Chance Pell Grants. "This is," said Senate Majority Leader George Mitchell of the crime bill, "a Democratic bill. The principal author of the bill is a Democrat. The principal supporter for this bill is a Democratic president."[6]

Yet, Clinton's racial project was not done. In 1996, fifteen years after Reagan declared that "government is not the solution to our problem; government is the problem," Clinton used the State of the Union address to declare that "the era of big government is over." Ten months later, Clinton signed into law the Personal Responsibility and Work Opportunity Act, fulfilling his campaign pledge "to end welfare as we know it." The act so drastically cut provisions to poor people that even Senator Daniel Patrick Moynihan voted against it. Nonetheless, due to the mood of the era, both measures received bipartisan support and were heralded as just the type of progressive reforms a "colorblind" nation needed. In the end, as Randall Robinson writes, "poor children were poorer under Clinton than they had been twenty years before in the age of Reagan. Their raw numbers had been expanded as well."[7]

If the Colorblind Age's posture of racial progressiveness accomplished anything, it merely made our nation more racially oblivious, and that obliviousness made our war on Black people all the more punitive. In the Colorblind Age, the symbol of America's racialized justice evolved from the lynch to an entire network of warehouses that kept Black fathers and sons, mothers and daughters in cages constructed of cement and steel. Mass incarceration devastated the lives of inmates and sent seismic waves through Black communities across America. While some Black Americans thrived, that by 2014 there would be more Black men in prison, on parole, or on probation than were enslaved in 1850 displays just how punitive our nation's progress remained. Mass incarceration demands mass reparations.[8]

As America placed Black people in prison, it preached the theory of trickle-down economics from decade to decade, promising that—at least theoretically—abundance could come to all. But poverty in Black America was never theoretical. By 1991, poverty was the third leading cause of death among Black men and the fourth leading cause of death for Black women.[9] By 2000, 176,000 people per year were dying from the devastation wrought within racially segregated communities.[10]

From the 1980s onward, economic and racial inequalities rose to ever increasing heights. "When the Constitution was written, a strange formula to determine taxes and representation declared that the Negro was 60 percent of a person," mused Martin Luther King Jr. in 1967. "Today another curious formula seems to declare he is 50 percent of a person. Of the good things in life he has approximately one-half those of whites; of the bad he has twice

those of whites."[11] Instead of the Colorblind Age bringing an end to the racial inequalities slavery and segregation had spawned, it compounded those
inequalities. As white America slowly learned to celebrate King during the
Colorblind Age, Black Americans' average wealth plummeted to 10 percent
of the wealth of their white counterparts and then further still to 5 percent,
Black dimes and nickels to white dollars.[12]

As the dreams of the Civil Rights Movement and the pursuit of the Great
Society devolved into a nightmare, the political response of Black America
and her political, intellectual, and emotional leaders sometimes varied. For
some, the nightmare seemed to contaminate the well of the soul. A few Black
idealists turned into cynics, and a few Black radicals began talking like white
conservatives. However, for all the diversity within Black America, there
remained a remarkable amount of unity and a determined defiance to the
racial politics of white backlash.

In 1972, second-term Congresswoman Shirley Chisholm became the face
of that defiance by running for president. Her campaign slogan was "Un-
bought and Unbossed," and her platform envisioned a party led by the "have-
nots" who prioritized antipoverty initiatives, exiting the Vietnam War, national health insurance, and a commitment to women's rights that included
their rightful claim to powerful cabinet positions. As Chisholm's campaign
exhibited, during the 1970s and '80s, the movement that rose when Rosa Parks
sat often became more radical and inclusive as its determination became increasingly steely. In 1984, Jesse Jackson followed suit, introducing a Rainbow
Coalition consisting of "the desperate, the damned, the disinherited, the dis-
respected, and the despised," which sought to realize an egalitarian and interracial democracy that could rise from the ashes of the Reagan Revolution.

The dark night of the soul inaugurated by the Colorblind Age brought
clarity to Black leaders, intellectuals, and artists. "Survival is not an academic
skill," Audre Lorde wrote as she envisioned a wide-ranging coalition of society's marginalized people. Survival, she continued, "is learning how to take
our differences and make them strengths. *For the master's tools will never
dismantle the master's house.*"[13] From Lorde to Manning Marable, Angela
Davis, Toni Morrison, Cornel West, and Vincent Harding, Black America
continued to strive to make America see that, in the words of Robin D. G.
Kelley, "another world was possible."[14]

At the grass roots, radical visions were stirring. On September 26, 1987,
only nine days after the House of Representatives passed the package of

reparations for Japanese Americans, the founding meeting of the National Coalition of Blacks for Reparations in America (N'COBRA) gathered. Picking up reparations' torch, N'COBRA committed "to win full Reparations for Black African Descendants residing in the United States and its territories for the genocidal war against Africans."[15] In 1989, N'COBRA's fight came to the floor of Congress through Representative John Conyers of Detroit. Conyers's bill was titled the Commission to Study and Develop Reparation Proposals for African Americans Act.

Few congressional members were better positioned to understand the urgency of reparations for Black America than Detroit's Conyers—for no city better embodied the destruction wrought by the toxic combination of America's racism and new economic direction than Motown. After racial inequality and police brutality led to a Black revolt in 1967, white flight spread like wildfire. Disinvestment followed white flight, sending Detroit's city center into rapid decay. And that was before deindustrialization. Between 1963 and 1992, three-quarters of Detroit's manufacturing jobs disappeared. As the tax base dwindled, city services paid the price—particularly the school system. While the education system was defunded and employment opportunities evaporated, crime increased. Despite the uptick in crime in the community, the most criminal aspect of Detroit was often its cops, who often doubled as drug dealers. Despite white flight making Detroit a predominately Black city, the city's police department remained 73 percent white.[16] Year by year, Detroit was dying and killing the Black people whom "colorblind" progress left behind. Proposed cures to confront Detroit's wounds rarely amounted to more than placing Band-Aids over bullet holes.[17]

As the act's title indicated, Conyers had little interest in superficial solutions. The act's vision was vast, calling for the United States

> to acknowledge the fundamental injustice, cruelty, brutality, and inhumanity of slavery in the United States and the 13 American colonies between 1619 and 1865 and to establish a commission to examine the institution of slavery, subsequent de jure and de facto racial and economic discrimination against African Americans, and the impact of these forces on living African Americans, to make recommendations to the Congress on appropriate remedies, and for other purposes.[18]

Conyers fought for the repentance, research, and strategizing necessary for public policies to make the work of racial atonement transformative. Despite Congress's having passed reparations for Japanese Americans with popular and bipartisan support, by the end of 1990, Conyers was able to secure only four cosponsors outside the Congressional Black Caucus.[19] With meaningful but rare exceptions, our nation preferred to lock Black truths in the closet and throw away the key.

Despite our nation's resistance to racial justice, Conyers's radical edge in the fight for equality never dulled. As America refused to seriously engage her racial crisis, Detroit's decay continued unabated. By 2000, the once-vibrant city ranked seventy-three out of seventy-seven cities in median income and became the most segregated metropolitan area in America. Life expectancy in parts of urban Detroit plummeted to sixteen years lower than it was in Detroit's suburbs.[20] If Detroit was the epitome of Black communal suffering in the Colorblind Age, it was in no way the exception. Horror stories traversed the nation in Black communities from East Coast to West Coast, North to South, and everywhere in between. So year after year for thirty years, Representative Conyers kept reintroducing his bill, refusing to allow white indifference to extinguish reparations' torch.

In the eyes of many commentators, the political potential of the "colorblind" worldview reached its mountaintop moment in the election of a Black president. Obama embraced Reagan's notions of American exceptionalism and carefully followed the rules of the Colorblind Age by consistently refusing to prioritize the pursuit of Black justice. Nonetheless, having a Black man in the Oval Office radicalized the game as yet another racial revolution brewed. When President Obama took the oath of office, the last racialized murders etched into mainstream white memory were of the martyrs of the Civil Rights generation: Medgar, Malcolm, and Martin. Yet, under Obama's watch, a new list of names was seared onto the public conscience: Trayvon Martin, Michael Brown, Sandra Bland, the Charleston Nine. Due to phone cameras, the list continued to increase as America began witnessing numerous murders of unarmed Black people. The list now seems endless. Yet it continues to grow.

In 2013, after Trayvon Martin's murderer was declared innocent, Black women led a movement into the street declaring that Black Lives Matter. Their truth shook our world. And that shaking was the death rattle of the Colorblind Age's racial illusions.

Enduring the radical dignity of Barack and Michelle Obama and witnessing Black people take their hurt and rage to the streets was more than many white Americans were able to bear. White America was ready to make America great all over again—even if making America great demanded reentering the most racist elements of our history and electing a leader who embodied a reckless endangerment of democracy itself. Under President Donald Trump, the very ideas of freedom and liberty continued to devolve. White privilege began being equated with a right to absolute recklessness. Somewhere between the chants of "Black Lives Matter" and "Make America Great Again," the Colorblind Age and the consensus worldview that Ronald Reagan had crafted came to an end. And there is no going back.

Truth can remain closeted for only so long. The movement that had taken Black truths out of the closet and into the streets beginning with Trayvon Martin and Michael Brown shattered historical precedents following the murders of Breonna Taylor and George Floyd. While Civil Rights era protesters numbered in the hundreds of thousands, protesters in summer 2020 are estimated to have ranged from fifteen to twenty-six million. And no longer did these protests consist almost exclusively of Black and Brown faces. "It looks, for all the world, like these protests are achieving what very few do: setting in motion a period of significant, sustained, and widespread social, political change," Stanford University sociologist Douglas McAdam told the *New York Times*. "We appear to be experiencing a social change tipping point—that is as rare in society as it is potentially consequential."[21]

As the Colorblind Age comes to an end and we search for a way forward, we must remember the power that the decisions we make today possess to shape our future. There always existed alternatives to the Reagan Revolution and the reviving of the racial mythologies of slavery and lynching in the Colorblind Age. Alternatives existed to the ideas represented in the Moynihan Report, Nixon's rhetoric of "law and order," and Reagan's quest to make America great again through wars on communism, welfare, and drugs. There was the Kerner Report and there was the politics of Ella Baker and the wisdom of Shirley Chisholm. America *chose* to reject Black wisdom and renounce a more radical pursuit of an egalitarian, interracial democracy.

In looking back, we must imagine where our nation would be if we had more wisdom. Where would our nation be if we designed our tax code to produce equity rather than enrich millionaires and billionaires, if we feared the very real kings of tax evasion more than mythical "welfare queens"? Where would our nation be if instead of creating corporate loopholes and investing in the multiplication of prisons, we aimed to create the greatest public education system in the world and provide young moms with the support they need? Where would we be if we heeded Martin Luther King Jr.'s warnings concerning the threats of racism, materialism, and militarism and adjusted our budgets accordingly? In the Colorblind Age, under the sway of our nation's racial mythologies, we often feared all the wrong things. And our racial fears marred our nation's future.

These hypothetical questions give birth to today's questions that are anything but theoretical. How can we make reparations for continually considering Black Americans acceptable civilian casualties in the pursuit of "colorblind" politics? How can we make reparations for white America's thirst for misinformation and our refusal to face the racial crimes our nation continues to perpetuate? How can we atone for our government's complicity in flooding inner-city communities with drugs and the millions of years lost from the lives of fathers and mothers, sons and daughters, in Black communities? How do we make reparations for paddy wagons becoming the Middle Passage made modern?

No one living today is completely responsible for the racial crimes of the Colorblind Age. However, *everyone* living today is responsible for how we respond to our shared past and the present realities that will continue to haunt our life together if we fail to act. Despite the heartbreaking and repetitive nature of America's racial mythologies and the crimes they inspired from the times of Thomas Jefferson to today, we are free to choose to begin writing a different future. Unbinding the American experiment from the claws of white supremacy will not be the work of one year, one decade, perhaps not even one lifetime. But as Black America has continually reminded our nation, *a different world is possible* when we embrace the work and sacrifice an interracial and egalitarian democracy demands.

From shackles, to lynchings, to the Colorblind Age of prisons and poverty, Black America demanded our nation take responsibility for our racial crimes, knowing that freedom is inseparable from responsibility. Today, the name of that responsibility is reparations. If our *choices* after slavery led to the age of lynching and our *choices* after the age of lynching led to the Colorblind Age of prisons and poverty, we *must now* make choices that lead to a Reparative Age. Will the Colorblind Age give way to an age of democratic repair? Or will the next age continue our nation's journey on the path to self-destruction? The answer to that question is in how we respond to the racial crimes of our nation's past and present. And it is to imagining how racial healing can replace America's repetitive racial crimes that we now turn.

IV

Remaking America

Reparations and a Reparative Age

No matter what we are going to do, unless we have reparations, we will never be able to do anything.

—Queen Mother Audley Moore, Philadelphia, 1968

Not everything is lost. Responsibility cannot be lost, it can only be abdicated. If one refuses abdication, one begins again.

—James Baldwin, *Just Above My Head*, 1979

13

Birthing Pains

> All around us worlds are dying and new worlds are being born;
> all around us life is dying and life is being born . . . when worlds
> crash and dreams whiten to ash. The birth of a child—life's most
> dramatic answer to death—this is the growing edge incarnate.
> Look well to the growing edge!
>
> —Howard Thurman, *The Growing Edge*, 1956

IN *REBIRTH OF A NATION*, we have witnessed the persistent war against Black America throughout America's history. From slavery's shackles to segregation's lynchings to the growth of Black prisons and poverty in the Colorblind Age, that war never ended. As the Colorblind Age comes to an agonizing end, we stand together at another inflection point in American history. A new racial age is emerging that offers a remarkable opportunity for our nation to be reborn by engaging in the work necessary to pull an antiracist future out of a remarkably racist past.

Personally, this journey together was born out of a debt to a community in Houston's Fifth Ward, where I lived and worked for nearly twenty years. In the Fifth Ward, a Black community opened their arms to my family and me, and in their embrace, we discovered a new world and way of life. Though we were strangers when we met, our lives were already tied together through the invisible bonds of a past that binds Black and white America to each other. Over the years, relationships reforged our bond and blurred the line between friend and kin. One day at a time, impersonal Black statistics became particular people and families, became the Johnsons, Robertses, and Combses. Intimacy replaced indifference.

But *Rebirth of a Nation* was also driven by my commitment to traumatized white Americans. For many white Americans, the decade of publicized Black death and the radicalization of politics under President Donald J. Trump introduced a season of personal crisis and brought an end to cherished illusions about ourselves and the nation we love. For those of us awakened from our self-deception, attempts to deny, downplay, or dodge proved salt water for the thirsty. Instead, the crisis quickened a desire for a deeper understanding of how our society became so sick and what we can do about it. *Rebirth of a Nation* was born from that thirst.

Times of crisis offer a remarkable opportunity to be remade—both as individuals and as a society. It is, of course, only when we know that we are deeply sick that we are prepared to embrace the risks that healing requires. Today, an estimated 21 percent of white Americans support reparations. Others are curious. Many are very resistant.[1] But for anyone ready to wrestle with our nation's obligations, I want to write in a way that helps increase our social and historical awareness so that moral clarity can cut through our moral fog and better position us to participate in an age committed to reparations. *Rebirth of a Nation* is *not* an intellectual exercise. It is instead part of a movement determined to atone for our racial nightmare through the work of reparations and solidarity with the struggle for Black justice and national renewal.

In *Rebirth of a Nation,* we have seen how moments of history that are pregnant with possibility often birth new forms of white supremacy. That cycle creates doubt that a new way of life is possible. Where is the hope that the emerging racial age can disentangle our national experiment from white supremacy's grasp?

In the days of Emmett Till, a generation of Black people arose and forced mainstream white America to see our nation's life together through the lens of Black suffering. Today, we have again witnessed acts of racial brutality we will never unsee, and now similar movements for Black freedom are crisscrossing our nation. Due to the work of organizations like the Black Lives Matter movement and Mothers of the Movement, due to the protests arising from the murders of Breonna Taylor, George Floyd, and Ahmaud Arbery, a new consciousness is percolating with the potential to transform America's political possibilities.

For white people, hope is found when we refuse to unsee and unfeel Black suffering; hope is found when what we witness challenges and changes the racial loyalties we inherited. The possibility of transformation always depends on how the witnesses of injustice respond—and our nation is responding. Once upon a time, solidarity with Black justice demanded that white abolitionists help shatter slavery's chains. Later, that solidarity demanded joining the work to overthrow Jim Crow's laws and rituals. Today, that solidarity demands participating in the creative minority laboring to realize reparations and bring about the birth of a Reparative Age.

The rumblings of a Reparative Age began June 19, 2019, as Congresswoman Sheila Jackson Lee of Houston's Fifth Ward invited our nation to stand in solidarity with the pursuit of Black justice by holding the first-ever congressional hearing on reparations for the descendants of the formerly enslaved. If the hearing represented a turning point in a long struggle for reparations, it also demonstrated our nation's deeply entrenched resistance to Black justice. That resistance demands we honestly face the objections to reparations. Not all objections are created equal. Some objections might be sincere. But that morning, most objections simply repeated the arguments that once justified slavery and segregation.

On that Juneteenth morning, the best summary of the objections to reparations came in the opening remarks by an up-and-coming political power broker, the future House Speaker Mike Johnson of Louisiana. Before he was named by the *New York Times* "the most important architect of the Electoral College objections" for his lawyerly and nuanced attempt to upend the 2020 presidential election,[2] Johnson's public face was that of neither an angry radical nor a cold cynic. Instead, Congressman Johnson effectively styled himself as the loving father next door. He is a conservative who took the time to give Ta-Nehisi Coates's work on reparations an appreciative reading. He positioned himself as desiring to hold a candid conversation. But from his introduction to his conclusion that morning, Congressman Johnson displayed just how difficult an open and honest conversation can be in a nation whose political imagination is so thoroughly warped by racial myths.

In Congressman Johnson's remarks, rather than representing reparations as a transformative opportunity to pursue justice through a reparative *process* of redress for *the continual history* of racial policies, reparations was reduced to a one-time payment to the descendants of the enslaved *exclusively* for the sin of slavery. Like the falling of neatly aligned dominoes, after this insufficient framing, Congressman Johnson laid out a series of objections that are now familiar:

> Putting aside the injustice of monetary reparations from current taxpayers for the sins of Americans from many generations ago . . . the fair distribution

would be nearly impossible once one considers the complexity of the American struggle to abolish slavery. . . . Tens of millions of today's non-African-Americans . . . arrived after slavery ended . . . [and] only a small percentage [of white Americans] were slave owners. For these reasons and many others, such an approach has been widely unpopular.[3]

Congressman Johnson never explained why monetary compensation for crimes with momentous monetary consequences represented an injustice or exactly when America's anti-Black crimes ceased. Instead, within two minutes, his argument was running at a sprinter's pace toward a dispiriting and predetermined conclusion.

Despite his haste, not all his statements were false. Johnson was correct that financial justice is complicated. So too was landing on the moon, but despite the complexity, we created the political will to pursue space travel. Complexity never absolves justice's demands, and, thankfully, due to the tireless efforts of reparations advocates, much of the due diligence to navigate the complexities has been accomplished.[4]

Congressman Johnson was correct that reparations are unpopular. But so was ending slavery and ending segregation. Committed abolitionists and civil rights advocates were never the popular majority. They were the creative minority. He was also correct that only a small minority of white Americans held slaves. But instead of slavery and anti-Black crimes incriminating the few and providing innocence to the many, these crimes received popular and religious support as well as every judicial, legislative, and executive blessing America could offer. That support and those blessings made the entire nation accomplices in slavery's crimes against Black Americans.[5]

It is also historically true, as Johnson pointed out, that many non-Black Americans today came from the waves of immigrants flowing to America in the years following the Civil War. But even though these nonwhite Americans were not present for and did not participate in slavery's crimes, anyone who is engrafted into the citizenship of a nation bears both the blessing and the responsibilities of that nation's complex history. Though America offered immigrants rich opportunities, it never offered them communion with an innocent nation.

At a deeper level, immigrant innocence is often an illusion because slavery was the beginning, not the ending, of the nation's anti-Black crimes. In these crimes, post–Civil War immigrants were often eager participants. Throughout our nation's history, *no* immigrant group consistently stood in solidarity with Black America, for no group desired to be a target of our nation's racial wrath. And this truth makes both European and non-European immigrants complicit in the nation's racial crimes. That complicity demands reparations, and this is why reparations are about the crimes of us as a people, not the crimes of individual persons.[6]

Running uphill in the wrong direction, Congressman Johnson pressed his opposition from additional angles, claiming that reparations distracted "from the persistent causes of racial disparities" that reside "in social and cultural dynamics which are negatively influenced by well-intended governmental policies." His linking of Black suffering to Black "social and cultural" pathologies echoed the racial convictions of enslavers like Thomas Jefferson, eugenicists like Madison Grant, committed liberals like Daniel Patrick Moynihan, and committed conservatives like Charles Murray. Rather than crafting new insights, Congressman Johnson's remarks remind us of the long history of racist ideas that justified white supremacy for four hundred years.

As he continued, Congressman Johnson employed his personal experiences to paint his vision of racial right and wrong as radiating from an inclusive and humanitarian heart. He narrated how he and his wife came to love a Black teenage boy and claimed to have adopted him.[7] Revealing an intimate portrait of his family life proved an emotional moment for the congressman. But, tragically, it also displayed a toxic level of obliviousness. The congressman viewed his relationship to racism according to his good deeds rather than his support for public policies that deepen Black suffering. Loving particular Black *people* while embracing public policies that perpetuate Black suffering is a historical hallmark of white supremacy. The irony is that even though Congressman Johnson loved a young Black man as a son, he was adamantly opposed to public policies that would remediate the poverty that leads so many Black children to be separated from loving but impoverished Black families. Like many white Americans, he failed to fathom the price Black children pay for white congressmen's refusal to support robust public policies that support Black families and ease Black suffering.

As Congressman Johnson continued, he highlighted the obstacles to reparations. He raised constitutional objections and the Supreme Court's previous rulings that seemed antithetical to reparations. He highlighted the lack of consensus and predicted white backlash. He said he thought it naive to think that reparations would give birth to a racial utopia. Yet, what Congressman Johnson failed to comprehend was that it is precisely these realities of racial animosity and racist laws that demand reparation and yearn for repair. The aim for reparations is justice, not consensus. Rather than utopia, reparations simply aim to bring the promises of the Constitution's preamble—"to form a more perfect Union, establish Justice, ensure domestic Tranquility . . ."—to bear on *all* Americans for the first time in our nation's history.

For whatever facts Congressman Johnson marshalled, as he continued, his rationality was increasingly poisoned by the racial fantasy that positioned white people as earning their wealth and Black people as simply refusing to work their way out of poverty. Congressman Johnson presented racial inequalities in terms of a footrace. How should Black people catch up? Work hard while white people sleep. Save Black dimes while white America rakes in white dollars. For Congressman Johnson, Black dignity could be found only by burning the midnight oil. Of course, the reality that wealthy white people make more money while sleeping than Black people make while working the night shift makes Congressman Johnson's formula for racial equity a moral monstrosity and mathematical impossibility. Rubbing salt in Black wounds, Johnson quoted King and spoke of a Black tradition of self-reliance that included Frederick Douglass, Booker T. Washington, and W. E. B. Du Bois as if his wisdom harmonized with the wisdom of the radical Black tradition rather than with the racist logics of enslavers and segregationists.

As we saw in Part III, when Japanese Americans received reparations, the nation spoke of her commitment to the Constitution and the moral clarity that the nation "can never fully right the wrongs of the past. But we can take a clear stand for justice." Yet when Congressman Johnson imagined Black reparations, he trembled at the "risks [of] communicating . . . a worldview that says external forces from a century and a half ago are directing the fate of Black Americans today." Despite his inclusive posture, the only power Congressman Johnson's racialized imagination could conceive of reparations possessing was incentivizing Black sloth and dependence.

As Congressman Johnson came to a close, it was clear he desired to distance himself from the racism of the nation's past. In fact, despite his detailed objections to reparations, he failed to mention how enmeshed his personal history is with our nation's worst racial instincts. He never mentioned how his family fought for the Confederacy and enslaved approximately twenty people, or how his Southern Baptist community of faith originated to protect the religious leadership of enslavers.[8] He never mentioned how lethal his state of Louisiana was for Black people; when it comes to lynchings, it hosted over five hundred, with his county ranking the third highest in the nation.[9] Congressman Johnson also never mentioned how his high school became infamous in 1992 for continuing to hold segregated reunions despite being founded after integration.[10] Rather than publicly and penitently detailing his inheritance, Congressman Johnson attempted to bury it.

Yet despite his work to distance himself from his haunted history, his comments simply reiterated the same worldview that had produced the racial terror of previous generations. Once again, Black justice was pitted against white rights. Once again, Black America was imagined as constructing its own barriers to self-reliance and racial equality. Throughout his presentation, Congressman Johnson failed to acknowledge his own responsibility in the present moment and how a failure to stand with Black justice today sends the sins of the past into the future. In this failure and in his basic arguments to delegitimize reparations, Congressman Johnson stands within a white American multitude.

On June 19, 2019, an invitation to join the work to realize reparations was extended, and a white man claiming a Black son rejected it.

⸻

If there is legitimate disappointment at the stark resistance to reparations within the white American multitude, there is little surprise. But the good news is that from California to New York, and from corporations to colleges to cities everywhere in between, the efforts to make a serious conversation about reparations impossible has failed. As we move to envisioning how a process of reparations will lead to our nation's rebirth, we will investigate the practical next steps in the work of healing our nation from the inside out by using three interdependent frameworks. First, the process of reparations and rebirth begins by constructing a moral framework for reparations through the soul work of *repentance*. It is repentance that makes personal and political transformation inevitable. Second, the financial framework of *repayment* involves identifying how we viably close the racial wealth gap at an individual level. Lastly, is the continual and ongoing public policy work to *repair* our nation by reimagining American society and reinvesting in Black communities. Through such a process, we can welcome in a Reparative Age that remakes America into a land of liberty and justice for *all*.

Over and over, what deeply investigating reparations makes clear is that the costly work of reparations is as pragmatic as it is redemptive and restorative. After exploring the process of reparations and the resources available to bring them about, the question is not if racial justice and socioeconomic equality in America are *possible*. The question is if they are *desired*. The question is if we believe deeply enough in our national possibilities to do the work and make the investments necessary to inaugurate a Reparative Age. As we examine the process of reparations, we begin with the most difficult and determinative aspect: repentance.

14

Repentance

> We must search ourselves to find how we have been guilty, not
> for the sake of wallowing in our guilt but for the sake of facing
> the fact that the future of our culture, of our country, does not
> depend so much on what black people do as it does depend on
> what white people do. This is a hard lesson. That the choice as to
> whether or not we will rid the country of racism is a choice that
> white America has to make.
>
> —Ella Baker, Southern Conference Education Fund,
> April 24, 1968

REBIRTH BEGINS IN REPENTANCE. And repentance returns us to where we
began, in the funeral parlor that holds the open caskets of American history.
The greatest challenge in the work of reparations has little to do with dollars
and everything to do with finding the courage to confront the truth and
trauma of our history and society. Repentance demands that, as a people, we
find the courage to vulnerably and penitently face the guilt and endure the
grief of becoming intimate with the realities from which we wanted to hide.
Repentance begins the work of becoming a people and society who not only
atone for our past crimes but also ensure our crimes and the crimes of our
forebears never repeat themselves in the future. *Repentance is the soul work
required to re-create our society.* Soul work hurts. But those unable to experience guilt and grief cannot grow. Those unable to mourn cannot mature.
It is through repentance that a new conscience and consciousness is forged
and new political possibilities are born.

In talking of repentance and the centrality of guilt, grief, and confession,
I am not recommending wallowing in white shame and self-hate. Instead,
I am talking about something much more costly. I am talking about the pro-
cess of facing our current moment with integrity, grace, and fortitude. I am

talking about the readiness to enter a refiner's fire that transforms the people we are and the society we are becoming.

My work in seriously considering the role of repentance in reparations began through a conversation with Patty Combs from Houston's Fifth Ward. She is one of the least sentimental people I know. She suffers no fools. Her grandfather was a white doctor with families on both sides of the train tracks in her family's Louisiana hometown. The family on the white side of the tracks her grandfather claimed as his own, and he wrapped them in wealth and comfort. The family on the Black side of the tracks he abandoned, and they struggled to survive. She is now the grandmother of an exceptionally gifted family. But they failed to beat the odds. Due to America's racialized systems of family protective services, housing, education, and employment, intergenerational poverty is an unbroken chain in her family just as strong today as it was when her white grandfather left them on the altar of a pitiless world.

Grandma Combs's intimacy with the depth of Black suffering placed her at the top of my list of interviews regarding reparations. During our time together, I asked her what national repentance would mean to her. The response I anticipated was: "White people can keep their apologies." Instead of this, the very mood of our conversation grew more earnest. There was a focused silence followed by a radical vulnerability born of years of silent suffering. After taking a deep pause, Grandma Combs confessed: "It would mean a lot, Joel. It would mean a lot." Somewhere deep inside, Grandma Combs seemed convinced that until our nation repented of the crimes we committed against her and her ancestors, our nation stood ready to commit those same crimes against her children, grandchildren, and generations yet unborn. In that conviction, Grandma Combs reprioritized my thinking concerning the centrality of repentance in the work of reparations.

In time, I learned that Grandma Combs was not unique in insisting on the centrality of repentance in reparations. Black America always understood that Black people were dying of a national disease. And that national disease resided in how the virus of white supremacy infected white minds and morality. Black people paid for the sickness of our nation's soul with their very lives. In the Black Freedom Movement, Black suffering was never reduced to a commodity to be purchased. At the very heart of the reparations movement was the work of repentance to open the door to national renewal. This is true not only of faith-based reparations advocates like the Rev. Dr. Martin Luther King and Malcolm X but also of Black radicals like David Walker, Queen Mother Audley Moore, James Baldwin, and Ta-Nehisi Coates. For Coates, a committed atheist, the nation's spiritual renewal is perhaps the most important aspect of reparations work.

As we examine the work of repentance, the framework I will employ is shaped by the Jewish tradition, which is centered on accountability for the violator and the dignity of the violated. In the Jewish tradition, guilt for past misdeeds must be experienced and confessions within a communal context made to the party that has been wronged. To receive forgiveness for such sins, atonement to the offended must be made for the crimes committed, and the crimes must never be repeated. The process offers no do-overs for repeat offenders. To think seriously about the role of repentance within reparations requires more than imagining how we confess communal guilt for past crimes. We must imagine how we can politically repent in such a way as to prevent our nation's recidivism into white supremacy's bondage. We must imagine how we can politically repent in such a way that makes us new people unable to recommit the crimes of the past.

As we move forward to imagine repentance in America, I will examine three critical ingredients at both the personal and public levels. The first ingredient of repentance we will analyze is the need to break the intergenerational curse of white supremacy by *rooting our national self-understanding in our past and present treatment of our most vulnerable people.* Second, repentance will require non-Black people to begin *learning from and creating relationships within Black-led spaces and institutions.* Intimacy is the most powerful antidote to indifference and the most powerful ingredient for personal reformation. This personal work prepares the ground for the final ingredient: *penitent politics.* Penitent politics intentionally works to empower a robust and united democracy by rooting repentance in the very rhythms of American life.

The repentance of antiracists is often deeply personal before it becomes politically powerful. In our nation, repentance has proven to possess the potential to be revolution in utero. The birthing pains of racial revolution begin as personal repentance takes on political power. As will be discussed, this process has happened to varying degrees in our history and is currently underway across our nation. The challenge before us is to widen and deepen these movements of repentance to transform our collective consciousness and national memory and move us toward a deeper interracial and egalitarian democracy. Because once a context is created that moves repentance from our nation's margins to the core of our national consciousness, a context is created to transform political possibilities and give birth to a Reparative Age.

Our Intergenerational Curse and Rewriting National Identity

Throughout our nation's history, we enslaved, lynched, imprisoned, and impoverished Black people. There is no telling what our nation will do next. Yet, neither the 135 million years Black people paid with their lives for the crime of slavery, nor the more than 10 million Black Americans devoured by convict leasing schemes, nor the intentionally crafted public policies that drove millions of Black people into prisons and entrapped even more in poverty were the worst aspects of our nation's racial crimes. White Americans desired to frame the nation's racial violence as inevitable, as if no crime had occurred and no guilt had accrued. And thus the greatest aspect of our crime resided in our attempt to make repentance impossible by rooting our very identity in an illusionary innocence and exceptionalism. Our failure as a nation to repent ensured we would repeat our racial crimes and that white supremacy would metastasize into an intergenerational cancer. And the only way to break this cycle is to fundamentally rewrite our nation's identity and self-understanding.

Our racial crisis today and our inability to repent as a nation are inseparable from a popular version of history that attempts to bury the sins of the past. By refusing to deal with the realities of our racial past, we lose the ability to understand the present and lack the tools to navigate our nation's racial and social injustices with wisdom and grace. However, we are learning that though history may be written by national apologists who erase our nation's crimes against Black people, national crimes leave national wounds. And no amount of denial will make these wounds disappear. For whatever else is possible with our history—from burying its truths to denying its relevancy—it can never be unlived.

To create a context that makes repentance possible and begin tending to our nation's racial, mental, and moral wounds, we must learn to more truthfully tell our story in relationship to our most oppressed people. This demands a readiness to engage with the perspectives and wisdom of Black writers, activists, artists, and intellectuals. It is not that Black wisdom and perspectives can provide our nation with a perfect self-understanding free from human error. But Black writers, activists, artists, and intellectuals can provide a *perfecting* perspective that illuminates our national wounds and provides a context in which to tend to those wounds by making repentance possible.[1]

It must be said that in a nation that often takes our oaths on Bibles, we should know that more penitent approaches to the stories that shape our self-understanding are possible. According to the Hebrew Scriptures, we dare not forget the sins of the past, because oppressed people know that when it comes to national crimes, forgetting is always the first step toward repetition. There is a reason why Jews worked to make the world aware of the sins of Kings David and Solomon while Americans hid the crimes of Presidents George Washington and Thomas Jefferson. By using history as an opportunity to learn from their forefathers' sins, Jews sought to create a community that would not be condemned to repeat their transgressions. From a penitential perspective, communal amnesia is a communal crime. For the United States, it is the perspectives of communities like the Fifth Ward and survivors like Grandma Combs that provide the potential to form citizens for whom human equality is not merely a heralded ideology but also a formative conviction.

Thankfully, a more repentant perspective of our history and society is already leaving an indelible mark on our nation. As Black writers play an increasingly prominent role in shaping historical and social consciousness, they are combating American amnesia and opening the door for repentance by telling history from the perspective of the persecuted. Debates now rage across the country about how history should be told. Participants in these debates range from professional historians to state legislatures and educational boardrooms, resulting in bans on any honest telling of history that might trouble white consciences.

Perhaps the most notable backlash of professional historians occurred when five prominent historians—including Princeton University's James McPherson and Brown University's Gordon Wood—authored an open letter insisting on corrections to The 1619 Project in a manner that called the very veracity of the project into question. Yet, since The 1619 Project is rooted in rigorous research and historically valid interpretations, the letter's outcry seems to amount to little more than the conviction that radical Black people should not be trusted as credible interpreters of fundamental aspects of our nation's history—from the reasons for the American Revolution to the Constitution's relationship to slavery to the Great Emancipator's relationship to Black America.[2] Though unstated, the white historians seemed to understand that if the historical interpretations of Black radicals were taken seriously, so too would be their recommendations for politically tending to the nation's travesties.

Likewise, in the movement to ban critical race theory and more accurate accounts of history from schools across the nation, what infuriated white parents and politicians seem to demand is that we hide the inconvenient truth that at the very heart of the American story are people who are not white and whose stories matter. Implicit in this movement and explicit in the legislation is the demand that white people's history should cause neither grief nor mourning nor feeling Black Americans' pain as our own.[3]

By seeking to make repentance impossible, legislation that bans critical race theory provides a perfect educational blueprint to pass our society's racial atrocities forward to the next generation. Such work represents the highest crime against a child's mind, spirit, and imagination and threatens to rob the next generation of precious pieces of their humanity that many white parents and politicians lost not so long ago.

There is, of course, nothing easy in examining the trauma of our history and society in a manner that facilitates repentance. Our history and society are living, breathing realities intertwined with our identity, inheritance, and family. The furor in the debate about our history is a testament to our fears regarding the cost of confessing that white identity is neither innocent nor nonviolent. It is to confess that those who loved us the most often raised us on half-truths and whole lies.

If we begin confessing the violence we have long denied, if we speak of the centrality of slavery's terror to the founding of our nation, of how America's anti-Black propaganda and public policies helped inspire the Nazis' genocidal quest, of how we allowed the War on Crime and War on Drugs to dismember Black and Brown communities, where does it stop? Race never existed as an isolated island in American history but at intersections that implicated every aspect of our life together. Learning to tell our history through the stories of the oppressed will demand a serious mental, social, economic, and ethical reconstruction. For many white people, that is simply too high a price to pay for healing. So white minds close and hearts harden to realities we believe we cannot bear.

In watching the white backlash to The 1619 Project and the efforts to prevent our education system from confronting the trauma of our racial past, it is easy to dismiss the possibility of national repentance. That despair is understandable. Yet, transformation never overtook a nation through mainstream modes of transportation. It came from those ready to sacrifice for hopes that were deemed impossible and those ready to live by convictions that existed only in the wilderness of public opinion. It came from radical abolitionists who were deemed enemies of the state. It came from civil rights advocates who believed their lives were not too high a price to pay to realize liberty and justice for all. When public schools refuse to teach the truths of history and the halls of power refuse to help facilitate the work of repentance, this is nothing new. That refusal simply requires repentant white people to seek other means of education and unsanctioned modes of repentance.

And this is happening. The silver lining in these ominous times is that more white people are learning to repent and seek a new way forward. From Trayvon Martin and Michael Brown to the Charleston Nine and Sandra Bland to Breonna Taylor and George Floyd, we have witnessed acts of racial violence that many white people will never be able to unsee. In a way previously unexperienced in our nation's history, an increasing number of white people appear ready to repent and begin learning how to live out the creed of human equality. In a real way, the legislative movement to ban critical race theory from schools is an acknowledgment that repentance with the potential to transform our nation's political possibilities—the type of repentance we have long needed and consistently rejected—is again at our doorstep.

And this readiness to repent has landed at a time rich in resources as white Americans welcome the words and wisdom of Black America in a manner utterly unique in our nation's history. A cover article Ibram X. Kendi wrote for *Time* magazine refers to the remarkable constellation of Black talent in America today as the "Black Renaissance." Black artists, writers, and intellectuals are simply the best in the business—and that is wonderful news for our nation. Through Black art, film has become a powerful weapon in the work of repentance. Marvel's *Black Panther* broke new ground, providing Black excellence a worldwide platform. Barry Jenkins's miniseries *The Underground Railroad* brings to life the fight for freedom during the days of slavery. The documentaries *I Am Not Your Negro* and *King in the Wilderness* bring viewers into James Baldwin's and Martin Luther King's struggle to survive Jim Crow and its aftermath. Other documentaries such as *13th*, *Crack*, and *LA 92* detail the racial crimes against Black people and communities during the Colorblind Age through the testimony of leading Black historians and activists. These movies not only move their audience but also shake the very foundations of our nation's racial narratives, creating spaces in which we can imagine new ways forward.

Simultaneous to the remarkable work of Black artists is the emergence of a legion of remarkably gifted Black writers and intellectuals who empower their readers to see the world and analyze our nation's racial crisis through their brilliance. Local bookstores make it clear that from leading intellectuals to popular writers, Black people have grabbed the mic and gained an audience to a degree previously unexperienced in American history. Isabel

Wilkerson, Jesmyn Ward, and Carol Anderson. Keisha N. Blain and Kellie Carter Jackson. Dorothy Roberts, Khalil Gibran Muhammad, Jelani Cobb, and Hanif Abdurraqib. This list represents an abundance of Black brilliance, and it is only a small sampling of the Black talent writing and working today. Thanks to the labors of remarkable Black Americans and their diverse allies, the question is not whether our nation has access to the necessary tools to begin the work of repentance. The question is whether we are ready to begin using the resources at our disposal in the work to save our nation from our self-inflicted wounds.

As we begin the work of repentance and rewriting our nation's identity, we must start imagining life after we have healed from the toxic illusions of innocence and exceptionalism. And what we may imagine on the other side of the death of our illusions is the world's first interracial and antiracist democracy.

Black Space: Building Transformative Alliances

How can white learning be more than an intellectual exercise? How can repentance's work within white people run deeper than showing up to a protest, burying one's nose in the right Black books, or streaming Black movies? We must reach deeper than what Hanif Abdurraqib refers to as "liberal performance for point scoring."[4] There are no straight lines or linear progress as repentance begins transforming people and societies. But there are invitations that must be received and open doors into Black communities that white people can find the courage to walk through. Repentance is fundamentally *relational work*. In the work of repentance, no one needs to walk alone. Reimagining white life requires immersive experiences in Black organizations and institutions. Building relationships through such community engagement is a critical ingredient in the work of repentance. Segregation was intentionally designed to make the relational intimacy necessary to upend white supremacy's reign nearly impossible to imagine, let alone foster. Yet, for repentance to deepen, white people must begin intentionally puncturing their white bubbles and begin learning from within Black spaces. Not all Black institutions or communities are eager to open their doors to white participation. Black havens can and should be protected. But when Black institutions welcome interracial participation, a space is created to incubate new ways forward guided by Black understanding and experience.

Predominately Black institutions, organizations, and communities provide life to Black philosophies and wisdom forged in the struggle to survive and thrive against all odds. At their best, Black spaces provide buffers against nihilism and despair by fostering what Cornel West refers to as a "Black love" strong enough to survive a world that often seems loveless and where "hope is a joke." Rarely racially exclusive enclaves, Black institutions often welcome interracial alliances and solidarity when they are grounded in Black leadership, dignity, and equality. "Anytime you talk about Black love, Black freedom, Black history," West reminds us, "there has always been vanilla brothers and sisters who have thoroughly immersed themselves into Black history, Black sensibilities. Black love is always all-embracing."[5] For mainstream white people accustomed to communities where individualism, self-interest, and white people reign, Black institutions provide ever present reminders across our nation that a different world is possible.

For white Christians, repentance demands participation in Black spiritual communities to free their faith formation from the clutches of white supremacy. Within the context of Black sacred spaces, Scripture's familiar stories land on white ears with a new ring and white Christians are forced to explore new dimensions of their faith. Within these spaces, white Christians are called to remember that Jesus's favorite passages of Hebrew Scripture are all about justice for the oppressed and good news for the poor. It was Jesus who echoed Leviticus's command that we are to make reparations to neighbors before requesting forgiveness from God.[6] In white spaces, sacred texts centered on justice are often strangled by racial commitments that dull their prophetic edge. In Black spaces, these same texts often provide the very backbone of religious life.

In Black churches, Scripture's command to love our neighbor as ourself sounds more earthly than spiritual. Zacchaeus's repaying the debts of his crimes comes across as essential rather than coincidental. The good Samaritan's refusal to pass by on the far side of the street takes on a more troubling relevance. Christian convictions about societal sins, Jesus's solidarity with the persecuted, and the believer's calling to work for the flourishing of their city develop a present-tense urgency unattainable in white havens.

Black sacred spaces open a new world in an ancient faith for those whose Christianity has been nurtured in white sanctuaries. Within this new world, white Christians must wrestle anew with weightier understandings of what repentance actually looks like and reengage the depths of Christian witness through the works of Augustine, Aquinas, and Calvin and the ancient Christian dictum that "without restitution, no remission."[7]

Within this new world, white Christians draw one step closer to seeing the possibilities of repentance through the eyes of Harriet Tubman, Ida B. Wells, and Martin Luther King Jr. In such a context, white people can more fully receive Rabbi Danya Ruttenberg's wisdom that "the work of repentance, all the way through, is the work of transformation. It's the work of facing down false stories and engaging with painful reality."[8] But if repentance is about facing the painful stories of our past that we longed to ignore, it is also about creating new stories and possibilities in the here and now that we can proudly pass forward to our children.

In addition to Black communities of faith is the essential work of Black nonprofits and communities of activism. Across America, Black nonprofits are transforming local landscapes to give voice to the voiceless and hope to those our nation desired to leave behind. Through Black activists in the Black Lives Matter Movement, more white people are embracing the invitation to be activated for racial justice's cause by standing in solidarity with their Black neighbors. A full 95 percent of Black Lives Matter protests during the 2020 racial reckoning occurred in counties that were majority white.[9] Black political organizers and leaders like William Barber II and Stacey Abrams are translating our moment in history into a movement that deepens Black political power and tends to our democratic wounds in real time. If virulent white backlash is one side of the coin in today's political context, the other side of that coin is that white participation in the fight for Black justice and political power has rarely, if ever, been more widespread.

For white parents, communal repentance transforms family decisions ranging from where to live to where to send children to school, which sports leagues to join, and which after-school programs to select. Within a family context and the rhythms of the daily grind, we learn the relational depths that distinguish professional diversity initiatives from a way of life that fosters diverse intimacies. It is a context of diverse intimacies that empowers white parents to better tend to the wounds of their racial inheritance and learn how to raise children better equipped to continue the work of building communities shaped by peace and justice.

For young adults, repentance may mean night classes at a local HBCU, where classes provide a rigorous challenge to white rationality. Historically, HBCUs provided an alternative ecosystem for nurturing the minds of both Black leaders and white allies. For white professionals, repentance means engaging in organizations ranging from the National Urban League to local African American chambers of commerce that fight for new ways of doing business in which Black people and communities are empowered to thrive. When white people develop connections on Black turf, unique relationships are fostered capable of confronting white worldviews with Black perspectives that reveal that alternatives to white domination were available to us all along. That revelation empowers repentance and modes of life in which we exchange the fear of our neighbor for the risks inherent in building the beloved community. Though such vulnerability and interracial intimacies are never far from danger, in the beauty and brokenness of the work of fostering these relationships, antiracist paths that we so desperately need are forged.

For me, it was through immersive experiences in Black churches, Black nonprofits, Black media, and HBCUs that repentance was made possible and my life was transformed and enriched. In these spaces I was provided with the opportunity to rethink my life and convictions and how to use the gifts entrusted to my care. I was immersed in an environment that demanded I consider our nation's great brokenness *and* her bewildering possibilities. Rather than administering tests regarding my ideological purity, the question Black organizations posed was whether I was ready to follow Black leadership and use my time and talent in the fight for Black education, health, housing, and justice. Though now much of my work is with words, words cannot express how these experiences reoriented my world.

And I am not alone. Within Black spaces, I worked with white friends of all kinds whose experiences echoed my own. Within the context of Black communities and organizations, I learned from white academics who committed their careers to serving Black and Brown communities. Their commitment sharpened their work as it reoriented their lives. I witnessed real estate developers begin working for aims higher than profits after glimpsing a deeper vision of community and realizing their talents could help create neighborhoods for Black people of all income levels to thrive. I watched white lawyers recenter their practices to fight for racial and economic justice even though such fights pay little and cost much. I watched gifted business leaders commit their skill sets to building equitable companies instead of simply repeating the patterns of the past. And I worked with gifted white students who immersed themselves in the life of Black communities in a manner that changed the very trajectory of their lives and careers. In each case, the depth of personal and professional transformation was directly related to the depth of antiracist intimacies they fostered. These lives testify that the way things are is not the way things have to be. These lives testify that miracles happen. They happen every day.

Black institutions and opportunities for interracial intimacies provide a path for non-Black people to wade deeper into the healing waters of repentance. It was through interracial alliances that the work of repentance began shattering slavery's chains. It was through Black churches that interracial networks were forged that brought Jim Crow's reign to an end. The work of social revolution is not the work of singular superheroes. It is instead the work of entire communities and networks of unlikely allies who embrace the price to transform the vision and hopes entrusted to their care from the fantasies of the few into the future all will share.

The Power of Penitent Politics

As repentance remakes people, it tills the ground for a more penitent form of politics. When it comes to race in America, repentance always demands a political response. And just as we can see societal repentance beginning as white people become more willing to learn from Black Americans, so too we are seeing repentance take on political power. Until recently, white leaders were unified under the bipartisan illusion of national innocence. In the 2013 words of Democrat Samantha Power: "America is the greatest country in the world, and we have nothing to apologize for."[10] Until recently, the thinnest of logic justified indifference to racial inequality. Why shouldn't we pursue reparations? To answer this question with the words of Republican senator Mitch McConnell, who descends from enslavers: the Civil War, civil rights, and "we elected a Black president."[11] But repentance is beginning to shatter these points of consensus, and the upending of white consensus provides the possibility of a humbler approach to our power.

America's crimes against her own citizens demand politicians ready to lead a national commitment to repentance. We need leaders unafraid to face their complicity in deepening our nation's racial wounds. We need politicians who understand that the colors at the root of our racial inequalities are not Black and Brown but red, white, and blue; who understand what must change is *not* pathological Black people but our nation's pathological racial politics and practices. Courageous and penitent leadership is needed to begin righting our nation's racial wrongs and tending to our racial wounds. We require leadership that moves from confession of our crimes to creating a context for repentance to bring about a redemptive reckoning. At the threat of repetition, penitence is not impotence—it is instead where the power to renew our nation resides.

It was in 2009 that the Senate issued its first confession to the crime of slavery by passing *Apologizing for Slavery and the Segregation of African Americans* by unanimous consent. Though the resolution took one step in the right direction, it carried with it a disclaimer clarifying that the apology in no way implied support for reparations. That disclaimer provided the political context that ensured the apology was limited to a one-time act that excluded the work of atonement. In essence, the Senate-approved apology stopped just short of where the work of repentance begins. Such apologies, Angelique Davis writes, "covertly thwart reparations or other racial justice for [B]lack Americans while providing the illusion of substantive racial progress. . . . They give the appearance of recognizing the harm while doing nothing to repair it."[12]

What has become clear is that repentance requires more. Our racial crimes were more than individual acts. They were brutal rituals born out of earnest racial convictions repeated from one generation to the next. These racist rituals were politically empowered and protected. They organized our communities, North and South, and provided the rhythms for the entire American way of life. Thus, the work of repentance must also be politically empowered, protected, and intertwined with our daily rhythms and routines.

We can learn from religious traditions and use the yearly calendar to craft what Black historian Stephen G. Hall refers to as a "calendar of remembrance."[13] In some ways, our national calendar already contains the beginnings necessary to start the work of political repentance. We already have a Martin Luther King Jr. Day. It is time we remember him more accurately. We already have a Black History Month. It is time we expand our remembrances of Black history beyond the notable accomplishments of exceptional Black people to include everyday Black folks' noble struggle to survive in a remarkably racist nation.

Unsurprisingly, the work to expand our calendar and collective memory is already underway in Black-led spaces like the Equal Justice Initiative, which launched a *History of Racial Injustice Calendar*. Such work needs political empowerment at local, state, and federal levels. In Louisiana, the Opelousas Massacre of September 28, 1868—in which over 150 Black Americans and white Americans supporting them were murdered and a blueprint was provided that led to the overthrow of interracial democracy across the South—

demands its spot on local, state, and national calendars. In New York, July 11 to 16 deserve annual commemoration to ensure remembrance of the New York Draft Riots of 1863, in which Black people were fed to the flames and Black babies were thrown to the ground from windows four stories high. In Washington, DC, June 28 marks the collapse of the Freedman's Bank in 1874 due to the corruption of white board members. Memorializing this tragedy in the very city shaping our future can help make us more cognizant of the concrete ways in which our nation pillaged Black people to build its wealth even after slavery's fall.

We need not only dates from the distant past, for across our nation, there is a racialized crime for every month in our current historical era. On January 30, 2020, William H. Green was murdered *after* being handcuffed by Maryland police. February 26 should be Trayvon Martin Day in Florida. March 13—Breonna Taylor Day in Kentucky. On April 21, 2021, Idaho became the first state to ban critical race theory, setting off a movement across the nation seeking to secure white supremacy for the next generation. May 25—George Floyd Day in Minnesota. On June 25, 2013, the Supreme Court deemed in *Shelby County v. Holder* that the voting protections of the Voting Rights Act of 1965 were unconstitutional due to the declining significance of racism. In the same month only two years later, Dylann Roof murdered nine Black people who welcomed him into their Bible study at Mother Emanuel AME in Charleston, South Carolina. July 13—Sandra Bland Day in Texas. August 9—Michael Brown Day in Missouri. Botham Jean was murdered in his apartment in Dallas, Texas, on September 6, 2018. On October 6, 2009, Keith Bardwell, a justice of the peace in Louisiana, refused to perform an interracial marriage. On November 2, 2004, Alabama voters rejected the removal of segregation and poll taxes from their state constitution. December 22—Andre Hill Day in Ohio. From Tanisha Anderson to Akai Gurley and Samuel DuBose, every province within our nation has racial crimes worthy of their place on a calendar. Like Martin Luther King Jr. Day, local acts of remembrance may lead to national memorial as well. This is one way we keep the caskets of our racial crimes open, and it is through the pain of such remembrances that we slowly develop the conscience and consciousness capable of imagining a new way forward.

However, we need political power that does more than rewrite our calendars. We need political support to multiply the memorials like the Equal

Justice Initiative's National Memorial for Peace and Justice dedicated to the Black Americans we enslaved, lynched, segregated, and incarcerated. How can we memorialize the accounts contained in the Ku Klux Klan Report of 1871 and what we ignored or failed to implement in the Kerner Report of 1968 and the Kerry Report of 1988? Surely, we need more museums like the National Museum of African American History and Culture on the Mall in Washington, DC. How do we memorialize the racial crimes of the FBI and their harassment of civil rights workers beginning during the Red Scare and running through their assaults on the Black Panthers? We must declassify the CIA files that deal with the agency's complicity in heroin and cocaine trafficking to understand the depth of the agency's role in the destruction of Black people and communities across America.

We need more tours like the Enslaved People of Mount Vernon Tour and the Slavery at Monticello Tour that refine our understandings of our Founding Fathers. We need the work of the Hidden History Tours of New Orleans and Take 'Em Down NOLA that helps us reengage our cities' complicity in human bondage and racial violence.[14] Such memorials, museums, and tours not only empower mourning and grief; they also begin shaping our physical landscape in a way that cries out to our nation the true character of white supremacy's reign. Increasing such remembrances and memorialization marks the beginning of creating a political atmosphere and moral imagination that move American politics in a more penitent and antiracist direction.

To deepen this work, there are international road maps and over forty truth-and-healing commissions worldwide that offer us practical and courageous next steps.[15] Perhaps the two most prominent examples of nations that displayed the courage to confront the horrific crimes white supremacy inspired in their lands are South Africa and Germany. In different ways and with different degrees of success, these nations walked the path of repentance toward a fundamentally different future. And there are lessons to be gleaned from both their successes and their shortcomings.

After the fall of apartheid in South Africa, the nation transitioned to a free and interracial democracy and developed a process of dealing with their traumatizing history in a way that created room for repentance through the Truth and Reconciliation Commission. From 1995 to 2002, the commission provided public space for testimonies from the nation's victims and perpetrators of gross human rights violations. The report from the Truth and Reconciliation Commission deals profoundly with the complexities of repentance, reparations, and restoration in a nation devastated by the crimes of the terroristic apartheid regime.

Page after page, the report details the questions South Africa was forced to face. How do we reconstruct our society after the very infrastructure of our life together has been deemed a crime? How do we create a morally responsible society after such monstrous crimes against humanity? How do we think about restorative justice amid the wounds left behind by systemically engineered suffering? How can wrestling with our criminal history ensure such atrocities are never repeated? "In short," the report reads, "what is required is a moral and spiritual renaissance capable of transforming moral indifference, denial, paralyzing guilt and unacknowledged shame into personal and social responsibility."[16] In the United States, this work is precisely the role repentance plays in the process of reparations. The lessons of South Africa provide touchstones for critically thinking about how repentance and reparations can help give birth to an antiracist conscience and consciousness.

In Germany, the process of repentance was much more secular. The reckoning began with the Nuremberg trials, but it proved a long road between reckoning and repentance. Just as in the Southern states of the US following the Civil War, Germans following World War II often imagined themselves as the greatest victims of the war and proved unwilling to confront the shame of being both the "loser and perpetrator."[17] In 1950, a survey found that only 5 percent of West Germans felt "guilty" for the nation's crimes against the Jewish people and only 29 percent believed West Germany owed restitution for their crimes. As Alexandra Senfft, the granddaughter of a Nazi war criminal, wrote:

> As a rule, the older generation studiously avoided a dialog with younger people. Instead, they romanticized, denied, and maintained a steely silence. That did not, however, remove all traces of guilt and shame; rather it transferred these feelings, verbally or non-verbally, to the emotional worlds of their children and grandchildren.[18]

Nonetheless, in 1952, the work of financial reparations began. In the 1960s, the work to mend a deeply broken society expanded as the grandchildren of the Nazis undertook the responsibility of repentance, ended their society's hallowed silence, and sought to make right crimes they themselves had not committed. In what was referred to as "working off the past," families whose forebears were either active or complicit in the Nazi regime's crimes began "the long march" to create "a spate of institutionalized atonement ceremonies."[19] Along with ceremonies, the art and academic communities got involved to rectify Germany's self-understanding about the atrocities their families committed on German soils and throughout Europe. Repentant Germans understood that it was only by taking such magnanimous responsibility for the sins of their forebears that a future worthy of their children could be built.

By the 1980s, the acts of public repentance, academic labor, and artistic expression matured into a political paradigm shift. On May 8, 1985, the fortieth anniversary of World War II's end, President Richard von Weizsäcker declared that the end of the war also represented liberation for Germany from "the inhumanity and tyranny of the National-Socialist regime."[20] Weizsäcker's speech celebrating the end of the Nazi regime represented a new epoch in Germany. As the decade wore on, it became untenable for Germans in Germany to paint themselves as the victims of the war. The reunification of East and West Germany only intensified national efforts to work off the past. West Germany followed East Germany's lead in spreading memorials throughout the nation. In 1990, article 2 of Germany's reunification treaty carried with it a continuation of the reparations program in the form of monthly payments of €580 from Germany to victims of the Holocaust.[21] As the grandchildren of Nazis began working off the crimes of their past, they began writing a fundamentally new future for Germany's children. No utopia was born in Germany. But reparations and repentance transformed a nation of Nazis into one of the world's primary examples of the power of penitent politics.[22]

When we think about what penitent politics can look like in America and how to create a context that deepens the work of repentance, we should remember that penitent politics is not about perfect solutions. Penitent politics is about the art of creating new political possibilities, about creating a context to reforge a racist past into a reparative future. Penitent politics is what the work of democracy is all about—a never-ending journey toward a more perfect union.

To face history with integrity, what white people must remember is that intertwined with our tragic history is a white antiracist tradition that stood in solidarity with the Black Freedom Movement. When this happened, our nation witnessed the power that is unleashed when the thirst for human rights leads people to repent. Such repentance provided sparks that helped set our nation ablaze. In our history, when white antiracists stood in solidarity with the Black Freedom Movement, the possibilities of an interracial and egalitarian democracy burned brightly. Despite our repeated failure to travel fully through the purifying fires, the flame of antiracist possibility still burns. Our nation lives at a crossroads where we must choose between embracing the refiner's fire or resigning ourselves to perpetuating acts of racial terrorism against our own people.

Throughout American history, the Black Freedom Movement and the white antiracist tradition helped bring the sparks of repentance to America's doorstep. And wherever there are sparks of a redemptive revolution, there is the potential to fan those sparks into a movement with the force of a wildfire. Of this, our history itself bears witness. Against all odds, in the age of the shackle, a committed minority of white radicals developed the courage to repent and listen to Black truths. Through repentance, illusions of innocence and callous indifference to Black suffering gave way to solidarity, engrafting white radicals into the struggle for Black freedom.

A white preacher named Lyman Beecher instilled antislavery convictions that radicalized his children Harriet and Henry. Harriet Beecher Stowe wrote *Uncle Tom's Cabin*, setting the nation ablaze. Henry Beecher provided rifles—known as "Beecher's bibles"—to ensure the fire would not be snuffed out. Raised by a single mother, William Lloyd Garrison lived with a price on his head and was beaten to a pulp for his commitment to bringing slavery to an end. That price tag and those beatings only deepened his resolve to spread freedom's fire. "I am in earnest," wrote Garrison as he began his costly journey in 1831. "I will not equivocate. I will not excuse. I will not retreat a single inch. I will be heard."[23] And he was.

Yet, the most revered white antiracist of the 1800s was named neither Garrison nor Beecher but Brown. W. E. B. Du Bois referred to John Brown as "the man who of all Americans has perhaps come nearest to touching the real souls of Black folk."[24] Brown widened freedom's fire by moving the strategy of arming freed people from the realms of the theoretical to the pragmatic at Harpers Ferry. In recalling Brown's self-sacrifice, Frederick Douglass brought the full power of his oratorical brilliance to bear: "His zeal for my race . . . was as the burning sun . . . stretched away to the boundless shores of eternity. I could live for the slave, but he could die for them." For Douglass, Brown represented nothing less than "the force of a moral earthquake."[25] Eventually Brown's sacrifice culminated in Abraham Lincoln arming Black people in the Union army to fight for both their own freedom and the perfection of our nation. The more Lincoln moved toward the strategy and politics of John Brown, the closer our nation moved toward its opportunity for a new birth of freedom.

Many of the most committed abolitionists, like Lucretia Mott, came from white family lines long committed to Black freedom. Other radicals, like Sarah and Angelina Grimke, came from slaveholding families. Leading radical abolitionist Wendell Phillips hailed from the aristocrats' most elite echelon. Others were middle-class. Some were raised in impoverished and broken homes. None embodied antiracist ideological perfection. Many left deep wounds on their Black colleagues. But despite their shortcomings and failures, what they held in common was a readiness to repent and use their talents, resources, and very lives in the fight for Black justice.

As personal convictions translated into political power, the commitment of abolitionists provided a meaningful momentum in the struggle to eradicate chattel slavery. Upon their work, the political careers of Thaddeus Stevens and Charles Sumner were founded. Stevens and Sumner represent perhaps the most antiracist white politicians the nation has ever known and opened the door to an even deeper yet still unfinished racial revolution.

It seems impossible, but white antiracists emerged in the era of lynching as well when radical white allies' desire for justice outweighed their need for innocence. Repentant and courageous white radicals gave their very lives to cut down the lynching trees and tear down the walls of segregation. In 1915, the Rev. A. J. Muste helped create the Fellowship of Reconciliation, leading him to serve alongside the transformative Black leaders Bayard Rustin and James Farmer and work in solidarity with the Black Freedom Movement. His most notable gift to the movement would be his helping bring Gandhian nonviolent direct action to the Civil Rights Movement. "The current emphasis on nonviolent direct action in the race relations field," claimed Martin Luther King, "is due more to A. J. than to anyone else in the country."[26]

Andrew Goodman and Michael Schwerner were Jewish activists who proved ready to die alongside James Chaney for the cause of Black justice. Viola Liuzzo was raised in dire poverty but clawed her way out and secured the comfort of a middle-class family life. Yet, rather than resting in white comfort, she joined the NAACP and later headed south. The price she paid for Black freedom was her very life. At the heart of the work of King's Southern Christian Leadership Conference was Jewish businessman and lawyer Stanley Levison, who was a close friend and adviser to King. "Stan Levison was one of the closest friends Martin King and I ever had," confessed Andrew Young upon Levison's death. "Of all the unknown supporters of the civil rights movement, he was perhaps the most important."[27] When Bob Zellner traced his family roots, they led directly to the Ku Klux Klan. Nonetheless, through the Student Nonviolent Coordinating Committee, Zellner joined forces with Ella Baker, Stokely Carmichael, Diane Nash, and Bob Moses in the struggle to realize a more antiracist nation in the belly of the beast, the

Mississippi Delta. These white antiracists came from different walks of life and possessed different ideological convictions, but what tied their lives together was repentance and their readiness to sacrifice their lives to play a role in killing Jim Crow.

In *All about Love,* as bell hooks argues for white people's ability to change, she writes that her convictions were forged by history's flames, from John Brown's bullets, to A. J. Muste's Gandhian nonviolence, to the self-sacrifice of scores of known and unknown white allies. And as she examines these diverse white allies, she sees a common thread: "What made these individuals exceptional was not that they were any smarter or kinder than their neighbors." There was something else that was essential. "They were willing to live the truth of their values."[28] Expanding the ability to embody the truths our nation has long declared is precisely what the work of repentance and reparations is all about.

A racial reckoning is brewing, and we will face it one way or the other. The question is not whether the debt will be paid, but how and by whom. Like previous generations, we can choose to reentrench our racial wounds and continue down the path of self-destruction. Or we can get to work. And if we do decide to risk getting off the path of self-destruction and lean fully into reparations and repentance as a way forward, that means we must address repayment. For reasons both symbolic and substantive, reparations without repayment is as meaningless as repentance without atonement. It is to repayment we now turn.

15

Repayment

> A monetary sum and words alone cannot restore lost years or erase painful memories; neither can they fully convey our Nation's resolve to rectify injustice and to uphold the rights of individuals. We can never fully right the wrongs of the past. But we can take a clear stand for justice.
>
> —President George H. W. Bush, "Letter of Reparations to Japanese Americans," October 1990

REPAYMENT DEEPENS THE WORK OF REPENTANCE through the work of atonement by monetary means and acts as a downpayment for a Reparative Age. Repayment is essential to prevent white supremacy's evolution. Until we stand ready to pay for our racial crimes, we stand ready to repeat them.

There is a story in the Talmud about a stolen beam around which a beautiful building was built. Two rabbis argue about how the thief should make atonement. Could the thief pay for the stolen beam? Or should the entire structure the thief designed be destroyed by forcing the thief to take down the beam and return it to its rightful owner? When the rabbis confer, they argue that mercy provides the best path into the future and recommend allowing the building to stand and for the thief to return the value of the beam as the next step in his rehabilitation. In the Talmud, repayment *replaces* vengeance in meeting justice's demands.[1]

The ideology of white supremacy and the crimes of slavery—the theft of human dignity, family, life, and labor—acted as a primary supporting beam upon which the American experiment was built. Similar to the rabbis, when Black Americans looked at what justice itself demanded from a nation founded on racial brutality, many called for Black America to be paid for what had been stolen. With rare exceptions, Black Americans refused the path of vengeance and the call for national destruction. Today, we must understand repayment for what it is: a merciful way to tend to our nation's self-inflicted wounds.

If beginning the work of repentance is the most difficult aspect of reparations, repayment represents the most practical and straightforward task in the process. Yet, despite the clear case for reparations, it is precisely the step many deem the most impossible.

Why is repayment often considered impossible? Unsurprisingly, the reason is not predominately monetary.[2] Rather than rehashing an analysis that ties resistance to reparations to white supremacy, we can instead display why the determinative obstacle toward making reparative repayments to Black America is *not* monetary in nature. If we decide to take the call for racial justice seriously, the path to reparations has been made clear, and most of the numbers needed to implement repayment to Black America have been calculated. Neither the path to repayment nor the calculations are overly complex. Perhaps the best book-length analysis of the financial calculations for reparations is *From Here to Equality* by William A. Darity Jr. and A. Kirsten Mullen. The authors argue that since reparations is more likely to fail without broad popular support, establishing the framework for reparations should begin in Congress.[3]

In measuring the monetary value Congress should aim to allocate for reparations, *From Here to Equality* analyzes various measurements, including uncompensated labor and the economic value of the enslaved. Though both metrics provide rough estimates of the economic damage incurred via slavery, the authors believe the better measurement for monetary reparations is simpler still. For Darity and Mullen, the best measure for reparations is simply *"the racial wealth gap . . . the most robust indicator of the cumulative economic effects of white supremacy in the United States."*[4] What is important to note up front—and for my argument moving forward—is that the racial wealth gap addresses inequalities at a family level, not structural and institutional inequalities that create fundamentally different worlds between neighboring Black and white communities.

Today, the wealth gap between white and Black America stands at $841,900 per household, or $357,000 per individual. This represents a current repayment figure estimated at $14.3 trillion.[5] Remediating the racial wealth gap requires investing more than chump change—the gap represents a little more than 55 percent of the GDP in 2022. This sum represents a real-world financial price tag for four hundred years of racial oppression.[6]

But is it financially doable? The answer is yes. And there is more than one way to go about it.[7] Most advocates for reparations believe repayments will need to stretch out over a decade, meaning payments of roughly $35,000 per year distributed directly to Black Americans and held in trusts for young Black Americans until they come of age. One way this repayment would transform Black lives is by simply providing a household income on par with white income for a decade. We must remember that since Black Americans make on average 74¢ of income for every white dollar, the difference in median income between white and Black families stands at nearly $30,000 per year.[8] In addition to bringing Black household income in line with white household income, Black children would also be provided the economic cushion that is now too often limited to white children.

And there are significant collateral benefits to financially buttressing Black families. Research indicates that "if racial gaps for Blacks had been closed 20 years ago, U.S. GDP could have benefitted by an estimated $16 trillion."[9] In the future, investments that enrich Black Americans will continue to enrich our nation as well, as such investments are predicted to lead to an estimated 4 to 6 percent boost in overall economic growth.[10] In short, repayment can be engineered into an economic a win-win.

Darity and Mullen envision multiple ways to finance this investment.[11] But it is no coincidence that as a nation undergoes a racial reckoning, the groundwork has been laid for the greatest transfer of wealth in recorded history as the boomer generation prepares to pass off $68 to $84 trillion to the next generation among overwhelmingly white families.[12] That wealth crystallizes the magnitude of the financial plunder during the Colorblind Age, as white baby boomers and their children intentionally chose a political path that concentrated wealth in white hands even as Black poverty and destitution grew increasingly dire. As detailed in Part III, that accumulation was made possible by the public policies of the United States that provided the largest tax loopholes and the least responsibility to the most affluent among us.

In a land that deprived millions of Black people of equitable education, housing, and health care, the radical accumulation of white wealth was never a victimless crime. And we stand at a point in history where the most feasible way of righting this historical wrong is to return inheritance taxes on the wealthiest families to their pre-Reagan levels. Such a tax level could help fund reparations while providing resources for additional economic and environmental justice investments.

If we take an inheritance tax seriously as a path toward reparations, we need to wrestle with the rights of wealthy white children that we so rarely discuss in detail. For the children of multimillionaires, can $1, $2, $3 million be sufficient inheritance and a taxing plan of 50, 60, 70 percent afterward be acceptable? For the children of billionaires, can $999 million in inheritance be an acceptable ceiling? If $999 million is an insufficient inheritance, what would a sufficient inheritance for the children of multibillionaires look like?

We must remember that between 1942 and 1976, our maximum inheritance tax was 77 percent, the estate tax exemption was a mere $60,000 in 1970, and the highest income tax was 91 percent from 1944 to 1963. During this era, our economy grew stronger as it grew more equitable. As inheritance taxes along with income and corporate tax rates began to nosedive under Reagan, racial inequality began to skyrocket. As of this writing, inheritance taxes are nearly nonexistent for estates below $27 million and a modest 40 percent on any additional wealth. These policy choices are driving reasons why the wealth of the average white family is now ten to twenty times the wealth of the average Black family.[13]

With these practicalities in mind, I desire to highlight two points. First, when we set the case for adjusting the inheritance tax code to empower reparations and foster equity next to the case of wealthy white families for protecting our current tax structure that concentrates wealth in a few families, reparations and equity have a much more compelling case. Though the most compelling case has been on the losing side for the last forty years, what history teaches us is that that can change. Doubling our inheritance tax and radically reducing the estate tax exemption is not only possible, but it is very similar to the tax code that reigned for forty years. At the threat of repetition, that tax code strengthened our economy while creating a more equitable nation.

Second, we must understand that those driving the resistance about what our nation cannot afford are often precisely the people protecting fortunes beyond our ability to fathom. Feigning economic powerlessness has been the staple propaganda technique for protecting the wealthiest families throughout our nation's history. To combat that misinformation, practical questions of what the children of the wealthy are entitled to are the kinds of questions we must wrestle with as a society if we ever desire to begin mending our racial and economic divisions. Adjusting the inheritance tax structure to fund the work of racial and economic justice would in no way disempower parents from financially providing for future generations, nor would it penalize thrift. But it would disincentivize the radical accumulation of wealth that threatens the economic viability of children and families across our nation.

Third, a simple picture to encapsulate the enormity of the economic injustice that exists in the relationship between Black poverty and America's wealthiest white families: When the Black wealth of a city is in keeping with national averages, white billionaires possess more wealth than the city's entire Black citizenship. This is true not only in smaller cities like Omaha, home to billionaire Warren Buffett, but also for the four largest cities in the United States—New York, Chicago, Los Angeles, and Houston. For instance, in Houston, the six richest billionaires are each likely much wealthier than the cumulative wealth of the city's 590,000 Black residents.[14] This reality is a mathematical and moral monstrosity that is the result of explicit engineering at local, state, and federal levels. This monstrosity is symptomatic of the crimes of the boomer and millennial generations, who pretended that political and economic policies that concentrated wealth in the fewest hands was a victimless crime. The best remediation to this inequitable engineering is an inheritance tax that funds racial and economic equity in general and reparation repayments to Black families in particular.

Examining the intersection of race, wealth, and public policy shows once again how white wealthy people and Black poor people are often treated as two fundamentally different species of humanity. For the wealthy, who are predominately white, radical wages and wealth were justified to incentivize work. But for disproportionately poor Black people, menial wages and scarce public assistance were justified to prevent sloth. The need to incentivize the work of the predominately white and wealthy and prevent the sloth of the disproportionately Black and poor displays how the political rationalizations linking work, rewards, and public assistance were filtered through racial lenses that corrupted our common sense. Such corruption is not easily overcome, but one of the greatest gifts reparations can provide is cleansing us of the deeply ingrained convictions that privilege the wealthy and punish the poor.

Since racialized inequality was intentionally designed, it is not an injustice that can ever be undone without enacting an equally specific plan for equity. The best first step at achieving the racial equity so long denied is a death tax that corrects how a broken tax system empowered an unjust accumulation of wealth over a lifetime. Such a tax would protect the majority of white families and *all* families who are poor and middle-class. In the past, conservative opponents mounted a successful campaign against inheritance taxes precisely by dubbing it a "death tax" and arguing that it represented double taxation. Though I love the term "death tax," the notion that it is an unjust, double tax on rich children is absurd for two reasons. First, the radical accumulation of wealth is the result of a refusal to insist that wealthy people pay a proportionate amount of our nation's tax burden for the past forty years. Second, there is simply no injustice in demanding that the children of wealth reinvest in the nation that made their fortunes possible. If the opposition's reasoning was as solid as their rhetoric, a meaningful conversation would be possible. But it is precisely meaningful conversations that those who argue for unmitigated concentrations of wealth seek to avoid.

If taxing the rich and providing for the poor is simple in concept, it can be complex in execution in a globalized world where nations compete to act as havens for the vast fortunes of the wealthy. And this is true of inheritance taxes that include entire portfolios of nonmonetary assets such as family companies, land, and art. But just because the work is complex doesn't mean there are not improvements we can execute to make our system more equitable and sufficiently fund reparations and other urgent social and environmental investments. From the global solutions of Thomas Piketty of the London School of Economics and Gabriel Zucman at the University of California at Berkeley to the domestic vision cast by Emory University's Dorothy Brown's book *The Whiteness of Wealth*, there are ways to radically and effectively make our system more equitable.

Perfection may be beyond our reach, but a just system is not. Currently, the tax structure is designed at a systemic level to reward inequitable policies throughout our economy, while at an individual level our system incentivizes the radical accumulation of wealth well beyond the ability of any family to use for numerous generations. Using the fight for racial justice as a clarion call to begin shifting our tax structures to empower economic equity and disincentivize the concentration of wealth is one way that reparations can lead to a more equitable flourishing throughout our nation.

But do reparations—and my proposal about inheritance taxes in particular—represent class warfare? This concern was raised as I lunched with a beloved white colleague who had given multiple decades of his life to fight for Black justice and who embodied the principle of following Black leadership better than any other white person I know. He had given significant thought to reparations and seemed to share my previous instinctual resistance to both the principles at play and the practicality of being able to execute so grand a vision.

The concern that simmered beneath the surface of our conversation was the threat of dehumanizing white people, and wealthy white people in particular. His focused engagement in a Black community only deepened his commitment to respect the human dignity and rights of all people. Targeted taxes felt, to my friend, like class warfare. Knowing that it was safe to be passionate, he demanded, "Are you suggesting robbing children of the inheritance they are rightfully due?" I said no. He scoffed: "You suggest taking trillions from white families, and you are robbing no one?"

With his gloves off, it was time to take my guard down. In this work, I am learning that the best conversations with friends occur only when together we risk a brutal vulnerability. So rather than sharing the history of our broken tax code, I shared what I had learned from those I love.

Some of the greatest blessings in my life have come through experiencing rich and personal relationships with Americans from all walks of life. This is true of people who are very, very wealthy and white, to people who are very, very poor and Black, and others all along the spectrum in between. And what I learned through these relationships is that people across our nation's demographic spectrum share the same human passions of love, loneliness, and fear. Every demographic is capable of amazing compassion and courage as well as callousness and cruelty.

Through these relationships, I have seen how wealth provides protection from a wide spectrum of suffering and grief. But I have also witnessed first-hand how wealth failed to protect people I love from some of the greatest pain this life offers. It is not rare that the problems and pain of wealthy white people and their families are at the very top of my prayer list. The problems common to humanity—problems from which neither race nor wealth offer haven—are fully worthy of our compassion.

I know what it is to be white and still not be able to meet modest monthly bills. I know what it is to be white and wealthy. And I know what it is to be white and hurt. But despite what I know about the realities facing people at different income levels, I learned something by living all my adult life in poor Black and Brown communities and working nearly as long for economically marginalized Black organizations. And what I have learned is that Black suffering in America is unique and anything but universal.

Regardless of how intimate with pain I become, I will never experience the particularity of Black suffering. The particularity I will never know is living in a society that attempts to rob me of the dignity of my humanity beginning the moment I am born. The particularity I will never experience is playing a rigged game in which I must be twice as good to gain half as much. The particularity I will never know is being blamed for my own predicament when I prove human rather than exceptional.

I do not know the fear Black parents experience as they attempt to raise kids in a racist world. I do not know the fear involved in raising children whom cops instinctually fear instead of instinctually protect. I do not know what it is like to send my child to school fearing the school will attempt to bury their talent rather than unleash it. I will never know what it is like to try to make a marriage work within a nation that systematically fails families like mine. Being Black in a racist world is an altogether different predicament than the problems that are common to all humanity.

After confessing to my friend that many people I love are very wealthy and sharing what I have witnessed living and working in poor Black and Brown communities, I confided with him one last conviction born of experience: "I know inheriting millions and billions in wealth will not heal wealthy people's wounds." I paused. "It is my hope that redirecting that wealth toward racial and economic justice can begin to help heal our nation and position Black families and poor people in our nation to more fully thrive." My friend listened patiently and was able to empathize with my experiences with the understanding of someone who lived and worked within the racial divides of our fractured nation. A just and progressive tax system does not represent class warfare. It represents what the love of a nation and moral integrity can look like in a nation as wealthy, beautiful, and broken as our own.

My conversation with my friend failed to construct a consensus on the best path forward. Yet it seemed to us the type of conversation from which a new future could be built. So we left lunch and went back to work.

When it comes to making monetary recompense to Black America, the question is not whether it is possible. It is. To not understand that multiple paths are possible to make reparations is to not understand the enormity of American wealth. The question is not whether monetary compensation is politically possible in a nation still enmeshed in white supremacy. It is not. The question is how to begin blurring the line between impossibility and possibility and then between possibility and inevitability.

If history can lead us to despair, it also can frighten us with the truth that the line between the impossible, possible, and inevitable can prove more permeable than we dare to imagine. And that reality endows us with the responsibility to fight and sacrifice for acts of justice that we have been told are impossible. That reality provides the imperative to grab shovels and attack mountains we have been told will never move. That reality means we are never simply spectators of this world's realities but participants capable of carving out a more just path into the future.

In James Baldwin's *The Fire Next Time*, he writes:

I know that what I am asking is impossible. But in our time, as in every time, the impossible is the least that one can demand—and one is, after all, emboldened by the spectacle of history in general, and American Negro history in particular, for it testifies to nothing less than the perpetual achievement of the impossible.[15]

Can white Americans committed to racial justice embrace the imperative to fight for the impossible? The truth we seem slow to learn is that when the terms "justice" and "impossible" collide, what is revealed is not the laws of nature but the narrow prison cells in which our minds operate and our reticence to embrace radical and redemptive change. What is revealed is that our imaginations need liberation and that our deepest hopes must call forth our deepest resolve.

I am not seeking to undersell the difficult struggle to achieve repayment or to paint integrity with a simplistic brush. I understand repayment and integrity are impossible without repentance. Both are the work of a lifetime and will remain unfinished business for my generation. Nor am I seeking to oversell the payment of reparations to Black Americans as either the cure-all that alone heals Black communities or the silver bullet that slays white supremacy. The racial injustices of our nation—the robbing of dignity, the raping of generations of women, the rituals of terror—can never be fully righted by monetary reparations. But monetary reparations will help eliminate that which it is designed to eliminate: the racial wealth gap at an individual and family level. Monetary reparations will provide an economic foundation from which Black people can begin building a new future and lead our nation into a Reparative Age.

If rebirth begins in repentance, new life begins in repayment. It is time to begin again—it is time for repair.

16

Repair

> The reparations movement must aim at undoing the damage where that damage has been most severe and where the history of race in America has left its most telling evidence. . . . The reparations movement must, therefore, focus on the poorest of the poor. It must finance social recovery for the bottom-stuck.
>
> —Charles J. Ogletree Jr.,
> "Litigating the Legacy of Slavery," 2002

"AN OLD WORLD IS DYING, and a new one, kicking in the belly of its mother, time, announces that it is ready to be born." Looking into the future, James Baldwin continued: "This birth will not be easy and many of us are doomed to discover that we are exceedingly clumsy midwives. No matter, so long as we accept that our responsibility is to the newborn: the acceptance of responsibility contains the key to the necessarily evolving skill."[1] In a very real way, repayment represents the day of the new national life Baldwin envisioned so long ago. But as Baldwin knew, rebirth brings the responsibility to attend to a newborn nation and the work to ensure that a Reparative Age does not allow recidivism back into white supremacy. This is the work of repair, of reimagining American society and reinvesting in Black communities.

If repayment addresses the racial wealth gap that is a festering wound infecting the whole body of our nation, repair deals with American society as a whole and the places where the pain and pus of America's racist ways concentrate in impoverished Black communities. To speak of reparations and a new life for our nation and not look at additional ways of addressing the country's systemic dysfunctions and the festering wounds within Black communities is simply to hope that our deepest racial wounds will heal themselves once Black families have a little money in their pockets. In a society like ours, that hope might prove naive. Erasing the racial wealth gap will not heal all the wounds inflicted through racialized practices of our education, employment, housing, criminal justice, health care, and child welfare systems.

To create a Reparative Age demands we repair our life together by thinking about reparations in communal, societal, and institutional terms as well. In the history of reparations, this is not a novel idea. Black advocates for reparations have long demanded that in addition to payments to Black families, we think about reparations in terms of the long game and invest in structural, institutional, and communal transformation.[2] When we come to repair, we enter ongoing activism and the long-game policy work that requires creativity, imagination, and social depth perception to eradicate elements of white supremacy interwoven into the fabric of our nation. Without repairing the machinery—the founding documents, public policies, institutions, and information systems—that concentrates poverty in under-resourced Black spaces, the justice of individual reparations can still be made subservient to white supremacy's deeper and more systemic forms.

To get a sense of how systemic racism formed two different white and Black worlds, we can look at snapshots that compare impoverished Black communities to the cities in which they reside.

Today, Congresswoman Sheila Jackson Lee of Houston's Fifth Ward is the sponsor of reparations legislation before Congress. Houston is not Detroit's mirror image, but the family resemblance is eerie. In 2011, a report produced by the Fifth Ward Community Redevelopment Corporation in partnership with Rice University revealed the community's scar-filled truths. Most households survive on less than $25,000 a year, and most adults over twenty-four had less than a high school education. By 2011, the Fifth Ward was no longer the Wild West the Geto Boys rapped about. But community residents were still three times more likely than the average Houstonian to die from a firearm-related death while being 2.5 times less likely to have health insurance to provide for their care if their wounds were less than lethal.[3] All of this in a city where there is a twenty-year difference in life expectancy between zip codes.[4] Houston, a city with many billionaires and many more millionaires, a city where governmental dollars launched a white man to the moon, continues to deny far too many of its Black children an equitable education, Black parents a living-wage job, and Black families a healthy and affordable place to live. These crimes are not merely the symptoms of the city's racial wealth gap. Instead, they represent how systemic racism is woven into the DNA of America's most diverse city.

At a community level, Houston's racial inequalities are tragic. They are traumatic. But they are typical. When George Floyd left Houston for Minneapolis–St. Paul, he exchanged one city of racial nightmares for another. In Minneapolis–St. Paul, the median income of majority-white neighborhoods was twice that of majority-Black neighborhoods.[5] In cities across America, the average life expectancy differential between majority-white neighborhoods and majority-Black neighborhoods is a full seven years. In Omaha, that differential is ten years. Life differentials between a predominately white neighborhood in Chicago and a predominately Black neighborhood is thirty years. Across America, different zip codes often represent fundamentally different universes within the same city.[6]

Though these community snapshots are stark, they are certainly not surprising. Between 1970 and 2010, the concentration of poverty became an increasingly dire threat to communities across America. The number of people living in poor neighborhoods doubled while the number of impoverished neighborhoods tripled.[7] These realities are precisely the outcomes the Kerner Commission warned against over fifty years ago. And just as Kerner demanded fifty years ago that we attack white racism at systemic, institutional, and communal levels under the umbrella of the War on Poverty, so too we must repair our racial divisions and democracy by seeking holistic, radical, and systemic solutions under the umbrella of reparations and the work of a Reparative Age.

As we seek to transform our nation's politics, we must remember that the primary reason America's social systems never produced equitable results is that from our founding documents to our current public policies, racial justice and economic equity were rarely explicit aims. Our Constitution never aimed for racial or economic equity. It was designed to ensure the opposite.[8] The policies that guide economic policy, public education, health care, and criminal justice rarely aim for racial equity. In practice, they often ensure the opposite. This means we must change the very aims of our public policies and community institutions. This means, in the words of Ella Baker once again, that

for poor and oppressed people to become a part of a society that is meaningful, the system under which we now exist has to be radically changed. This means we are going to have to learn to think in radical terms. I use the term radical in its original meaning—getting down to and understanding the root cause. It means facing a system that does not lend itself to your needs and devising means by which you change the system.[9]

The crucial long-term work of repair is this work to radically recalibrate the very aims of a democracy that refuses to help the people it breaks.

There are many aspects of our democracy that need to be repaired to ensure an antiracist future. From the federal to the local level, we must radically reevaluate our guiding principles and rethink the very purpose of our politics and public institutions. This is the work of a generation and not an election cycle. Since a comprehensive evaluation of repairs is beyond the scope of this brief chapter, I will simply provide snapshots of the possibilities we can imagine in a Reparative Age as well as realistic ways these investments can be financed. For our purposes, I will focus on three spheres of systemic and communal influence that need repair and what we can do. They are: (1) revising our founding documents, (2) reckoning with the intersection of public policy and institutional racism, and (3) reimagining our racial and social awareness.

Amending Our Constitution: Creating an Economic and Social Bill of Rights

We begin with a basic historical fact: our Constitution was intentionally and explicitly designed to be amended. As the Constitution was finalized, it was none other than Benjamin Franklin who warned that despite the strengths of the Constitution, it "inevitably" would possess all the Founders' "prejudices, their passions, their errors of opinion, . . . and their selfish views."[10] Despite many other failures, our founders understood that perfecting the nation required a commitment to continuous moral growth and involved perfecting its founding documents by evolving them to meet the demands of new generations. And no tradition has taken this fact more seriously and urgently than the Black Freedom Movement, whose radical visions of our nation's potential have often involved revising our founding documents through various modes.

In the nineteenth century, as many white abolitionists decried the Constitution, calling for its erasure and demanding the nation start again from scratch, Frederick Douglass instead counseled that the Constitution be amended to align its body with its preamble. And that was the purpose of the Thirteenth, Fourteenth, and Fifteenth Amendments. In so doing, Douglass helped open the door for the nation to be reborn. Throughout the nineteenth, twentieth, and twenty-first centuries, the rhetoric of Black Americans also continually rewrote the Declaration of Independence with the document's own words by demanding Black inclusion in its equation of human equality. This was the work of Ella Baker, Fannie Lou Hamer, Diane Nash, John Lewis, Stokely Carmichael, Bob Moses, Malcolm X, and Martin Luther King Jr. And through this struggle, seas of Black people opened the door to imagine a more interracial and egalitarian democracy once more.

Yet, in King's final days, including Black folks in the Declaration of Independence's equality clause and the Constitution's Thirteenth, Fourteenth, and Fifteenth Amendments proved insufficient. Like Douglass before him, he too wanted to continue improving the Constitution. For King, the movement had matured and entered

> a terrain where the voice of the Constitution is not clear. We have left the realm of constitutional rights and we are entering the area of human rights. The Constitution assured the right to vote, but there is no such assurance of the right to adequate housing, or the right to an adequate income. And yet in a nation which has a gross national product of $750 billion a year, it is morally right to insist that every person have a decent house, an adequate education, and enough money to provide basic necessities for one's family.

To make the Constitution worthy of the nation, King believed we must provide "a contemporary social and economic Bill of Rights to supplement the Constitution's political Bill of Rights."[11] King understood, with penetrating foresight, that not only must the work of civil rights grow more radical and move into human rights, but that even the victories the civil rights already won would remain insecure until we repair our nation's foundation by amending the Constitution to include an economic and social Bill of Rights.

In speaking of amending the Constitution, many in America believed King had lost his mind. But unsurprisingly, he was right. In a historical sense, the ink of the civil rights legislation of 1964 and 1965 had barely dried when the work to make the grand achievement meaningless began. Like Lincoln, we have accepted our Constitution in its current state as a nearly perfect document without the need for amendment for far too long. That assumption is no longer viable and will prove as disastrous in the twenty-first century as it proved in the eighteenth, nineteenth, and twentieth centuries.

During this time of national upheaval, we must bring our founding documents' ideologies of human equality from the realms of the theoretical down to earth. Reparations' work of repairing our life together demands that the

Declaration of Independence's proclamation of human equality be finally enshrined as a constitutional principle by our amending our Constitution to protect human dignity and to hold our public policies accountable for working to realize racial and economic equity. An economic and social Bill of Rights is needed to ensure an equitable education for *all* students, living wages for *all* workers, food, housing, and health care for *all* families, the right to vote for *all* citizens, and that *all* forms of gerrymandering are understood as what they are—an act of treason against democracy. Such a vision is not utopian but the lived reality of developed nations around the globe. Such a vision is homegrown and rooted in the "all" of the most famous declaration of human dignity in history: "that all men are created equal and endowed with inalienable rights."

It is only through a commitment to continually tend to our nation's founding documents that we can stay truthful to our founders' vision of a morally maturing nation. It was, after all, the author of the Declaration of Independence who counseled:

> Laws and institutions must go hand in hand with the progress of the human mind. As . . . new truths [are] discovered . . . and opinions change . . . , institutions must advance also to keep pace with the times. We might as well require a man to wear still the coat which fitted him when a boy as civilized society to remain ever under the regimen of their barbarous ancestors.[12]

As the Founders knew, a society's refusal to morally mature is a sign not of national exceptionalism but of decay and death.

Part of this repair is imagining a Constitutional Convention with Benjamin Banneker, Ida B. Wells, and Ella Baker at the table. Part of this repair is placing frontline workers for racial justice today at the table of political power and learning how to craft amendments that place the Constitution on the side of justice instead of the side of an unjust status quo. A repaired nation cannot claim that the wealthiest country on earth must allow her children to go hungry, force her mothers to live in deprivation, and condemn her working poor to destitution. Children eating healthy food, families having affordable access to life's necessities, and people receiving an honest day's pay for an honest day's work should not be a utopian dream. It must be a constitutional demand.

All of this is to say we must seek to perfect the Constitution by adding amendments that engraft a commitment to an interracial and equitable democracy into the nation's very marrow.

Reckoning with Public Policy and Institutional Racism

When we think of public policy issues and institutional racism, we often think in well-defined silos—education, housing, health, criminal justice, employment. Unsurprisingly, what becomes infuriating for the most gifted and dedicated public servants is that society's wounds often refuse to align with the simplicity of our thinking. Instead of existing in silos, the nation's racial wounds exist within a complex history and a tightly entangled network of social and economic forces. This knot is not easily disentangled. Incarceration is directly related to education. Education is intimately connected to housing. Housing options are tied to wages. Wages are in a complex relationship with race and education. For those in the trenches, there are few more frustrating experiences than pulling on your special string with all your soul and strength, only for the knot to grow stronger with the passing of time. This is why national repair demands transformative public investments in the wide array of public services and institutions that shape our life together.

Rather than detail a litany of investments we must make, I will limit my attention to the crisis of public policy and systemic racism at the intersection of education and incarceration. Some of the richest legacies of the Black freedom struggle reside at this intersection. From W. E. B. Du Bois to Mary McLeod Bethune to Ida B. Wells to Michelle Alexander and Bryan Stevenson, the Black Freedom Movement has consistently placed reinvesting in Black education and reforming the criminal justice system at the center of the fight for racial justice. Thanks to the work of today's tireless advocates, there is growing awareness that Black America did not fail our education system but that our education system failed Black America. Likewise, pervasive public awareness exists that in today's criminal justice system, it is much safer to be wealthy, white, and guilty than it is to be poor, Black, and innocent.

Reparations help us translate this raised public awareness to public policies that begin the work to repair the damage of institutional racism. We start with our education system. At the heart of Black America's vision for an antiracist democracy is an equitable and excellent public education system from pre-K through college. Currently, the quality of education a child in America receives is nearly predetermined by the private wealth and race of their parents. The basis of educational funding must shift from parental race and wealth to students' needs. For all the financial crimes of our nation's history, perhaps none has inflicted more damage than the funding mechanisms for primary and secondary education. Unlike in other nations, public education funding in the United States runs through the local tax base in ways that were designed to create inequitable public schools. And the design has fulfilled its intention, as the United States perpetuates one of the most inequitable education systems in the world. Today, our state school funding models have created a racial funding gap that is estimated at $23 billion per year.[13] This translates to an average per-student state investment for predominately white school districts that is $2,000 higher than it is for their nonwhite counterparts—that is, 18 percent more.

Yet, to understand the wounds we have inflicted and the impact of $23 billion less a year and $2,000 less per student, we must think historically—think in terms of decades, not years; groups, not individuals. For instance, when a predominately Black high school graduating class is in keeping with national norms of around two hundred students, that graduation ceremony not only marks a remarkable accomplishment; it also marks the devastating underinvestment of approximately $5.2 million. And we know that underinvestment will have consequences even among those celebrating their remarkable accomplishment.[14]

But compounding this injustice is the reality that an *equitable* education system seeks more than equal investment: it seeks to meet students' *needs*. This means the most marginalized students must receive the most comprehensive educational, social, and emotional investments. These investments must include committing the top talent and resources to our most marginalized schools and students. After white parents responded to integration by redrawing district lines and creating new municipalities to ensure a disproportionate share of public dollars went toward their children's education, a myth arose that funding was not a primary cause for our Black students' educational woes. From disinterested Black parents to dysfunctional teachers and disengaged students, white politicians and pundits crafted stories to justify the criminally poor education we provide in poor Black communities and to distract from the crime of public disinvestment in Black education. Though money alone may not heal all educational inequalities, funding for research-driven interventions that empower on-the-ground educators can have transformative results. Research indicates that wisely investing 25 percent more in impoverished schools can eliminate the achievement gap between poor and nonpoor students.[15]

Despite such research, as myths arose, so too did deeply flawed solutions to the nation's public education crisis. Instead of prioritizing deeply investing in and resourcing impoverished schools, educational leaders became captivated by a school "choice" movement that too often focused on radically "rethinking" public education. Heroic charter schools were heralded as the solution to failing under-resourced Black community schools. The movement was captivating, and some of the nation's most brilliant and committed young public servants hopped on board and committed their lives to the self-sacrificial work of providing Black and Brown students a chance at an excellent educational experience.

And while some charter schools achieved exceptional results through self-sacrificial and brilliant work, the movement mainly transferred deeply flawed and racialized economic ideas into the education system. In the charter school movement, the undergirding societal failures and national disinvestments that broke public education were often left untouched and unexplored. Mythology fed upon mythology in a manner that complicated the work of remediating the deep shortcomings of a system that bears not only the scars of our nation's racist educational history but also the wounds students carry from racialized employment, housing, and health practices.

Currently, the cumulative impact of the underfunding and under-resourcing of Black education is that by the time many impoverished Black students turn eighteen, the doors to a quality education and economic independence have been slammed shut. And when that door locks, the giftedness of poor students is imprisoned. That is not simply a crime against children. Burying the talents of our youth is a crime against the very soul of our democracy.

Yet, educational problems only get worse after high school. College is free to students whose parents are ready and able to pay skyrocketing tuition rates and a few academically exceptional students. For everyone else, college education is provided usually at the price of student debts that financially penalize students for the rest of their lives. Often lost in the conversation concerning publicly funding college is the simple truth that no student can afford college today. To restrict college education to the wealthiest or the academically exceptional among us while financially punishing everyone else with educational ambitions is another generational crime against our children of the highest magnitude. And that crime disproportionately damages the educational and wealth potential of Black people.[16] For too many Black communities, our nation's educational dysfunction is destruction by design.

However, as it stands, this is not our greatest crime against students in Black communities. Our most callous crimes occur at the intersection of Black educational disinvestment and mass incarceration. Currently, the most significant investment our nation proves ready to make in the lives of poor Black students is incarcerating them. In poor Black communities across the nation reside underfunded high schools whose students are often as likely to go to jail as they are to graduate from college. Over the past forty years, we have constructed a school-to-prison pipeline that damned the ambitions of generations of gifted Black and Brown people. We need not only end the flow of that pipeline; we must also reverse the tide by transforming our incarceration system into an education system that prevents recidivism and empowers economic viability beyond prison walls.

Precisely such a transformation is underway and demands robust public support. In 2015, the Obama administration resurrected the Second Chance Pell Grant program, which provides college educational opportunities to people behind bars. Shuttered during the punitive Clinton era, Second Chance Pell Grants prove to drastically reduce recidivism and provide a social and economic boon to the communities most deeply impacted by violence and mass incarceration. Under Obama, the Second Chance Pell Grant program began as an experiment with sixty-seven institutions. The Trump administration broadened the program by doubling institutional partners and serving seventeen thousand students. The Biden administration likewise expanded the program by seventy-three institutions, including twenty-four HBCUs. After the program produced a strong track record through incremental growth, in the summer of 2023, the door opened to all colleges and Pell Grant–eligible incarcerated people. Constructing the prison-to-school pipeline can now begin in earnest with the opportunity to transform the lives of hundreds of thousands of students and families. This opportunity must now receive robust protections from the propaganda and political power of the $87 billion prison industry, whose bread and butter is incarcerating Black men and creating repeat customers through a system designed to produce recidivism.

This opening to construct a prison-to-school pipeline is also an invitation to reimagine our criminal justice system from the bottom up. Currently, America's criminal justice system is nothing less than a crime against humanity, as it represents both the highest incarceration rate in the world and one of the world's most racially biased systems. Black young men are five times more likely to be arrested than their white counterparts and serve, on average, nearly 20 percent longer jail sentences for the same offenses. The crime this represents is that our nation stands ready to spend billions upon billions of dollars to place Black men in a cage, while it balks at social investments that would unleash these men's gifts and talents for the benefit of their families, their communities, and our nation.[17] But the crime of our criminal justice system runs much deeper than robbing men behind bars of years of their life. Currently, one of the cruelest crimes of our criminal justice system is that it fundamentally fails the victims and survivors of violent crimes—survivors, victims, and communities that are too often Black.

In *Until We Reckon,* Danielle Sered of Common Justice recenters our conversation concerning prison reform by listening to the desires and needs of those left behind in the wake of violent crimes. Through rigorous research and stories spanning decades of personal experiences, Sered reveals that the greatest needs and desires of victims and their communities are often simple: they are safety and ensuring that the violence they experienced is less likely to occur in the future. Yet, centering the conversation on survivors' need for a sense of safety and security leads in an unexpected direction for those unfamiliar with the devastating impact of the prison industrial complex on vulnerable communities. Instead of expressing a desire for an endless extension of prison sentences, the cry of victims and communities is repeatedly for a system that focuses on rehabilitation rather than incarceration. Here is the kicker. Black communities most intimate with violence often know what research shows: rather than our current addiction to incarceration reducing violence, our prisons and punitive approaches to justice are perfectly designed to deepen trauma and accelerate violence, making impoverished communities more dangerous.

Sered writes: "If we listened deeply and well and asked open-ended questions" to victims of violence, we would develop a criminal justice system "characterized by accountability, by safety, by justice, and by healing. And it would look very little like what we have today."[18] To take seriously what victims, survivors, and traumatized communities say demands we convert our criminal justice system's *aim* from being one of the most *punitive* in the world to becoming one of the most *reparative*. Such a system in no way underplays the seriousness of crimes committed or what victims have survived. It prioritizes what victims and survivors say they need and desire.[19]

Additionally, reimagining our criminal justice system around the needs of the victims and survivors of violence does not erase the need to uphold the rights and dignities of the incarcerated. It demands it. Placing victims, survivors, and communities at the center of our priorities reconstructs our criminal justice equations and can make incarceration the last option rather than the first. From sentencing to treatment to educational offerings, we must learn to protect the rights and dignity of those currently in cages.

Currently, nearly 80 percent of male inmates lack a high school diploma, and 70 percent are functionally illiterate. Most inmates were impoverished, with a full 66 percent living off of less than $12,000 a year. Between 60 and 80 percent of those imprisoned suffer from addiction and substance abuse. The majority of inmates are parents and were the primary provider for their family. Nearly two hundred thousand are veterans. Another two hundred thousand have a history of severe mental illness. Though Black men make up only 6.5 percent of the total US population, they make up a full 40 percent of the nation's prison population. In sum, the prison population consists largely of those whom our society has deeply failed and traumatized. And for the most part, prison simply deepens that failure and trauma. Until we set accountability, justice, and healing as the foundational principles of our criminal justice system, it will continue to be an engine of injustice—reflecting and deepening our society's brokenness while offering no repair or healing for the people and communities it is mandated to serve.[20]

Finally, respecting the voices of the survivors of crime and the rights of the incarcerated and accused requires rethinking the whole network of relationships within the criminal justice system and the training of judges, prosecutors, and public defenders, who are endowed with a godlike power over marginalized communities. Currently, neither law school nor continuing-education requirements offer sufficient tools and resources to foster the social depth perception equal to the responsibility entrusted to the power brokers. Though law schools are responsible for the initial training of those who shape the criminal justice system, very few take seriously enough their responsibility for the profound social wounds our failed system of training inflicts on our most vulnerable communities. And there are, to my knowledge, no requirements for community engagement and investment for those seeking to be judges, prosecutors, or public defenders. Simply put, within the criminal justice system, those whose decisions most deeply impact Black communities are consistently those least impacted by the fallout their decisions produce.

Currently the greatest collaborative injustice resulting from the relational misalignment between the power brokers within the criminal justice system and impoverished communities are plea deals. A full 98 percent of convictions stem from plea deals.[21] Plea deals provide victims too little voice and the accused too little leverage. When we think of criminal convictions, we often think of courtrooms. We should think of hostage negotiations in which defendants who cannot afford an adequate defense regularly give away years of their life to avoid risking the loss of decades.

In the rare instance that a case goes to trial before "a jury of our peers," the role of judges, prosecutors, and public defenders still often reduces victims and defendants alike to pawns in the hands of professionals. To achieve justice, it is not too much to require the criminal justice system to implement educational, professional, and experiential qualifications that ensure that those entrusted to provide justice possess a knowledge of the people that runs as deep as their knowledge of the law. A society riven by wealth and race can never be repaired by public servants of justice with a superficial understanding of the people and communities they are mandated to serve and protect.

In my encounters with people who work within the criminal justice system, I often meet exceptional people. Yet, on other occasions I walk away with an eerie feeling. It is the feeling that the very people who live at the mercy of the system are repeatedly in the hands of those who understand their circumstances the least. The different worlds of those who work in the criminal justice system and those on whom the criminal system works are perfectly engineered to produce the types of systemic injustice that typify the criminal justice system. That systemic injustice is a symptom of a society segregated by race and wealth. These relationships must be righted.

Repairing our society by dealing explicitly with public policies and institutional racism means remaking the very infrastructure that binds our life together. As seen in education and incarceration, our public policies and institutions cry out for healing and repair. But what also must be emphasized is that if injustices exist within an interconnected network of relationships that makes progress in any one area difficult to achieve, we should not be surprised if in an age committed to reparations and repair we uncover healing multipliers. Improvement in any one area—education, employment, housing, health care, incarceration—can create a chain reaction of collateral benefits that produce a transformative momentum.

Currently, brilliant and dedicated advocates are pushing on all fronts. What these advocates deserve and their communities cry out for is the empowerment that only a commitment to reparations and a reckoning with public policies and systemic reparations can provide. Again, the radical repair of public policy and institutional racism is not a utopian dream. As in the days of the fall of slavery and segregation, it is an inevitability as soon as our nation's political will matches our moment in history.

Reimagining Our Racial and Social Awareness

In addition to amending our Constitution and reckoning with public policy and institutional racism, we must engage in the essential work of continuing to reimagine, sharpen, and shape our nation's awareness regarding our racial and social violence *and* our democratic and restorative possibilities. From Occupy Wall Street to the New Jim Crow to the Green New Deal, from #Me-Too to Black Lives Matter, the work of raising public consciousness about sicknesses within our society has prepared the ground for the possibility of a societal reconstruction unique in our nation's history. And yet despite the awakening that is occurring, there is significant work left to do to combat what poverty abolitionist Matthew Desmond refers to as "the propaganda of capitalism."[22] To counter capitalism's propaganda, we need a robust campaign of public awareness that personalizes the power of public assistance, commits to tying the minimum wage to a living wage, and harmonizes our understanding of both corporations and our nation's financial health with the demand for racial and economic equity.

First, we must repair our public imagination concerning the realities of welfare. Despite all that we now know, our society's mental image of public assistance is still scarred by the mythology of dependence. Research consistently provides data-driven evidence that rather than creating dependence, welfare provides a helping hand during terrible times. But this research has largely failed to mend our mental images. The tantalizing images of welfare queens and other mythologies are hard to unsee—especially for those whose lived experiences are segregated from impoverished communities.

When it comes to public assistance, our moral imagination needs intensive care. To date, advocates for public assistance have lost the battle for the public narrative, having failed to infuse into the public imagination the personal stories of people for whom public assistance was a lifeline. Yet, those who support a public helping hand during people's times of great need have great stories to tell. One example. We live in a nation that brutally deprives our children. Among industrialized nations, Turkey and Chile stand among the rare few countries with slightly higher child poverty rates than the US. Within the past decade, child poverty rates hovered around 15 percent—even after government assistance. In 2018, well over a million of our children were homeless. That is nearly five times the amount of the entire homeless population only forty years ago. Neither the power of our economy nor the minimal provisions of our social safety net provided a cure to this destitution.[23]

Yet, as Matthew Desmond narrates in *Poverty, by America*, during a pandemic and a global economic crisis in 2020 and 2021, something remarkable happened. We cut childhood poverty nearly in half as swift interventions prevented the economy from entering into a free fall. Our ability to provide for children in the face of global fears could have pleasantly shocked us into the awareness that we have it in our power to protect our nation's children and families from the nightmare of poverty. Sensing our power, we could have committed to the work of abolishing child poverty. We could have learned about the families and told the stories of those newly protected from poverty's ravages. But that is not what happened.

When employment shortages hit, public backlash did as well. And from newscasts to op-eds to social media posts, an age-old story resurrected, linking worker sloth to the shortages of service workers. The inconveniences customers experienced were heralded as proof positive that governmental provisions for the poor produced dependence and destroyed people's willingness to work. Several states went into action and cut provisions for their residents. Unsurprisingly, the states that cut provisions failed to improve their employment statistics. However, they did damage their economy, as consumer spending declined because fewer people possessed the cash for life's necessities.

As Desmond writes:

> Why, I wonder, did we so readily embrace a narrative that blamed high unemployment on government aid when so many other explanations were available to us? Why didn't we figure people weren't returning to work because they didn't want to get sick and die? Or because their jobs were lousy to begin with? Or because they were tired of sexual harassment and mistreatment? Or because their children's schools had closed, and they lacked reliable childcare? When asked why many Americans weren't returning to work as fast as some people would have liked, why was our answer *Because they are getting $300 extra each week?*[24]

Desmond points to the challenge we face: Currently, we possess the statistics of poverty but too often lack intimacy with the stories of those seeking to survive. We know the numbers but usually do not know the names and thus have difficulty making their stories known. And this shortcoming plays directly into the hands of corporate propagandists who seek to erase the lives of those who have no place in their calculus.

It is hard, if not impossible, to overstate how the disinformation of the propaganda of capitalism has wounded our nation. Such propaganda has flipped our mental and moral maps to make compassion look like cruelty and cruelty compassion. We must learn to personalize our stories concerning public assistance and tattoo the conviction on the nation's heart that poverty is a public problem, not merely a personal failure. Public wounds demand public compassion and care.

Second, besides seeing and sharing the ways in which public assistance provides critical help to our poorest people and families, we must raise awareness of the realities faced by the working poor and the need to ensure that minimum wages equal a living wage. The main driver of poverty is neither sloth nor unemployment. The main driver of poverty is the lack of a living wage for American workers. The economic world in which boomers and Generation X were raised is starkly different than the world they created. In 1968, full-time workers on a minimum wage protected a family of three from falling below the poverty line. Since then, workers have become much, much more productive. But since productivity increased 3.5 times the rate of workers' wages, instead of worker productivity securing a living wage, that productivity translated to radical increases in executive pay and corporate profits that enrich investors who provide no sweat equity. Today, economic logics and public policies have reduced full-time minimum wages such that full-time work fails to protect a family of two.

Nearly 15 percent of Black workers receive wages that fail to meet their basic needs. For white workers, that number is nearly 10 percent.[25] If there were one lever to lean fully into to begin reimagining our racial world and healing the racial, economic, and social wounds of the nation, it would be to ensure that wages are racially equitable and that minimum wages are robust. Here's the upshot: If hard work more consistently translated to an economically stable life, America would not need to worry much about the curse of poverty and its attendant social consequences of child neglect, drug addiction, homelessness, and violent crime. These social wounds are a byproduct of buying into the corporate propaganda that companies with record profits are nonetheless powerless to fight against the poverty of their own employees whose sweat has proved so profitable.

Our current state of affairs regarding unlivable wages begs the question of what we can do about it. The solution is tragically simple: the cure to this crisis is a phased-in approach that ties the federal minimum wage to local living wage requirements.[26] Unlike many countries, the US possesses no legislative prerequisite to regularly revisit the minimum wage to ensure that full-time work protects from full-time poverty. Evidence-based research routinely points to the social benefits and lack of economic or employment hardships associated with robust wages. It also makes a strong business case that links living wages to decreased turnover, stronger company morale, and improved employee health and productivity.[27] Additional research is underway concerning the bottom-line returns to the company, and the early indications are encouraging.[28] However, such evidence has again failed to overcome the power of capitalistic propaganda that keeps minimum wages in line with economic destitution. It is ironic that a country so deeply anxious about welfare dependency is so deeply resistant to ensuring robust wages that empower self-sufficiency.

Finally, we must raise awareness regarding corporate and national measures of racial and economic equity. For far too long, our corporations and our nation have measured their performance through fundamentally insufficient measures. And while there is a wide array of initiatives underway and many more we can imagine, there is a very low-hanging fruit: corporate and national equity scorecards.

Corporate scorecards. Similar to how the S&P 500 Environmental & Socially Responsible Index empowers ethical opportunities for investors, an index is needed for everyday consumers. This scorecard can provide consumers with key performance indicators such as wage standards, minority leadership, compensation comparisons between executives and frontline workers, and environmental impact. Corporate equity scorecards targeted to consumers would provide for our institutions what nutritional labels provide for our food: transparency about the core ingredients that make up the final product.

National scorecards. When it comes to our nation, public awareness of America's financial health is shaped through measures reported to and through news outlets ranging from the GDP, the stock market, unemployment metrics, and other similar statistics. What these statistics too often hold in common is they divorce public awareness from issues of racial equity, justice, and social and environmental responsibility. When it comes to racial justice and economic equity, these measurements conceal more than they reveal. We desperately need a national equity scorecard that keeps the public aware of our nation's racial, economic, and environmental realities. We are a nation with remarkably wealthy individuals and remarkably poor people. Through national equity scorecards, our nation can begin developing the social and moral sensibilities that are required to embody the conviction of human equality in a nation divided by race and wealth.

The refusal to either provide public help to people in need or pay workers a living wage is not an inherent feature of a capitalistic society. It was, after all, in *The Wealth of Nations* that Adam Smith wrote, "No society can surely be flourishing and happy of which the far greater part of the members are poor and miserable." He continues: "It is but equity, besides, that they who feed, clothe, and lodge the whole body of the people, should have such a share of the produce of their own labour as to be themselves tolerably well fed, clothed, and lodged."[29] We must mature to recognize that the propaganda of

US capitalism has placed us on a path to choose a particular kind of capitalism that values corporations and profits over communities and people.

But capitalism's propaganda is not all-powerful. We must imagine a nation in which the scars of capitalism's propaganda are repaired as poverty is personalized, wages become dignified, and racial and social awareness are realized. We must imagine a nation fully aware of not simply the *value* of brand-name labels but the *values* of the brand name. We must imagine a nation in which Gross Domestic Poverty is as important an index as our Gross Domestic Product. We can create the political will necessary for justice, equity, and dignity to replace punishment, scarcity, and bootstraps in our nation's political calculus.

Of course, these are only a few of the numerous ways to promote the racial and social awareness needed to repair racist and classist public policies. For additional steps in the process, multiple reports already exist that provide a more holistic picture of American life. The National Urban League releases its *State of Black America* report every year, providing a map of not only where we are but also how we got here. The Kerner Report continues to demand a preeminent place in policy considerations, and reparations must include translating its recommendations for employment, education, welfare, and housing into more concrete public policies.

Just as in the days of the Kerner Commission, the question rightly arises: How can the nation afford such deep investments to ensure institutional equity? This question is particularly poignant after calling for reparational payments of $14.3 trillion to be paid to Black people and families. And that leads us to examine our nation's resources and confront capitalism's largest lie: that we cannot afford to fix our nation's brokenness.

Our Nation's Economic Engine and Funding the Work of Repair

Our nation's economic engine is spelled I-R-S. When combined, these are perhaps the least popular letters in the alphabet. Yet, we cannot achieve an economically healthy and robust nation without a healthy and robust economic engine. No other agency is positioned to empower a more economically equitable and viable nation than the IRS, for it is the agency tasked with ensuring that the nation can meet her bills and that every American pays their fair share.

Due to the popular disdain for the agency, the decimation of the IRS over the past decade and a half is a too rarely told story—but it is of singular importance. Beginning in 2008, a radical defunding began, and over the course of the next ten years, over $2 billion would be cut from the agency's annual budget. Rather than a singular drastic cut occurring, it was death by a hundred slashes as the IRS's budget dwindled year after year. In time, the agency decayed into a former shell of itself. By 2017, the agency employed only 9,500 people, a full third fewer auditors than it had when the cuts began. It was the first time the IRS had employed fewer than 10,000 auditors since 1953, when the nation's GDP was about 2 percent of what it was in 2017.

The results were predictable. Allow those with the highest bills to kill the accounts payable division, and your revenue stream begins evaporating. The agency audit rate plummeted 42 percent, conducting 675,000 fewer audits than it had in 2010. Of course, no one benefitted more from the cuts than the wealthy. Audits of millionaires plummeted a full 71 percent.[30] Despite the IRS's inability to hold the wealthy accountable, the poor remained heavily audited, accounting for 36 percent of audits in 2017 as legislators continued to fear that it was welfare cheats who were robbing public coffers. As Alan Rappeport of the *New York Times* noted, this fear led directly to Black people becoming the most audited demographic in the nation. "Audit rates for Black Americans," he wrote in 2023, "are three to five times higher than for other taxpayers, with audits focused on the tax credit being a major driver of the disparity."[31] Unsurprisingly, auditing the poor provides a negative return on investment and places additional stress on the citizens who can least afford it. And though it is no simple or cheap task to audit the wealthy, research from the years 2010–2014 shows that the average return on investment is absurd: ranging from 318 to 620 percent. And this return fails to take into account indirect returns on investment when a rigorous atmosphere of accountability is provided.

What all of this means is that even with the current tax laws that benefit the wealthy, the IRS reports that the nation is still cheated out of $1 trillion annually. It is not simply that we refuse to implement an equitable tax structure. It is also that we refuse to enforce the tax structure we already have in place. Clearly a more equitable tax structure is needed, but reparations repair of our nation can begin simply by empowering the IRS to collect the current and back taxes that are owed to the national treasury. This would position us to collect the $1 trillion in revenue we currently lose, as well as the taxes we failed to collect over the last decade. Reports estimate the ability to collect $5 to $7.5 trillion from back taxes in addition to penalties.

Thankfully, the importance of the IRS has moved closer to center stage. In 2022, the Inflation Reduction Act added $80 billion to the IRS's budget over a ten-year time frame. Yet, by 2023, negotiations reduced that investment by

$20 billion, threatening to place the nation back on the path of fiscal reckless-ness. A commitment to repairing our nation and tending to our racial and social wounds demands a commitment to repairing our nation's economic engine.[32]

Many reparations repairs will save our nation money in the short run. Nearly all the repairs will strengthen our economy in the long run. None-theless, the price to repair a house is not cheap. Especially when that house is our nation. Yet, any serious look at the combined failures to fund the IRS and construct an equitable tax code reveals the fact that our nation can, in fact, fund much more radical interventions to eradicate poverty and the racial wealth gap than we do. We can, in fact, make our nation more equitable and economically stable. There are now nearly twenty-two million millionaires in America.[33] That so many people fail to understand that we can afford to repay Black families, reimagine American society, and reinvest in Black communities exposes how capitalism's propaganda has crippled our moral imagination. Make no mistake: the obstacle to reparations and repairing our life together is not economic in nature. The question is not whether we can afford racial equity. The first question is if we desire it.

Reparations is about the work of repair to remake America. It is about revising our Constitution and creating an economic and social Bill of Rights. It is about reckoning with racist public policies and institutional racism. It is about reimagining racial and social awareness. Reparations is about the rebirth of a nation.

17

Rebirth

If we merge mercy with might, and might with right, then love
becomes our legacy and change our children's birthright.

—Amanda Gorman

REPENTANCE. REPAYMENT. REPAIR. Reforging the nation's conscience and
consciousness. Erasing the nation's racial wealth gap. Reconstructing the
nation's most devastated neighborhoods and communities. Healing our democracy. This is the work of reparations.

Justice will never be freely given. Rebirth is the stuff of struggle and strife,
of sweat and blood, of enduring the pain of failure and heartbreak, of killing
off the old ways of life so that new ways of living can be born. Understanding
both what is needed and the mechanisms of how our nation can be reborn
will require vulnerability, creativity, and determination that we too often lack
but that we can and must foster. Through the lives of Sojourner Truth, Harriet Tubman, Ida B. Wells, Callie House, and Ella Baker, I began to see that
part of the difficult work of changing a society is the difficult work of growing
and maturing into the type of person and people who make change possible.
Reparations and a Reparative Age are not fanciful ideals. Reparations and
a Reparative Age are the inevitable end point of our life together when we
become the people our moment in history demands.

At one level, thinking about the practicalities of reparations and reimagining our life together can feel like nothing more than an exercise in futility.
What good is it to imagine Banneker, Wells, and Baker at the Constitutional
Convention? What good is it to imagine the New Deal shaped more by Black
brilliance than white racism or to imagine the War on Poverty shaped more
by the Kerner Commission than by the Moynihan Report? Until we learn
to imagine how different our nation's past could have been, we will be ill-
equipped to imagine how different our future can be. The truth is that our

racial and economic ways can change, but those changes must be envisioned before they can be actualized.

As seen throughout the history of the Black Freedom Movement, revolutionaries come in all shapes and sizes. But what they share is the clarity and courage to see the possibility of a new way of life and the readiness to make the sacrifices necessary today to transform tomorrow. Sometimes societal change is quick. At other times, it is wrought slowly over decades. Ending slavery, beginning the New Deal, women receiving the right to vote, taking down segregation, initiating the War on Poverty, the Americans with Disabilities Act—each was impossible, until it wasn't.

Throughout history, paradigm shifts emerge in times of crisis and confusion, when worldviews and deep-seated convictions become untenable and our world groans for new ways forward. In our current crisis, the paradigm-shifting ideas we so deeply need are already emanating from society's margins. Crisis and untapped sources of wisdom can impel us to reshape our worldview and culture in a way that brings them into deeper harmony with democracy's convictions. Our wounded nation yearns for a better way forward as our accumulating crises are proving unbearable.[1]

Reparations offers us the paradigm shift we must embrace if we are to thrive as a nation. The paradigm shift repentance represents is the conviction that penitence provides our nation's best path to transforming our political possibilities and aligning our life together with our democratic ideals. It is the conviction that our future freedom depends on taking responsibility for our past crimes. It is the conviction that a society's health is best measured by its treatment of its most vulnerable, not its glitter or its gold. The paradigm shift of repayment reflects the principle that Black people deserve economic justice and that economic equity is the only viable economic cornerstone for a sustainable future. It is the principle that it is through atonement rather than amnesia that we must attend to our moral, ethical, and historical wounds. And repair represents the proposition that reimagining American society and reinvesting in Black communities is the only way we can reconstruct a society whose very foundation was broken by white supremacy. It is the proposition that the struggle for racial and economic equity was never utopian. It was and is—everywhere and always—the most democratic, pragmatic, and long-visioned politics imaginable.

Perhaps as much as anything, the question that reparations demands we answer is if we can begin thinking in generational terms and make sacrifices now for the sake of tomorrow. For if we fail to make reparations—if we fail to repent for our sins, repay our debts, and repair our life together—we will leave a society to our children that is on a path to self-destruction. There comes a time in a society's life when its most cherished beliefs have brought it to a dead end. We now stand at that moment in history.

The antiracists of previous ages, both Black and white, became intimate with heartbreak, despair, and bewilderment. And though they never reached the land for which they labored, no one who faithfully gives their lives for truth and justice ever fails. Instead, they pass the work forward to future generations to continue and deepen their quest for a more just and antiracist world.

Few embodied this principle more intentionally than Queen Mother Audley Moore. Queen Mother Moore invested her life working in the wilderness with her colaborers for an expansive vision of reparations. Like many who fought against slavery and lynching before her, Queen Mother Moore knew she would not live to see the promised land where reparations would be realized. And so her last acts focused on passing the torch that carried freedom's fire to the next generation.

Attending N'COBRA's conference in Michigan in 1990 and 1994, she welcomed her sisters in the struggle to her bedside for a conversation about reparations and activism. And it was in Detroit—that city that so epitomizes America's racial crimes—that her caregivers would wheel her onstage to give her final public comments to those gathered to carry forth the struggle for reparations. As Ashley Farmer narrates the scene: "A 'solemn hush' fell over the crowd. . . . Queen Mother Moore proclaimed: 'Reparations, Reparations . . . Keep on. Keep on. We've got to win!'"[2] And the responsibility to realize reparations was passed to the next generation, who took the torch and moved reparations' cause to center stage in America's political imagination.

Justice is calling for a national reckoning and rebirth. A debt is owed. An opportunity is at hand. The question is not if we will pay for the crimes of our past or if we are forming the future. The question is how. May we have the wisdom, courage, and imagination to enter the work of reparations so that we can answer, "With liberty and justice for all."

Acknowledgments

My acknowledgments begin with the One who gives dreams and sustains us through the struggle. *Rebirth of a Nation* began in a dream in the middle of August 2019. When I awoke the work of writing this book began in earnest, and it was a journey that impacted nearly every waking hour ever since. Little did I know then—and hardly can I believe now—that the door would open for me to partner with the literary force and writer's warrior that is my agent, Charlotte Sheedy. To Charlotte, Ally, and the entire Sheedy team, you gave me room to grow as a writer and stuck with me through the birthing pains of a book that proved a great challenge to bring into the world. I am honored to be a part of the Sheedy Literary family, and I have been immeasurably enriched by your investment in my life and work.

Early in the process, I reached out to the most vicious editor I knew to provide a helping hand. At the time, I did not know Stephen Hall well, but from 2020 to today, Stephen has become not only my editor but my professor, pastor, and psychologist. I have learned so much about writing and life from you, Stephen. Thank you for the way you pour your gifts into the world.

To the Eerdmans team of James Ernest and Andrew Knapp, who believed in *Rebirth of a Nation* and worked to improve it: I cannot tell you how humbled I am by the opportunity to work together. My gratitude to Angela Baggetta for partnering with us.

Outside of the *Rebirth*'s official team were transformative friends who read early drafts and opened doors that seemed sealed shut. My deepest indebtedness is to Khalil Gibran Muhammad. We know why. Some of my favorite writers and scholars—Phillip Luke Sinitiere, Mary Pipher, Guy Mount Emerson, David Romine, David Gushee, and Keisha Blain—took time to read troublesome sections of the manuscript and offered helpful feedback. Additional friends from all walks of life agreed to read the first draft of the manuscript. A big shout-out to DZ Cofield. Your kindness and mentorship are one of the greatest gifts I ever received. Shout-outs to Omkari Williams,

Todd Litton, Anthony Emerson, Blake Thomas, Peter Swarr, Kim Milton, Steve Bezner, Marty Troyer, Monica Blaumueller, Frank Becht, and Chris Caldwell. Numerous scholars answered pesky emails as I sought to get my head around their remarkable work. A special thanks to Jonathan Spiro and James Q. Whitman. Deep gratitude to Aimee Muller at the Ronald Reagan Presidential Library. To all the above: time is precious. You took time for me, and I cherish you.

And then there are the musicians. I rely on Marvin Sapp to get by. The artist who feeds my soul, under whose work I write, and whose support has been unwavering is my friend and brother Victor Gaddie, who also created the cover image.

Institutions play a critical role in helping writers survive. A shout-out to Alan Dettlaff of the University of Houston's Graduate School of Social Work, who allowed me to be a visiting scholar to access the university's research facilities. While writing, I also attended and graduated from the University of Texas's LBJ School of Public Policy. This would have been impossible without the patience and understanding of Jermi Suri, who went the extra mile. Last on the list but first in my heart is the only comeback HBCU in American history: Simmons College of Kentucky. While I was writing *Rebirth of a Nation*, Simmons brought me onto the faculty and into the family of the college. To my colleagues: I am a slow writer and worker—thank you for your patience. I pray *Rebirth* makes Simmons Nation proud.

I am grateful for the kindness and support of the cloud of witnesses— Rev. William Barber II, Mary Frances Berry, Michelle Dunster, Carol Anderson, David Roediger, Tim Tyson, and William Darity Jr. Like the friends listed above, your work has shaped my life, and no stamp of approval means more than the mentors we model our work after. Thank you for helping to provide this work a platform.

To my family: Sarah Ann, in loving you, I came to understand what abundance means. Naomi, your superpower the past several years has been sunshine, and I needed your radiance. Samuel Roger, you allowed me to cuddle you close and tight, and your love helped hold me together. Our family has been the most magical experience of my life.

Finally, to my readers: thanks for sharing in this journey. The road will be long and rocky, but the best is yet ahead.

Notes

Preface

1. James Baldwin, *Notes of a Native Son* (Boston: Beacon, 2012), 28.
2. Vincent Harding, *There Is a River: The Black Struggle for Freedom in America* (San Diego: Harcourt Brace, 1981), xix.
3. Guy Emerson Mount, "Can Reparations Save American Politics?," *Black Perspectives*, June 27, 2017.

Introduction

1. Quoted in Timothy B. Tyson, *The Blood of Emmett Till* (New York: Simon & Schuster, 2017), 66. Tyson's remarkable work informed much of my analysis of Mamie Till-Mobley and Emmett Till's story.
2. Tyson, *Blood of Emmett Till*, 178.
3. One of the most troubling books on the War on Crime and the War on Drugs is Elizabeth Hinton's *From the War on Poverty to the War on Crime: The Making of Mass Incarceration in America* (Cambridge, MA: Harvard University Press, 2016), where she details how racist public policies touched ground in places like Houston and communities like the Fifth Ward.
4. Richard West, "Only the Strong Survive," *Texas Monthly*, February 1979.
5. The stories of these families are used with permission. Names have been changed.
6. The story of the racialization of America's child welfare policies is brilliantly captured in Dorothy Roberts's *Shattered Bonds: The Color of Child Welfare* (New York: Basic, 2002).
7. Jared Sharpe, "UMass Amherst/WCVB Poll Finds Nearly Half of Americans Say the Federal Government Definitely Should Not Pay Reparations to the Descendants of Slaves," University of Massachusetts Amherst, April 29, 2021, https://www.umass.edu/news/article/umass-amherstwcvb-poll-finds-nearly-half.
8. Ta-Nehisi Coates, "The Case for Reparations," *Atlantic*, June 2014, 201.
9. Ta-Nehisi Coates, *We Were Eight Years in Power* (New York: One World, 2017), 202, 207.
10. W. E. B. Du Bois, *The Souls of Black Folk* (New York: Signet Classic, 1995), 227.
11. Howard Thurman, *The Mood of Christmas and Other Celebrations* (Richmond, IN: Friends United, 2001), 37.
12. James Baldwin, from an interview for *Ebony*, 1970, quoted in Eddie S. Glaude Jr.,

Begin Again: James Baldwin's America and Its Urgent Lessons for Our Own (New York: Crown, 2020), 145.

Chapter 1

1. Jon Meacham, *And There Was Light: Abraham Lincoln and the American Struggle* (New York: Random House, 2022), 9.

Chapter 2

1. Annette Gordon-Reed, *The Hemingses of Monticello: An American Family* (New York: Norton, 2008), 145

2. Clint Smith, *How the Word Is Passed: A Reckoning with the History of Slavery Across America* (New York: Little, Brown, 2021), 21.

3. Thomas Jefferson to John Adams, June 10, 1815, quoted in Jack McLaughlin, *Jefferson and Monticello: The Biography of a Builder* (New York: Henry Holt, 1990), 395.

4. See Gordon-Reed, *Hemingses of Monticello*, 111–13.

5. Benjamin Isaac, *The Invention of Racism in Classical Antiquity* (Princeton: Princeton University Press, 2004), 107, 195, 214; Thomas Jefferson, *Thomas Jefferson: Writings* (New York: Library of America, 1984), 96, 1341–43, 1431, 1436.

6. John Locke, *An Essay Concerning Human Understanding* (New York: Penguin, 1997), 403. Insulting political rivals by comparing them to monkeys was as ancient as the Greeks and was revived by church leaders to insult pagans, but in the Enlightenment this insult becomes racialized and weaponized against Black people and "savages."

7. For an extended discussion of Locke and the American experiment, see the chapter "John Locke: Institutionalizing and Aristocratic—& Racist—Revolution," in Joel Edward Goza, *America's Unholy Ghosts: The Racist Roots of Our Faith and Politics* (Eugene, OR: Cascade, 2019), 68–104.

8. Locke was not the only Enlightenment philosopher memorialized at Monticello who wrote of women taking monkeys for lovers. Voltaire, whose bust adorns the entrance hall, wove a similar myth into his novel *Candide*, which became one of the most important novels in the Western canon. In *Candide*, women from savage nations take monkeys as lovers. The story goes like this: "The sun went down" on Candide. He "heard some little cries which seemed to be uttered by women." Were the noises from the dark women's joy or pain? Candide did not know, but "the noise was made by two naked girls. . . . Two monkeys were pursuing them and biting their buttocks." Candide grabs his gun. *Bang. Bang. Bang.* "God be praised!" Candide declares, "I have rescued those two poor creatures." Yet to his horror, "he saw the two girls tenderly embracing the monkeys, bathing their bodies in tears, and rending the air with the most dismal lamentations." The servant Cacambo arrives: "Master . . . you have slain the sweethearts of those two young ladies. . . . Why should you think it so strange that in some countries there are monkeys which insinuate themselves into the good graces of the ladies?" Voltaire, *Candide* (New York: Boni and Liveright, 1918), 69–70.

9. Jefferson was brilliant. But Jefferson's significance when it comes to America is not mainly the originality of his thoughts on freedom, equality, slavery, or race. He was a man

of his time who swam in the Enlightened river in the same direction as his contemporaries, building upon their work but rarely breaking new ground. The new ground that Jefferson did break was in bringing the most racist aspects of Europe's Enlightenment onto American soil in a way that fundamentally intertwined slavery and white supremacy into our nation's DNA. Perhaps this would have happened without Jefferson. Nonetheless, Jefferson was white supremacy's leading intellectual in colonial America.

10. Thomas Jefferson, *Notes on the State of Virginia* (Philadelphia: Prichard and Hall, 1848), 173.

11. As Jon Meacham writes: "Beginning with Robert Carter, the planter who freed his slaves in 1791, some Virginians of Jefferson's class recognized that the blight of slavery had to go and did what was in their power by emancipating their slaves. . . . The politicians of the North were steadily creating a climate in which antislavery rhetoric and sentiment could take root. . . . The debate over Missouri suggested that antislavery forces were gathering strength. . . . It is not as though Jefferson lived in a time or in places where abolition was the remotest or most fanciful of prospects. It had not only been thought of but had been brought into being in his lifetime in lands he knew intimately." Jon Meacham, *Thomas Jefferson: The Art of Power* (New York: Random House, 2012), 478.

12. This is clearly shown in Ta-Nehisi Coates's "The Case for Reparations." "Quakers in New York, New England, and Baltimore went so far as to make membership 'contingent upon compensating one's former slaves'" Coates, "Case for Reparations," 176–77.

13. "Many consider it the most important American book written before 1800. Jefferson originally composed the work in 1781 in answer to queries posed by a French diplomat, and then revised and expanded it into a description and defense of the young United States as interpreted through a Virginia lens." Robert P. Forbes, "*Notes on the State of Virginia* (1785)," Encyclopedia Virginia, https://www.encyclopediavirginia.org/Notes_on_the _State_of_Virginia_1785.

14. "Deep rooted prejudices entertained by the whites; ten thousand recollections, by the blacks, of the injuries they have sustained; new provocations; will divide us into parties . . . and produce convulsions which will probably never end but in the extermination of the one or the other race." Thomas Jefferson, *Notes*, 147.

15. Jefferson, 148.

16. Nell Irvin Painter, *The History of White People* (New York: Norton, 2010), 87.

17. Jefferson, *Notes*, 148.

18. Anthony Slide, *American Racist: The Life and Films of Thomas Dixon* (Lexington: University Press of Kentucky, 2004), 143.

19. Jefferson, *Notes*, 154.

20. Like other racial myths, the emphasis on the purity of the master race can also be traced to the ancient Greeks. Isaac, *Invention of Racism*, 129.

21. It is important to note that Jefferson's predatory sexuality in no way began with Sally Hemings. This becomes obvious in his letter to a friend in 1764: "For St. Paul only says that it is better to be married than to burn. Now I presume that if that apostle had known that providence would at an after day be so kind to any particular set of people as to furnish them with other means of extinguishing their fire than those of matrimony, he would have earnestly recommended them to their practice." According to Jefferson, Paul would have encouraged the practice of white masters freely having sex with any slave of their choosing. That is a predatory piety. Thomas Jefferson to William Fleming, March

20, 1764, https://founders.archives.gov/documents/Jefferson/01-01-02-0009. See Goza, *America's Unholy Ghosts*, 120.

22. Jefferson, *Notes*, 148.

23. Daina Berry, *The Price for Their Pound of Flesh: The Value of the Enslaved, from Womb to Grave, in the Building of a Nation* (Boston: Beacon, 2017), 18.

24. Henry Bibb, *Narrative of the Life and Adventures of Henry Bibb, an American Slave* (New York: privately printed, 1849), 136.

25. Again, we must keep in mind that Jefferson's predatory behavior extended well beyond Sally Hemings. It was a hallmark of his life. In addition to the aforementioned letter in which he valorizes the life of singleness coupled with sex with slaves, he also wrote to John Wayles in 1820 commending the procurement of female slaves for the profit via reproduction. And he pursued multiple married women, including Betsy Walker and Maria Cosway.

26. David Walker, *David Walker's Appeal, in Four Articles* (Mansfield Centre, CT: Martino, 2015), 10.

27. See Gregory D. Smithers, *Slave Breeding: Sex, Violence, and Memory in African American History* (Gainesville: University Press of Florida, 2012).

28. Jefferson, *Notes*, 148–49.

29. Dorothy Roberts, *Fatal Invention: How Science, Politics, and Big Business Recreate Race in the Twenty-First Century* (New York: New Press, 2011), 83–84, 92. In her brilliant book, writer, professor, and activist Dorothy Roberts directly engages with Jefferson on the topic: "Jefferson was not misusing a biological category of race he had discovered in nature; he was helping to *invent* it for political reasons. Attributing blacks' poor health to inherent racial difference allowed whites like Jefferson both to ignore how disease is caused by political inequality and to justify an unequal system by pointing to the inherent racial difference that disease supposedly reveals." Jefferson helped write this lie, and it was a lie that never died. *Fatal Invention* traces the power of racial lies to shape modern medicine. "One of the most enduring and disturbing medical beliefs about blacks," writes Roberts, "is that they are impervious to pain. This myth has excused surgical experimentation without anesthesia on blacks, as well as providing blacks with inadequate pain relief for their injuries and illnesses."

30. Jefferson, *Notes*, 149, 152.

31. Benjamin Banneker to Thomas Jefferson, August 19, 1791, https://founders.archives .gov/documents/Jefferson/01-22-02-0049.

32. For more on Benjamin Banneker, see Reed, *Hemingses of Monticello*, 474–78; and Manisha Sinha, *The Slave's Cause: A History of Abolition* (New Haven: Yale University Press, 2016), 144–46.

33. Jefferson, *Notes*, 153.

34. See note 21, above.

35. Quoted in Smith, *How the Word Is Passed*, 31.

36. Jefferson, *Notes*, 154.

37. Thomas Jefferson to Edward Coles, August 25, 1814, https://founders.archives.gov /documents/Jefferson/03-07-02-0439. See also Peter S. Onuf and Annette Gordon-Reed, *"Most Blessed of Patriarchs": Thomas Jefferson and the Empire of the Imagination* (New York: Liveright, 2017), 285.

38. The leading candidate to compete with Jefferson for antislavery writings in the orbit of the Founding Fathers would be Thomas Paine. For analysis on Thomas Paine and

abolition, see James V. Lynch, "The Limits of Revolutionary Radicalism: Tom Paine and Slavery," *Pennsylvania Magazine of History and Biography* 123, no. 3 (July 1999): 177–99. Lynch writes: "To be sure, Thomas Paine *in no way supported slavery*, indeed he found it repulsive and sincerely hoped for its eradication. But so did many late-eighteenth-century intellectuals. It might even be argued that Thomas Jefferson, vilified in recent historical literature for his ambivalence about race, tried harder than Paine to challenge chattel slavery."

39. It bears repeating that despite the impotence of the fight for racial justice, the path to freedom was not impossible within the Revolutionary generation. Many leading lights—the Quakers, Benjamin Franklin, John Jay, Rufus King, Theodore Dwight, Benjamin Rush, and Samuel Hopkins—called for an end to slavery and the dawning of a new day.

40. David McCullough, *John Adams* (New York: Simon & Schuster, 2002), 419.

41. John Adams to Thomas Jefferson, May 22, 1785, https://founders.archives.gov/doc uments/Adams/06-17-02-0062.

42. See John Hope Franklin and Franklin A. Moss Jr., *From Slavery to Freedom: A History of African Americans* (New York: Knopf, 2000), 74–78.

43. Paul J. Polgar, "A Clash of Principles: The First Federal Debate over Slavery and Race, 1790," *Federal History Journal* 14 (2022): 31–32.

44. Thomas Jefferson to John Holmes, April 22, 1820, https://founders.archives.gov/doc uments/Jefferson/03-15-02-0518.

45. In the Declaration of Independence, Jefferson writes as much by blaming Britain for America's addiction to slavery. That passage on slavery was struck from the Declaration of Independence's final version.

46. Thomas Jefferson to James Madison, September 6, 1789, https://founders.archives .gov/documents/Madison/01-12-02-0248.

47. "Plunder" in this context is a favorite term not only for Ta-Nehisi Coates but also for a host of other Black writers, such as Hosea Easton and Frederick Douglass.

48. Thomas Jefferson to Frances Wright, August 7, 1825, https://founders.archives.gov /documents/Jefferson/98-01-02-5449.

49. See Meacham, *And There Was Light*, 62–63.

50. Thomas Jefferson to Jared Sparks, February 4, 1824, https://founders.archives.gov /documents/Jefferson/98-01-02-4020; Joseph J. Ellis, *American Sphinx: The Character of Thomas Jefferson* (New York: Vintage, 1998), 320. In 1973, the Harvard economist Claudia Dale Goldin estimated the value of slaves in America at $1.3 billion in 1850 and $2.7 billion in 1860. Goldin's calculations display how the cost of racial justice increased in time— doubling within a ten-year time frame. Claudia Dale Goldin, "The Economics of Emancipation," *Journal of Economic History* 33, no. 1 (1973): 74–75.

51. Jefferson joined James Madison in arguing that if slavery spread to places such as Missouri, it would hasten slavery's demise. The pursuit of self-justification produces self-deception. See Thomas Jefferson to William Branch Giles, December 26, 1825, https:// founders.archives.gov/documents/Jefferson/98-01-02-5771; and James Madison to Robert Walsh Jr., November 27, 1819, https://founders.archives.gov/documents/Madison /04-01-02-0504.

52. Other notable racial compromises include the Missouri Compromise of 1820 and the Compromise of 1850, as well as the Mexican-American War and the Kansas-Nebraska Act of 1854.

53. Frederick Douglass, "On the Mission of the War," *Douglass' Monthly*, January 13, 1864.

54. His fellow revolutionary John Adams passed on the same day.

55. Ellis, *American Sphinx*, 280.

56. Walker, *Appeal*, 28.

57. John Hope Franklin, "Who Divided This House?," *Chicago History* 19, nos. 3–4 (Fall and Winter 1990–91): 35.

Chapter 3

1. Shane Bauer, *American Prison: A Reporter's Undercover Journey into the Business of Punishment* (New York: Penguin, 2018), 98.

2. James M. McPherson, "Who Freed the Slaves?," *Proceedings of the American Philosophical Society* 139, no. 1 (March 1995): 3.

3. Harding, *There Is a River*, 117.

4. Quoted in Kellie Carter Jackson, *Force and Freedom: Black Abolitionists and the Politics of Violence* (Philadelphia: University of Pennsylvania Press, 2019), 33.

5. "Raced-Based Legislation in the North," PBS, https://www.pbs.org/wgbh/aia/part4/4p2957.html; Wendy S. Walters, "Lonely in America," in *The Fire This Time: A New Generation Speaks about Race*, ed. Jesmyn Ward (New York: Scribner, 2017), 45.

6. The law declared: "If any person or persons shall bring, or cause to be brought into this state, any negro or mulatto slave, whether said slaver is free or not, [he] shall be liable to an indictment."

7. Jackson, *Force and Freedom*, 7.

8. No one knows the body count the riots left, but the estimates range from the hundreds to over a thousand. The quote above is from Mattie Griffith to Mary Anne Estlin, July 27, 1863, quoted in Eric Foner, *Reconstruction: America's Unfinished Revolution, 1863–1877* (New York: HarperPerennial, 2014), 32–33; and Ida Giddings, *Ida: A Sword Among Lions* (New York: Amistad, 2008), 234. Griffith continued: "The negroes—the poor negroes! They have been the worst sufferers—no one helped them. They were recklessly shot down, hanged, burned, roasted alive—every device and refinement of cruelty practiced upon them, and no one dared interpose in their behalf."

9. John Hope Franklin and Loren Schweninger, *Runaway Slaves: Rebels on the Plantation* (New York: Oxford University Press, 2000), 281–82.

10. Frederick Douglass, "The Fugitive Slave Law," in *The Essential Douglass: Selected Writings and Speeches*, ed. Nicholas Buccola (Indianapolis: Hackett, 2016), 72.

11. Carl Sandburg, "Text of Carl Sandburg's Address on Lincoln Before a Joint Session of Congress," *New York Times*, February 13, 1959.

12. Doris Kearns Goodwin, *Team of Rivals: The Political Genius of Abraham Lincoln* (New York: Simon & Schuster, 2006), 52; Meacham, *And There Was Light*, 22.

13. William Lloyd Garrison, "The American Union," *Liberator*, January 10, 1845. See https://teachingamericanhistory.org/document/the-american-union/.

14. Quoted in David W. Blight, *Frederick Douglass: Prophet of Freedom* (New York: Simon & Schuster, 2018), 214.

15. Abraham Lincoln, "Speech on Internal Improvements," June 20, 1848, in *Speeches and Writings, 1832–1858*, ed. Don E. Fehrenbacher (New York: Library of America, 1989), 196.

16. Abraham Lincoln, "Speech on the Kansas-Nebraska Act at Peoria, Illinois," October 16, 1854, https://www.nps.gov/liho/learn/historyculture/peoriaspeech.htm.

17. With rare exception, slavery was not a stumbling block for the Revolutionary generation, and for most founders, slavery was a cornerstone that every other principle of life together must square. The largest slaveholders in the nation—North and South—signed the Declaration of Independence: forty-one of the fifty-six delegates who signed, in fact, enslaved people. The Constitution, by design, made enslaving people increase states' power. In no meaningful way were our founders "hostile" to slavery.

18. Joshua F. Speed to William H. Herndon, December 6, 1866, in Douglas L. Wilson and Rodney O. Davis, eds., *Herndon's Informants: Letters, Interviews, and Statements about Abraham Lincoln* (Champaign: University of Illinois Press, 1997), 499.

19. Abraham Lincoln and Dan Stone, "Protest in Illinois Legislature on Slavery," presented to the Illinois House of Representatives, March 3, 1837, https://papersofabraham lincoln.org/documents/D200101.

20. At his Lyceum address on January 27, 1838, less than three months after the Lovejoy murder, Lincoln mourned mob rule without morning the loss of Elijah Lovejoy. "In any case that arises, as for instance, the promulgation of abolitionism," Lincoln said, never is "mob law, either necessary, justifiable, or excusable." That is not much of a eulogy for an event the *Boston Recorder* compared to Lexington and Concord. His brothers penned *Liberty's Martyr* in Elijah's memory, and John Quincy Adams provided the introduction. For more on Lincoln, Illinois, and abolition, see Goodwin, *Team of Rivals*, 91.

21. Elmer Gertz, "The Black Laws of Illinois," *Journal of the Illinois State Historical Society (1908–1984)* 56, no. 3 (Fall 1963): 469–72; Andrew Delbanco, *The War Before the War: Fugitive Slaves and the Struggle for America's Soul from the Revolution to the Civil War* (New York: Penguin, 2018), 212.

22. Goodwin, *Team of Rivals*, 128.

23. Abraham Lincoln to Joshua F. Speed, August 24, 1855, in *Speeches and Writings, 1832–1858*, 360; Meacham, *And There Was Light*, 143.

24. Abraham Lincoln, *Lincoln-Douglas Debates*, Sixth Joint Debate, Quincy, IL, October 13, 1858, https://www.civiced.org/lincoln-lesson/sixth-joint-debate-between-abraham -lincoln-and-stephen-a-douglas-at-quincy-october-13-1858.

25. See Painter, "American School of Anthropology," in *History of White People*, and her analysis of Samuel Morton, Josiah Nott, and Louis Agassiz.

26. Perhaps the most prominent expression of this work was The American Anti-Slavery Society, founded by William Lloyd Garrison, Frederick Douglass, and Arthur Tappan in 1833. The society relied on moral suasion rooted in religion and personal testimonies of slavery's horrors.

27. Jackson, *Force and Freedom*, 80.

28. Quoted in Harding, *There Is a River*, 142.

29. Abraham Lincoln, "The First Inaugural," March 4, 1861, in *Speeches and Writings, 1859–1865*, ed. Don E. Fehrenbacher (New York: Library of America, 1989), 224.

30. Frederick Douglass, "The Inaugural Address," *Douglass' Monthly*, April 1861.

31. Lincoln to Speed, in *Speeches and Writings, 1832–1858*, 361.

32. Abraham Lincoln to Albert G. Hodges, April 4, 1864, in *Speeches and Writings, 1859–1865*, 585.

33. Jessie Benton Frémont, *The Letters of Jessie Benton Frémont*, ed. Pamela Herr and Mary Lee Spence (Champaign: University of Illinois Press, 1992), 246.

34. Congressional Joint Resolution on Compensated Emancipation, April 10, 1862.

35. Frederick Douglass, "Horse Democracy," *Douglass' Monthly*, October 1860.

36. Frederick Douglass, "The War and How to End It," *Douglass' Monthly*, March 1862.

37. Harriet Tubman, as recorded by Lydia Maria Child in a letter to John G. Whittier, January 21, 1862, Lydia Maria Child Papers, Library of Congress, Washington, DC. Quoted in Kate Clifford Larson, *Bound for the Promised Land: Harriet Tubman, Portrait of an American Hero* (New York: One World, 2003), 206.

38. Quoted in Blight, *Frederick Douglass*, 363.

39. John Hope Franklin, *The Emancipation Proclamation* (Wheeling, IL: Harlan Davidson, 1995), 31.

40. Abraham Lincoln, quoted in Meacham, *And There Was Light*, 383.

41. Many African Americans supported emigration rather than colonization. Blacks had immigrated to Haiti in the 1820s and the 1850s as well as supported emigration efforts from the United States to South and Central America proposed by Martin Delany. Members of this meeting were supporters of emigration. This, too, was a part of the Black response to the violence of the slavocracy and the desire to live freely beyond the boundaries of the United States.

42. Quoted in Franklin, *Emancipation Proclamation*, 30.

43. Significant racial work transpired in both the theological and scientific intellectual guilds, but that work attempted to cement white supremacy and reinforce a human hierarchy along racial lines.

44. Frederick Douglass, "The President and His Speeches," *Douglass' Monthly*, September 1862.

45. Quoted in Ibram X. Kendi, *Stamped from the Beginning: The Definitive History of Racist Ideas in America* (New York: Nation, 2016), 219.

46. Even after the emancipation, Lincoln considered removing the issue of slavery from the proposed peace settlement altogether. Louis Masur, *Lincoln's Last Speech: Wartime Reconstruction and the Crisis of Union* (New York: Oxford University Press, 2015), 118.

47. Quoted in Franklin, *Emancipation Proclamation*, xiv.

48. Quoted in Franklin, *Emancipation Proclamation*, 80.

49. Neither colonization nor compensation evaporated in the mind of the emancipator. Lincoln carried the potential of compensation with him through his final meetings with his Cabinet, but neither idea proved capable of gaining the needed traction. Franklin, *Emancipation Proclamation*, 129.

50. Robert Engs, "The Great American Slave Rebellion" (paper, Civil War Institute, Gettysburg College, Pennsylvania, June 27, 1991), 3.

51. Quoted in Blight, *Frederick Douglass*, 409.

52. Frederick Douglass, "On the Mission of the War." David Blight writes that as the Civil War pressed toward a close, the ideological and rhetorical similarities between Douglass and Lincoln made it seem as if they often worked "from the same script." David W. Blight, *Race and Reunion: The Civil War in American Memory* (Cambridge, MA: Belknap, 2001), 18.

53. Quoted in Meacham, *And There Was Light*, 373.

54. For more on Lincoln and Douglass's meetings, see Blight, *Frederick Douglass*, 406–10, 435–38.

55. Abraham Lincoln, "Gettysburg Address," Gettysburg, PA, November 19, 1863, https://www.loc.gov/resource/rbpe.24404500/?st=text.

56. Abraham Lincoln, "Annual Message to Congress," December 8, 1863, in *Speeches and Writings, 1859–1865*, 552.

57. Abraham Lincoln, "Annual Message to Congress," December 6, 1864, in *Speeches and Writings, 1859–1865*, 661.

58. Abraham Lincoln, "Proclamation of Amnesty and Reconstruction," December 8, 1863, in *Writings and Speeches, 1859–1865*, 555.

59. Lincoln, "Proclamation of Amnesty and Reconstruction," 557.

60. Foner, *Reconstruction*, 36.

61. Wendell Phillips, "Review of the President's Proclamation: Mr. Lincoln Considered No Leader," *New York Times*, December 23, 1863. Remarks delivered at the Cooper Institute in New York.

62. Quoted in Blight, *Frederick Douglass*, 432.

63. Christopher Bonner, interview in *Lincoln: Divided We Stand*, episode 5, "The Dogs of War," directed by Jon Hirsch, aired spring 2021 on CNN.

64. Abraham Lincoln, "The Second Inaugural," March 4, 1865, https://teachingameri canhistory.org/document/second-inaugural-address-1865-2/.

65. Meacham, *And There Was Light*, 354.

66. Quoted in James M. McPherson, *Tried by War: Abraham Lincoln as Commander in Chief* (New York: Penguin, 2008), 263.

67. For more on Fairbank, see Blight, *Race and Reunion*, 233. Fairbank served seventeen years in the Kentucky State Penitentiary, where he reportedly received thousands upon thousands of lashes for his solidarity with freedom's cause.

68. Frederick Douglass, "Oration of Frederick Douglass Delivered on the Occasion of the Unveiling of the Freemen's Monument in Memory of Abraham Lincoln," Washington, DC, April 14, 1876, in *Essential Douglass*, 241.

69. W. E. B. Du Bois, "Again, Lincoln," *Crisis*, September 1922, 200.

Chapter 4

1. Painter, *History of White People*, 194.

2. This estimate is based on census data that began in 1790. Every decade saw an increase in the number of people enslaved in America. Thus, for a conservative estimate, you can take the number of people enslaved according to the census and multiply that number by ten through the 1850 census. The 1860 census can be multiplied by four to harmonize with the Emancipation Proclamation.

3. Jefferson Davis's bail was paid by an unlikely collaboration of twenty patrons from the North and South. The freedom of Robert E. Lee was recommended by Ulysses S. Grant. Full presidential pardons would be forthcoming on Christmas Day 1968.

Chapter 5

1. Quoted in Elizabeth Brown Pryor, *Reading the Man: A Portrait of Robert E. Lee Through His Private Letters* (New York: Penguin, 2007), 152.

2. Quoted in Foner, *Reconstruction*, 82.

3. For those baptized under the Enlightenment's myths regarding Black sexuality and Black

inability for intimacy, the lengths to which the newly emancipated went to reestablish the broken bonds provided a clue that what America had believed about Black people had been a lie.

4. For a more thorough account, see Foner, *Reconstruction*, 88–110.

5. The first governmental agency established to provide for the basic needs of American citizens, the Freedmen's Bureau was tasked with helping provide education and land to the newly freed people. Against great odds, the bureau's meager provisions proved capable of meaningfully contributing to the well-being of the Black community through coordinating education, legal assistance, and emergency health care needs. But after four short years, the director of the Freedmen's Bureau, General Oliver Howard, moved to close up shop. In Howard's estimation, the bureau had fought a "war on dependence" and successfully shut its doors before empowering "pauperism." Howard displayed pride in the self-control the bureau exhibited by denying so many freed people assistance and providing economic aid to "so few."

6. Not only did Congress fail to appropriate sufficient funds to the Freedmen's Bureau; often what little funds were received were directed to relatives of deceased Confederates. "Less than 1 percent of aid went to freed Blacks—about five thousand rations for a population of more than three hundred thousand people." Robert Samuels and Toluse Olorunnipa, *His Name Is George Floyd: One Man's Life and the Struggle for Racial Justice* (New York: Viking, 2022), 37.

7. See W. Caleb McDaniel's *Sweet Taste of Liberty: A True Story of Slavery and Restitution in America* (New York: Oxford University Press, 2019) for Wood's full story.

8. Amos 5:24 and Gal. 3:28 NIV.

9. Nearly all other nations in the Western Hemisphere freed their slaves long before Lincoln's Emancipation Proclamation. Saint-Domingue ended slavery in 1803, Mexico in 1814, Central America in 1824, Bolivia in 1831, England (where enslavers received compensation in an amount not to exceed £20 million) in 1833, Uruguay in 1842, and Peru in 1855. Even Russia emancipated its serfs in 1861.

10. Keri Leigh Merritt, "Land and the Roots of African-American Poverty," *Aeon*, March 11, 2016.

11. Quoted in Christopher Petrella and Ameer Hasan Loggins, "'This is a Country for White Men': White Supremacy and U.S. Politics," *Black Perspectives*, January 5, 2017, https://www.aaihs.org/this-is-a-country-for-white-men-white-supremacy-and-u-s-politics/.

12. Blight, *Race and Reunion*, 45.

13. Harding, *There Is a River*, 309. Ida B. Wells provides a brief history of the Ku Klux Klan: "The events which have led up to the present wide-spread lawlessness in the South can be traced to the very first year Lee's conquered veterans marched from Appomattox to their homes in the Southland. They were conquered in war, but not in spirit. They believed as firmly as ever that it was their right to rule black men and dictate to the National Government. The Knights of White Liners and the Ku Klux Klans were composed of veterans of the Confederate army who were determined to destroy the effect of all the slave had gained by the war." Ida B. Wells, "Lynch Law in All Its Phases," in *The Light of Truth: Writings of an Anti-Lynching Crusader*, ed. Mia Bay (New York: Penguin, 2014), 111.

14. For an analysis of the ways in which the pre–Civil War legal system terrorized poor white people in the South, see Keri Leigh Merritt, *Masterless Men: Poor Whites and Slavery in the Antebellum South* (New York: Cambridge University Press, 2017), 179–251.

15. Horace Greeley, "Let Us Clasp Hands Across the Bloody Chasm," *Harper's Weekly*, September 21, 1872.

16. This phrase is from Confederate veteran John C. Underwood. Quoted in Blight, *Race and Reunion*, 139, 205.

17. The key cases were the Slaughterhouse Cases in 1873, *United States v. Cruikshank* in 1876, and the Civil Rights Cases in 1883. Under Justice Miller, the Slaughterhouse Cases sharply distinguished between federal citizenship rights and state citizenship rights in regard to the Fourteenth Amendment. The Fourteenth Amendment, the Supreme Court concluded, protected narrow federal rights—like running for federal office and the freedom to navigate ports and waterways. States' rights covered almost every other aspect of citizenship, from voting to education to labor, and those were not protected under the Fourteenth Amendment. The verdict blew the door open for racial discrimination without federal intervention. Justice Stephen Field dissented, writing simply that the verdict reduced the Fourteenth Amendment to "a vain and idle enactment, which accomplished nothing."

Under Justice Waite, the *Cruikshank* decision freed the perpetrators of the Colfax massacre, who had been convicted in a federal court. The majority opinion claimed the federal courts that had convicted the murderers had lacked jurisdiction. The upshot of the *Cruikshank* decision was that it essentially legalized vigilante justice by placing racialized violence under local, rather than federal, jurisdiction. Despite the *Cruikshank* decision providing the greatest blow to the protection of African Americans' rights since *Dred Scott*, the *New York Times* praised the verdict as demonstrating the "utmost fidelity to the highest interest of the whole people."

The final judicial nail in Reconstruction's coffin came in 1883, when the Supreme Court declared unconstitutional the Civil Rights Act of 1875, which had barred segregation. In the blatantly racist majority opinion written by Justice Joseph P. Bradley, the court divorced current acts of discrimination from America's history of racial oppression. "After giving to these questions all the consideration which their importance demands," Justice Bradley wrote, "we are forced to the conclusion that such an act of refusal has nothing to to do with slavery."

18. For more analysis, see Foner, *Reconstruction*, 575–87.

19. Frederick Douglass, "This Decision Has Humbled the Nation" (speech), Civil Rights Mass-Meeting, Lincoln Hall, Washington, DC, October 22, 1883.

20. W. E. B. Du Bois, *Black Reconstruction in America, 1860–1880* (New York: Free Press, 1998), 30.

Chapter 6

1. Dixon grew up in a clerical family in North Carolina. His father was a venerated preacher who owned slaves, and his mother heralded from wealthy plantation owners in South Carolina. In addition to Thomas, two other Dixon children—Benjamin Franklin Dixon and Amzi Clarence Dixon—would enter the ministry. Benjamin would fight for the Confederacy, and Amzi would coedit a set of ninety essays titled *The Fundamentals* (Chicago: Testimony, 1910–1915), perhaps the most influential theological work written in America, as it formed the foundation of modern Christian fundamentalism.

2. From Adams, Dixon encountered racial history ideas such as "germ theory" and

racial history theories such as the genius of the Teutonic people. These theories later inspired and informed the eugenics movement in America and Nazism in Germany. See Joel Williamson, *The Crucible of Race: Black-White Relations in the American South since Emancipation* (New York: Oxford University Press, 1985), 153–54.

3. Thomas Dixon Jr., "A Note to the Reader," in *The Flaming Sword* (Lexington: University Press of Kentucky, 2013).

4. Dixon's breaking point was seeing *Uncle Tom's Cabin* acted out as a play. He reportedly wept at the play's portrayal of the brutality of Southern life and committed himself to taking action to reframe the South as a land of Christian chivalry.

5. Quoted in Giddings, *Ida*, 87; Frederick Douglass, "A Day and a Night in 'Uncle Tom's Cabin,'" *Frederick Douglass' Paper*, March 4, 1853.

6. Quoted in E. F. Harkins, *Little Pilgrimages Among the Men Who Have Written Famous Books*, 2nd series (Boston: Page, 1903), 121.

7. Quoted in Grace Elizabeth Hale, *Making Whiteness: The Culture of Segregation in the South, 1890–1940* (New York: Pantheon, 1998), 79; Michele K. Gillespie and Randal L. Hall, eds., *Thomas Dixon Jr. and the Birth of Modern America* (Baton Rouge: Louisiana State University Press 2006), 1.

8. Thomas Dixon Jr., *The Leopard's Spots: A Romance of the White Man's Burden—1865–1900* (New York: Doubleday, Page, 1902), 5.

9. Dixon, *Leopard's Spots*, 39–40.

10. It is important to understand that white supremacy united white Christians across ideological and regional divides. Dixon's own family is a case in point. Dixon was a progressive Christian from the Social Gospel tradition, and his theology fit well with New York and New England liberals. His brother Amzi was one of the editors of the most famous fundamentalist Christian collections of texts in American history, one that was simply titled *The Fundamentals*. The Dixon brothers' relationship was bitter, but they were united on white supremacy.

11. Frederick Douglass, "The Nation's Great Act," *National Republican*, April 18, 1885.

12. W. E. B. Du Bois, "Religion in the South," in Booker T. Washington and W. E. Burghardt DuBois, *The Negro in the South: His Economic Progress in Relation to His Moral and Religious Development* (Philadelphia: George W. Jacobs, 1907), 174.

13. For a full treatment of how white Christianity fueled a racist national reconciliation, see Edward J. Blum, *Reforging the White Republic: Race, Religion, and American Nationalism, 1865–1898* (Baton Rouge: Louisiana State University Press, 2005).

14. His novel *Sins of the Father* refers to white men's failure to withstand being seduced by Black women. The book was likely of unique personal importance to Dixon, as Dixon's father was rumored to have had an interracial child. See John David Smith, "Dixon and His African American Critics," in Gillespie and Hall, *Thomas Dixon Jr.*, 52.

15. Duke was the editor of the *Montgomery Herald*, a Black newspaper. "We greatly suspect," he wrote about the increasing intimacies between Black men and white women, "it is the growing appreciation of the white Juliet for the colored Romeo, as he becomes more and more intelligent and refined." When the editorial hit the stands, Duke was forced to hit the road to save his life. Giddings, *Ida*, 153.

16. Dixon, *Leopard's Spots*, 146.

17. Dixon, *Leopard's Spots*, 108.

18. Du Bois, *Black Reconstruction*, 428. This section of Du Bois's masterpiece inspired

the introduction to Ta-Nehisi Coates's *We Were Eight Years in Power*, in which Coates analyzes how the same dynamic was at work throughout Obama's presidency.

19. In truth, most bayonets left the South, and the racist backlash from the white community against Black elected officials typically left Black public servants in poverty rather than with privileges.

20. Dixon, *Leopard's Spots*, 242, 335, 394.

21. Dixon, *Leopard's Spots*, 127–28.

22. Dixon, *Leopard's Spots*, 85.

23. Blight, *Race and Reunion*, 109.

24. Ida B. Wells, "Lynch Law in America," *Arena*, January 1900.

25. Ida B. Wells, "Southern Horrors: Lynch Law in All Its Phases," in *Light of Truth*, 70.

26. Ida B. Wells, "The Negro's Case in Equity," *Independent*, April 5, 1900.

27. Wells, "Southern Horrors," 70.

28. Dixon, *Leopard's Spots*, 160.

29. Ida B. Wells, "A Red Record," in Wells, *Light of Truth*, 223.

30. In *The Negro a Beast*, Carroll argues within the racist pre-Adamist tradition that white people are descendants of Adam, while Black people descended from apes.

31. "Dixon's *Leopard's Spots*," Institute for Advanced Technology in the Humanities at the University of Virginia, http://utc.iath.virginia.edu/proslav/dixonhp.html; Slide, *American Racist*, 33.

32. Meacham, *And There Was Light*, 180.

33. Thomas Dixon Jr., *The Clansman* (Lexington: University Press of Kentucky, 1970), 56.

34. Kelly Miller of Howard University expressed this hope most poignantly: "These misstatements of fact are not of so much importance in themselves, as that they serve to warn the reader against the accuracy and value of your general judgments. . . . You will not blame the reader for not paying much heed to your sweeping generalizations, when you are at such little pains as to the accuracy of easily ascertainable data." Kelly Miller, *As to* The Leopard's Spots*: An Open Letter to Thomas Dixon Jr.* (Washington, DC: Hayworth, 1905), 18.

35. Goodwin, *Team of Rivals*, 258, 293.

36. Dixon, *Clansman*, 29, 31.

37. Franklin, *Emancipation Proclamation*, 57.

38. Dixon, *Clansman*, 290.

39. Quoted in Painter, *History of White People*, 127.

40. Dixon, *Clansman*, 117. On the Freedmen's Bureau's favoritism of the white poor over freed people, see Nancy Isenberg, *White Trash: The 400-Year Untold History of Class in America* (New York: Viking, 2016), 178.

41. Ta-Nehisi Coates, *The Water Dancer: A Novel* (New York: Random House, 2019), 35.

42. US Supreme Court Justice Samuel Miller summed up the irony: "The pretense is that the negro won't work [unless] he is compelled to do so, and this pretense is made in a country and by the white people, where the negro has done all the work for four generations and the white man makes a boast of the fact that he will *not* labour." Quoted in Carol Anderson, *White Rage: The Unspoken Truth of Our Racial Divide* (New York: Bloomsbury, 2016), 27.

43. Frederick Douglass, Speech at Concert Hall, Philadelphia, April 14, 1875, in *Centennial Anniversary of the Pennsylvania Society for Promoting the Abolition of Slavery, the*

Relief of Free Negroes, Unlawfully Held in Bondage, and for Improving the Condition of the African Race (Philadelphia: Grant, Faires & Rodgers, 1875), 25.

44. Grant quoted in Harding, *There Is a River*, 239. The remanent Union troops in the South often proved indifferent to the racial violence occurring under their noses. Mob rule became a communal right in the South. Following the 1866 race riots in Memphis, 47 freed citizens lay dead; the New Orleans Massacre of 1866 added 34 victims; 200 freed people were slaughtered in the Opleousas Massacre of 1868; and Colfax added another 150 victims in 1873. Following these riots and the over 425 murders they represented, no meaningful justice ensued. Yet, absolving the South of 425 murders was only the tip of the iceberg. Everything was bigger in Texas. Between 1865 and 1868, 1,000 citizens were lynched in the Lone Star State. Though 500 white men were indicted on the charge of murder, none were convicted. As one observer noted: "Murder is considered one of their inalienable state rights." Anderson, *White Rage*, 30; Foner, *Reconstruction*, 204, 242, 262, 263, 437.

45. The soldier in Dixon's narrative named August Caesar feels loosely based on the historical lynching victim Jim Williams. Williams had escaped from slavery and led Union troops.

46. Dixon, *Clansman*, 217.

47. August's rule over eighty thousand men is but one example of the absurd historical delusions Dixon sought to foster, as at the time in which this part of the story is set, there were not much more than eighty thousand Union soldiers left in all the South. "From June 1865 to January 1866, the occupation force in the South shrank from roughly 270,000 to 87,550 soldiers." Mark L. Bradley, *The Army and Reconstruction, 1865–1877* (Washington, DC: Center of Military History, 2015), 15.

48. Dixon, *Clansman*, 304.

49. Dixon, *Clansman*, 314.

50. Dixon, *Clansman*, 314.

51. Dixon, *Clansman*, 323.

52. Dixon, *Clansman*, 343, 374.

53. Douglas Blackmon, *Slavery by Another Name: The Re-Enslavement of Black Americans from the Civil War to World War II* (New York: Random House, 2009), 267.

54. Sutton E. Griggs, *The Hindered Hand: or, The Reign of the Repressionist* (Nashville: Orion, 1905), 228.

55. W. Fitzhugh Brundage, "American Proteus," in Gillespie and Hall, *Thomas Dixon Jr.*, 31.

56. It is important to note that Dixon's literary output was developing in lockstep with the more sophisticated works of academic history and the racial sciences of his age. But neither the "academic" in "academic history" nor the "science" in "racial sciences" were antidotes to white supremacy's mythologies. Racist mythologies provided *the* lens of all academic work that intersected with race, politics, and religion. The Columbia School in New York translated Reconstruction in precisely the same way as Dixon. The racial sciences used biology to buttress arguments of the beast-like nature of Black Americans, but neither the Columbia School nor the racial sciences proved able to paint their ideas with the same power as Dixon.

57. See Kendi, *Stamped from the Beginning*, 287, 306; James H. Cone, *The Cross and the Lynching Tree* (New York: Orbis, 2013), 5; John Hope Franklin, "History as Propaganda,"

in *Race and History: Selected Essays, 1938–1988* (Baton Rouge: Louisiana State University Press, 1991), 16–17.

58. Slide, *American Racist*, 198.

59. Quoted in Slide, *American Racist*, 95.

60. Joshua Rothman, "When Bigotry Paraded Through the Streets," *Atlantic*, December 4, 2016.

61. W. E. B. Du Bois, *Dusk of Dawn*, in *Writings*, ed. Nathan Huggins (New York: Library of America, 1986), 730.

62. David Levering Lewis, *W. E. B. Du Bois: The Fight for Equality and the American Century, 1919–1963* (New York: Owl, 2000), 86–87.

63. Donovan Ramsey, *When Crack Was King: A People's History of a Misunderstood Era* (New York: One World, 2023), 94.

64. Thomas Leonard, *Illiberal Reformers: Race, Eugenics, and American Economics in the Progressive Era* (Princeton: Princeton University Press, 2016), 122.

65. Miller, *As to* The Leopard's Spots, 20.

66. Griggs, *Hindered Hand*, 337.

67. Equal Justice Initiative, *Lynching in America: Confronting the Legacy of Racial Terror*, 3rd ed. (Montgomery, AL: Equal Justice Initiative, 2017), 4.

68. Richard Wright, *Black Boy* (New York: Harper Perennial, 1993), 203.

69. See Slide, *American Racist*, 5, 209–12; Gillespie and Hall, *Thomas Dixon Jr.*, 13.

70. Quoted in John David Smith, "Dixon and His African American Critics," in Gillespie and Hall, *Thomas Dixon Jr.*, 62.

71. Frank Smethurst, "Americans in Black, White and Red," *Raleigh News and Observer*, August 6, 1939.

72. Quoted in Smith, "Dixon and His African American Critics," 71.

Chapter 7

1. Reconstruction officially ended with the Compromise of 1877 that secured the election of Rutherford B. Hayes. It was another classic American political compromise that crucified Black people. In it, the contested 1876 presidential election found closure through Hayes's promise to remove the final remnants of federal troops from the South after he entered office. True to his word, Hayes placed Black lives back into the hands of unrepentant enslavers.

2. Isabel Wilkerson, "The Great Migration," in *Four Hundred Souls: A Community History of African America, 1619–2019*, ed. Ibram X. Kendi and Keisha N. Blain (New York: One World, 2021), 279.

3. Painter, *History of White People*, 111.

4. For a deeper analysis, see Matthew Frye Jacobson, *Whiteness of a Different Color: European Immigrants and the Alchemy of Race* (Cambridge, MA: Harvard University Press, 1999), 22.

5. The French and English participated in the work, but America and Germany provided arguably the richest research and training grounds in these sciences. Leading racial scholars often developed strong ties to both nations.

6. Painter, *History of White People*, 193.

7. From 1820 to 1870, immigration dramatically increased in America, but northern Europe accounted for well over 90 percent of immigrants and again increased Anglo-Saxon dominance. After 1870, immigration's aggressive growth continued, but its Anglo-Saxon dominance waned. Immigration aggressively increased in the latter half of the nineteenth century. From 1900 to 1910, America received more immigrants than it had from 1820 to 1870 *combined.*

8. Leonard, *Illiberal Reformers*, 4.

9. Khalil Gibran Muhammad, *The Condemnation of Blackness: Race, Crime, and the Making of Modern Urban America* (Cambridge, MA: Harvard University Press, 2019), 8, 10.

10. Madison Grant, *The Passing of the Great Race*, 4th ed. (New York: Scribner's, 1923), 79. This quote does not appear in the original edition. All other citations of this work are to the original edition, reprinted by Martino in 2017.

11. Quoted in Jonathan Spiro, *Defending the Master Race: Conservation, Eugenics, and the Legacy of Madison Grant* (Burlington: University of Vermont Press, 2009), 158.

12. The term "race suicide" becomes central to Madison Grant's thinking. The term was first coined in 1900 by Edward A. Ross.

13. Michael Kohlman, "Evangelizing Eugenics: A Brief Historiography of Popular and Formal American Eugenics Education (1908–1948)," *Alberta Journal of Educational Research* 58, no. 4 (Winter 2012): 380.

14. Spiro, *Defending the Master Race*, xi, 164.

15. Roberts, *Fatal Invention*, 42; Spiro, *Defending the Master Race*, iii, 142, 154.

16. For more analysis on the conflicts and discrepancies within European racial mythologies, see George L. Mosse, *Toward the Final Solution: A History of European Racism* (New York: H. Fertig, 1978); Léon Poliakov, *The Aryan Myth: A History of Racist and Nationalist Ideas in Europe*, trans. Edmund Howard (London: Sussex University Press, 1974); and Spiro, *Defending the Master Race*, chap. 7.

17. See Kendi, *Stamped from the Beginning*, 209–11; and Herbert Spencer, *The Principles of Biology*, vol. 1, chap. 12, "Indirect Equilibration" (London and Edinburgh: Williams and Norgate, 1864).

18. Francis Galton, "Probability, the Foundation of Eugenics," Herbert Spencer Lecture, University of Oxford, June 5, 1907, in Francis Galton, *Essays in Eugenics* (London: Eugenics Education Society, 1909), 99.

19. Madison Grant, *The Passing of the Great Race* (Eastford, CT: Martino, 2017), 87. Francis Galton delineates why inferior races cannot benefit from public investment: "But a barbarian has none of these facilities: his interests are few; his dress, such as it is, is intended to stand the wear and tear of years, and all weathers; it is relatively very costly, and is an investment, one may say, of his capital rather than of his income; the invention of his people is sluggish, and their arts are few, consequently he is perforce taught to be conservative, his ideas are fixed, and he becomes scandalised even at the suggestion of change." Francis Galton, *Inquiries into Human Investment* (New York: Macmillan, 1883), 180.

20. As will be discussed, both social Darwinists and eugenicists believed in obliterating the unfit. The main difference was that eugenics also imagined the "positive" work of bringing together the best people to breed. In time, however, even most eugenicists believed positive eugenics was more utopian than realpolitik.

21. Craniology, the study of the measurement of skulls, was a means by which racial

scientists attempted to demonstrate that white people possessed the largest brains and therefore the highest intelligence. The theory of recapitulation in biology states that the stages an organism passes through during its embryonic development repeat the evolutionary stages of structural change in its ancestral lineage. In the racial sciences, the rage was to display how Black Americans more closely resembled the ape to prove that Black people represented a less evolved species.

22. Edward Franklin Frazier, "The Pathology of Race Prejudice," *Forum* 77, no. 6 (June 1927): 857.

23. Frazier, "The Pathology of Race Prejudice," 857.

24. Grant, *Passing of the Great Race*, 228.

25. Grant, *Passing of the Great Race*, 23, 187 (emphasis mine).

26. Madison Grant, "The Racial Transformation of America," *North American Review* 219, no. 820 (March 1924): 352.

27. Grant, *Passing of the Great Race*, 74–75.

28. As the leading Nazi theorist Eugen Fischer remarked: "The Jew is such an alien and, therefore, when he wants to insinuate himself, he must be warded off. This is self-defense. In saying this, I do not characterize every Jew as inferior, as Negroes are, and I do not underestimate the greatest enemy with whom we have to fight." Quoted in Edwin Black, *War against the Weak: Eugenics and America's Campaign to Create a Master Race* (Washington, DC: Dialog, 2003), 317.

29. Grant, *Passing of the Great Race*, 27.

30. Madison Grant, *The Conquest of a Continent* (London: Ostara, 2018), 19–20.

31. W. E. B. Du Bois, "The Technique of Race Prejudice," *Crisis*, August 1923, 153.

32. W. E. B. Du Bois, "Americanization," *Crisis*, August 1922, 154.

33. W. E. B. Du Bois, *Darkwater: Voices from within the Veil* (New York: Harcourt, Brace and Howe, 1920), 120.

34. Grant, "Racial Transformation of America," 350.

35. Grant, *Passing of the Great Race*, xvi (emphasis mine).

36. Madison Grant, "America for Americans," *Forum* 74, no. 3 (September 1925): 351.

37. Grant, "America for Americans," 352.

38. Grant, *Passing of the Great Race*, 14.

39. Grant, *Passing of the Great Race*, 16.

40. This passage proved influential on Hitler, who in *Mein Kampf* writes: "But it is a scarcely conceivable fallacy of thought to believe that a Negro or a Chinese, let us say, will turn into a German because he learns German and is willing to speak the German language in the future and perhaps even give his vote to a German political party. . . . Surely no one will call the purely external fact that most of this lice-ridden [Jewish] migration from the East speaks German a proof of their German origin and nationality." See Black, *War against the Weak*, 275.

41. Grant, *Passing of the Great Race*, 45 (emphasis mine).

42. Grant, *Passing of the Great Race*, 69.

43. See William A. Darity Jr., "Many Roads to Extinction: Early AEA Economists and the Black Disappearance Theory," *History of Economics Review* 21, no. 1 (January 1994): 47.

44. Grant, *Passing of the Great Race*, 47.

45. Grant, *Passing of the Great Race*, 47, 49 (emphasis mine).

46. Quoted in Painter, *History of White People*, 186.

47. Quoted in J. R. LeMaster and Donald D. Kummings, eds., *Walt Whitman: An Encyclopedia* (New York: Routledge, 1998), 568.

48. Charles Darwin, *The Descent of Man, and Selection in Relation to Sex* (Norwalk: The Easton Press, 1979), 139.

49. Herbert Spencer, *First Principles: Sixth and Final Edition* (Honolulu: University of the Pacific, 2000), 427–28.

50. When the 1890 census displayed a two-percentage-point decrease in the number of Blacks in America, it was confirmation that such scientific hopes were not in vain. America's fittest people would survive and Black Americans would die. Francis Amasa Walker, a Union army officer and the superintendent of the 1870 and 1880 census who later rose to the presidency of the Massachusetts Institute of Technology, interpreted the 1890 census in harmony with the Black extinction hypothesis. Walker believed better days lay in store for those seeking the eradication of Black Americans: "The diminution of marriages or persistence in the criminal practices, which diminishes the birth rate, is more than likely to accelerate the death rate.... Hence we may say wherever the *raison d'être* of the colored man ... [a] rapid decline in this element ... is to be expected." With this eager expectation, white America waited for a whiter future. Muhammad, *Condemnation of Blackness*, 32; Francis A. Walker, *Discussions in Economics and Statistics: The Colored Race in the United States* (New York: Henry Holt, 1999), 135.

51. Quoted in Matthew Connelly, *Fatal Misconception: The Struggle to Control World Population* (Cambridge, MA: Belknap, 2008), 44.

52. Grant, *Passing of the Great Race*, 16. See also Isaac, *Invention of Racism*, 118–21.

53. Adolf Hitler, *Mein Kampf*, vol. 1, trans. Ralph Manheim (New York: Mariner, 1971), 285. See also Black, *War against the Weak*, 274–75.

54. Richard Weikart, "The Role of Darwinism in Nazi Racial Thought," *German Studies Review* 36, no. 3 (October 2013): 541.

55. Spiro, *Defending the Master Race*, 137.

56. Grant, *Conquest of a Continent*, 221, 223.

57. W. E. B. Du Bois, "The Superior Race (An Essay)," *The Smart Set: A Magazine of Cleverness* 70, no. 4 (April 1923).

58. Spiro, *Defending the Master Race*, 160.

59. Unsurprisingly, neither craniology's claim that larger brains possess more brainpower nor the superiority of the shape of Anglo-Saxon heads held up to scrutiny over time. Eventually, explaining away the exceptions to the rules of the game kills people's confidence in the rules themselves.

60. See Stephen Jay Gould, *The Mismeasure of Man* (New York: Norton, 1996), 181. For the larger context of IQ tests, see chapter 5, "The Hereditarian Theory of IQ: An American Invention."

61. Leonard, *Illiberal Reformers*, 73.

62. The administration of IQ tests highly impacts their results. Binet's tests were designed for a licensed administrator to sit one-on-one with a student to ensure accuracy. Such rigor was impracticable when administering them in large numbers under tight timelines. Unsurprisingly, the best conditions for taking the tests were provided to native-born white soldiers. Language barriers were brutal, impacting soldiers from immigrant families, and the high illiteracy rates among Black soldiers coupled with the way the tests were administered made them nearly impossible to take.

63. Though few elite schools possess a racially innocent past, it is Princeton University that is considered the Ivy League of the South and was the last to integrate. Princeton long recruited from the South's leading families and depended on their donations. Paul Robeson, who was born and raised in Princeton, referred to it as the "Northernmost town in the South, . . . spiritually located in Dixie." The Black community would set a curfew for their children because the streets were filled with the "drunken rich" and were not safe for Black children. See Fred Jerome and Rodger Taylor, *Einstein on Race and Racism* (New Brunswick, NJ: Rutgers University Press, 2006), chap. 3, "The Other Princeton."

64. Spiro, *Defending the Master Race*, 216, 220.

65. Horace Bond, "Intelligence Tests and Propaganda," *Crisis*, May 30, 1924, 61.

66. Spiro, *Defending the Master Race*, 220.

67. Against great odds, many of the *St. Louis's* passengers survived the war waged for their annihilation, though 234 did not. Dara Lind, "How America's Rejection of Jews Fleeing Nazi Germany Haunts Our Refugee Policy Today," *Vox*, January 27, 2017.

68. Spiro, *Defending the Master Race*, 370.

69. See Isabel Wilkerson, *Caste: The Origins of Our Discontents* (New York: Random House, 2020), 78; and Spiro, *Defending the Master Race*, xii.

70. W. E. B. Du Bois, *Darkwater*, 34, 50.

71. Langston Hughes, "Nazi and Dixie Nordics," in *Langston Hughes and the Chicago Defender: Essays on Race, Politics, and Culture, 1942–62*, ed. Christopher C. De Santis (Champaign: University of Illinois Press, 1995), 80.

72. Carol Anderson, *Eyes Off the Prize: The United Nations and the African American Struggle for Human Rights, 1944–1955* (Cambridge: Cambridge University Press, 2003), xxx.

73. Spiro, *Defending the Master Race*, 167.

74. Grant's victories in immigration predated the Immigration Restriction Act of 1924. With help from friends, Grant secured the passage of literacy test requirements for immigrants in 1917 despite President Wilson's veto. Grant's influence would finally be broken by the Hart-Celler Act of 1965 during Lyndon B. Johnson's presidency. Emmanuel Celler was a freshman in Congress who began fighting for immigrant rights during Grant's infamous quest to ensure the passage of the Immigration Restriction Act of 1924.

75. Much of the unemployment inequality along racial lines resided in the North and West, as sharecropping and other forms of servitude inflated Black employment figures without easing Black economic agony.

76. Spiro, *Defending the Master Race*, 250.

77. See William A. Sundstrom, "Black Unemployment in the Great Depression," *Journal of Economic History* 52 (1992): 422; Daina Ramey Berry and Kali Nicole Gross, *A Black Women's History of the United States* (Boston: Beacon, 2020), 139.

78. See chapter 3, "Burning Brown to the Ground," and chapter 4, "Rolling Back Civil Rights," in Carol Anderson's *White Rage*.

79. Spiro, *Defending the Master Race*, xiii, 250.

Chapter 8

1. When Germany rejected American jurisprudence, it was usually because Amer-

ican jurisprudence proved too racist and laws like the one-drop rule too radical for German tastes.

2. Ronald J. Pestritto and William J. Atto, *American Progressivism: A Reader* (Lanham, MD: Lexington, 2008), 1–2.

3. Hitler, *Mein Kampf*, 184.

4. James Q. Whitman, *Hitler's American Model: The United States and the Making of Nazi Race Law* (Princeton: Princeton University Press, 2017), 6.

5. Martin Luther King Jr., "Letter from Birmingham City Jail," in *A Testament of Hope: The Essential Writings and Speeches of Martin Luther King Jr.*, ed. James M. Washington (New York: HarperOne, 1986), 295.

6. Douglas Blackmon estimates that at least two hundred thousand Black Americans were subjected to the convict leasing system in Alabama. Over the eighty-year period before the system was formally ended in 1941, he estimates that tens of millions of Black Americans nationwide were either forced to live on a farm or in a lumber camp or forced into convict leasing by the justice system. Douglas Blackmon, "Book: American Slavery Continued Until 1941," interview by Imani Cheers, *Newsweek*, July 13, 2008.

7. Anderson, *Eyes Off the Prize*, 180.

8. Ida B. Wells, "Lynch Law in America," *Arena*, January 1900.

9. See Mary Francis Berry, *My Face Is Black Is True: Callie House and the Struggle for Ex-Slave Reparations* (New York: Vintage, 2006).

10. Du Bois, "Americanization," 155.

11. Quoted in Barbara Ransby, *Ella Baker and the Black Freedom Movement: A Radical Democratic Vision* (Chapel Hill: University of North Carolina Press, 2003), 1.

Chapter 9

1. Quoted in Jason Sokol, *The Heavens Might Crack: The Death and Legacy of Martin Luther King Jr.* (New York: Basic, 2018), 38.

2. Robert Caro, *The Passage of Power: The Years of Lyndon Johnson*, vol. 4 (New York: Knopf, 2012), xiv, 406.

3. Lyndon B. Johnson to Martin Luther King Jr., phone conversation, November 25, 1963, https://www.discoverlbj.org/item/tel-00056.

4. Ramsey, *When Crack Was King*, 36, 38.

5. Quoted in Keisha Blain, *Until I Am Free: Fannie Lou Hamer's Enduring Message to America* (Boston: Beacon, 2021), 71.

6. For more on Oscar Lewis and other theorists of the era, see Mitchell Duneier, *Ghetto: The Invention of a Place, the History of an Idea* (New York: Farrar, Straus and Giroux, 2017).

7. Daniel Patrick Moynihan, *The Negro Family: The Case for National Action* (Washington, DC: Office of Policy Planning and Research, US Department of Labor, 1965), 5.

8. Moynihan, *Negro Family*, 12.

9. The concept of a "tangle of pathology" began with the Black sociologist E. Franklin Frazier, on whom Moynihan builds much of his argument. And yet Moynihan's employment of Frazier's ideas lacks the nuance and care of Frazier's original work and provides an example of how Black people's writings and arguments can be reappropriated to support white ideas antithetical to their original designs. For more on Moynihan and Frazier, see

Tony Platt, "E. Franklin Frazier and Daniel Patrick Moynihan: Setting the Record Straight," *Contemporary Crises* 11 (September 1987): 265–77.

10. Moynihan, *Negro Family*, 5, 30.

11. Moynihan, *Negro Family*, 29.

12. Quoted in Alice O'Connor, *Poverty Knowledge: Social Science, Social Policy, and the Poor in Twentieth-Century U.S. History* (Princeton: Princeton University Press, 2001), 207.

13. Hinton, *From the War on Poverty*, 75; Ramsey, *When Crack Was King*, 50.

14. Hinton, *From the War on Poverty*, 79.

15. Ramsey, *When Crack Was King*, 37.

16. Jelani Cobb, *The Essential Kerner Commission: The Landmark Study on Race, Inequality, and Police Violence* (New York: Liveright, 2021), 16.

17. "When asked whether the War on Poverty was designed specifically to help urban blacks, Adam Yarmolinsky, a key advisor to Kennedy and Johnson, commented that administration planners in 1963 paid less attention to the problems of the ghettoes than to Appalachia. 'Color it Appalachian,' he concluded, 'if you are going to color it anything at all'" Ronald Eller, *Uneven Ground: Appalachia since 1945* (Lexington: University Press of Kentucky, 2008), 88.

18. In interviews with local white officials, the responses consistently displayed a remarkable level of either obliviousness or indifference to the needs of officials' Black constituency, who often lacked any Black representation.

19. Quoted in Steve Gillon, *Separate and Unequal: The Kerner Commission and the Unraveling of American Liberalism* (New York: Basic, 2018), 101.

20. National Advisory Commission on Civil Disorders, *The Kerner Report* (Princeton: Princeton University Press, 2016), 1.

21. *Kerner Report*, 2.

22. Ramsey, *When Crack Was King*, 37.

23. Quoted in Hinton, *From the War on Poverty*, 140–42.

24. Moynihan, *Negro Family*, 47.

25. James T. Patterson, *Freedom Is Not Enough: The Moynihan Report and America's Struggle over Black Family Life from LBJ to Obama* (New York: Basic, 2010), 124.

Chapter 10

1. David S. Broder and Stephen Hess, *The Republican Establishment: The Present and Future of the G.O.P.* (New York: Harper & Row, 1967), 272.

2. Ronald Reagan, *Where's the Rest of Me?* (New York: Karz, 1981), 12–13.

3. Reagan, *Where's the Rest of Me?*, 12.

4. See Stephen Vaughn, "Ronald Reagan and the Struggle for Black Dignity in Cinema, 1937–1953," *Journal of Negro History* 77, no. 1 (Winter 1992): 1, 11, 13.

5. Harry Truman to Charles Bolte, August 28, 1946, https://www.trumanlibrary.gov/library/public-papers/214/letter-chairman-american-veterans-committee-concerning-discrimination. See also Anderson, *Eyes Off the Prize*, 68.

6. Reagan, *Where's the Rest of Me?*, 160.

7. Reagan, *Where's the Rest of Me?*, 161, 163. I originally came across this quote in David T. Byrne, *Ronald Reagan: An Intellectual Biography* (Lincoln, NE: Potomac, 2018), 20.

8. See Milton Friedman, "What Is Barry Goldwater's View of Economics?," *New York Times*, October 11, 1964; "Klan to Back Goldwater Despite His Repudiation," *New York Times*, August 14, 1964 (official endorsement from Imperial Wizard Robert M. Shelton).

9. H. W. Brands, *Reagan: The Life* (New York: Anchor, 2016), 105.

10. Byrne, *Ronald Reagan*, 31.

11. Not many Black Americans joined the Communist Party, but some did. In the South, the Communist Party, which consisted mainly of impoverished Black people, was simply referred to as "the nigger party." The commitment of poor Black people to communism was inextricably bound to their deeper commitments to interracial democracy, civil and workers' rights, and the teachings of Jesus. Just as Black people repurposed white Christianity for their own spiritual and political needs, sometimes communism itself was recrafted and repurposed in Black people's fight for a more egalitarian and antiracist nation.

12. The communists would fight against lynching and provide legal defense for Black people wrongfully accused of rape, most famously in the Scottsboro case. As Robin D. G. Kelley details in his classic, *Hammer and Hoe: Alabama Communists during the Great Depression* (Chapel Hill: University of North Carolina Press, 1990), when communism did take root in Black communities, it was tailored more to the needs and context of Black people's experience rather than to the dictates of Russia. For Black communists in the South, communism provided a helpful and coherent worldview to help frame their fight against starvation. Over time, however, communism lost its credibility even among its Black constituency. In the buildup to World War II, Black communists became disillusioned by mounting evidence that communism's commitment to Black Americans amounted to little more than political convenience. For Du Bois and communism, see David Levering Lewis, *W. E. B. Du Bois: A Biography* (New York: Holt, 2009), 669.

13. These quotes are from Hughes, *Langston Hughes*: "A Portent and a Warning to the Negro People from Hughes," February 5, 1949, 184; "A Thorn in the Side," May 15, 1948, 183; "Faults of the Soviet Union," August 3, 1946, 178; "Are You a Communist?," September 13, 1947, 181.

14. Reagan, *Where's the Rest of Me?*, 194.

15. Reagan, *Where's the Rest of Me?*, 164.

16. Quoted in Rick Perlstein, *The Invisible Bridge: The Fall of Nixon and the Rise of Reagan* (New York: Simon & Schuster, 2015), 373.

17. Broder and Hess, *Republican Establishment*, 251.

18. Quoted in Perlstein, *Invisible Bridge*, 372; Brands, *Reagan*, 110.

19. Thomas W. Evans, *The Education of Ronald Reagan: The General Electric Years and the Untold Story of His Conversion to Conservatism* (New York: Columbia University Press, 2006), 22; David S. Broder, "Always Goldwater," *Washington Post*, June 2, 1998.

20. Evans, *Education of Ronald Reagan*, 22.

21. As Rick Perlstein writes, for Reagan, "freedom was always on the verge of extinction; in 1948, the predators were the tax evaders; the prey was the common man. By 1960, the lion and the lamb had switched places: now it was the likes of Standard Oil and Hollywood who were the put-upon martyrs—moral role models, in fact." Perlstein, *Invisible Bridge*, 393.

22. GE's propaganda machine included a managed news program that not only placed periodicals and opinion pieces in local and national publications but also produced weekly

newspapers and magazines for GE's employees and spheres of influence. Evans, *Education of Ronald Reagan*, 50.

23. Evans, *Education of Ronald Reagan*, 57–58.

24. Evans, *Education of Ronald Reagan*, 4.

25. Ronald Reagan, *An American Life* (New York: Simon & Schuster, 1990), 129.

26. Quoted in Lou Cannon, *President Reagan: The Role of a Lifetime* (New York: Public Affairs, 2000), 740.

27. Adam Smith, *The Wealth of Nations* (New York: Modern Library, 2000), 287.

28. For Smith, the titans of industry represented "an order of men . . . who have generally an interest to deceive and even to oppress the public, and who accordingly have, upon many occasions, both deceived and oppressed it." Smith, *Wealth of Nations*, 288.

29. John T. Flynn, *The Road Ahead: America's Creeping Revolution* (New York: Devin-Adair, 1949), 103.

30. Reagan, *American Life*, 132.

31. Quoted in Perlstein, *Invisible Bridge*, 400.

32. See Thomas Jefferson to Tadeusz Kosciuszko, April 16, 1811, https://founders.ar chives.gov/documents/Jefferson/03-03-02-0439.

33. See Perlstein, *Invisible Bridge*, 400–403; and Kim Phillips-Fein, *Invisible Hands: The Businessmen's Crusade Against the New Deal* (New York: Norton, 2009), 114.

34. Rick Perlstein, *Before the Storm: Barry Goldwater and the Unmaking of the American Consensus* (New York: Nation, 2009), 402.

35. Quoted in Perlstein, *Before the Storm*, 312.

36. Jackie Robinson, "Murder, Hate, Violence Will Be Weapons of GOP," *Indianapolis Recorder*, July 25, 1964.

37. See Broder and Hess, *Republican Establishment*, 273; and chapter 8, "Kidding on the Square," in Cannon, *President Reagan*, 94–114.

38. Ronald Reagan, "A Time for Choosing" (speech), October 27, 1964, https://www .reaganlibrary.gov/reagans/ronald-reagan/time-choosing-speech-october-27-1964.

39. Quoted in Perlstein, *Invisible Bridge*, 407.

40. Quoted in John A. Daly, *Advocacy: Championing Ideas and Influencing Others* (New Haven: Yale University Press, 2011), 266.

41. Reagan's memory also sometimes got him in trouble. It was nearly photographic but full of faulty information that was not fact-checked. See Cannon, *President Reagan*, 102.

42. Perlstein, *Invisible Bridge*, 555–56.

43. Broder and Hess, *Republican Establishment*, 253.

44. All quotes in this paragraph and the next three are from Ronald Reagan, "The Myth of the Great Society," http://www.poorrichardsprintshop.com/wiki/MythOfTheGreatSoci ety.ashx. According to the Ronald Reagan Presidential Library, the exact date and location of this speech are unknown, but the library believes it was in New York in 1966. View the video recording at https://www.c-span.org/video/?476893-1/the-myth-great-society.

45. Broder and Hess, *Republican Establishment*, 274.

46. Lee Edwards, *Reagan: A Political Biography* (Houston: Nordland, 1981), 123.

47. California Task Force to Study and Develop Reparation Proposals for African Americans, *The California Reparations Report*, June 29, 2023, p. 219, https://oag.ca.gov /ab3121/report.

48. Taylor Branch, *At Canaan's Edge: America in the King Years, 1965–68* (New York: Simon & Schuster, 2007), 481.

49. Quoted in Cannon, *President Reagan*, 458.

50. "Reagan Walks Out," Associated Press, March 7, 1966.

51. Perlstein, *Before the Storm*, 312; Doug Rossinow, *The Reagan Era: A History of the 1980s* (New York: Columbia University Press, 2015), 13; Perlstein, *Invisible Bridge*, 553; Lou Cannon, *Governor Reagan: His Rise to Power* (New York: Public Affairs, 2003), 142.

52. Quoted in Broder and Hess, *Republican Establishment*, 267.

53. Martin Anderson, quoted in Cannon, *President Reagan*, 106–7.

54. Quoted in Perlstein, *Invisible Bridge*, 556.

55. Quoted in Theodore Hamm, *Rebel with a Cause: Caryl Chessman and the Politics of the Death Penalty in Postwar California, 1948–1974* (Berkeley: University of California Press, 2001), 147.

56. Broder and Hess, *Republican Establishment*, 268.

57. Quoted in Eddie S. Glaude Jr., *Democracy in Black: How Race Still Enslaves the American Soul* (New York: Crown, 2016), 97.

58. Quoted in Branch, *At Canaan's Edge*, 550.

59. Peniel E. Joseph, *Stokely: A Life* (New York: Basic Civitas, 2014), 163.

60. Martin Luther King Jr., "The Three Evils" (speech), National Conference on New Politics, Chicago, August 31, 1967.

61. Martin Luther King Jr., *Where Do We Go from Here: Chaos or Community?* (Boston: Beacon, 2010), 2.

62. Peniel E. Joseph, *The Sword and the Shield: The Revolutionary Lives of Malcolm X and Martin Luther King Jr.* (New York: Basic, 2020), 60; King, "Three Evils"; King, *Where Do We Go from Here?*, 197.

63. Martin Luther King Jr., Speech, Monmouth College, Monmouth, IL, October 6, 1966, https://www.monmouth.edu/about/wp-content/uploads/sites/128/2019/01/MLK JrSpeechatMonmouth.pdf.

64. Martin Luther King Jr., "A Testament of Hope," in *Testament of Hope*, 315.

65. King, *Where Do We Go from Here?*, 95; Martin Luther King Jr., "Why We Can't Wait," in *Testament of Hope*, 113; Michael Dyson, *I May Not Get There with You: The True Martin Luther King* (New York: Free Press, 2001), 12.

66. Charles Blow, "The Most Dangerous Negro," *New York Times*, August 28, 2013.

67. Nick Kotz, *Judgment Days: Lyndon Baines Johnson, Martin Luther King Jr., and the Laws That Changed America* (Boston: Houghton Mifflin, 2005), 76; Sokol, *Heavens Might Crack*, 232; Ronnie Dugger, *On Reagan: The Man and His Presidency* (New York: McGraw-Hill, 2003), 200; Anthony Lewis, "Abroad at Home; the Real Reagan," *New York Times*, October 24, 1983; Joseph, *Sword and the Shield*, 9.

68. Roper Center of Public Opinion, "Assassination Nation: Public Responses to King and Kennedy in 1968," Roper Center, June 5, 2019, https://ropercenter.cornell.edu/blog/as sassination-nation-public-responses-king-and-kennedy-1968.

69. King, *Where Do We Go from Here?*, 10.

70. Quoted in Cannon, *Governor Reagan*, 265; Broder and Hess, *Republican Establishment*, 275.

71. Brands, *Reagan*, 166, quoting the *Los Angeles Times*, May 19, 1968.

72. Ronald Reagan, *"Face the Nation* with Governor Ronald Reagan," CBS News, aired June 16, 1968, https://www.c-span.org/video/?443905-1/face-nation-governor-ronald-reagan.

73. Reagan, *"Face the Nation."*

74. Quoted in Cannon, *Governor Reagan*, 264.

75. Edwards, *Reagan*, 200; Perlstein, *Invisible Bridge*, 410.

76. Duggar, *On Reagan*, 294.

77. Quoted in Cannon, *Governor Reagan*, 342, 349; Duggar, *On Reagan*, 293.

78. See Duggar, *On Reagan*, 292–98.

79. J. Alfred Smith, personal correspondence, August 16, 2021, used with permission.

80. Anderson Lanham, "A Haven for Communist Sympathizers, Protesters and Sex Deviants," *Daily Californian*, November 15, 2016.

81. Quoted in Perlstein, *Invisible Bridge*, 89–90; Rick Perlstein, *Nixonland: The Rise of a President and the Fracturing of America* (New York: Scribner, 2009), 384–85.

82. Ramsey, *When Crack Was King*, 98.

83. Rick Perlstein, "Infamous 1981 Interview on the Southern Strategy," *Nation*, November 13, 2012.

84. Quoted in Duggar, *On Reagan*, 201.

85. Quoted in Cannon, *President Reagan*, 457.

86. See Nicholas M. Horrock, "Reagan Resists Financial Disclosure," *New York Times*, August 13, 1976; and Dennis J. Ventry Jr., "Tax Shelter Opinions Threatened the Tax System in the 1970s," *Tax Notes*, May 15, 2006.

87. Quoted in O'Connor, *Poverty Knowledge*, 209.

88. Quoted in Brands, *Reagan*, 186.

89. Ronald Reagan, *In His Own Hand: The Writings of Ronald Reagan That Reveal His Revolutionary Vision for America*, ed. George P. Shultz (New York: Free Press, 2001), 351, 259, 241; Duggar, *On Reagan*, 476.

90. Reagan, *In His Own Hand*, 390–92, 394; Duggar, *On Reagan*, 497.

91. Quoted in Brands, *Reagan*, 186–87.

Chapter 11

1. James Baldwin, "An Open Letter to Jimmy Carter," *New York Times*, January 23, 1977.

2. Quoted in Steven Levingston, *Kennedy and King: The President, the Pastor, and the Battle over Civil Rights* (New York: Hachette, 2017), xi.

3. Chuck Stone, "Carter's Paternalistic Racism and the Inept Presidency," *Black Scholar*, March 1978; Manning Marable, *Race, Reform, and Rebellion: The Second Reconstruction and Beyond in Black America, 1945–2006*, 2nd ed. (Jackson: University Press of Mississippi, 1991), 168–69. Funding for historically Black colleges and universities provides but one example of why African Americans felt betrayed by Carter. Whereas Nixon and Ford passed legislation providing federal funds to help with nearly 75 percent of HBCUs' budgets, Carter cut the funding down to a meager 18 percent by 1980.

4. Rick Perlstein, *Reaganland: America's Right Turn, 1976–1980* (New York: Simon & Schuster, 2020), 569, 590, 594, 570, 575.

5. Perlstein, *Reaganland*, 665–66.

6. Quoted in Perlstein, *Reaganland*, 749; Robert Scheer, "Reagan's Views Issues at Home, Abroad," *Los Angeles Times*, March 6, 1980.

7. Ronald Reagan, "Address Accepting the Presidential Nomination at the Republican National Convention in Detroit," Republican National Convention, Detroit, July 17, 1980, https://www.presidency.ucsb.edu/documents/address-accepting-the-presidential-nomination-the-republican-national-convention-detroit.

8. Pearlstein, *Reaganland*, 830; Cannon, "Reagan Makes Appeal for Black Votes," *Washington Post*, August 6, 1980; Lou Cannon, "Reagan Visits Jordan, Says He Is Doing Well," *Washington Post*, August 5, 1980.

9. Martin Luther King Jr., July 24, 1964, quoted in Neely Tucker, "Mississippi Turning," *Washington Post*, June 16, 2005.

10. Ronald Reagan, Speech at the Neshoba County Fair, Philadelphia, MS, August 3, 1980, https://neshobademocrat.com/stories/ronald-reagans-1980-neshoba-county-fair-speech,49123. See Susan Neiman, *Learning from the Germans: Race and the Memory of Evil* (New York: Farrar, Straus and Giroux, 2019), 299; Lou Cannon, "Reagan Campaigning from County Fair to Urban League," *Washington Post*, August 4, 1980; Perlstein, *Reaganland*, 830–34.

11. Andrew Young, "Chilling Words in Neshoba County," *Washington Post*, August 11, 1980.

12. Reagan writes in his 1965 autobiography, *Where's the Rest of Me?*, that "every morning Nancy and I turn to see what [columnist Carroll Righter] has to say about people of our respective birth signs." After rising to president, Reagan's commitment to astrology was an open secret and the depth to which it shaped his presidency an open question. See Paul Houston, "Reagan Denies Astrology Influences His Decisions," *Los Angeles Times*, May 4, 1988.

13. Lou Cannon writes about the Therapeutic Abortion Act Reagan signed. In 1967, when the measure was enacted, there were only 518 legal abortions in California. In 1980, the year Reagan was elected president, 199,089 abortions were performed in California hospitals and clinics. The total number of abortions performed from 1968 to 1980 was 1,444,778. Cannon, *Governor Reagan*, 213.

14. "Seeking to eliminate the strife and deception often associated with the legal regime of fault-based divorce, Reagan signed the nation's first no-fault divorce bill. . . . But no-fault divorce also gutted marriage of its legal power to bind husband and wife, allowing one spouse to dissolve a marriage for any reason—or for no reason at all. In the decade and a half that followed, virtually every state in the Union followed California's lead and enacted a no-fault divorce law of its own. This legal transformation was only one of the more visible signs of the divorce revolution then sweeping the United States: From 1960 to 1980, the divorce rate more than doubled—from 9.2 divorces per 1,000 married women to 22.6 divorces per 1,000 married women." W. Bradford Wilcox, "The Evolution of Divorce," *National Affairs*, Fall 2009, https://www.nationalaffairs.com/publications/detail/the-evolution-of-divorce.

15. In 1976, Carter's presidential campaign inspired the *Newsweek* cover story "The Year of the Evangelical."

16. In Michael Emerson and Christian Smith's *Divided by Faith*, the authors contend that the three most critically important cultural tools in the white evangelical tool kit are "accountable freewill individualism," "relationalism," and "antistructualism," tools that, in

addition to white supremacy, fit perfectly with the Reagan Revolution. Michael Emerson and Christian Smith, *Divided by Faith: Evangelical Religion and the Problem of Race in America* (New York: Oxford University Press, 2000), 76.

17. Jerry Falwell, *Falwell: An Autobiography* (Lynchburg, VA: Liberty House, 1997), 312.

18. Frances FitzGerald, "A Disciplined, Charging Army," *New Yorker*, May 18, 1981.

19. James Robison, "National Affairs Briefing," August 13, 1980, https://www.youtube.com/watch?v=lH1eoxxRRbk.; Perlstein, *Reaganland*, 845.

20. Quoted in Rossinow, *Reagan Era*, 25.

21. James Baldwin, "Notes on the House of Bondage," in *Collected Essays* (New York: Library of America, 1988), 803.

22. Baldwin, "Notes on the House of Bondage," 804.

23. Baldwin, "Notes on the House of Bondage," 806.

24. James Reston, "Reagan's Dramatic Success," *New York Times*, January 21, 1981.

25. Ronald Reagan, "First Inaugural Address" (speech, Washington, DC, January 20, 1981).

26. If the goal was to make HUD impotent, in selecting Samuel Pierce, Reagan made a savvy appointment. Pierce, one of the few African Americans in the Reagan administration, earned the name "Silent Sam" and used his position mainly to funnel federal funds to corporations and Republican consultants. In eight years on the job, Reagan was so disinterested in the work of Housing and Urban Development that he never visited the department. Cannon, *President Reagan*, 104–5; Marable, *Race Reform and Rebellion*, 197–98.

27. Matthew Desmond, *Poverty, by America* (New York: Crown, 2023), 109.

28. Schweiker was a progressive Republican. Too conservative for liberals. Too liberal for conservatives. But he was loyal, and for that reason he was selected as Reagan's VP pick in 1976 to widen Reagan's appeal to more moderate voters. "As long as I'm on the plane on the takeoff, I'll be the first one out defending it after the crash," he had promised Reagan when he joined the 1976 ticket. From 1981 to 1983, Schweiker made good on his word and supported the president's cuts to his department while protecting everything he could. Upon Schweiker's resignation, Senator Edward Kennedy remarked: "As secretary of HHS, he has too often been a lonely voice of compassion and humanity. The country may never know how much greater the damage to social programs would have been without Dick Schweiker as secretary." Rich Spencer, "Schweiker Resigning as HHS Secretary, Officials Say," *Washington Post*, January 12, 1983.

29. Edward Fiske, "Education Secretary Bell's View of a Department in Transition," *New York Times*, February 3, 1981.

30. Edward Fiske, "Reagan Record in Education: Mixed Results," *New York Times*, November 14, 1982.

31. Mark Lawrence, "Bennett Defends Controversial Style," *Los Angeles Times*, September 7, 1988.

32. Ramsey, *When Crack Was King*, 240.

33. Jake Taper, "William Bennett Defends Comment on Abortion and Crime," ABC News, November 1, 2007.

34. Jonathan Kozol, *Savage Inequalities: Children in America's Schools* (New York: Broadway, 1991), 5.

35. Sandro Galea et al., "Estimated Deaths Attributable to Social Factors in the United States," *American Journal of Public Health* 101, no. 8 (August 2011): 1456.

36. Rossinow, *Reagan Era*, 42.

37. See Rossinow, *Reagan Era*, 42, 143; Marable, *Race, Reform, and Rebellion*, 177–81; RobertPear, "Reagan Ousts Three from Civil Rights Panel," *New York Times*, October 26, 1983.

38. Any talk of hungry children "was purely political." For Meese, "the real question is, if people are hungry, if there are such individuals, particularly children, then why are they hungry?"—as if the only explanation was personal irresponsibility. When he was later informed that his Christmastime declaration inspired comparisons to Ebenezer Scrooge from Charles Dickens's *A Christmas Carol*, Meese embraced the comparison. After all, they both had suffered from simply "bad press." Meese offered a rereading of Dickens in which Scrooge embodied entrepreneurial heroism. "Let's be fair to Scrooge," Meese declared, "he had his faults, but he wasn't unfair to anyone." Like his boss, Meese was often funny—and always ruthless. David Hoffman, "Discussing Hunger in U.S., Meese Sparks a Firestorm," *Washington Post*, December 10, 1983; Paul Hendrickson, "Meese Gets the Dickens Humbug!," *Washington Post*, December 17, 1983.

39. Phillip Shenon, "Meese Sees Racism in Hiring Goals," *New York Times*, September 18, 1985.

40. Reagan would take similar approaches in his relationships with Haiti, Guyana, and Jamaica.

41. Ronald Reagan to Otis Carney, November 1981, in Ronald Reagan, *Reagan: A Life in Letters* (New York: Free Press, 2003), 259–60; Perlstein, *Reaganland*, 679.

42. Sandra Evans, "Tutu Says He Wants to Meet with Reagan, Hill Panel Gives Bishop Rare Ovation," *Washington Post*, December 5, 1984.

43. Desmond Tutu, "The current crisis in South Africa" (hearing before the Subcommittee on Africa of the Committee on Foreign Affairs, US House of Representatives, Ninety-Eighth Congress, second session, December 4, 1984); Marable, *Race, Reform, and Rebellion*, 179; Rossinow, *Reagan Era*, 7.

44. Perhaps the two preeminent cases that best display the division in the Supreme Court of that era were the rulings in *University of California v. Bakke* (1978), which disallowed specific racial quotas in college admissions, and in *United Steelworkers v. Weber* (1979), which upheld the legality of preferencing minorities and women in hiring decisions.

45. Edwin Meese, "The Case for Originalism," The Heritage Foundation, June 6, 1985; Robert Post and Reva Seigel, "Originalism as a Political Practice: The Right's Living Constitution," *Fordham Law Review* 75 (2006): 545–74.

46. Rossinow, *Reagan Era*, 178–79.

47. Marable, *Race, Reform, and Rebellion*, 195.

48. Antonin Scalia, "The Disease as Cure: 'In Order to Get beyond Racism, We Must First Take Account of Race,'" *Washington University Law Quarterly* 147 (1979): 153; Yanan Wang, "Where Justice Scalia Got the Idea That African Americans Might Be Better Off at 'Slower-Track' Universities," *Washington Post*, December 10, 2015; Richard Posner, "The Court of Celebrity," *New Republic*, May 5, 2011.

49. Thurgood Marshall, "Remarks Made at the Second Circuit Judicial Conference, September 8, 1989," *Trotter Review* 4, no. 3 (1990): 3.

50. Dr. Joseph Giordano was the surgeon.

51. Barry Sussman, "Shooting Gives Reagan Boost in Popularity," *Washington Post*, April 2, 1981.

52. Rossinow, *Reagan Era*, 57–58.

53. Ronald Reagan, "Program for Economic Recovery" (speech, Joint Session of Congress, April 28, 1981), https://www.reaganlibrary.gov/archives/speech/address-joint-session-congress-program-economic-recovery-april-1981; Haynes Johnson, "Reagan Thanks Nation for Its Compassion," *Washington Post*, April 29, 1981.

54. Martin Tolchin, "The Troubles of Tip O'Neill," *New York Times*, August 16, 1981.

55. Ronald Reagan, "Remarks on Signing the Economic Recovery Tax Act of 1981 and the Omnibus Budget Reconciliation Act of 1981," Santa Ynez, CA, August 13, 1981, https://www.reaganlibrary.gov/archives/speech/remarks-signing-economic-recovery-tax-act-1981-and-omnibus-budget-reconciliation.

56. Marable, *Race, Reform, and Rebellion*, 179–80; Rossinow, *Reagan Era*, 59–60; Fisk, "Reagan Record in Education."

57. Quoted in Brands, *Reagan*, 469.

58. Rossinow, *Reagan Era*, 61–62.

59. Robert McIntyre, *Corporate Income Taxes in the Reagan Years: A Study of Three Years of Legalized Corporate Tax Avoidance* (Washington, DC: Citizens for Tax Justice, 1984).

60. The greatest raise came during the Obama years, as the estate tax exemption grew from $1 million to $5 million. Trump more than doubled Obama's generosity and put the exemption at over $11 million, representing a 7,000 percent growth since 1980.

61. Robin Kaiser Schatzlein, "This Is How America's Richest Families Stay That Way," *New York Times*, September 24, 2021.

62. Richard Cowen, "Reagan's Life Style Contradicts Policies," *Washington Post*, September 15, 1981.

63. Marian Wright Edelman, *Families in Peril: An Agenda for Social Change* (Cambridge, MA: Harvard University Press, 1987), 29. This book was developed from Edelman's 1986 W. E. B. Du Bois Lectures at Amherst College.

64. Edelman, *Families in Peril*, 35.

65. Edelman, *Families in Peril*, 29.

66. Edelman, *Families in Peril*, 69.

67. Meg Kunde, "Making the Free Market Moral: Ronald Reagan's Covenantal Economy," *Rhetoric and Public Affairs* 22, no. 2 (Summer 2019): 237; Ronald Reagan, "Remarks at the Annual Meeting of the National Alliance of Business," October 5, 1981, https://www.reaganlibrary.gov/archives/speech/remarks-annual-meeting-national-alliance-business.

68. Edelman, *Families in Peril*, 38.

69. "Reagan Opposes National Holiday for Martin Luther King Birthday," *Boston Globe*, January 23, 1983; Sokol, *Heavens Might Crack*, 228.

70. During the morning gathering, Coretta Scott King declared, "We must demand justice in Harlem and in the Bronx . . . in the barrios of Los Angeles . . . but also in El Salvador" in a not-so-veiled slap at Reagan.

71. "20th Anniversary March on Washington," video, C-SPAN, August 27, 1983, https://www.c-span.org/video/?88744-1/20th-anniversary-march-washington.

72. In 1983, Reagan wrote to a friend regarding King that "the perception of too many people is based on an image, not reality. Indeed, to them the perception is reality." Francis Clines, "Reagan's Doubts on King Disclosed," *Washington Post*, October 22, 1983.

73. "We're committed to a society in which all men and women have equal opportunities to succeed," said Reagan. "And so we oppose the use of quotas. We want a colorblind

society, a society that, in the words of Dr. King, judges people 'not by the color of their skin, but by the content of their character.'" Ronald Reagan, "Radio Address to the Nation on Martin Luther King Jr. and Black Americans," January 18, 1986, https://www.reaganlibrary .gov/archives/speech/radio-address-nation-martin-luther-king-jr-and-black-americans.

74. Reagan, "Radio Address to the Nation."

75. Roger Wilkins, "A Dream Still Denied," *Los Angeles Times*, January 19, 1986; Sokol, *Heavens Might Crack*, 234.

76. "Reagan Quotes King Speech in Opposing Minority Quotas," Associated Press, January 19, 1986.

77. Wilkins, "Dream Still Denied"; Sokol, *Heavens Might Crack*, 234.

78. Ibram X. Kendi, "The Second Assassination of Martin Luther King Jr.," *Atlantic*, October 14, 2021.

79. The Black conservative was nothing new. In *Where Do We Go from Here?*, King wrote explicitly about the threats those leaders represented as he accused Black leaders of "aloofness and absence of faith in their people. The white establishment is skilled in flattering and cultivating emerging [Black] leaders. It presses its own image on them and finally . . . a deeper strain of corruption develops. . . . He changes from the representative of the Negro to the white man into the white man's representative to the Negro. The tragedy is that too often he does not recognize what has happened to him." King, *Where Do We Go from Here?*, 168-69.

80. John Baum, "Legalize It All," *Harper's Magazine*, April 2016.

81. "John Erlichman Settles a Few Scores," *Washington Post*, January 24, 1982. White House Counsel John Dean concurred: "I was cranking out that bullshit on Nixon's crime policy before he was elected. And it was bullshit, too. . . . We knew it." Quoted in Hinton, *From the War on Poverty*, 140.

82. Robert A. Hahn et al., "Poverty and Death in the United States, 1973-1991," *International Journal of Health Services* 26, no. 4 (October 1996): 681.

83. See Lance Hannon and James DeFronzo, "The Truly Disadvantaged, Public Assistance, and Crime," *Social Problems* 45 (1998): 389; Lance Hannon and James DeFronzo, "Welfare Assistance Levels and Homicide Rates," *Homicide Studies* 2, no. 1 (February 1998): 31.

84. Ronald Reagan, "Remarks Announcing Federal Initiatives Against Drug Trafficking and Organized Crime," October 14, 1982, https://www.reaganlibrary.gov/archives/speech /remarks-announcing-federal-initiatives-against-drug-trafficking-and-organized-crime.

85. See Michelle Alexander, *The New Jim Crow: Mass Incarceration in the Age of Colorblindness* (New York: New Press, 2010), 78-80; Hinton, *From the War on Poverty*, 310-14; Eric Blumenson and Eva Nilsen, "Policing for Profit: The Drug War's Hidden Economic Agenda," *University of Chicago Law Review* 65, no. 1 (Winter 1998): 72-76; Dan Baum, *Smoke and Mirrors* (Boston: Back Bay, 1997), 249.

86. Ramsey, *When Crack Was King*, 8-11.

87. Ronald Reagan, "Remarks on Signing the Anti-Drug Abuse Act of 1986," October 27, 1986, https://www.reaganlibrary.gov/archives/speech/remarks-signing-anti-drug-abuse -act-1986; Ramsey, *When Crack Was King*, 216.

88. Ellen Goodman, "Crack Baby Hyperbole," *Washington Post*, January 11, 1992.

89. Alexander, *New Jim Crow*, 49-50; US Department of Justice, Office of Justice Programs, Bureau of Justice Statistics, "State Corrections Expenditures, FY 1982-2010," December 2012, revised April 30, 2014, https://bjs.ojp.gov/content/pub/pdf/scefy8210.pdf.

90. "Economics of Incarceration," Prison Policy Initiative, https://www.prisonpolicy
.org/research/economics_of_incarceration/ ($80.7 billion in public prisons + $3.9 billion
in private prisons + $2.9 billion in phone charges).

91. Alexander, *New Jim Crow*, 7.

92. Alexander, *New Jim Crow*, 5.

93. Janet Dewart, ed., *The State of Black America, 1990* (New York: National Urban
League, 1990), quoted in Alexander, *New Jim Crow*, 5–6.

94. After McCoy testified before Congress prior to the book's release, the CIA intervened to halt Harper and Row from publishing the work. After the CIA reviewed the
manuscript and proved unable to refute any of its research or conclusions, Harper and
Row went to print without alteration.

95. Brian Barger and Robert Parry, "Reports Link Nicaraguan Rebels to Cocaine Trafficking," Associated Press, December 20, 1985. Also included in the reporting was a well-
known and well-connected Panamanian doctor, Dr. Hugo Spadafora. Dr. Spadafora was
so concerned about what he had witnessed that he was able to set up a secret meeting to
lay out to US intelligence agencies the details of the Contras' network. Shortly after the
meeting, Dr. Spadafora was brutally assassinated.

96. Peter Kornbluh, "Crack, the Contras and the CIA: The Storm over 'Dark Alliance,'" *Columbia Journalism Review*, January/February 1997, https://nsarchive2.gwu.edu
/NSAEBB/NSAEBB113/storm.htm.

97. Committee on Foreign Relations, *Drugs, Law Enforcement and Foreign Policy* (aka
the Kerry Report), Washington, DC, December 1988, 38.

98. Alfred W. McCoy, *The Politics of Heroin: CIA Complicity in the Global Drug Trade*
(Chicago: Lawrence Hill, 2003), 488.

99. McCoy, *Politics of Heroin*, 492.

100. Kerry Report, 8.

101. Ramsey, *When Crack Was King*, 306.

102. See Ebony Underwood and Miriam Aroni Krinsky, "Millions of Children Lose
Their Parents to Incarceration. That Doesn't Have to Happen," *The Appeal*, October 24,
2019, https://theappeal.org/millions-of-children-lose-their-parents-to-incarceration-that
-doesnt-have-to-happen/; and Clio Chang, "Incarcerated Fathers and the Children Left
Behind," Century Foundation, September 3, 2014, https://tcf.org/content/commentary/in
carcerated-fathers-and-the-children-left-behind/.

103. James Forman Jr., *Locking Up Our Own: Crime and Punishment in Black America*
(New York: Farrar, Straus and Giroux, 2017), 45.

104. Ruth Marcus and Helen Dewar, "Reagan Vetoes Civil Rights Restoration Act," *New
York Times*, March 17, 1988.

105. T. R. Reid, "Most States Allow Furloughs from Prison," *New York Times*, June 24, 1988.

106. Eric Yamamoto et al., *Race, Rights, and Reparation: Law and the Japanese American
Internment*, 2nd ed. (Boston: Aspen, 2013), 319; "Japanese Internment—Memorandum for
Kenneth M. Duberstein from Joseph R. Wright. Subject: H. R. 442 and S. 1 09—Relocation
of Japanese-Americans During World War II," Reagan Library, Kenneth M. Duberstein
Files (Chief of Staff), Box 2, January 19, 1988.

107. "Japanese Internment—Letter from Governor Thomas Kean to Ronald Reagan,"
Reagan Library, Kenneth M. Duberstein Files (Chief of Staff), Box 2, February 6, 1987.

108. Civil Liberties Act of 1988, Pub. L. No. 100–383, 102 Stat. 904 (1988).

109. Julie Johnson, "President Signs Law to Redress Wartime Wrong," *New York Times*, August 11, 1988.

110. Ronald Reagan, "Farewell Address to the Nation," January 11, 1989, https://www .reaganlibrary.gov/archives/speech/farewell-address-nation.

111. Rossinow, *Reagan Era*, 281. By 2021, the number of billionaires would surpass six hundred. See "Billionaires by the Numbers," Americans for Tax Fairness, https://ameri cansfortaxfairness.org/billionaires/.

112. John Hope Franklin, *The Color Line: Legacy for the Twenty-First Century* (Columbia: University of Missouri Press, 1993), 20. See also Forbes's list of richest Americans, which began in 1982.

113. Roberta Ann Johnson, "African Americans and Homelessness: Moving Through History," *Journal of Black Studies* 40, no. 4 (March 2010): 598.

114. Hahn et al., "Poverty and Death," 680.

115. James Barron, "A Search for Solutions to the Housing Squeeze," *New York Times*, July 12, 1987.

116. Marable, *Race, Reform, and Rebellion*, 205; Desmond, *Poverty, by America*, 18.

117. Ibram X. Kendi, *How to Be an Antiracist* (New York: One World, 2019), 9.

Chapter 12

1. Richard J. Herrnstein, "IQ," *Atlantic*, September 1971.

2. Charles A. Murray, *Losing Ground: American Social Policy, 1950–1980* (New York: Basic, 1984).

3. "Losing More Ground," *New York Times*, February 3, 1985.

4. For a thorough review of *Losing Ground*, see William A. Darity Jr. and Samuel L. Myers Jr., "Book Review: *Losing Ground: American Social Policy, 1950–1980*," *Review of Black Political Economy* 14, nos. 2–3 (December 1985): 167–77.

5. Richard J. Herrnstein and Charles A. Murray, *The Bell Curve: Intelligence and Class Structure in American Life* (New York: Free Press, 1994), 550.

6. Ramsey, *When Crack was King*, 266, 276–78.

7. Randall Robinson, *The Reckoning: What Blacks Owe to Each Other* (New York: Plume, 2003), 42, 212.

8. Max Ehrenfreund, "There's a Disturbing Truth to John Legend's Oscar Statement about Prisons and Slavery," *Washington Post*, February 23, 2015.

9. Hahn et al., "Poverty and Death," 683.

10. Galea et al., "Estimated Deaths," 1456.

11. King, *Where Do We Go from Here?*, 559.

12. "The Pew Research Center estimates that white households are worth roughly 20 times as much as black households." Coates, "Case for Reparations."

13. Audre Lorde, *Sister Outsider* (London: Penguin, 2019), 112 (emphasis mine).

14. Kelley, *Hammer and Hoe*, xii.

15. "Our Mission," N'COBRA, https://www.ncobraonline.org, retrieved December 5, 2023.

16. In 1973, twenty-two police officers were indicted and ten were charged with trafficking heroin into the city.

17. John Lowell, "Detroit: That Sinking Feeling," *Newsweek*, October 1976, https://po licing.umhistorylabs.lsa.umich.edu/s/crackdowndetroit/page/drug-corruption.

18. Commission to Study and Develop Reparation Proposals for African-Americans Act, H. R. 40, 116th Cong. (2019–2020), https://www.congress.gov/bill/116th-congress /house-bill/40/text.

19. In total, the bill received twenty-four cosponsors. The four cosponsors outside the CBC included the Japanese allies Norman Mineta and Robert Matsui and the white allies Andrew Jacobs and Jim Bates.

20. See Kevin Boyle, "The Ruins of Detroit: Exploring the Urban Crisis in the Motor City," *Michigan Historical Review* 27, no. 1 (Spring 2001): 110–20; Christine MacDonald and Charles E. Ramirez, "Life Span for Detroit's Poor among Shortest in Nation," *Detroit News*, June 2, 2016; "Detroit," Black Demographics, https://blackdemographics.com/cities -2/detroit-black-pupulation/, retrieved September 14, 2021.

21. Larry Buchanan, Quoctrung Bui, and Jugal K. Patel, "Black Lives Matter May Be the Largest Movement in U.S. History," *New York Times*, July 3, 2020.

Chapter 13

1. In a study following the summer of 2020, 49 percent of white Americans believed racism was still a significant factor in American life. Yet, only 21 percent supported reparations. "White and Black Americans Far Apart on Racial Issues," Ipsos, August 27, 2020, https://www.ipsos.com/en-us/news-polls/npr-racial-inequality-issues.

2. Steve Eder, David D. Kirkpatrick, and Mike McIntire, "They Legitimized the Myth of a Stolen Election—and Reaped the Rewards," *New York Times*, October 3, 2022.

3. For full transcript of the hearing, visit https://www.govinfo.gov/content/pkg/CHRG -116hhrg41178/html/CHRG-116hhrg41178.htm.

4. From estimates of unpaid wages to lists of current racial inequalities, we possess every tool we need to navigate the complexity of considering economic remuneration with a great degree of precision, sophistication, and integrity.

5. See Edward Baptist, *The Half Has Never Been Told: Slavery and the Making of American Capitalism* (New York: Basic, 2014); and Muhammad, *Condemnation of Blackness*.

6. See Jacobson, *Whiteness of a Different Color*; and Matthew Frye Jacobson, *Barbarian Virtues: The United States Encounters Foreign Peoples at Home and Abroad, 1876–1917* (New York: Hill and Wang, 2000).

7. Congressman Johnson's narration of his relationship with a young Black man would undergo increased scrutiny after he rose to Speaker of the House. He would be forced to clarify that he never technically adopted the young man but that he mentored him as a father figure and brought him into his family's life. See Adam Nagourney, "On Race, Mike Johnson Says His Views Were Shaped by Raising a Black Child," *New York Times*, October 27, 2023.

8. Tom Lasseter, "House Speaker Johnson among US politicians with ancestral ties to slavery," Reuters, December 20, 2023.

9. Equal Justice Initiative, *Lynching in America*, 40–41.

10. Barbara Kantrowitz, "Still Separate After 20 Years," *Newsweek*, September 6, 1992.

Chapter 14

1. This is not to suggest that white voices have nothing to add to the conversation concerning our history and potential ways forward. The contributions of white antiracist historians such as Eric Foner, David Blight, and Howard Zinn provide a treasure trove of resources for antiracist work.

2. See Jake Silverstein, "We Respond to the Historians Who Critiqued The 1619 Project," *New York Times*, December 20, 2019. In some ways, The 1619 Project simply made academic histories, such as Black historian Gerald Horne's *The Counter-Revolution of 1776*, available to the mass market. That many recalcitrant white historians aimed the fury of their critiques at the spearheading journalist Nikole Hannah-Jones and not Gerald Horne or other leading historians within the project displayed the politics of their protest.

3. See Joel Edward Goza, "Why We Must Oppose Politics like SB 138 That Seek to Shrink Young Minds," *Louisville Courier Journal*, February 23, 2022.

4. Hanif Abdurraqib, *They Can't Kill Us Until They Kill Us* (Columbus: Two Dollar Radio, 2017), 240.

5. Cornel West, "Black Love: A Love Like No Other" (lecture), MasterClass, November 28, 2021, https://www.masterclass.com/classes/black-history-black-freedom-and-black-love/chapters/black-love-a-love-like-no-other#class-info.

6. See Matt. 5:23–24 and Luke 19:8–9.

7. See Duke L. Kwon and Gregory Thompson, *Reparations: A Christian Call for Repentance and Repair* (Grand Rapids: Brazos, 2021), 149–51.

8. Danya Ruttenberg, *On Repentance and Repair: Making Amends in an Unapologetic World* (Boston: Beacon, 2022), 43.

9. Heather McGhee, *The Sum of Us: What Racism Costs Everyone and How We Can Prosper Together* (New York: One World, 2021), 237.

10. Quoted in Perlstein, *Invisible Bridge*, xix.

11. Sandy Mazza, "In McConnell's Boyhood Town Where His Family Owned Slaves, the Reparations Debate Thrives," *USA Today*, July 13, 2019.

12. Quoted in Ruttenberg, *On Repentance and Repair*, 111.

13. Stephen G. Hall, from a conversation with the author, January 2022.

14. See Smith, *How the Word Is Passed*, 4–51.

15. Ruttenberg, *On Repentance and Repair*, 117.

16. Truth and Reconciliation Commission, *Truth and Reconciliation Commission of South Africa Report*, vol. 1, October 28, 1998, https://www.justice.gov.za/trc/report/finalreport/volume%201.pdf., 132. For perspectives on the Truth and Reconciliation Commission, a special thanks is due to the Rev. Peter Storey, former president of the South African Council of Churches and author of *Protest at Midnight*. Storey highlighted that one of the greatest historical tragedies of the Truth and Reconciliation Commission is how few white people chose to participate. In the words of former President P. W. Botha: "I only apologize for my sins before God." See also Paul Harris, "Apartheid Leader Refuses Apology," *AP News*, January 23, 1998.

17. Alexandra Senfft, quoted in Neiman, *Learning from the Germans*, 42.

18. Alexandra Senfft, *The Long Shadow of the Perpetrator* (unpublished manuscript), 2.

19. Neiman, *Learning from the Germans*, 72.

20. President Richard von Weizsäcker, Speech at the Ceremony Commemorating the Fortieth Anniversary of the End of War in Europe and of National-Socialist Tyranny, Bund-

estag, Bonn, May 8, 1985. https://www.bundespraesident.de/SharedDocs/Downloads/DE /Reden/2015/02/150202-RvW-Rede-8-Mai-1985-englisch.pdf?__blob=publicationFile.

21. For more information, see "Article 2 Fund: Overview & History," Claims Conference, https://www.claimscon.org/our-work/compensation/background/article2-article2 /article2-history/.

22. For a detailed analysis of Germany's story and what it offers to the United States, see Susan Neiman's *Learning from the Germans*.

23. William Lloyd Garrison, "To the Public," *Liberator*, January 1, 1831.

24. W. E. B. Du Bois, preface to *John Brown: A Biography* (New York: Modern Library, 2001), xxv.

25. Frederick Douglass, "John Brown," in *Essential Douglass*, 261, 264.

26. Quoted in Leilah Danielson, *American Gandhi: A. J. Muste and the History of Radicalism in the Twentieth Century* (Philadelphia: University of Pennsylvania Press, 2014), 15.

27. "Stanley Levison, 67, Adviser to Dr. King," *New York Times*, September 14, 1979. The Andrew Young quote continues: "He never pushed his own views on us, but was always willing to be critical and to think through ideas with us. Stan and his wife and his son have been part of my family."

28. bell hooks, *All about Love: New Visions* (New York: Perennial, 2001), 90.

Chapter 15

1. For more on the interconnection of reparations and the Talmud, see Rabbi Sharon Brous, "Our Country Was Built on a Stolen Beam: The Call for a National Reckoning," IKAR, September 22, 2017.

2. Though more than one reason for the difficulty of enacting reparations exists, the preeminent logjam for any progressive legislation throughout the course of our history has been the Senate. Just as the Senate once secured slavery and protected the ritual of lynching, the Senate continues to stifle the work of racial justice, from reparations to voting rights. What the Senate represents is the necessity for progressive change to not only receive popular support, but also for that popular support to reach levels at or near a supermajority. For monetary reparations to be implemented through Congress, it must become a dominant demand.

3. An additional path that must be taken seriously is engagement with the United Nations and the call for sanctions against the United States until progress is made on racial equality. In South Africa, it was both domestic and international pressure that placed the apartheid regime on the way to extinction. Black America explored employing this strategy throughout the twentieth century. What is needed now, particularly now that presidential candidates run on whether they support reparations, is a president who is willing to leverage international pressure to achieve domestic racial justice. It must be admitted that throughout the twentieth century, it was rare for domestic pressure to be sufficient for achieving racial and economic justice for oppressed people.

4. William A. Darity Jr. and A. Kirsten Mullen, *From Here to Equality: Reparations for Black Americans in the Twenty-First Century* (Chapel Hill: University of North Carolina Press, 2020), 263.

5. See Darity and Mullen, *From Here to Equality*, 263; and Dorothy Brown, *The Whiteness of Wealth: How the Tax System Impoverishes Black Americans—and How We Can Fix*

It (New York: Crown, 2021), 217. It is important to note that Darity and Mullen insist we use the mean wealth difference rather than the median, as the median excludes both the white poor and the white ultrawealthy.

6. See William A. Darity Jr., A. Kirsten Mullen, and Lucas Hubbard, eds., *The Black Reparations Project: A Handbook for Racial Justice* (Oakland: University of California Press, 2023), 13, 19, 206; William A. Darity Jr., A. Kirsten Mullen, and Marvin Slaughter, "The Cumulative Costs of Racism and the Bill for Black Reparations," *Journal of Economic Perspectives* 36, no. 2 (Spring 2022): 116–18.

7. For a vision of reparations via tax credits, see Dorothy Brown's *The Whiteness of Wealth*.

8. Desmond, *Poverty, by America*, 60.

9. McGee, *Sum of Us*, 277.

10. Nick Noel et al., "The Economic Impact of Closing the Racial Wealth Gap," McKinsey Institute for Black Economic Mobility, August 13, 2019, https://www.mckinsey.com/indus tries/public-sector/our-insights/the-economic-impact-of-closing-the-racial-wealth-gap.

11. The simplest way forward would be that "*congress could direct the Federal Reserve to fund black reparations in part or in total.*" Darity and Mullen, *From Here to Equality*, 263, 265.

12. See Cerulli Associates, "Cerulli Anticipates $84 Trillion in Wealth Transfers Through 2045," January 20, 2022, https://www.cerulli.com/press-releases/cerulli-anticipates-84-tril lion-in-wealth-transfers-through-2045; Hillary Hoffower, "There are 618,000 millennial millionaires in the US, and they're on track to inherit even more wealth from the richest generation ever," *Business Insider*, October 18, 2019; and Scott Reyburn, "A 'Great Wealth Transfer' Is Coming. What Will It Mean for Art?," *New York Times*, December, 18, 2019.

13. Amelia Josephson, "A Guide to the Federal Estate Tax for 2024," SmartAsset, December 20, 2023, https://smartasset.com/taxes/all-about-the-estate-tax; "Federal Estate and Gift Tax Rates, Exemptions, and Exclusions, 1916–2014," Tax Foundation, February 4, 2014, https://taxfoundation.org/federal-estate-and-gift-tax-rates-exemptions-and -exclusions-1916-2014/.

14. Wealth statistics in the United States are at national levels, not local. According to the Federal Reserve System, the average Black wealth per family in America is approximately $24,100. With the average family size of 3.3, the average Black wealth per individual is $7,303. For the Black wealth of Houston to be equivalent to that of Rich Kinder, the wealthiest white billionaire in Houston, the average Black person's wealth in Houston would need to be $13,085, almost double the national average. For the Black wealth of New York to be equivalent to that of Michael Bloomberg, the average Black person's wealth would have to be $29,500. For the Black wealth of Los Angeles to be equivalent to that of Peter Parker, the average Black person's wealth would have to be $50,544. For the Black wealth of Chicago to be equivalent to that of Ken Griffen, the average Black person's wealth would have to be $12,543.

15. James Baldwin, *The Fire Next Time* (New York: Vintage, 1993), 104.

Chapter 16

1. James Baldwin, *No Name in the Streets* (New York: Vintage, 2007), 196.

2. See Ashley Farmer, "'Somebody Has to Pay': Audley Moore and the Modern Reparations Movement," *Palimpsest* 7 (2018): 104–34.

3. See TIRZ 18, *The Fifth Ward Housing Study: Our Space is a Great Place*, Houston, 2012.

4. Katie Watkins, "Life Expectancy in Houston Can Vary Up to 20 Years Depending on Where You Live," Houston Public Media, March 4, 2019.

5. Patrick Sharkey, Keeanga-Yamahtta Taylor, and Yaryna Serkez, "The Gaps Between White and Black America in Charts," *New York Times*, June 19, 2020.

6. Paul Cline, "Chicago Life Expectancy Gap Driven by Race, Segregation, Says Researcher," NPR Chicago, July 22, 2019.

7. Joe Cortright, "Lost in Place: Why the Persistence and Spread of Concentrated Poverty—Not Gentrification—Is Our Biggest Urban Challenge," *City Observatory*, September 12, 2014.

8. See Charles A. Beard, *An Economic Interpretation of the Constitution of the United States* (Mineola, NY: Dover, 2004); Nancy MacLean, *Democracy in Chains: The Deep History of the Radical Right's Stealth Plan for America* (New York: Viking, 2017); Michael Klarman, *The Framers' Coup: The Making of the United States Constitution* (New York: Oxford University Press, 2016).

9. Quoted in Ransby, *Ella Baker*, 1.

10. Quoted in Klarman, *Framers' Coup*, 1.

11. King, *Where Do We Go from Here?*, 139, 211.

12. Thomas Jefferson to Samuel Kercheval, July 12, 1816, https://teachingamericanhistory.org/document/letter-to-samuel-kercheval/.

13. EdBuild, "$23 Billion," February 2019, https://edbuild.org/content/23-billion; Laura Meckler, "Report Finds $23 Billion Racial Funding Gap for Schools," *Washington Post*, February 26, 2019.

14. $2,000 × 200 students × 13 years (K–12) = $5,200,000. See Linda Darling-Hammond, "Unequal Opportunity: Race and Education," Brookings Institution, March 1, 1998, https://www.brookings.edu/articles/unequal-opportunity-race-and-education/; and Tom Vander Ark, "What's the Right High School Size and Structure?," *Forbes*, June 4, 2021.

15. "Closing America's Funding Gaps," Century Foundation, July 22, 2020, https://tcf.org/content/report/closing-americas-education-funding/; Bruce D. Baker, "How Money Matters for Schools," Learning Policy Institute, July 17, 2018; C. Kirabo Jackson, Rucker C. Johnson, and Claudia Persico, "The Effects of School Spending on Educational and Economic Outcomes: Evidence from School Finance Reforms," *Quarterly Journal of Economics* 131, no. 1 (February 2016): 160.

16. See Andre M. Perry, Marshall Steinbaum, and Carl Romer, "Student loans, the racial wealth divide, and why we need full student debt cancellation," Brookings Institution, June 23, 2021, https://www.brookings.edu/articles/student-loans-the-racial-wealth-divide-and-why-we-need-full-student-debt-cancellation/.

17. See Michelle Alexander's *The New Jim Crow* and Elizabeth Hinton's *From the War on Poverty to the War on Crime*.

18. Danielle Sered, *Until We Reckon: Violence, Mass Incarceration, and a Road to Repair* (New York: Free Press, 2019), 48.

19. A full 69 percent of survivors of violence desire alternatives beyond prison, such as mental health and substance abuse treatment, and report 80 to 90 percent satisfaction rates with restorative processes as opposed to the standard 30 percent satisfaction rate with the traditional court and incarceration system. Sered, *Until We Reckon*, 48, 141.

20. See Gerald Young, "The Dream Re-imagined: Historically Black Colleges and Univer-

sities Releasing Purpose to Prisoners (A Case Study on the Second Chance Pell Grant Program at Wiley College, Marshall Texas)" (PhD diss., Union University and Institute, 2022), 49.

21. See American Bar Association, *2023 Plea Bargain Task Force Report*, https://www.americanbar.org/groups/criminal_justice/committees/taskforces/plea_bargain_tf /; Carrie Johnson, "The vast majority of criminal cases end in plea bargains, a new report finds," NPR, February 22, 2023; and Sered, *Until We Reckon*, 30.

22. Desmond, *Poverty, by America*, 85.

23. Desmond, *Poverty, by America*, 18; Kalee Burns, Liana Fox, and Danielle Wilson, "Child Poverty Fell to Record Low 5.2% in 2021," United States Census Bureau, September 13, 2022, https://www.census.gov/library/stories/2022/09/record-drop-in-child-poverty.html; Peter G. Peterson Foundation, "What Are the Economic Costs of Child Poverty?," October 24, 2023, https://www.pgpf.org/blog/2023/10/what-are-the-economic-costs-of-child-poverty.

24. Desmond, *Poverty, by America*, 83.

25. David Cooper, "Workers of Color Are Far More Likely to Be Paid Poverty-Level Wages than White Workers," Economic Policy Institute, June 21, 2018, https://www.epi.org/blog /workers-of-color-are-far-more-likely-to-be-paid-poverty-level-wages-than-white-workers/.

26. In this approach, the federal minimum wage would be adjusted to the local cost of living.

27. See A. Barford et al., *The Case for Living Wages: How Paying Living Wages Improves Business Performance and Tackles Poverty* (Cambridge: University of Cambridge Institute for Sustainability Leadership & Shift, 2022).

28. See Ray Fisman and Michael Luca, "The Case for Higher Wages in Hard Times," *Wall Street Journal*, January 21, 2021, https://www.wsj.com/articles/the-case-for-higher -wages-in-hard-times-11611241084.

29. Smith, *Wealth of Nations*, 90.

30. "Chart Book: The Need to Rebuild the Depleted IRS," Center on Budget and Policy Priorities, revised December 16, 2022, https://www.cbpp.org/research/federal-tax/the -need-to-rebuild-the-depleted-irs.

31. Alan Rappeport, "I.R.S. Changes Audit Practice That Discriminated Against Black Taxpayers," *New York Times*, September 18, 2023.

32. Alan Rappeport, "The U.S. Is Losing $1 Trillion Annually to Tax Cheats," *New York Times*, April 13, 2021 (updated October 13, 2021); "The Tax Gap," IRS, https://www.irs.gov /newsroom/the-tax-gap; Paul Kiel and Jesse Eisinger, "How the IRS Was Gutted," *ProPublica*, December 11, 2018; Alan Rappeport, "I.R.S. Unveils $80 Billion Plan to Overhaul Tax Collection," *New York Times*, April 6, 2023; Catherine Rampell, "How Much Did Congress Lose by Defunding the IRS? Way More Than We Thought," *Washington Post*, June 14, 2023.

33. Charlotte Wold, "The Number of Millionaires Continues to Increase," Investopedia, November 21, 2021, https://www.investopedia.com/news/number-millionaires -continues-increase/.

Chapter 17

1. For more on paradigm shifts, see Thomas Kuhn's *The Structure of Scientific Revolutions*.

2. Farmer, "Somebody Has to Pay," 125.

Bibliography

Abdurraqib, Hanif. *They Can't Kill Us Until They Kill Us*. Columbus: Two Dollar Radio, 2017.

Alexander, Michelle. *The New Jim Crow: Mass Incarceration in the Age of Colorblindness*. New York: New Press, 2010.

American Bar Association. 2023 *Plea Bargain Task Force Report*. https://www.americanbar .org/groups/criminal_justice/committees/taskforces/plea_bargain_tf /.

Anderson, Carol. *Eyes Off the Prize: The United Nations and the African American Struggle for Human Rights, 1944–1955*. Cambridge: Cambridge University Press, 2003.

———. *White Rage: The Unspoken Truth of Our Racial Divide*. New York: Bloomsbury, 2016.

"Article 2 Fund: Overview & History." Claims Conference. https://www.claimscon.org/our -work/compensation/background/article2-article2/article2-history/.

Baker, Bruce D. "How Money Matters for Schools." Learning Policy Institute, July 17, 2018.

Baldwin, James. *The Fire Next Time*. New York: Vintage, 1993.

———. *No Name in the Streets*. New York: Vintage, 2007.

———. *Notes of a Native Son*. Boston: Beacon, 2012.

———. "Notes on the House of Bondage." In *Collected Essays*, 799–807. New York: Library of America, 1988.

———. "An Open Letter to Jimmy Carter." *New York Times*, January 23, 1977.

Baptist, Edward. *The Half Has Never Been Told: Slavery and the Making of American Capitalism*. New York: Basic, 2014.

Barford, A., R. Gilbert, A. Beales, M. Zorila, and J. Nelson. *The Case for Living Wages: How Paying Living Wages Improves Business Performance and Tackles Poverty*. Cambridge: University of Cambridge Institute for Sustainability Leadership & Shift, 2022.

Barger, Brian, and Robert Parry. "Reports Link Nicaraguan Rebels to Cocaine Trafficking." Associated Press, December 20, 1985.

Barron, James. "A Search for Solutions to the Housing Squeeze." *New York Times*, July 12, 1987.

Bauer, Shane. *American Prison: A Reporter's Undercover Journey into the Business of Punishment*. New York: Penguin, 2018.

Baum, Dan. *Smoke and Mirrors*. Boston: Back Bay, 1997.

Baum, John. "Legalize It All." *Harper's Magazine*, April 2016.

Beard, Charles A. *An Economic Interpretation of the Constitution of the United States*. Mineola, NY: Dover, 2004.

Berry, Daina Ramey. *The Price for Their Pound of Flesh: The Value of the Enslaved, from Womb to Grave, in the Building of a Nation*. Boston: Beacon, 2017.

Berry, Daina Ramey, and Kali Nicole Gross. *A Black Women's History of the United States*. Boston: Beacon, 2020.

Berry, Mary Frances. *My Face Is Black Is True: Callie House and the Struggle for Ex-Slave Reparations*. New York: Vintage, 2006.

Bibb, Henry. *Narrative of the Life and Adventures of Henry Bibb, an American Slave*. New York: privately printed, 1849.

"Billionaires by the Numbers." Americans for Tax Fairness. https://americansfortaxfairness .org/billionaires/.

Black, Edwin. *War against the Weak: Eugenics and America's Campaign to Create a Master Race*. Washington, DC: Dialog, 2003.

Blackmon, Douglas. "Book: American Slavery Continued Until 1941." Interview by Imani Cheers. *Newsweek*, July 13, 2008.

———. *Slavery by Another Name: The Re-Enslavement of Black Americans from the Civil War to World War II*. New York: Random House, 2009.

Blain, Keisha N. *Until I Am Free: Fannie Lou Hamer's Enduring Message to America*. Boston: Beacon, 2021.

Blight, David W. *Frederick Douglass: Prophet of Freedom*. New York: Simon & Schuster, 2018.

———. *Race and Reunion: The Civil War in American Memory*. Cambridge, MA: Belknap, 2001.

Blow, Charles. "The Most Dangerous Negro." *New York Times*, August 28, 2013.

Blum, Edward J. *Reforging the White Republic: Race, Religion, and American Nationalism, 1865–1898*. Baton Rouge: Louisiana State University Press, 2005.

Blumenson, Eric, and Eva Nilsen. "Policing for Profit: The Drug War's Hidden Economic Agenda." *University of Chicago Law Review* 65, no. 1 (Winter 1998): 35–114.

Bond, Horace. "Intelligence Tests and Propaganda." *Crisis*, May 30, 1924.

Bonner, Christopher. Interview in *Lincoln: Divided We Stand*, dir. Jon Hirsch. CNN Miniseries. Aired spring 2021.

Boyle, Kevin. "The Ruins of Detroit: Exploring the Urban Crisis in the Motor City." *Michigan Historical Review* 27, no. 1 (Spring 2001): 109–27.

Bradley, Mark L. *The Army and Reconstruction, 1865–1877*. Washington, DC: Center of Military History, 2015.

Branch, Taylor. *At Canaan's Edge: America in the King Years, 1965–68*. New York: Simon & Schuster, 2007.

Brands, H. W. *Reagan: The Life*. New York: Anchor, 2016.

Broder, David S. "Always Goldwater." *Washington Post*, June 2, 1998.

Broder, David S., and Stephen Hess. *The Republican Establishment: The Present and Future of the G.O.P.* New York: Harper & Row, 1967.

Brous, Rabbi Sharon. "Our Country Was Built on a Stolen Beam: The Call for a National Reckoning." IKAR, September 22, 2017.

Brown, Dorothy. *The Whiteness of Wealth: How the Tax System Impoverishes Black Americans—and How We Can Fix It*. New York: Crown, 2021.

Buchanan, Larry, Quoctrung Bui, and Jugal K. Patel. "Black Lives Matter May Be the Largest Movement in U.S. History." *New York Times*, July 3, 2020.

Burns, Kalee, Liana Fox, and Danielle Wilson. "Child Poverty Fell to Record Low 5.2% in 2021." United States Census Bureau, September 13, 2022. https://www.census.gov/library/stories/2022/09/record-drop-in-child-poverty.html.

Byrne, David T. *Ronald Reagan: An Intellectual Biography*. Lincoln, NE: Potomac, 2018.

California Task Force to Study and Develop Reparation Proposals for African Americans. *The California Reparations Report*. June 29, 2023. https://oag.ca.gov/ab3121/report.

Cannon, Lou. *Governor Reagan: His Rise to Power*. New York: Public Affairs, 2003.

———. *President Reagan: The Role of a Lifetime*. New York: Public Affairs, 2000.

———. "Reagan Campaigning from County Fair to Urban League." *Washington Post*, August 4, 1980.

———. "Reagan Visits Jordan, Says He Is Doing Well." *Washington Post*, August 5, 1980.

Caro, Robert. *The Passage of Power: The Years of Lyndon Johnson*. Vol. 4. New York: Knopf, 2012.

Cerulli Associates. "Cerulli Anticipates $84 Trillion in Wealth Transfers Through 2045." January 20, 2022. https://www.cerulli.com/press-releases/cerulli-anticipates-84-trillion-in-wealth-transfers-through-2045.

Chang, Clio. "Incarcerated Fathers and the Children Left Behind." Century Foundation, September 3, 2014. https://tcf.org/content/commentary/incarcerated-fathers-and-the-children-left-behind/.

"Chart Book: The Need to Rebuild the Depleted IRS." Center on Budget and Policy Priorities. Revised December 16, 2022. https://www.cbpp.org/research/federal-tax/the-need-to-rebuild-the-depleted-irs.

Civil Liberties Act of 1988, Pub. L. No. 100–383, 102 Stat. 904 (1988).

Cline, Paul. "Chicago Life Expectancy Gap Driven by Race, Segregation, Says Researcher." NPR Chicago, July 22, 2019.

Clines, Francis. "Reagan's Doubts on King Disclosed." *Washington Post*, October 22, 1983.

"Closing America's Funding Gaps." Century Foundation, July 22, 2020. https://tcf.org/content/report/closing-americas-education-funding/.

Coates, Ta-Nehisi. "The Case for Reparations." *Atlantic*, June 2014.

———. *The Water Dancer: A Novel*. New York: Random House, 2019.

———. *We Were Eight Years in Power: An American Tragedy*. New York: One World, 2017.

Cobb, Jelani. *The Essential Kerner Commission: The Landmark Study on Race, Inequality, and Police Violence*. New York: Liveright, 2021.

Committee on Foreign Relations. *Drugs, Law Enforcement and Foreign Policy* (aka the Kerry Report). Washington, DC, December 1988.

Cone, James H. *The Cross and the Lynching Tree*. New York: Orbis, 2013.

Connelly, Matthew. *Fatal Misconception: The Struggle to Control World Population*. Cambridge, MA: Belknap, 2008.

Cooper, David. "Workers of Color Are Far More Likely to Be Paid Poverty-Level Wages than White Workers." Economic Policy Institute, June 21, 2018. https://www.epi.org/blog/workers-of-color-are-far-more-likely-to-be-paid-poverty-level-wages-than-white-workers/.

Cortright, Joe. "Lost in Place: Why the Persistence and Spread of Concentrated Poverty—Not Gentrification—Is Our Biggest Urban Challenge." *City Observatory*, September 12, 2014.

Cowen, Richard. "Reagan's Life Style Contradicts Policies." *Washington Post*, September 15, 1981.

Daly, John A. *Advocacy: Championing Ideas and Influencing Others*. New Haven: Yale University Press, 2011.

Danielson, Leilah. *American Gandhi: A. J. Muste and the History of Radicalism in the Twentieth Century*. Philadelphia: University of Pennsylvania Press, 2014.

Darity, William A., Jr. "Many Roads to Extinction: Early AEA Economists and the Black Disappearance Theory." *History of Economics Review* 21, no. 1 (January 1994): 47–64.

Darity, William A., Jr., and A. Kirsten Mullen. *From Here to Equality: Reparations for Black Americans in the Twenty-First Century*. Chapel Hill: University of North Carolina Press, 2020.

Darity, William A., Jr., A. Kirsten Mullen, and Lucas Hubbard, eds. *The Black Reparations Project: A Handbook for Racial Justice*. Oakland: University of California Press, 2023.

Darity, William A., Jr., A. Kirsten Mullen, and Marvin Slaughter. "The Cumulative Costs of Racism and the Bill for Black Reparations." *Journal of Economic Perspectives* 36, no 2 (Spring 2022): 99–122.

Darity, William A., Jr., and Samuel L. Myers Jr. "Book Review: *Losing Ground: American Social Policy, 1950–1980*." *Review of Black Political Economy* 14, nos. 2–3 (December 1985): 167–77.

Darling-Hammond, Linda. "Unequal Opportunity: Race and Education." Brookings Institution, March 1, 1998. https://www.brookings.edu/articles/unequal-opportuni ty-race-and-education/.

Darwin, Charles. *The Descent of Man, and Selection in Relation to Sex*. Norwalk: The Easton Press, 1979.

Delbanco, Andrew. *The War Before the War: Fugitive Slaves and the Struggle for America's Soul from the Revolution to the Civil War*. New York: Penguin, 2018.

Desmond, Matthew. *Poverty, by America*. New York: Crown, 2023.

"Detroit." Black Demographics. Accessed September 14, 2021. https://blackdemographics .com/cities-2/detroit-black-pupulation/.

Dewart, Janet, ed. *The State of Black America, 1990*. New York: National Urban League, 1990.

Dixon, Thomas, Jr. *The Clansman*. Lexington: University Press of Kentucky, 1970.

———. *The Flaming Sword*. Lexington: University Press of Kentucky, 2013.

———. *The Leopard's Spots: A Romance of the White Man's Burden—1865–1900*. New York: Doubleday, Page, 1902.

"Dixon's *Leopard's Spots*." The Institute for Advanced Technology in the Humanities at the University of Virginia. http://utc.iath.virginia.edu/proslav/dixonhp.html.

Douglass, Frederick. "A Day and a Night in 'Uncle Tom's Cabin.'" *Frederick Douglass' Paper*, March 4, 1853.

———. "The Fugitive Slave Law." In *The Essential Douglass: Selected Writings and Speeches*, edited by Nicholas Buccola, 72–75. Indianapolis: Hackett, 2016.

———. "Horse Democracy." *Douglass' Monthly*, October 1860.

———. "The Inaugural Address." *Douglass' Monthly*, April 1861.

———. "John Brown." In *The Essential Douglass: Selected Writings and Speeches*, edited by Nicholas Buccola, 258–75. Indianapolis: Hackett, 2016.

———. "The Nation's Great Act." *National Republican*, April 18, 1885.

———. "On the Mission of the War." *Douglass' Monthly*, January 13, 1864.

———. "Oration of Frederick Douglass Delivered on the Occasion of the Unveiling of the Freemen's Monument in Memory of Abraham Lincoln." Speech. Washington, DC, April 14, 1876. In *The Essential Douglass: Selected Writings and Speeches*, edited by Nicholas Buccola, 239–48. Indianapolis: Hackett, 2016.

———. "The President and His Speeches." *Douglass' Monthly*, September 1862.

———. Speech at Concert Hall, Philadelphia, April 14, 1875. In *Centennial Anniversary of the Pennsylvania Society for Promoting the Abolition of Slavery, the Relief of Free Negroes, Unlawfully Held in Bondage, and for Improving the Condition of the African Race*. Philadelphia: Grant, Faires & Rodgers, 1875.

———. "This Decision Has Humbled the Nation." Speech at the Civil Rights Mass-Meeting, Lincoln Hall, Washington, DC, October 22, 1883.

———. "The War and How to End It." *Douglass' Monthly*, March 1862.

Du Bois, W. E. B. "Again, Lincoln." *Crisis*, September 1922.

———. "Americanization." *Crisis*, August 1922.

———. *Black Reconstruction in America, 1860–1880*. New York: Free Press, 1998.

———. *Darkwater: Voices from within the Veil*. New York: Harcourt, Brace and Howe, 1920.

———. *Dusk of Dawn*. In *Writings*, edited by Nathan Huggins, 549–802. New York: Library of America, 1986.

———. *John Brown: A Biography*. New York: Modern Library, 2001.

———. "Religion in the South." In Booker T. Washington and W. E. Burghardt DuBois, *The Negro in the South: His Economic Progress in Relation to His Moral and Religious Development*, 126–91. Philadelphia: George W. Jacobs, 1907.

———. *The Souls of Black Folk*. New York: Signet Classic, 1995.

———. "The Superior Race (An Essay)." *The Smart Set: A Magazine of Cleverness* 70, no. 4 (April 1923): 55–60.

———. "The Technique of Race Prejudice." *Crisis*, August 1923.

Dugger, Ronnie. *On Reagan: The Man and His Presidency*. New York: McGraw-Hill, 2003.

Duneier, Mitchell. *Ghetto: The Invention of a Place, the History of an Idea*. New York: Farrar, Straus and Giroux, 2017.

Dyson, Michael. *I May Not Get There with You: The True Martin Luther King*. New York: Free Press, 2001.

"Economics of Incarceration." Prison Policy Initiative. https://www.prisonpolicy.org/research/economics_of_incarceration/.

Edelman, Marian Wright. *Families in Peril: An Agenda for Social Change*. Cambridge, MA: Harvard University Press, 1987.

Eder, Steve, David D. Kirkpatrick, and Mike McIntire. "They Legitimized the Myth of a Stolen Election—and Reaped the Rewards." *New York Times*, October 3, 2022.

Edwards, Lee. *Reagan: A Political Biography*. Houston: Nordland, 1981.

Ehrenfreund, Max. "There's a Disturbing Truth to John Legend's Oscar Statement about Prisons and Slavery." *Washington Post*, February 23, 2015.

Eller, Ronald. *Uneven Ground: Appalachia since 1945*. Lexington: University Press of Kentucky, 2008.

Ellis, Joseph J. *American Sphinx: The Character of Thomas Jefferson*. New York: Vintage, 1998.

Emerson, Michael, and Christian Smith. *Divided by Faith: Evangelical Religion and the Problem of Race in America*. New York: Oxford University Press, 2000.

Engs, Robert. "The Great American Slave Rebellion." Paper presented at the Civil War Institute at Gettysburg College, Pennsylvania, June 27, 1991.

Equal Justice Initiative. *Lynching in America: Confronting the Legacy of Racial Terror*. 3rd ed. Montgomery, AL: Equal Justice Initiative, 2017.

Evans, Sandra. "Tutu Says He Wants to Meet with Reagan, Hill Panel Gives Bishop Rare Ovation." *Washington Post*, December 5, 1984.

Evans, Thomas W. *The Education of Ronald Reagan: The General Electric Years and the Untold Story of His Conversion to Conservatism*. New York: Columbia University Press, 2006.

Falwell, Jerry. *Falwell: An Autobiography*. Lynchburg, VA: Liberty House, 1997.

Farmer, Ashley. "'Somebody Has to Pay': Audley Moore and the Modern Reparations Movement." *Palimpsest* 7 (2018): 108–34.

"Federal Estate and Gift Tax Rates, Exemptions, and Exclusions, 1916–2014." Tax Foundation, February 4, 2014. https://taxfoundation.org/federal-estate-and-gift-tax-rates -exemptions-and-exclusions-1916-2014/.

Fiske, Edward. "Education Secretary Bell's View of a Department in Transition." *New York Times*, February 3, 1981.

———. "Reagan Record in Education: Mixed Results." *New York Times*, November 14, 1982.

Fisman, Ray, and Michael Luca. "The Case for Higher Wages in Hard Times." *Wall Street Journal*, January 21, 2021. https://www.wsj.com/articles/the-case-for-higher-wages -in-hard-times-11611241084.

FitzGerald, Frances. "A Disciplined, Charging Army." *New Yorker*, May 18, 1981.

Flynn, John T. *The Road Ahead: America's Creeping Revolution*. New York: Devin-Adair, 1949.

Foner, Eric. *Reconstruction: America's Unfinished Revolution, 1863–1877*. New York: HarperPerennial, 2014.

Forbes, Robert P. "*Notes on the State of Virginia* (1785)." Encyclopedia Virginia. https://www .encyclopediavirginia.org/Notes_on_the_State_of_Virginia_1785.

Forman, James, Jr. *Locking Up Our Own: Crime and Punishment in Black America*. New York: Farrar, Straus and Giroux, 2017.

Franklin, John Hope. *The Color Line: Legacy for the Twenty-First Century*. Columbia: University of Missouri Press, 1993.

———. *The Emancipation Proclamation*. Wheeling, IL: Harlan Davidson, 1995.

———. "History as Propaganda." In *Race and History: Selected Essays, 1938–1988*, 10–23. Baton Rouge: Louisiana State University Press, 1991.

———. "Who Divided This House?" *Chicago History* 19, nos. 3–4 (Fall and Winter 1990–91): 24–35.

Franklin, John Hope, and Franklin A. Moss Jr. *From Slavery to Freedom: A History of African Americans*. New York: Knopf, 2000.

Franklin, John Hope, and Loren Schweninger. *Runaway Slaves: Rebels on the Plantation*. New York: Oxford University Press, 2000.

Frazier, Edward Franklin. "The Pathology of Race Prejudice." *Forum* 77, no. 6 (June 1927): 856–61.

Frémont, Jessie Benton. *The Letters of Jessie Benton Frémont*. Edited by Pamela Herr and Mary Lee Spence. Champaign: University of Illinois Press, 1992.

Friedman, Milton. "What Is Barry Goldwater's View of Economics?" *New York Times*, October 11, 1964.

Galea, Sandro, Melissa Tracey, Katherine Hoggatt, Charles DiMaggio, and Adam Karpati. "Estimated Deaths Attributable to Social Factors in the United States." *American Journal of Public Health* 101, no. 8 (August 2011): 1456–65.

Galton, Francis. *Essays in Eugenics*. London: Eugenics Education Society, 1909.

Garrison, William Lloyd. "The American Union." *Liberator*, January 10, 1845.

———. "To the Public." *Liberator*, January 1, 1831.

Gertz, Elmer. "The Black Laws of Illinois." *Journal of the Illinois State Historical Society (1908–1984)* 56, no. 3 (Fall 1963): 454–73.

Giddings, Ida. *Ida: A Sword Among Lions*. New York: Amistad, 2008.

Gillespie, Michele K., and Randal L. Hall, eds. *Thomas Dixon Jr. and the Birth of Modern America*. Baton Rouge: Louisiana State University Press, 2006.

Gillon, Steve. *Separate and Unequal: The Kerner Commission and the Unraveling of American Liberalism*. New York: Basic, 2018.

Glaude, Eddie S., Jr. *Begin Again: James Baldwin's America and Its Urgent Lessons for Our Own*. New York: Crown, 2020.

———. *Democracy in Black: How Race Still Enslaves the American Soul*. New York: Crown, 2016.

Goldin, Claudia Dale. "The Economics of Emancipation." *Journal of Economic History* 33, no. 1 (1973): 66–85.

Goodman, Ellen. "Crack Baby Hyperbole." *Washington Post*, January 11, 1992.

Goodwin, Doris Kearns. *Team of Rivals: The Political Genius of Abraham Lincoln*. New York: Simon & Schuster, 2006.

Gordon-Reed, Annette. *The Hemingses of Monticello: An American Family*. New York: Norton, 2008.

Gould, Stephen Jay. *The Mismeasure of Man*. New York: Norton, 1996.

Goza, Joel Edward. *America's Unholy Ghosts: The Racist Roots of Our Faith and Politics*. Eugene, OR: Cascade, 2019.

———. "Why We Must Oppose Politics like SB 138 That Seek to Shrink Young Minds." *Louisville Courier Journal*, February 23, 2022.

Grant, Madison. "America for Americans." *Forum* 74, no. 3 (September 1925): 346–55.

———. *The Conquest of a Continent*. London: Ostara, 2018.

———. *The Passing of the Great Race*. Eastford, CT: Martino, 2017.

———. "The Racial Transformation of America." *North American Review* 219, no. 820 (March 1924): 343–52.

Greeley, Horace. "Let Us Clasp Hands Across the Bloody Chasm." *Harper's Weekly*, September 21, 1872.

Griggs, Sutton E. *The Hindered Hand: or, The Reign of the Repressionist*. Nashville: Orion, 1905.

Hahn, Robert A., Elaine D. Eaker, Nancy D. Barker, Steven M. Teutsch, Waldemar A.

Sosniak, and Nancy Krieger. "Poverty and Death in the United States, 1973–1991." *International Journal of Health Services* 26, no. 4 (October 1996): 673–90.

Hale, Grace Elizabeth. *Making Whiteness: The Culture of Segregation in the South, 1890–1940.* New York: Pantheon, 1998.

Hamm, Theodore. *Rebel with a Cause: Caryl Chessman and the Politics of the Death Penalty in Postwar California, 1948–1974.* Berkeley: University of California Press, 2001.

Hannon, Lance, and James DeFronzo. "The Truly Disadvantaged, Public Assistance, and Crime." *Social Problems* 45, no. 3 (August 1998): 383–92.

———. "Welfare Assistance Levels and Homicide Rates." *Homicide Studies* 2, no. 1 (February 1998): 31–45.

Harding, Vincent. *There Is a River: The Black Struggle for Freedom in America.* San Diego: Harcourt Brace, 1981.

Harkins, E. F. *Little Pilgrimages Among the Men Who Have Written Famous Books.* 2nd series. Boston: Page, 1903.

Harris, Paul. "Apartheid Leader Refuses Apology." *AP News*, January 23, 1998.

Hendrickson, Paul. "Meese Gets the Dickens Humbug!" *Washington Post*, December 17, 1983.

Herrnstein, Richard J. "IQ." *Atlantic*, September 1971.

Herrnstein, Richard J., and Charles A. Murray. *The Bell Curve: Intelligence and Class Structure in American Life.* New York: Free Press, 1994.

Hinton, Elizabeth. *From the War on Poverty to the War on Crime: The Making of Mass Incarceration in America.* Cambridge, MA: Harvard University Press, 2016.

Hitler, Adolf. *Mein Kampf.* Vol. 1. Translated by Ralph Manheim. New York: Mariner, 1971.

Hoffman, David. "Discussing Hunger in U.S., Meese Sparks a Firestorm." *Washington Post*, December 10, 1983.

hooks, bell. *All about Love: New Visions.* New York: Perennial, 2001.

Horrock, Nicholas M. "Reagan Resists Financial Disclosure." *New York Times*, August 13, 1976.

Houston, Paul. "Reagan Denies Astrology Influences His Decisions." *Los Angeles Times*, May 4, 1988.

Hughes, Langston. *Langston Hughes and the* Chicago Defender*: Essays on Race, Politics, and Culture, 1942–62.* Edited by Christopher C. De Santis. Champaign: University of Illinois Press, 1995.

Isaac, Benjamin. *The Invention of Racism in Classical Antiquity.* Princeton: Princeton University Press, 2004.

Isenberg, Nancy. *White Trash: The 400-Year Untold History of Class in America.* New York: Viking, 2016.

Jackson, C. Kirabo, Rucker C. Johnson, and Claudia Persico. "The Effects of School Spending on Educational and Economic Outcomes: Evidence from School Finance Reforms." *Quarterly Journal of Economics* 131, no. 1 (February 2016): 157–218.

Jackson, Kellie Carter. *Force and Freedom: Black Abolitionists and the Politics of Violence.* Philadelphia: University of Pennsylvania Press, 2019.

Jacobson, Matthew Frye. *Barbarian Virtues: The United States Encounters Foreign Peoples at Home and Abroad, 1876–1917.* New York: Hill and Wang, 2000.

———. *Whiteness of a Different Color: European Immigrants and the Alchemy of Race.* Cambridge, MA: Harvard University Press, 1999.

Jefferson, Thomas. *Notes on the State of Virginia*. Philadelphia: Prichard and Hall, 1848. https://docsouth.unc.edu/southlit/jefferson/jefferson.html.

———. *Thomas Jefferson: Writings*. New York: Library of America, 1984.

Jerome, Fred, and Rodger Taylor. *Einstein on Race and Racism*. New Brunswick, NJ: Rutgers University Press, 2006.

"John Erlichman Settles a Few Scores." *Washington Post*, January 24, 1982.

Johnson, Carrie. "The vast majority of criminal cases end in plea bargains, a new report finds." NPR, February 22, 2023.

Johnson, Haynes. "Reagan Thanks Nation for Its Compassion." *Washington Post*, April 29, 1981.

Johnson, Julie. "President Signs Law to Redress Wartime Wrong." *New York Times*, August 11, 1988.

Johnson, Roberta Ann. "African Americans and Homelessness: Moving Through History." *Journal of Black Studies* 40, no. 4 (March 2010): 583–605.

Joseph, Peniel E. *Stokely: A Life*. New York: Basic Civitas, 2014.

———. *The Sword and the Shield: The Revolutionary Lives of Malcolm X and Martin Luther King Jr.* New York: Basic, 2020.

Josephson, Amelia. "A Guide to the Federal Estate Tax for 2024." SmartAsset, December 20, 2023 https://smartasset.com/taxes/all-about-the-estate-tax.

Kaiser-Schatzlein, Robin. "This Is How America's Richest Families Stay That Way." *New York Times*, September 24, 2021.

Kantrowitz, Barbara. "Still Separate After 20 Years." *Newsweek*, September 6, 1992.

Kelley, Robin D. G. *Hammer and Hoe: Alabama Communists during the Great Depression*. Chapel Hill: University of North Carolina Press, 1990.

Kendi, Ibram X. *How to Be an Antiracist*. New York: One World, 2019.

———. "The Second Assassination of Martin Luther King Jr." *Atlantic*, October 14, 2021.

———. *Stamped from the Beginning: The Definitive History of Racist Ideas in America*. New York: Nation, 2016.

Kiel, Paul, and Jesse Eisinger. "How the IRS Was Gutted." *ProPublica*, December 11, 2018. https://www.propublica.org/article/how-the-irs-was-gutted.

King, Martin Luther, Jr. "Letter from Birmingham City Jail." In *A Testament of Hope: The Essential Writings and Speeches of Martin Luther King Jr.*, edited by James M. Washington, 289–302. New York: HarperOne, 1986.

———. Speech. Monmouth College, Monmouth, IL, October 6, 1966. https://www.monmouth.edu/about/wp-content/uploads/sites/128/2019/01/MLKJrSpeechatMonmouth.pdf.

———. "A Testament of Hope." In *A Testament of Hope: The Essential Writings and Speeches of Martin Luther King Jr.*, edited by James M. Washington, 313–30. New York: HarperOne, 1986.

———. "The Three Evils." Speech. The National Conference on New Politics, Chicago, August 31, 1967. https://www.nwesd.org/ed-talks/equity/the-three-evils-of-society-address-martin-luther-king-jr/.

———. *Where Do We Go from Here: Chaos or Community?* Boston: Beacon, 2010.

———. "Why We Can't Wait." In *A Testament of Hope: The Essential Writings and Speeches of Martin Luther King Jr.*, edited by James M. Washington, 518–54. New York: HarperOne, 1986.

"Klan to Back Goldwater Despite His Repudiation." *New York Times*, August 14, 1964.

Klarman, Michael. *The Framers' Coup: The Making of the United States Constitution*. New York: Oxford University Press, 2016.

Kohlman, Michael. "Evangelizing Eugenics: A Brief Historiography of Popular and Formal American Eugenics Education (1908–1948)." *Alberta Journal of Educational Research* 58, no. 4 (Winter 2012): 657–90.

Kornbluh, Peter. "Crack, the Contras and the CIA: The Storm over 'Dark Alliance.'" *Columbia Journalism Review*, January/February 1997. https://nsarchive2.gwu.edu /NSAEBB/NSAEBB113/storm.htm.

Kotz, Nick. *Judgment Days: Lyndon Baines Johnson, Martin Luther King Jr., and the Laws That Changed America*. Boston: Houghton Mifflin, 2005.

Kozol, Jonathan. *Savage Inequalities: Children in America's Schools*. New York: Broadway, 1991.

Kunde, Meg. "Making the Free Market Moral: Ronald Reagan's Covenantal Economy." *Rhetoric and Public Affairs* 22, no. 2 (Summer 2019): 217–52.

Kwon, Duke L., and Gregory Thompson. *Reparations: A Christian Call for Repentance and Repair*. Grand Rapids: Brazos, 2021.

Lanham, Anderson. "A Haven for Communist Sympathizers, Protesters and Sex Deviants." *Daily Californian*, November 15, 2016.

Larson, Kate Clifford. *Bound for the Promised Land: Harriet Tubman, Portrait of an American Hero*. New York: One World, 2003.

Lasseter, Tom. "House Speaker Johnson among US politicians with ancestral ties to slavery." Reuters, December 20, 2023.

Lawrence, Mark. "Bennett Defends Controversial Style." *Los Angeles Times*, September 7, 1988.

LeMaster, J. R., and Donald D. Kummings, eds. *Walt Whitman: An Encyclopedia*. New York: Routledge, 1998.

Leonard, Thomas. *Illiberal Reformers: Race, Eugenics, and American Economics in the Progressive Era*. Princeton: Princeton University Press, 2016.

Levingston, Steven. *Kennedy and King: The President, the Pastor, and the Battle over Civil Rights*. New York: Hachette, 2017.

Lewis, Anthony. "Abroad at Home; the Real Reagan." *New York Times*, October 24, 1983.

Lewis, David Levering. *W. E. B. Du Bois: A Biography*. New York: Holt, 2009.

———. *W. E. B. Du Bois: The Fight for Equality and the American Century, 1919–1963*. New York: Owl, 2000.

Lincoln, Abraham. "Annual Message to Congress." Speech. Washington, DC, December 8, 1863. In *Speeches and Writings, 1859–1865*, edited by Don E. Fehrenbacher, 538–54. New York: Library of America, 1989.

———. "Annual Message to Congress." Speech. Washington, DC, December 6, 1864. In *Speeches and Writings, 1859–1865*, edited by Don E. Fehrenbacher, 646–52. New York: Library of America, 1989.

———. "The First Inaugural." Speech. Washington, DC, March 4, 1861. In *Speeches and Writings, 1859–1865*, edited by Don E. Fehrenbacher, 215–24. New York: Library of America, 1989.

———. "Gettysburg Address." Speech. Gettysburg, PA, November 19, 1863. https://www .loc.gov/resource/rbpe.24404500/?st=text.

———. *Lincoln-Douglas Debates.* Sixth Joint Debate, Quincy, IL, October 13, 1858. https://www.civiced.org/lincoln-lesson/sixth-joint-debate-between-abraham-lincoln-and-stephen-a-douglas-at-quincy-october-13-1858.

———. "The Second Inaugural." Speech. Washington, DC, March 4, 1865. https://teaching americanhistory.org/document/second-inaugural-address-1865-2/.

———. *Speeches and Writings, 1832–1858.* Edited by Don E. Fehrenbacher. New York: Library of America, 1989.

———. *Speeches and Writings, 1859–1865.* Edited by Don E. Fehrenbacher. New York: Library of America, 1989.

———. "Speech on Internal Improvements." June 20, 1848. In *Speeches and Writings, 1832–1858,* edited by Don E. Fehrenbacher, 187–98. New York: Library of America, 1989.

———. "Speech on the Kansas-Nebraska Act at Peoria, Illinois." October 16, 1854. https://www.nps.gov/liho/learn/historyculture/peoriaspeech.htm.

Lincoln, Abraham, and Dan Stone. "Protest in Illinois Legislature on Slavery." Presented to the Illinois House of Representatives, March 3, 1837. https://papersofabraham lincoln.org/documents/D200101.

Lind, Dara. "How America's Rejection of Jews Fleeing Nazi Germany Haunts Our Refugee Policy Today." *Vox,* January 27, 2017.

Locke, John. *An Essay Concerning Human Understanding.* New York: Penguin, 1997.

Lorde, Audre. *Sister Outsider.* London: Penguin, 2019.

"Losing More Ground." *New York Times,* February 3, 1985.

Lowell, John. "Detroit: That Sinking Feeling." *Newsweek,* October 1976. https://policing.um historylabs.lsa.umich.edu/s/crackdowndetroit/page/drug-corruption.

Lynch, James V. "The Limits of Revolutionary Radicalism: Tom Paine and Slavery." *Pennsylvania Magazine of History and Biography* 123, no. 3 (July 1999): 177–99.

MacDonald, Christine, and Charles E. Ramirez. "Life Span for Detroit's Poor among Shortest in Nation." *Detroit News,* June 2, 2016.

MacLean, Nancy. *Democracy in Chains: The Deep History of the Radical Right's Stealth Plan for America.* New York: Viking, 2017.

Marable, Manning. *Race, Reform, and Rebellion: The Second Reconstruction and Beyond in Black America, 1945–2006.* 2nd ed. Jackson: University Press of Mississippi, 1991.

Marcus, Ruth, and Helen Dewar. "Reagan Vetoes Civil Rights Restoration Act." *New York Times,* March 17, 1988.

Marshall, Thurgood. "Remarks Made at the Second Circuit Judicial Conference, September 8, 1989." *Trotter Review* 4, no. 3 (1990): 3–5.

Masur, Louis. *Lincoln's Last Speech: Wartime Reconstruction and the Crisis of Union.* New York: Oxford University Press, 2015.

Mazza, Sandy. "In McConnell's Boyhood Town Where His Family Owned Slaves, the Reparations Debate Thrives." *USA Today,* July 13, 2019.

McCoy, Alfred W. *The Politics of Heroin: CIA Complicity in the Global Drug Trade.* Chicago: Lawrence Hill, 2003.

McCullough, David. *John Adams.* New York: Simon & Schuster, 2002.

McDaniel, W. Caleb. *Sweet Taste of Liberty: A True Story of Slavery and Restitution in America.* New York: Oxford University Press, 2019.

McGhee, Heather. *The Sum of Us: What Racism Costs Everyone and How We Can Prosper Together.* New York: One World, 2021.

McIntyre, Robert. *Corporate Income Taxes in the Reagan Years: A Study of Three Years of Legalized Corporate Tax Avoidance.* Washington, DC: Citizens for Tax Justice, 1984.

McLaughlin, Jack. *Jefferson and Monticello: The Biography of a Builder.* New York: Henry Holt, 1990.

McPherson, James M. *Tried by War: Abraham Lincoln as Commander in Chief.* New York: Penguin, 2008.

———. "Who Freed the Slaves?" *Proceedings of the American Philosophical Society* 139, no. 1 (March 1995): 1–10.

Meacham, Jon. *And There Was Light: Abraham Lincoln and the American Struggle.* New York: Random House, 2022.

———. *Thomas Jefferson: The Art of Power.* New York: Random House, 2012.

Meckler, Laura. "Report Finds $23 Billion Racial Funding Gap for Schools," *Washington Post*, February 26, 2019.

Meese, Edwin. "The Case for Originalism." Heritage Foundation, June 6, 1985.

Merritt, Keri Leigh. "Land and the Roots of African-American Poverty." *Aeon*, March 11, 2016.

Miller, Kelly. *As to* The Leopard's Spots: *An Open Letter to Thomas Dixon Jr.* Washington, DC: Hayworth, 1905.

Mount, Guy Emerson. "Can Reparations Save American Politics?" *Black Perspectives*, June 27, 2017.

Moynihan, Daniel Patrick. *The Negro Family: The Case for National Action.* Washington, DC: Office of Policy Planning and Research, US Department of Labor, 1965.

Muhammad, Khalil Gibran. *The Condemnation of Blackness: Race, Crime, and the Making of Modern Urban America.* Cambridge, MA: Harvard University Press, 2019.

Murray, Charles A. *Losing Ground: American Social Policy, 1950–1980.* New York: Basic, 1984.

Nagourney, Adam. "On Race, Mike Johnson Says His Views Were Shaped by Raising a Black Child." *New York Times*, October 27, 2023.

National Advisory Commission on Civil Disorders. *The Kerner Report.* Princeton: Princeton University Press, 2016.

"N'Cobra Mission Statement." N'Cobra. Accessed September 13, 2021. https://www.ncobra online.org/about-ncobra.

Neiman, Susan. *Learning from the Germans: Race and the Memory of Evil.* New York: Farrar, Straus and Giroux, 2019.

Noel, Nick, Duwain Pinder, Shelley Stewart, and Jason Wright. "The Economic Impact of Closing the Racial Wealth Gap." McKinsey Institute for Black Economic Mobility, August 13, 2019. https://www.mckinsey.com/industries/public-sector/our-insights /the-economic-impact-of-closing-the-racial-wealth-gap.

O'Connor, Alice. *Poverty Knowledge: Social Science, Social Policy, and the Poor in Twentieth-Century U.S. History.* Princeton: Princeton University Press, 2001.

Onuf, Peter S., and Annette Gordon-Reed. *"Most Blessed of Patriarchs": Thomas Jefferson and the Empire of the Imagination.* New York: Liveright, 2017.

Painter, Nell Irvin. *The History of White People.* New York: Norton, 2010.

Patterson, James T. *Freedom Is Not Enough: The Moynihan Report and America's Struggle over Black Family Life from LBJ to Obama.* New York: Basic, 2010.

Pear, Robert. "Reagan Ousts Three from Civil Rights Panel." *New York Times*, October 26, 1983.

Perlstein, Rick. *Before the Storm: Barry Goldwater and the Unmaking of the American Consensus*. New York: Nation, 2009.

———. "Infamous 1981 Interview on the Southern Strategy." *Nation*, November 13, 2012.

———. *The Invisible Bridge: The Fall of Nixon and the Rise of Reagan*. New York: Simon & Schuster 2015.

———. *Nixonland: The Rise of a President and the Fracturing of America*. New York: Scribner, 2009.

———. *Reaganland: America's Right Turn, 1976–1980*. New York: Simon & Schuster, 2020.

Perry, Andre M., Marshall Steinbaum, and Carl Romer. "Student loans, the racial wealth divide, and why we need full student debt cancellation." Brookings Institution, June 23, 2021. https://www.brookings.edu/articles/student-loans-the-racial-wealth-divide -and-why-we-need-full-student-debt-cancellation/.

Pestritto, Ronald J., and William J. Atto. *American Progressivism: A Reader*. Lanham, MD: Lexington, 2008.

Peter G. Peterson Foundation. "What Are the Economic Costs of Child Poverty?" October 24, 2023. https://www.pgpf.org/blog/2023/10/what-are-the-economic -costs-of-child poverty.

Petrella, Christopher, and Ameer Hasan Loggins. "'This is a Country for White Men': White Supremacy and U.S. Politics." *Black Perspectives*, January 5, 2017. https://www.aaihs .org/this-is-a-country-for-white-men-white-supremacy-and-u-s-politics/.

Phillips, Wendell. "Review of the President's Proclamation: Mr. Lincoln Considered No Leader." *New York Times*, December 23, 1863.

Phillips-Fein, Kim. *Invisible Hands: The Businessmen's Crusade Against the New Deal*. New York: Norton, 2009.

Platt, Tony. "E. Franklin Frazier and Daniel Patrick Moynihan: Setting the Record Straight." *Contemporary Crises* 11 (September 1987): 265–77.

Polgar, Paul J. "A Clash of Principles: The First Federal Debate over Slavery and Race, 1790." *Federal History Journal* 14 (2022): 15–37.

Posner, Richard. "The Court of Celebrity." *New Republic*, May 5, 2011.

Post, Robert, and Reva Seigel. "Originalism as a Political Practice: The Right's Living Constitution." *Fordham Law Review* 75 (2006): 545–74.

Pryor, Elizabeth Brown. *Reading the Man: A Portrait of Robert E. Lee Through His Private Letters*. New York: Penguin, 2007.

"Race-Based Legislation in the North." PBS. https://www.pbs.org/wgbh/aia/part4/4p2957 .html.

Rampell, Catherine. "How Much Did Congress Lose by Defunding the IRS? Way More Than We Thought." *Washington Post*, June 14, 2023.

Ramsey, Donovan. *When Crack Was King: A People's History of a Misunderstood Era*. New York: One World, 2023.

Ransby, Barbara. *Ella Baker and the Black Freedom Movement: A Radical Democratic Vision*. Chapel Hill: University of North Carolina Press, 2003.

Rappeport, Alan. "I.R.S. Changes Audit Practice That Discriminated Against Black Taxpayers." *New York Times*, September 18, 2023.

———. "I.R.S. Unveils $80 Billion Plan to Overhaul Tax Collection." *New York Times*, April 6, 2023.

———. "The U.S. Is Losing $1 Trillion Annually to Tax Cheats." *New York Times*, April 13, 2021. Updated October 13, 2021.

Reagan, Ronald. "Address Accepting the Presidential Nomination at the Republican National Convention in Detroit." Speech. Republican National Convention, Detroit, July 17, 1980. https://www.presidency.ucsb.edu/documents/address-accepting-the -presidential-nomination-the-republican-national-convention-detroit.

———. *An American Life.* New York: Simon & Schuster, 1990.

———. "*Face the Nation* with Governor Ronald Reagan." CBS News, aired June 16, 1968. https://www.c-span.org/video/?443905-1/face-nation-governor-ronald-reagan.

———. "Farewell Address to the Nation." Speech. Washington, DC, January 11, 1989. https:// www.reaganlibrary.gov/archives/speech/farewell-address-nation.

———. "First Inaugural Address." Speech. Washington, DC, January 20, 1981.

———. *In His Own Hand: The Writings of Ronald Reagan That Reveal His Revolutionary Vision for America.* Edited by George P. Shultz. New York: Free Press, 2001.

———. "The Myth of the Great Society." Speech. Probably New York, 1966. http://www .poorrichardsprintshop.com/wiki/MythOfTheGreatSociety.ashx.

———. "Program for Economic Recovery." Speech. Joint Session of Congress, April 28, 1981. https://www.reaganlibrary.gov/archives/speech/address-joint-session-congress -program-economic-recovery-april-1981.

———. "Radio Address to the Nation on Martin Luther King Jr. and Black Americans." January 18, 1986. https://www.reaganlibrary.gov/archives/speech/radio-address -nation-martin-luther-king-jr-and-black-americans.

———. *Reagan: A Life in Letters.* New York: Free Press, 2003.

———. "Remarks Announcing Federal Initiatives Against Drug Trafficking and Organized Crime." October 14, 1982. https://www.reaganlibrary.gov/archives/speech/remarks -announcing-federal-initiatives-against-drug-trafficking-and-organized-crime.

———. "Remarks at the Annual Meeting of the National Alliance of Business." October 5, 1981. https://www.reaganlibrary.gov/archives/speech/remarks-annual-meeting -national-alliance-business.

———. "Remarks on Signing the Anti-Drug Abuse Act of 1986." October 27, 1986. https://www.reaganlibrary.gov/archives/speech/remarks-signing-anti-drug -abuse-act-1986.

———. "Remarks on Signing the Economic Recovery Tax Act of 1981 and the Omnibus Budget Reconciliation Act of 1981." August 13, 1981. https://www.reaganlibrary.gov /archives/speech/remarks-signing-economic-recovery-tax-act-1981-and-omnibus -budget-reconciliation.

———. Speech at the Neshoba County Fair, Philadelphia, MS, August 3, 1980, https://neshoba democrat.com/stories/ronald-reagans-1980-neshoba-county-fair-speech,49123.

———. "A Time for Choosing." October 27, 1964. https://www.reaganlibrary.gov/reagans /ronald-reagan/time-choosing-speech-october-27-1964.

———. *Where's the Rest of Me?* New York: Karz, 1981.

"Reagan Opposes National Holiday for Martin Luther King Birthday." *Boston Globe*, January 23, 1983.

"Reagan Quotes King Speech in Opposing Minority Quotas." Associated Press, January 19, 1986.

"Reagan Walks Out." Associated Press, March 7, 1966.

Reid, T. R. "Most States Allow Furloughs from Prison." *New York Times*, June 24, 1988.

Reston, James. "Reagan's Dramatic Success." *New York Times*, January 21, 1981.

Reyburn, Scott. "A 'Great Wealth Transfer' Is Coming. What Will It Mean for Art?" *New York Times*, December 18, 2019.

Roberts, Dorothy. *Fatal Invention: How Science, Politics, and Big Business Recreate Race in the Twenty-First Century*. New York: New Press, 2011.

———. *Shattered Bonds: The Color of Child Welfare*. New York: Basic, 2002.

Robinson, Jackie. "Murder, Hate, Violence Will Be Weapons of GOP." *Indianapolis Recorder*, July 25, 1964.

Robison, James. "National Affairs Briefing." August 13, 1980. https://www.youtube.com /watch?v=lH1eoxxRRbk.

Robinson, Randall. *The Reckoning: What Blacks Owe to Each Other*. New York: Plume, 2003.

Roper Center of Public Opinion. "Assassination Nation: Public Responses to King and Kennedy in 1968." Roper Center, June 5, 2019. https://ropercenter.cornell.edu/blog /assassination-nation-public-responses-king-and-kennedy-1968.

Rossinow, Doug. *The Reagan Era: A History of the 1980s*. New York: Columbia University Press, 2015.

Rothman, Joshua. "When Bigotry Paraded Through the Streets." *Atlantic*, December 4, 2016.

Ruttenberg, Danya. *On Repentance and Repair: Making Amends in an Unapologetic World*. Boston: Beacon, 2022.

Samuels, Robert, and Toluse Olorunnipa. *His Name Is George Floyd: One Man's Life and the Struggle for Racial Justice*. New York: Viking, 2022.

Sandburg, Carl. "Text of Carl Sandburg's Address on Lincoln Before a Joint Session of Congress." *New York Times*, February 13, 1959.

Scalia, Antonin. "The Disease as Cure: 'In Order to Get beyond Racism, We Must First Take Account of Race.'" *Washington University Law Quarterly* 147 (1979): 147–57.

Scheer, Robert. "Reagan's Views on Issues at Home, Abroad." *Los Angeles Times*, March 6, 1980.

Senfft, Alexandra. *The Long Shadow of the Perpetrator*. Unpublished manuscript.

Sered, Danielle. *Until We Reckon: Violence, Mass Incarceration, and a Road to Repair*. New York: Free Press, 2019.

Sharkey, Patrick, Keeanga-Yamahtta Taylor, and Yaryna Serkez. "The Gaps Between White and Black America in Charts." *New York Times*, June 19, 2020.

Sharpe, Jared. "UMass Amherst/WCVB Poll Finds Nearly Half of Americans Say the Federal Government Definitely Should Not Pay Reparations to the Descendants of Slaves." University of Massachusetts Amherst, April 29, 2021. https://www.umass .edu/news/article/umass-amherstwcvb-poll-finds-nearly-half.

Shenon, Phillip. "Meese Sees Racism in Hiring Goals." *New York Times*, September 18, 1985.

Silverstein, Jake. "We Respond to the Historians Who Critiqued The 1619 Project." *New York Times*, December 20, 2019.

Sinha, Manisha. *The Slave's Cause: A History of Abolition*. New Haven: Yale University Press, 2016.

Slide, Anthony. *American Racist: The Life and Films of Thomas Dixon.* Lexington: University Press of Kentucky, 2004.

Smethurst, Frank. "Americans in Black, White and Red." *Raleigh News and Observer,* August 6, 1939.

Smith, Adam. *The Wealth of Nations.* New York: Modern Library, 2000.

Smith, Clint. *How the Word Is Passed: A Reckoning with the History of Slavery Across America.* New York: Little, Brown, 2021.

Smithers, Gregory D. *Slave Breeding: Sex, Violence, and Memory in African American History.* Gainesville: University Press of Florida, 2012.

Sokol, Jason. *The Heavens Might Crack: The Death and Legacy of Martin Luther King Jr.* New York: Basic, 2018.

Spencer, Herbert. *First Principles: Sixth and Final Edition.* Honolulu: University of the Pacific, 2000.

———. *The Principles of Biology.* Vol. 1. London and Edinburgh: Williams and Norgate, 1864.

Spencer, Rich. "Schweiker Resigning as HHS Secretary, Officials Say." *Washington Post,* January 12, 1983.

Spiro, Jonathan. *Defending the Master Race: Conservation, Eugenics, and the Legacy of Madison Grant.* Burlington: University of Vermont Press, 2009.

"Stanley Levison, 67, Adviser to Dr. King." *New York Times,* September 14, 1979.

Stone, Chuck. "Carter's Paternalistic Racism and the Inept Presidency." *Black Scholar,* March 1978.

Sundstrom, William A. "Black Unemployment in the Great Depression." *Journal of Economic History* 52 (1992): 415–29.

Sussman, Barry. "Shooting Gives Reagan Boost in Popularity." *Washington Post,* April 2, 1981.

Taper, Jake. "William Bennett Defends Comment on Abortion and Crime." ABC News, November 1, 2007.

"The Tax Gap." IRS. https://www.irs.gov/newsroom/the-tax-gap.

Thurman, Howard. *The Mood of Christmas and Other Celebrations.* Richmond, IN: Friends United, 2001.

TIRZ 18. *The Fifth Ward Housing Study: Our Space Is a Great Place.* Houston, 2012.

Tolchin, Martin. "The Troubles of Tip O'Neill." *New York Times,* August 16, 1981.

Truth and Reconciliation Commission. *Truth and Reconciliation Commission of South Africa Report.* Vol. 1. October 28, 1998. https://www.justice.gov.za/trc/report/final report/volume%201.pdf.

Tucker, Neely. "Mississippi Turning." *Washington Post,* June 16, 2005.

Tutu, Desmond. "The current crisis in South Africa." Hearing before the Subcommittee on Africa of the Committee on Foreign Affairs, US House of Representatives, Ninety-Eighth Congress, second session, December 4, 1984.

"20th Anniversary March on Washington." Video. C-SPAN, August 27, 1983. https://www.c-span.org/video/?88744-1/20th-anniversary-march-washington.

Tyson, Timothy B. *The Blood of Emmett Till.* New York: Simon & Schuster, 2017.

Underwood, Ebony, and Miriam Aroni Krinsky. "Millions of Children Lose Their Parents to Incarceration. That Doesn't Have to Happen." *The Appeal,* October 24, 2019. https://theappeal.org/millions-of-children-lose-their-parents-to-incarceration -that-doesnt-have-to-happen/.

US Department of Justice, Office of Justice Programs, Bureau of Justice Statistics. "State Corrections Expenditures, FY 1982–2010." December 2012, revised April 30, 2014. https://bjs.ojp.gov/content/pub/pdf/scefy8210.pdf.

Vander Ark, Tom. "What's the Right High School Size and Structure?" *Forbes*, June 4, 2021.

Vaughn, Stephen. "Ronald Reagan and the Struggle for Black Dignity in Cinema, 1937–1953." *Journal of Negro History* 77, no. 1 (Winter 1992): 1–16.

Ventry, Dennis J., Jr. "Tax Shelter Opinions Threatened the Tax System in the 1970s." *Tax Notes*, May 22, 2006.

Voltaire. *Candide*. New York: Boni and Liveright, 1918. https://www.gutenberg.org/files /19942/19942-h/19942-h.htm.

Walker, David. *David Walker's Appeal, in Four Articles*. Mansfield Centre, CT: Martino, 2015.

Walker, Francis A. *Discussions in Economics and Statistics: The Colored Race in the United States*. New York: Henry Holt, 1999.

Walters, Wendy S. "Lonely in America." In *The Fire This Time: A New Generation Speaks about Race*, edited by Jesmyn Ward, 33–58. New York: Scribner, 2017.

Wang, Yanan. "Where Justice Scalia Got the Idea That African Americans Might Be Better Off at 'Slower-Track' Universities." *Washington Post*, December 10, 2015.

Watkins, Katie. "Life Expectancy in Houston Can Vary Up to 20 Years Depending on Where You Live." Houston Public Media, March 4, 2019.

Weikart, Richard. "The Role of Darwinism in Nazi Racial Thought." *German Studies Review* 36, no. 3 (October 2013): 537–56.

Weizsäcker, President Richard von. Speech. Ceremony Commemorating the Fortieth Anniversary of the End of War in Europe and of National-Socialist Tyranny, Bundestag, Bonn, May 8, 1985. https://www.bundespraesident.de/SharedDocs /Downloads/DE/Reden/2015/02/150202-RvW-Rede-8-Mai-1985-englisch.pdf ?__blob=publicationFile.

Wells, Ida B. "Lynch Law in All Its Phases." In *The Light of Truth: Writings of an Anti-Lynching Crusader*, edited by Mia Bay, 96–114. New York: Penguin, 2014.

———. "Lynch Law in America." *Arena*, January 1900.

———. "The Negro's Case in Equity." *Independent*, April 5, 1900.

———. "A Red Record." In *The Light of Truth: Writings of an Anti-Lynching Crusader*, edited by Mia Bay, 218–312. New York: Penguin, 2014.

———. "Southern Horrors: Lynch Law in All Its Phases." In *The Light of Truth: Writings of an Anti-Lynching Crusader*, edited by Mia Bay, 57–82. New York: Penguin, 2014.

West, Cornel. "Black Love: A Love Like No Other." Lecture. MasterClass, November 28, 2021. https://www.masterclass.com/classes/black-history-black-freedom-and -black-love/chapters/black-love-a-love-like-no-other#class-info.

West, Richard. "Only the Strong Survive." *Texas Monthly*, February 1979.

"White and Black Americans Far Apart on Racial Issues." Ipsos, August 27, 2020. https:// www.ipsos.com/en-us/news-polls/npr-racial-inequality-issues.

Whitman, James Q. *Hitler's American Model: The United States and the Making of Nazi Race Law*. Princeton: Princeton University Press, 2017.

Wilcox, W. Bradford. "The Evolution of Divorce." *National Affairs*, Fall 2009. https://www .nationalaffairs.com/publications/detail/the-evolution-of-divorce.

Wilkerson, Isabel. *Caste: The Origins of Our Discontents*. New York: Random House, 2020.

———. "The Great Migration." In *Four Hundred Souls: A Community History of African America, 1619–2019*, edited by Ibram X. Kendi and Keisha N. Blain, 278–82. New York: One World, 2021.

Wilkins, Roger. "A Dream Still Denied." *Los Angeles Times*, January 19, 1986.

Williamson, Joel. *The Crucible of Race: Black-White Relations in the American South since Emancipation.* New York: Oxford University Press, 1985.

Wilson, Douglas L., and Rodney O. Davis, eds. *Herndon's Informants: Letters, Interviews, and Statements about Abraham Lincoln.* Champaign: University of Illinois Press, 1997.

Wold, Charlotte. "The Number of Millionaires Continues to Increase." Investopedia, November 21, 2021. https://www.investopedia.com/news/number-millionaires-continues-increase/.

Wright, Richard. *Black Boy.* New York: Harper Perennial, 1993.

Yamamoto, Eric, Margaret Chon, Carol Izumi, Jerry Kang, and Frank Wu. *Race, Rights, and Reparation: Law and the Japanese American Internment.* 2nd ed. Boston: Aspen, 2013.

Young, Andrew. "Chilling Words in Neshoba County." *Washington Post*, August 11, 1980.

Young, Gerald. "The Dream Re-imagined: Historically Black Colleges and Universities Releasing Purpose to Prisoners (A Case Study on the Second Chance Pell Grant Program at Wiley College, Marshall Texas)." PhD diss., Union University and Institute, 2022.

Index

Abdurraqib, Hanif, 247

abolitionism, 27, 45–46, 47–48, 51, 54, 58–59, 82–83, 234–35, 256–58; American Anti-Slavery Society, 45, 299n26; Christian, 82–83, 88; and the Constitution, 43, 272–73; and Jefferson's *Notes*, 24, 33, 34, 36–37, 295n11; Lincoln and, 39, 42–44, 46, 47–48, 51–52, 54, 58–59, 299n20; Lovejoy's murder in Illinois, 44, 299n20; Pennsylvania's Gradual Abolition Act of 1780, 41; and Reconstruction, 55; and Stowe's *Uncle Tom's Cabin*, 80

Abrams, Stacey, xiv–xv, 249

Adams, Henry Baxter, 78, 303–4n2

Adams, John, 32

affirmative action, 193–94, 195, 199, 203

Alexander, Michelle, 137, 211, 275

All about Love (hooks), 259

American Anti-Slavery Society, 45, 299n26

American Economic Association, 114, 135

American Eugenics Society, 135

America's Unholy Ghosts: The Racist Roots of Our Faith and Politics (Goza), 8

Anderson, Carol, 247

Anderson, Tanisha, 253

And There Was Light (Meacham), 57

Anglo-Saxonism, 102, 103–5, 308n7; Dixon and, 85, 94; Founding Fathers and, 103–5; Grant and, 102, 106, 109, 112

Anti-Drug Abuse Act (1986), 208, 209

Anti-Drug Abuse Act (1988), 210

anti-immigrant racism, 105–6, 108, 110–15, 120–21, 122–23, 308n7; Grant

and, 106, 110–15, 122–23, 126, 311n74; racial sciences and "criminality," 105–6; racial sciences and IQ tests, 120–21

antilynching legislation, 88, 97

antimiscegenation laws, 88, 98, 126, 127–28, 130

Apologizing for Slavery and the Segregation of African Americans (2009 congressional resolution), 252

Arbery, Ahmaud, 234

Aristotle, 21, 22

Associated Press, 204, 212–13

Atlantic, 9, 221

Atwater, Lee, 182, 216

Baker, Ella, 130, 136, 229, 240, 258, 271–72, 273, 274, 289

Baldwin, James, xii, 1, 139, 231, 241, 246, 267–68, 269; on hope, 11; on King's assassination, 139; open letter to President Carter, 186; warning to the nation about a Reagan presidency, 190–91

Banneker, Benjamin, 29–30, 37, 97, 274, 289

Barbé-Marbois, François, 23

Barber, William, III, xiv–xv, 249

Bardwell, Keith, 253

Barger, Brian, 212

Beecher, Henry, 257

Beecher, Lyman, 257

Bell, T. H., 192

Bell Curve, The (Herrnstein and Murray), 221–23

Benezet, Anthony, 37

Bennett, William, 192–93

Berry, Mary Frances, 193, 201

Bethune, Mary McLeod, 275

Bias, Len, 208, 209

Bibb, Henry, 27

Biden, Joe, 224, 278

Bill of Rights, 34, 41, 272–74, 288; economic and social, 272–74, 288

Binet, Alfred, 120–21, 310n62

Birth of a Nation, The (film), 95–96, 97, 101, 154, 156

Black Boy (Wright), 98–99

Black churches, 190, 248–49, 251; Houston's Fifth Ward, 6; and King's work and worldview, 176; Reconstruction era, 69; and white Christians' participation in Black sacred spaces, 248–49

Black Codes, 71, 74

Black education, 275–79; *Brown v. Board of Education*, 127, 170; HBCUs, 249–50, 278, 317n3; the intersection of educational disinvestment and mass incarceration, 224–25, 277–79; and public education funding, 127, 192–93, 197, 219, 275–79; Reagan's budget cuts, 192–93, 197, 219; Reconstruction era, 69; and school integration, 5; schools of Houston's Fifth Ward, 5, 6; Second Chance Pell Grant program, 224–25, 278. *See also* schools

"Black extinction hypothesis," 116–17, 118, 122, 310n50

Black Freedom Movement, xiv–xv, 11, 176, 241, 256–59, 272–73, 275, 290. *See also* Civil Rights Movement

Black Haitian Revolution (1791–1804), 41

Black History Month, 252

Black Laws in Northern states, 41, 71, 298n6

Black Lives Matter movement, 228, 229, 234, 249, 282

Blackmon, Douglas, 94, 312n6

Black nonprofits, 249

Black Panther (film), 246

Black Panther Party, 181, 254

Black Power activists, 175

Black Reconstruction in America (Du Bois), 40

"Black Renaissance," 246–47

Black Scholar, 186

Black spaces, 242, 247–51

Black unemployment rates: early twentieth century, 126, 311n75; the 1970s, 182; Reagan era, 193

Black Union soldiers, 52–53, 92–93, 257

Black urban uprisings of the 1960s, 141, 145–48, 179; and the Kerner Report, 146–48, 254; Reagan and, 179

Blain, Keisha N., 247

Bland, Sandra, 228, 246, 253

Blight, David, 85, 300n52, 326n1

Bliss, George, 183

"Bloody Thursday" (1969 People's Park protest at Berkeley), 181–82

Bond, Horace Mann, 122

Bonner, Christopher, 56

Booth, John Wilkes, 58, 63, 136

Boulware, Lemuel, 162–64, 166, 167

Bradford, William, 193

Bradley, Joseph P., 75, 303n17

Brandt, Karl, 124

Brigham, Carl C., 121, 122

Broder, David, 168

Brokaw, Tom, 209

Brown, Dorothy, 265

Brown, John, 45, 53, 59, 62, 257, 259

Brown, Michael, 228, 229, 246, 253

Brown, Pat, 171, 175

Brown v. Board of Education (1954), 127, 170

Bryan, William Jennings, 168

Buck, Carrie, 127

Buck v. Bell (1927), 127

Buffett, Warren, 264

Burger, Earl, 194–95

Bush, George H. W., 192, 213, 216–17, 260

"calendar of remembrance," national, 252–53

California Republicans, 171–75

Candide (Voltaire), 294n8

Cannon, Lou, 318n13

capital punishment, 210

Carmichael, Stokely, xiv–xv, 136, 139, 175, 204, 258, 273

Carnegie, Andrew, 77

Caro, Robert, 140

Carroll, Charles R., 87

Carter, Jimmy, 175, 186–87, 189–91, 317n3

"Carter's Paternalistic Racism and the Inept Presidency" (Stone), 186

"Case for Reparations, The" (Coates), 9–10

Caste (Wilkerson), 76

CBS Evening News, 184

Celler, Emmanuel, 311n74

Central Intelligence Agency (CIA), 211–14, 254; complicity with drug traffickers and cartels, 211–14, 254; McCoy's *The Politics of Heroin in Southeast Asia*, 211, 213, 323n94; and Reagan's War on Drugs, 211–14

Chandler, Elizabeth Margaret, 82

Chaney, James, 130, 188–89, 258

Charleston church shooting (2015), 253

Charleston Nine, 228, 246

charter schools, 276–77

Chasnoff, Ira, 208–9, 210

Chicago Defender, 101

Chicago Tribune, 183

child poverty rates, 197, 199–201, 218, 219, 225, 282–83

Chisholm, Shirley, 221, 226, 229

Cincinnati Enquirer, 69, 147

Civil Liberties Act (1988), 216

Civil Rights Act (1875), 303n17

Civil Rights Act (1964), 139, 140, 141, 171, 172

Civil Rights Cases (1883), 74–75, 303n17

Civil Rights Movement, 129, 136, 176, 192, 198, 224, 258; and Emmett Till's 1955 lynching, 1–3; Muste and Gandhian nonviolent direct action, 258, 259; Poor People's Campaign, 177, 179; Reagan and, 153–54, 175–78, 179, 201–5. *See also* Black Freedom Movement; King, Martin Luther, Jr.

Civil Rights Restoration Act, 216

Civil War: America and slavery on the eve of, 40–42; Black Union soldiers, 52–53, 92, 257; Confederate defeat and the end of, 58, 63, 67–69, 302n13; Lincoln and, 47–58, 257, 300n52; postwar national misinformation campaign about, 72–73. *See also* Reconstruction

Clansman, The (Dixon), 78, 81, 88–95

Clinton, Bill, 221–22, 224–25, 278

Coates, Ta-Nehisi, 9–10, 91, 235, 241–42

Cobb, Jelani, 247

cocaine, 96–97, 208–9, 212–14. *See also* crack epidemic

Cofield, D. Z., 8

Colbert, Burwell, 36

Coles, Edward, 32, 37

Colfax Massacre (1873), 303n17, 306n44

colonial Virginia, 23–24, 295n11. *See also* *Notes on the State of Virginia* (Jefferson)

Colorblind Age, 129, 139–57, 153–85, 186–220, 221–30, 233; Clinton and, 221–22, 224–25, 278; Herrnstein and Murray's *The Bell Curve*, 221–23; and Johnson's War on Poverty, 140–49, 183–84, 313n17; Kerner Commission and Kerner Report, 142, 146–49, 184, 229, 254, 271, 286; the lasting legacy of, 221–30; and mass incarceration, 224–25; Moynihan's 1965 report on *The Negro Family*, 142–46, 149–50, 183–84, 223–24, 229, 312n9; myth of Black pathology, 143–46, 149–50, 185, 223–24; Nixon and, 149–51; Obama and, 228; Reagan and, 151–52, 153–55, 172–73, 219–20, 221, 223–26; social transformation and unrest of the 1960s, 139–42; Trump and, 228–29

Columbia University, 102, 306n56

Combs, Grandma (Patty), 7, 241, 244

Commission to Study and Develop Reparation Proposals for African Americans Act (1989), 227–28, 325n19

Common Justice, 279

communism: Billy Graham on, 190; Black Americans and, 159–60, 314n11, 314n12; Dixon's fear of, 99; first Red Scare and anticommunist propaganda, 99, 128, 159; Grant's fear of, 99, 128; Reagan and the communist threat, 158–61, 165, 166–67, 170, 181, 212, 215; second Red Scare, 128, 151, 155, 158–61, 165, 166–67, 181, 223, 254

Communist Party, 159, 160, 314n11

Comprehensive Anti-Apartheid Act, 194

Comprehensive Crime Control Act (1984), 207–8

Compromise of 1877, 307n1

Condemnation of Blackness, The (Muhammad), 105

Congressional Black Caucus, 204, 228

Connor, Bull, 153, 154

Conquest of a Continent, The (Grant), 111

Constitutional Convention, 23, 32–33, 104

Convention of National Negro Republicans, 172

convict leasing schemes, 71, 74, 75, 87, 134, 243, 312n6

Conyers, John, 202, 227–28

Coolidge, Calvin, 77

corporate capitalism, 164–65, 176

corporate equity scorecards, 285

corporate tax rates, 197–98, 263

Cowen, Richard, 198

Crack (documentary film), 246

crack epidemic: "crack babies" propaganda, 209, 210, 214; and Houston's Fifth Ward, 5; Reagan's War on Drugs, 5, 208–10, 211

craniology, 109, 120, 308–9n21

Crime Bill (1994), 224–25

criminal justice system: failures for Black victims and survivors of violence, 6, 279–80, 330n19; intersection of Black educational disinvestment and, 224–25, 277–79; legacy of Reagan's War on Drugs, 210–11, 215; plea deals, 280–81. *See also* mass incarceration

Crisis (NAACP magazine), 112

critical race theory, 244–45, 246, 253

"culture of poverty" thesis, 143, 183–84

Darity, William A., Jr., 261–62

Darkwater (Du Bois), 112

Darwin, Charles, 107–8, 116

Davis, Angela, 181, 226

Davis, Angelique M., 252

Davis, Loyal, 162

Dean, John, 322n81

"death tax," 264–65

Deaver, Michael, 185

Declaration of Independence, 18, 21, 37, 221, 273–74; Grant on the flaw of, 112–13; Jefferson and the racial ideologies of, 21, 23, 31–32, 221, 297n45; proclamation of equality ("all men are created equal"), 19, 21, 23, 53, 61, 274

Defending the Master Race (Spiro), 118

DeFronzo, James, 207

Democracy in America (Tocqueville), 90

Democratic Party, 156–57, 171, 224

Descent of Man, The (Darwin), 116

Desmond, Matthew, 282–83

Detroit, Michigan, 227–28, 291

divorce, no-fault, 189, 318n14

Dixon, Amzi Clarence, 303n1, 304n10

Dixon, Benjamin Franklin, 303n1

Dixon, Thomas, Jr., 75–77, 78–100, 131–33, 154; Anglo-Saxonism, 85, 94; background and family, 75–77, 78–80, 303n1, 304n10; *The Clansman*, 78, 81, 88–95; fear of socialism, 80, 88, 99, 131; and Griffith's *The Birth of a Nation*, 95–96; and Jefferson, 79–80; and the Ku Klux Klan, 80, 85, 87, 94, 149; *The Leopard's Spots*, 78, 80, 81, 82–88, 95; and Lincoln, 80, 88; and lynching, 81, 85–87, 88, 97–99; Miller's open letter to, 78, 97, 305n34; on miscegenation, 79–80, 84–85; propagandistic novels about the white South following Reconstruction, 78, 79–100, 132; racial myths, 83, 87–88, 90–92, 93, 96–97; and Social Gospel movement, 76, 79, 132, 304n10; and Stowe's *Uncle Tom's Cabin*, 80, 304n4

Double V campaign, 135–36

Douglas, Stephen, 44

Douglass, Frederick, xiv–xv, 44, 45–46, 75, 91, 238; on Black Union soldiers, 52; on the Constitution and preamble, 43, 272; on the Fugitive Slave Act, 35–36, 42; on John Brown, 257; on Lincoln, 13, 46–47,

48, 49–50, 52–53, 59; on Reconstruction, 55, 75, 91; and Stowe's *Uncle Tom's Cabin*, 80; on white Christianity, 83
Dred Scott v. Sandford (1857), 35, 37, 194
drug cartels, 212–14
Drugs, Law Enforcement and Foreign Policy (1988 Kerry Report), 213–14, 254
Du Bois, W. E. B., xv, 40, 91, 99, 119, 238, 275; on "Americanization" and Grant's race hatred, 112; on *The Birth of a Nation*, 96; on Black hope, 11; comparisons of America and Nazi Germany, 124, 125; on John Brown, 257; on Lincoln, 39, 59; on Reconstruction, 75, 84; on white Christianity, 83; on white supremacy and democracy, 135
DuBose, Samuel, 253
Duke, Jesse, 83, 304n15
Dwight, Timothy, IV, 37
Dyer Anti-Lynching Bill (1918), 97

Economics in One Lesson (Hazlitt), 164
Edelman, Marian Wright, 199–201, 205
Ehrlichman, John, 205
Eisenhower, Dwight D., 178
Ellis, Joseph, 36
Emancipation Proclamation, 18, 41, 49–51, 54–55, 89–90
Emerson, Michael, 318–19n16
Emerson, Ralph Waldo, 116
Emmett Till Antilynching Act (2022), 97
Engs, Robert F., 51
Enlightenment, 20–23, 30, 36, 294n8, 294–95n9
Enslaved People of Mount Vernon Tour, 254
Equal Justice Initiative: *History of Racial Injustice Calendar*, 252–53; on lynching, 98; National Memorial for Peace and Justice, 253–54
Equal Opportunity Employment Commission, 193
Escobar, Pablo, 213
Essay on Human Understanding (Locke), 22
estate tax exemption, 198, 262–63, 321n60
eugenics movement, 102–3, 107–8, 114–19, 120–23, 125–29, 133, 143; Galton,

107–8, 221, 308n19; Grant and *The Passing of the Great Race*, 102–3, 107–8, 114–19, 125–29; and IQ tests, 120–23, 127, 221–22, 310n62; negative/positive eugenics, 115–16, 308n20; and social Darwinism, 108, 117, 133, 308n20; sterilizations, 127. *See also* racial sciences (scientific racism)
Eureka College (California), 156, 163
Evers, Medgar, 136, 139

Face the Nation (TV show), 179
Fairbank, Calvin, 59
Fair Housing Act (1968), 148
Falwell, Jerry, 190
Families in Peril (Edelman), 199–201
Farmer, Ashley, 291
Farmer, James, 258
Fatal Invention (Roberts), 296n29
Federal-Aid Highway Act (1956), 4
Federal Bureau of Investigation (FBI), 177, 207, 210, 254
Fellowship of Reconciliation, 258
Field, Stephen, 303n17
Fifteenth Amendment, 58, 69, 272–73
Fifth Ward Community Redevelopment Corporation (Houston), 270
54th Massachusetts Infantry Regiment, 52
Fire Next Time, The (Baldwin), 267–68
First Principles (Spencer), 116
Fischer, Eugen, 309n28
Flaming Sword, The (Dixon), 99
Fletcher, Arthur, 204
Floyd, George, 8, 229, 234, 246, 253, 271
Flynn, John T., 164, 165
Foner, Eric, 326n1
food stamps, 183, 185, 197, 198, 200
Force and Freedom (Jackson), 41
Ford, Gerald, 184
Forman, James, Jr., 215
Fortune magazine, 123
Founding Fathers (the Revolutionary generation), 23, 31–33, 36–38, 154; Anglo-Saxonism and racial hierarchies, 103–5; and the Constitution, 272; Reagan's comparison of Nicaraguan Contras to,

212; and the slavery debate, 31–33, 43, 60–61, 296–97n38, 297n39, 299n17. *See also* Jefferson, Thomas

Fourteenth Amendment, 58, 69, 272–73, 303n17

Franklin, Benjamin, 272

Franklin, John Hope, 19, 38

Frazier, Edward Franklin, 109–10, 312n9

Frazier, Garrison, 69

Freedman's Bank, 253

Freedmen's Bureau, 70–71, 90, 302n5, 302n6

Frémont, John C., 47

From Here to Equality (Darity and Mullen), 261–62

Fugitive Slave Act (1850), 35–36, 42, 44, 80

Fundamentals, The (1910–1915 essay collection), 303n1, 304n10

Galton, Francis, 107–8, 221, 308n19

Garnet, Henry Highland, 46

Garrison, William Lloyd, 43, 45–46, 58–59, 82, 257

General Electric (GE), 162–67, 197–98; *General Electric Theater* (TV show), 163; propaganda machine, 163, 314–15n22; Reagan as GE spokesman, 151, 162–67, 199

Germany: Dixon's education in German research methods, 78–79, 303–4n2; financial reparations to Holocaust victims, 255, 256; Grant and, 102, 107; Nuremberg trials, 62, 255; process of repentance following World War II, 62, 255–56; racial sciences, 102, 103, 107, 307n5; reunification treaty, 256. *See also* Nazi Germany

Gingrich, Newt, 202

Goddard, Henry Herbert, 120–21

Goebbels, Joseph, 123

Goldin, Claudia Dale, 297n50

Goldwater, Barry, 140, 155, 157, 162, 167, 169–70, 172, 174

Goodman, Andrew, 130, 188–89, 258

Gorman, Amanda, 289

Gould, Charles W., 121

Gould, Stephen Jay, 121–22

Gradual Abolition Act of 1780 (Pennsylvania), 41

Graham, Billy, 190

Grant, Madison, 75–77, 101–29, 131–33, 154, 237; anti-immigrant racism and policies, 106, 110–15, 122–23, 126, 311n74; background and white supremacy, 102–3; Du Bois on "Americanization" project, 112; and the eugenics movement, 102–3, 107–8, 114–19, 125–29; fear of socialism, 106, 128, 131; on the flaw in the Declaration of Independence, 112–13; and German racial sciences, 102, 107; influence on Hitler and Nazi Germany, 107, 117–18, 123–24, 132–33, 309n40; and IQ tests, 121; and Jefferson, 113; *The Passing of the Great Race*, 76, 101–3, 106–9, 110–20, 124, 125, 309n40; on "race suicide," 107, 110, 308n12; and the racial sciences, 76, 102–29; on slavery, 114–15; on the US Constitution, 112–13

Grant, Ulysses S., 92

Gray, William, 204

Great Depression, 162, 177, 206

Great Migration, 101

Great Society, 140, 144, 150, 169, 176

Greece, ancient, 20–23

Greeley, Horace, 72

Green, William H., 253

Green New Deal, 282

Griffith, D. W., 95

Griffith, Mattie, 41, 298n8

Griggs, Sutton, 94, 97

Grimke, Angelina, 58, 258

Grimke, Sarah, 58, 258

Gurley, Akai, 253

Haig, Alexander, 194

Haiti, 41, 300n41

Hall, Prescott, 117

Hall, Stephen G., 252

Hamer, Fannie Lou, 136, 143, 273

Hannah-Jones, Nikole, 326n2

Hannon, Lance, 207

Harding, Vincent, xiv, 11, 40, 226

Harding, Warren G., 77, 123
Harris, Joel Chandler, 79
Hart-Celler Act (1965), 311n74
Hayek, Friedrich A., 164
Hayes, Rutherford B., 307n1
Hazlitt, Henry, 164
HBCUs (historically Black colleges and universities), 249–50, 278, 317n3
Head Start, 140, 200
Hebrew Scriptures, 243–44, 248
Hemings, Harriet, 31
Hemings, James Madison, 31
Hemings, Sally, 31, 36, 295n21, 296n25
Hemings, Thomas Eston, 31
Hemings, William Beverly, 31
Herrnstein, Richard, 221–23
Hidden History Tours of New Orleans, 254
Hill, Andre, 253
Hinckley, John, Jr., 195
Hinton, Elizabeth, 146, 293n3
historically Black colleges and universities (HBCUs), 249–50, 278, 317n3
history, teaching of, 244–46, 326n2
History of Racial Injustice Calendar (Equal Justice Initiative), 252–53
History of White People, The (Painter), 24, 60
Hitler, Adolf, 107, 117–18, 132, 160, 309n40. *See also* Nazi Germany
Hitler's American Model (Whitman), 76
Holmes, Oliver Wendell, Jr., 127, 169
homelessness, 218, 282
Homestead Acts, 71
hooks, bell, 201, 259
Hoover, Herbert, 77
Hopper, Hedda, 161
Horne, Gerald, 326n2
Horton, Willie, 216
House, Callie, xv, 135, 289
Houston, Texas: Combs family, 7, 241, 244; Fifth Ward, 4–8, 11–12, 233, 235, 241, 244, 270–71; Johnson family, 6; racial inequalities, 4–8, 264, 270–71, 328n14; racial wealth gap, 264, 328n14; Roberts family, 6–7

Howard, Oliver, 302n5
Hughes, Langston, 101, 125, 160
Humphrey, Hubert, 157
Hunter, David, 47

I Am Not Your Negro (documentary film), 246
immigrants. *See* anti-immigrant racism
Immigration and Nationality Act (1965), 140
Immigration Restriction Act (1924), 123, 311n74
Indian Removal Act (1830), 40
infant mortality, 219
Inflation Reduction Act (2022), 287–88
inheritance taxes, 262–66
intelligence tests (IQ tests), 120–23, 127, 221–23, 310n62. *See also* racial sciences (scientific racism)
Internal Revenue Service (IRS), 183, 286–88
Invention of Racism in Classical Antiquity, The (Isaac), 21
Iran-Contra Affair, 212–14, 323n95
Isaac, Benjamin, 21
It's Happening Here (radio series), 157

Jackson, Andrew, 40, 107
Jackson, James, 33
Jackson, Jesse, 226
Jackson, Kellie Carter, 41, 45, 247
January 6th Capitol insurrection (2021), 98
Japanese American internment and reparations, 216–17, 227, 238
Jean, Botham, 253
Jefferson, Martha Skelton, 19–20, 31
Jefferson, Thomas, 17, 19–38, 60–61, 78, 154, 221, 237; and abolitionism, 24, 33, 34, 36–37, 295n11; and ancient Greek mythologies, 20–23; Anglo-Saxonism, 104; and the Declaration of Independence, 21, 23, 31–32, 221, 297n45; and Dixon, 79–80; and Enlightenment racial ideologies, 20–23, 30, 36, 294n8, 294–95n9; and Grant, 113; Lincoln's faith in, 43; Monticello mansion, 17, 20–21,

32; *Notes on the State of Virginia*, 19, 23–33, 34, 83, 221, 295n13; predatory sexuality, 31, 295n21, 296n25; proposals for emancipation, 32–33, 34–35; racial myths about Black people, 24–30, 36, 60–61, 73, 79, 83; Walker on influence of, 13, 36–37

Jenkins, Barry, 246

Jennings, Peter, 209

Jewish tradition, 242, 243–44, 260

Jim Crow laws, 117, 134, 251

Johns Hopkins University, 78, 97

Johnson, Andrew, 71, 92, 140, 192

Johnson, Jamarcus, 6

Johnson, James, 6

Johnson, James Weldon, 65

Johnson, Lyndon B., 139–49, 169–71, 175; Great Society, 140, 144, 150, 169, 176; and King, 140; War on Crime, 141, 144, 146, 148, 205; War on Poverty, 140–49, 183–84, 313n17

Johnson, Mike, 235–39, 325n7

Jones, Coryl, 209

Jordan, Vernon, 188

Junior Ku Klux Klan, 96

Kansas-Nebraska Act (1854), 43

Kelley, Robin D. G., 226, 314n12

Kendi, Ibram X., 107, 219, 246

Kennedy, Edward, 319n28

Kennedy, John F., 139, 186

Kennedy, Robert, 139

Kerner, Otto, 146

Kerner Commission, 146, 271, 286

Kerner Report (1968), 142, 146–49, 184, 229, 254, 271, 286

Kerry, John, 213–14

Kerry Report (1988), 213–14, 254

King, Coretta Scott, 202

King, Martin Luther, Jr., xiv–xv, 136, 153, 175–78, 186, 188, 241, 246, 249, 258; assassination, 136, 139, 141, 148, 177–78; on conservative Black leaders, 322n79; on the Constitution and a "social and economic Bill of Rights," 273; on economic and racial inequalities, 225–26, 273; and

Johnson, 140; and the Kerner Report, 148; and MLK Day, 202–5, 252, 253; on Muste and nonviolent direct action, 258; Poor People's Campaign, 177, 179; on the racism of white moderate, 133; Reagan's opposition to vision of, 153–54, 175–78, 179, 201–5, 321n72; Reagan's propaganda campaign to rewrite legacy, 201–5, 321n72, 321–22n73; on reparations, 177; "A Testament of Hope," 177; on the "triple evils," 176–77, 178, 229

King in the Wilderness (documentary film), 246

Koch, Christopher, 96–97

Kozol, Jonathan, 193

Ku Klux Kiddies, 96

Ku Klux Klan, 71–72, 135, 180; Dixon and, 80, 85, 87, 94, 149; and Griffith's *The Birth of a Nation*, 95–96, 156; Reagan's early opposition, 156–57; Reagan's embrace of Wilkinson and revival of, 189; Wells on history of, 87, 302n13

Ku Klux Klan Act (1871), 71–72

Ku Klux Klan Report (1871), 72, 214, 254

LA 92 (documentary film), 246

"law and order": Dixon on the Ku Klux Klan and, 85, 94, 149; Johnson's administration response to Watts uprising, 146; Nixon administration, 149, 150–51, 229; Reagan and, 207. *See also* War on Crime

Law Enforcement Assistance Act (1965), 146

Lee, Robert E., 58, 68, 91, 116

Lee, Sheila Jackson, 235, 270

Leopard's Spots, The (Dixon), 78, 80, 81, 82–88, 95

Levison, Stanley, 258, 327n27

Lewis, David Levering, 96

Lewis, John, xv, 202, 205, 273

Lewis, Oscar, 143

Lincoln, Abraham, 17–18, 39–59, 61–62, 154; and abolitionism, 39, 42–44, 46, 47–48, 51–52, 54, 58–59, 299n20; anti-Black racism, 39, 42, 44–45, 58, 59, 61–62; and the Civil War, 47–58, 257, 300n52; colonization and compensation schemes, 49–50, 300n41, 300n49; confidence in the Constitution, 42–43, 46; and Dixon's Reconstruction novels, 80, 88; Douglass on, 13, 46–47, 48, 49–50, 52–53, 59; early life, 17–18, 39, 42; Emancipation Proclamation, 39–40, 49–51, 54–55, 89–90; embrace of emancipation as military necessity, 48–51; faith in Jefferson and the Founders, 43; first inaugural address, 46–47, 57; and the Fugitive Slave Act, 44, 46; Gettysburg Address, 53–54; and passage of the Thirteenth Amendment, 57–58; Proclamation of Amnesty and Reconstruction, 39–40, 54–56, 58; second inaugural address, 56–57; and Stowe's *Uncle Tom's Cabin*, 80

Lincoln, Nancy, 17–18

Lincoln, Robert, 94

Lincoln, Thomas, 18

Lincoln: Divided We Stand (television docuseries), 56

Liuzzo, Viola, 258

Locke, John, 20, 22, 25

Locking Up Our Own (Forman), 215

Lorde, Audre, 226

Los Angeles Times, 161, 214

Losing Ground (Murray), 222

Lost Cause, The: A New Southern History of the Civil War (Pollard), 72–73

Lovejoy, Elijah, 44, 58–59, 299n20

Loving v. Virginia (1883), 98

Lynch, James V., 296–97n38

lynchings, 65, 67–68, 75, 81, 85–86, 97–99, 129, 130–36, 149, 173; antilynching bills, 88, 97; and Dixon, 81, 85–87, 88, 97–99; of Emmett Till, xii, 1–3; estimated deaths, 98; inspired by *The Birth of a Nation*, 97; Louisiana, 238; Texas, 306n44; Wells on, 65, 85–86, 134

Madison, James, 34, 297n50

Malcolm X, 136, 139, 204, 241, 273

Marable, Manning, 226

March on Washington, second (August 27, 1983), 202

Markie, Biz, 221

Marshall, Thurgood, 195

Martin, Trayvon, 228, 229, 246, 253

Martin Luther King, Jr. Day, 202–5, 252, 253

mass incarceration, 224–25, 275, 278–81; and Clinton's 1994 Crime Bill, 224–25; intersection of Black educational disinvestment and, 224–25, 277–79; prison-to-school pipeline, 278; and Reagan's War on Drugs, 210–11, 215; school-to-prison pipeline, 219, 278; and Second Chance Pell Grant program, 224–25, 278. *See also* criminal justice system

McAdam, Douglas, 229

McCarthy, Joseph, 155, 158

McConnell, Mitch, 251

McCoy, Alfred William, 211, 213, 323n94

McDowell, Calvin, 86

McGhee, Heather, 15

McPherson, James M., 40, 244

Meacham, Jon, 57, 295n11

Medellín Cartel, 213

Medicaid, 140, 200

Medi-Cal (California), 180

Medicare, 140, 200

Meese, Edwin, III, 193–94, 213, 320n38

Meet the Press (TV show), 173

Mein Kampf (Hitler), 107, 117–18, 132, 309n40

Memphis race riots (1866), 306n44

#MeToo movement, 282

Miller, Kelly, 78, 97, 122, 305n34

Miller, Samuel, 74, 303n17, 305n42

Minneapolis–St. Paul, Minnesota, 271

miscegenation: antimiscegnation laws, 88, 98, 126, 127–28, 130; Dixon on, 79–80, 84–85; Grant on, 113, 117, 127–28; Jefferson on, 25; Virginia's Racial Integrity Act of 1924, 127–28

Mismeasure of Man, The (Gould), 121–22

Missouri Compromise (1820), 35–36

Mitchell, George, 225

Moore, Queen Mother Audley, xv, 136, 231, 241, 291

Moral Majority, 190

Morgan, J. P., 77
Morrison, Toni, 137, 226
Morse, Arthur, 123
Moses, Bob, 258, 273
Moss, Tom, 86
Mother Emanuel African Methodist
    Church (Charleston, South Carolina), 253
Mothers of the Movement, 234
Mott, Lucretia, 58, 82, 257
Mount, Guy Emerson, xv
Moynihan, Daniel Patrick, 142–46,
    149–50, 185, 225, 237; and Clinton's
    welfare reform bill, 225; and Nixon's
    policy of "benign neglect" toward Black
    America, 150. *See also* Moynihan Report
    (*The Negro Family*)
Moynihan Report (*The Negro Family*),
    142–46, 149–50, 183–84, 223–24,
    229, 312n9; attributing Black poverty
    to pathological psychology, 142–46,
    223–24; on the "tangle of pathology,"
    145–46, 149–50, 312n9; tracing origin
    of family dysfunction to slavery, 145; on
    welfare dependence, 144–45, 183–84
Muhammad, Khalil Gibran, 105, 247
Mulford Act (1967), 181
Mullen, A. Kirsten, 261–62
Murray, Charles, 221–23, 237
Murray, Pauli, 136
Muste, A. J., 258, 259

NAACP, 112, 135, 258
*Narrative of the Life and Adventures of
    Henry Bibb, an American Slave*, 27
Nash, Diane, 136, 258, 273
National Coalition of Blacks for Repara-
    tions in America (N'COBRA), 227, 291
national equity scorecards, 285
National Ex-Slave Mutual Relief, Bounty
    and Pension Association, 135
National Memorial for Peace and Justice,
    253–54
National Museum of African American
    History and Culture (Washington, DC),
    254
National Recovery Agency, 126

National Urban League, 250; *State of
    Black America* reports, 211, 286
Nazi Germany: comparisons of America
    to, 124–25, 160; Grant's influence, 107,
    117–18, 123–24, 132–33, 309n40; Hughes
    on, 160; Nuremberg laws, 124; postwar
    German repentance and accountabil-
    ity, 62, 255–56; racial project, 76, 107,
    117–18, 123–25, 130, 132–33, 309n28,
    309n40, 311–12n1; racial science and
    eugenics, 107, 117–18, 132–33, 309n40;
    The Triumph of the Will (1932 film),
    132; US refusal to admit Jewish child
    refugees, 123; World War II, 123–25. *See
    also* Germany
Negro a Beast, The (Carroll), 87
*Negro Family, The: The Call for National
    Action. See* Moynihan Report (*The
    Negro Family*)
Neshoba County Fair (Philadelphia, Mis-
    sissippi), 188–89
New Deal, 126, 131, 133, 159, 169, 177, 192,
    198, 289
"New Democrats," 224
New England Journal of Medicine, 209
New Jim Crow, The (Alexander), 211
New Orleans Massacre (1866), 306n44
Newsweek, 209
New York Draft Riots (1863), 41, 253,
    298n8
New York Times, 97, 191, 214, 222, 229,
    235, 287
New York Tribune, 50
New York Urban League, 188
Nicaraguan Contras, 212–14
Nixon, Richard M., 149, 155, 180, 186;
    "benign neglect" policy toward Black
    America, 150; "law and order" policies,
    149, 150–51, 229; War on Crime, 149,
    150, 205, 211, 322n81; War on Drugs, 150,
    205, 211
Nordic race, so-called, 104, 110–15, 122,
    123, 125, 135, 154
Noriega, Manuel, 213
North, Oliver, 212, 213

"Notes on the House of Bondage" (Baldwin), 190–91
Notes on the State of Virginia (Jefferson), 19, 23–33, 34, 83, 221, 295n13
Nuremberg Laws, 124
Nuremberg trials in postwar Germany, 62, 255

Obama, Barack, 228, 278, 321n60
Obama, Michelle, 228
Occupy Wall Street, 282
O'Connor, Sandra Day, 194
Office of Redress Administration, 216
Ogletree, Charles J., Jr., 269
Omnibus Crime Control and Safe Streets Act (1968), 148
O'Neill, Tip, 196
One Woman (Dixon), 88
"Only the Strong Survive" (West), 5–6
On the Origin of Species (Darwin), 107, 108
Opelousas Massacre in Louisiana (September 28, 1868), 252–53, 306n44

Page, Thomas Nelson, 79
Paine, Thomas, 10, 296–97n38
Painter, Nell Irvin, 24, 60, 104
pain tolerance of Black people, 28, 29, 296n29
paradigm shifts, 256, 290
Parks, Rosa, 226
Parry, Robert, 212
Passing of the Great Race, The (Grant), 76, 101–3, 106–9, 110–20, 124, 125, 309n40; and eugenics, 102–3, 107–8, 114–19, 125–29; Grant's influence on Hitler and Nazi Germany, 107, 117–18, 123–24, 132–33, 309n40; and the racial sciences (scientific racism), 76, 102–3, 107, 110–20, 125
"Pathology of Race Prejudice, The" (Frazier), 109–10
Patterson, William L., 134, 136
Pelosi, Nancy, 224
Perlstein, Rick, 187, 314n21
Personal Responsibility and Work Opportunity Act (1996), 225

Philadelphia, Mississippi, 188–89
Phillips, Wendell, 55, 82, 258
Pierce, Samuel ("Silent Sam"), 192, 319n26
Piketty, Thomas, 265
Plato, 21, 22
plea deals, 280–81
Poindexter, John, 212
Politics of Heroin in Southeast Asia, The (McCoy), 211, 213, 323n94
Pollard, Edward Alfred, 72
Poor People's Campaign, 177, 179
Poverty, by America (Desmond), 282–83
Power, Samantha, 251
presidential election: of 1876, 307n1; of 1964, 140, 155, 167–70; of 1968, 149, 178–80; of 1972, 150, 226; of 1976, 182–84; of 1980, 186–91; of 1984, 202, 226
Princeton University, 121, 311n63
Princeton University Press, 121
prison to school pipeline, 278
Proclamation of Amnesty and Reconstruction, 39–40, 54–56, 58
Progressive Era, 77, 103, 131. *See also* Grant, Madison; racial sciences (scientific racism)
Prosser, Gabriel, 41
public education funding, 127, 192–93, 197, 219, 275–79

"race suicide," 107, 110, 308n12
Racial Integrity Act of 1924 (Virginia), 127–28
racial myths, xii, 15–18; about Black beauty, 24–25; about Black intelligence, xii, 17, 29–30, 120–23, 127, 221–23; about Black men as criminal beasts, xii, 74–75, 83, 87–88, 93, 96–97; about Black pathology, 143–46, 149–50, 185, 223–24; about Black people's pain tolerance, 28, 29, 296n29; about Black sexuality and Black families, xii, 17, 22, 25–28, 83, 301–2n3; about Black sloth, xii, 17, 29, 36, 73, 79, 90–92, 305n42; Dixon and, 83, 87–88, 90–92, 93, 96–97; Jefferson and, 24–30, 36, 60–61, 73, 79, 83
racial sciences (scientific racism), 102–29;

and Columbia School of Anthropology, 306n56; craniology, 109, 120, 308–9n21; and "criminality," 105–6; Darwin and, 107–8, 116; Founders' views of Anglo-Saxonism, 103–5; German, 102, 103, 107, 307n5; and Gould's *Mismeasure of Man*, 121–22; Grant and, 76, 102–29; Grant's *The Passing of the Great Race*, 76, 102–3, 107, 110–20, 125; IQ tests, 120–23, 127, 221–22, 310n62; Nazi Germany, 107, 117–18, 132–33, 309n40; and nineteenth-century European immigrants, 105–6, 108, 110–15, 120–21, 308n7; segregation and the "Black extinction hypothesis," 116–17, 118, 122, 310n50; and social Darwinism, 107–9, 117, 133, 308n20; theory of recapitulation, 109, 308–9n21. *See also* eugenics movement

racial wealth gap, 9, 261–65, 268, 269–70, 328n14; Colorblind Age, 226; and financial reparations, 261–65, 268, 269–70; and the New Deal, 126

Rainbow Coalition, 226

Randolph, A. Philip, 136

Rappeport, Alan, 287

Rat Extermination Act (1967), 175

Rather, Dan, 209

Ray, James Earl, 136

Reagan, Christine, 158

Reagan, Jack, 156

Reagan, Michael, 158

Reagan, Nancy, 162, 167, 198, 209, 219, 318n12

Reagan, Nelle, 156

Reagan, Ronald, 3, 151–52, 153–85, 186–220, 221, 223–26; acting career, 151, 156–57; astrology interests, 189, 318n12; attempted assassination of, 195–96; budget cuts to departments and social services, 192–93, 195–201, 218, 219; cabinet appointments, 192–94; as California governor, 180–82, 189, 191; campaign for California governor, 170–75; on communist threat, 158–61, 165, 166–67, 170, 181, 212, 215; as early liberal and Democratic Party supporter,

156–57; early life, 155–57; fight against communism in South America, 212, 215; first inaugural address, 191–92; as GE spokesman, 151, 162–67, 199; Iran-Contra Affair, 212–14, 323n95; and Japanese American reparations, 216–17; judicial appointments, 194–95; and the King Day holiday, 202–5; and the King legacy, 201–5, 321n72, 321–22n73; and the Ku Klux Klan, 156–57, 189; marriage to Nancy, 162, 167; mass incarceration, 210–11, 215; "The Myth of the Great Society" (speech), 170–71; opposition to Civil Rights Movement and King's message, 153–54, 175–78, 179, 201–5, 321n72; personal tragedies, 157–58; personal transformation from liberal to conservative, 157–67; as president, 186–220; presidential election of 1968, 178–80; presidential election of 1976, 182–84; presidential election of 1980, 186–91; presidential election of 1984, 202; and racism of the Colorblind Age, 151–52, 153–55, 172–73, 219–20, 221, 223–26; radio shows (1970s), 184–85; second presidential term, 205–20; and the second Red Scare, 151, 155, 158–61, 165, 166–67, 181, 223; "The Speech" at the 1964 Republican National Convention, 152, 168–70; tax cuts for the wealthy, 196, 197–98, 263; "trickle-down economics," 198; vetoing civil rights legislation, 216; War on Crime, 206–8; War on Drugs, 205–16, 219; and the War on Poverty, abandonment of, 183–84, 192, 198, 200–201, 224, 313n17; and welfare, 174, 180–81, 182–83, 185, 187–88, 200, 206–7, 222; and white evangelicals, 189–90, 318–19n16

Real World, Real Talk (Cofield radio show), 8

recapitulation, theory of, 109, 308–9n21

Reconstruction, 63, 68–77; abolitionists on, 55; Black Codes, 71, 74, 75; Black families and communal institutions, 69, 301–2n3; constitutional amendments,

58, 69, 73–74, 272–73, 303n17; convict leasing, 71, 74, 75, 87, 134, 243, 312n6; Dixon's propaganda novels on the white South, 78, 79–100, 132; Douglass on, 55, 75, 91; Du Bois on, 75, 84; end of, 101, 307n1; Freedmen's Bureau, 70–71, 90, 302n5, 302n6; Johnson's presidential appointments to thwart, 71, 192; Lincoln's Proclamation of Amnesty and Reconstruction, 39–40, 54–56, 58; reparations proposals, 70; rise of the Klan, 71–73; Sherman's Special Field Order No. 154, 69–70, 71; Supreme Court decisions favoring states' rights and white supremacy, 73–75, 303n17; and white supremacist misinformation campaign about the South and the Civil War, 72–73, 79, 86, 122. *See also* Dixon, Thomas, Jr.

Rector, James, 181–82

redlining, 4

Red Scare: first wave, 99, 128, 159; Reagan and, 151, 155, 158–61, 165, 166–67, 181, 223; second-wave, 128, 151, 155, 158–61, 165, 166–67, 181, 223, 254

Regan, Don, 197

Rehnquist, William, 194–95

Religious Right, 189–90

Religious Roundtable National Affairs Briefing (August 1980), 190

reparations, xiv–xvi, 3, 8–10, 62–63, 230; closing the racial wealth gap, 261–65, 268, 269–70; Coates's argument for, 9–10, 235; Congress and a framework for implementation, 261, 327n2; for the era of lynchings, 133–35; financing through a progressive tax code/tax structure, 262–67, 286–88; to Japanese Americans interned during World War II, 216–17, 227, 238; King on, 177; monetary compensation, 239, 260–68, 290; and N'COBRA, 227, 291; postwar Germany, 255, 256; Rep. Conyers's 1989 commission to study and develop, 227–28, 325n19; Rep. Johnson's 2019 objections, 235–39; Rep. Lee's sponsorship of reparations legislation, 235, 270; Stevens's proposal

during Reconstruction, 70; and the United Nations, 327n3; white America's resistance to, xi, xv, 8–9, 134–35, 234, 235–39, 325n1. *See also* Reparative Age

Reparative Age, 16, 230, 233–39, 240–59, 260–68, 269–88, 289–91; breaking the intergenerational curse of white supremacy, 242, 243–47, 326n1; building interracial relationships within Black-led spaces and institutions, 242, 247–51; changing the tax code, 262–67, 286–88; closing the racial wealth gap, 261–65, 268, 269–70; a paradigm shift, 290; the power of penitent politics, 242, 251–59; raising public awareness about corporate and national measures of racial and economic equity, 285–86; raising public awareness about minimum wage/living wages, 284–85; raising public awareness about poverty and public assistance, 282–84; reckoning with intersection of public policy and institutional racism, 275–81; repair (continual and ongoing public policy work), 269–88, 290; repayment (monetary compensation), 239, 260–68, 290; repentance, 62–63, 239, 240–59, 290; revising the Constitution to create an economic and social Bill of Rights, 272–74, 288

Report on Conditions in the South (Grant), 92

Republic (Plato), 21

Republican Party: California Republicans, 171–75; Radical Republicans and Reconstruction, 69, 70; Reagan's campaign for California governor and vision for, 170–75; Reagan's speech at the 1964 Republican National Convention, 152, 168–70; Southern Strategy, 182–83

Reston, James, 191

Rice University, 270

Road Ahead, The: America's Creeping Revolution (Flynn), 164

Road to Serfdom, The (Hayek), 164

Roberts, Dorothy, 247, 296n29

Roberts, Lamar, 6–7

Robeson, Paul, 136, 311n63
Robinson, Jackie, 153, 167–68, 171
Robinson, Randall, 201, 225
Robison, James, 190
Rockefeller, John D., 77
Roof, Dylann, 253
Roosevelt, Eleanor, 125
Roosevelt, Franklin D., 77, 126, 131, 133, 154, 156
Roosevelt, Theodore, 77, 96, 102, 106–7, 131
Rumford Fair Housing Act of 1963 (California), 171, 173
Rustin, Bayard, 258
Ruttenberg, Danya, 249

Sancho, Ignatius, 37
Sandburg, Carl, 42
Sandinista National Liberation Front, 212
Savage Inequalities (Kozol), 193
Scalia, Antonin, 195
schools: charter schools, 276–77; Houston's Fifth Ward, 5, 6; integration, 5; prison-to-school pipeline, 278; public education funding, 127, 192–93, 197, 219, 275–79; Reagan's budget cuts, 192–93, 197, 219; school "choice" movement, 276–77; school-to-prison pipeline, 219, 278. See also Black education
Schumer, Chuck, 224
Schweiker, Richard S., 192, 319n28
Schwerner, Michael, 130, 188–89, 258
Scottsboro Boys, 314n12
Screen Actors Guild, 158
Second Chance Pell Grant program, 224–25, 278
Senfft, Alexandra, 255
Sered, Danielle, 279
Seward, William Henry, 49, 57
Shakespeare, William, 46
Shelby County v. Holder (2013), 253
Sherman, William T., 69–70
Shultz, George, 194
Sins of the Father (Dixon), 304n14
1619 Project, The, 244, 245, 326n2
Slaughterhouse Cases (1873), 303n17

Slave Codes, 71
slavery, 9, 40–42, 301n2; Founding Fathers and the debate over, 31–33, 43, 60–61, 296–97n38, 297n39, 299n17; Fugitive Slave Act (1850), 35–36, 42, 44, 80; Grant on, 114–15; Moynihan Report and, 145; Thirteenth Amendment ending, 57–58, 69, 74, 87, 272–73
Slavery at Monticello Tour, 254
Smith, Adam, 164, 285, 315n28
Smith, Christian, 318–19n16
Smith, Henry, 86
Smith, J. Alfred, 181
Smith, William Loughton, 33
social Darwinism, 107–9, 117, 133, 308n20. See also racial sciences (scientific racism)
Social Gospel movement, 76, 79, 132, 304n10
socialism: Dixon on threat to America's racial order, 80, 88, 99, 131; Grant's fear of, 106, 128, 131; and the progressive tradition, 131
Social Security, 174
South Africa: apartheid regime, 194, 254, 327n3; Truth and Reconciliation Commission and repentance process, 254–55, 326n16
Southern Christian Leadership Conference (SCLC), 258
Southerner, The (Dixon), 80
Southern Strategy, 182–83
Sowell, Thomas, 204
Spadafora, Hugo, 323n95
Special Field Order No. 154 (forty acres and a mule), 69–70, 71
Spencer, Herbert, 107–8, 116
Spiro, Jonathan, 76, 107, 118, 125–26
Stamped from the Beginning (Kendi), 107
Stanton, Edwin, 69
State of Black America (National Urban League reports), 211, 286
Stevens, Thaddeus, 57, 58–59, 70, 258
Stevenson, Bryan, 275
Stewart, Will (Henry), 86
Stone, Chuck, 186

Storey, Peter, 326n16
Stowe, Harriet Beecher, 45, 80, 95, 96, 257
Student Nonviolent Coordinating Committee (SNCC), 258
Study of American Intelligence, A (Brigham), 121, 122–23
Sumner, Charles, 58–59, 258
Sutton, Belinda, 24

Taft, William Howard, 77
Take 'Em Down NOLA, 254
Taney, Roger B., 37, 194
Tappan, Arthur, 45
tax system/tax code: audit rates for Black Americans, 287; corporate tax rates, 197–98, 263; "death tax," 264–65; estate tax exemption, 198, 262–63, 321n60; financing reparations through, 262–67, 286–88; inheritance taxes, 262–66; Reagan's tax cuts for the wealthy, 196, 197–98, 263; tax evasion by the wealthy, 183, 287
Taylor, Breonna, 229, 234, 246, 253
Taylor, Linda, 183
"Testament of Hope, A" (King), 177
Texas Monthly, 5–6
Therapeutic Abortion Act of 1967 (California), 189, 318n13
13th (documentary film), 246
Thirteenth Amendment, 57–58, 69, 74, 87, 272–73; loophole, 74, 87
Thomas, Clarence, 193
Thornburgh, Dick, 216
Thornton, Tex, 147
Three-Fifths Compromise, 24, 32–33, 43, 52, 98, 112
Thurman, Howard, 11, 233
Thurmond, Strom, 155
Till, Emmett, xii, 1–3, 234
Till-Mobley, Mamie, 1–3
Time magazine, 209, 246
"Time of Choosing, A" (Reagan's 1964 speech), 152, 168–70
Tocqueville, Alexis de, 90
Trail of Tears, 40, 107
"trickle-down economics," 198, 225

Tri-K Klub, 96
Triumph of the Will, The (1935 film), 132
Truman, Harry, 157
Trump, Donald, 228–29, 233–34, 278, 321n60
Truth, Sojourner, xv, 44, 45, 289
truth and reconciliation commissions, 254–55; America's failure to create, 133; South Africa's, 254–55, 326n16
Tubman, Harriet, xv, 44, 46, 48, 60, 221, 249, 289
Turner, Nat, 41–42, 45
Tutu, Desmond, 194
Tyson, Tim, 2

Uncle Tom's Cabin (Stowe), 80, 96, 257, 304n4
Underground Railroad, 59, 101
Underground Railroad, The (miniseries), 246
United Nations, 125, 327n3
United States v. Cruikshank (1876), 303n17
United Steelworkers v. Weber (1979), 320n44
University of California at Berkeley, 181–82, 265
University of California v. Bakke (1978), 320n44
University of Virginia, 104, 195
Until We Reckon (Sered), 279
US Constitution: and abolition, 43, 272–73; amending through an economic and social Bill of Rights, 272–74, 288; Bill of Rights, 34, 41, 272–74, 288; Douglass on, 43, 272; Grant on, 112–13; King on, 225–26, 273; Lincoln on, 42–43, 46; preamble, 43, 237, 272; Reconstruction amendments, 58, 69, 73–74, 272–73, 303n17; Supreme Court's post–Civil War interpretations favoring states' rights and white supremacy, 73–75, 303n17
US Department of Defense, 192, 210
US Department of Education, 192–93
US Department of Health and Human Services, 192, 319n28

US Department of Housing and Urban Development, 192, 319n26

US Department of Justice, 193–94

US Department of State, 194

US Department of the Treasury, 197

US Supreme Court: *Buck v. Bell* (1927), 127; *Dred Scott v. Sandford* (1857), 35, 37, 194; ideological division on civil rights in the late 1970s, 194, 320n44; influence of Grant's racial science, 126–27; *Loving v. Virginia* (1883), 98; post–Civil War decisions favoring states' rights and white supremacy, 73–75, 303n17; Reagan's "originalist" appointees, 194–95; *Shelby County v. Holder* (2013) and voting protections of the Civil Rights Act, 253

Vanderbilt, Cornelius, 77

Vesey, Denmark, 41

Vietnam War, 141, 148, 149, 176, 177, 179, 182, 199, 224

Voltaire, 20, 294n8

Voting Rights Act (1965), 98, 139, 253

Wagner-Rogers Bill (1939), 123

Waite, Morrison R., 74, 303n17

Wake Forest College, 78

Walker, Alice, 186

Walker, David, 13, 27, 36–37, 241

Walker, Francis Amasa, 105, 310n50

Wallace, George, 153, 154, 155, 180

Wall Street Journal, 145

Ward, Jesmyn, 247

Ward, Zebulon, 70

Warmth of Other Suns, The (Wilkerson), 101

War on Crime, 5, 224; Johnson's, 141, 144, 146, 148, 205; Nixon's, 149, 150, 205, 211, 322n81; Reagan's, 206–8

War on Drugs: and the CIA, 211–14; and crack epidemic, 5, 208–10; drug sentencing laws, 208; and Iran-Contra, 212–14, 323n95; and the Kerry Report, 213–14, 254; mass incarceration and prison industrial complex as legacy of, 210–11, 215; National Urban League's

State of Black America report (1990), 211; Nixon's, 150, 205, 211; Reagan's, 205–16, 219

War on Poverty, 183–84, 289; Johnson's, 140–49, 183–84, 313n17; Reagan's abandonment of, 183–84, 192, 198, 200–201, 224, 313n17

Washington, Booker T., 238

Washington Post, 189, 196, 198, 209, 214

Water Dancer, The (Coates), 91

Watergate, 150–51, 175, 182, 209

Watts uprising in Los Angeles (1965), 145–46

wealth gap. *See* racial wealth gap

Wealth of Nations, The (Smith), 285

Webster, Delia, 58

Weizsäcker, Richard von, 256

welfare: Clinton's 1996 welfare reform bill, 225; Moynihan Report on welfare dependence, 144–45, 183–84; Murray's argument for eradication of, 222; raising public awareness about poverty and public assistance (Reparative Age), 282–84; Reagan and, 174, 180–81, 182–83, 185, 187–88, 200, 206–7, 222; "welfare queen" stories, 183, 187–88, 229

Wells, Ida B., xiv–xv, 67, 135, 249, 274, 289; on the Ku Klux Klan, 87, 302n13; on lynching, 65, 85–86, 134; and Stowe's *Uncle Tom's Cabin*, 80

West, Cornel, 201, 226, 248

West, Richard, 5–6

Wheatley, Phillis, 11, 37

Where Do We Go from Here: Chaos or Community? (King), 176, 322n79

Where's the Rest of Me? (Reagan), 318n12

Whig Party, 43–44

White, Walter, 136

white Christianity, 8, 82–85; and abolitionism, 82–83, 88; Carter and, 189; Dixon and, 82–85, 132, 304n10; Dixon's propaganda novels about Reconstruction and the South, 82–85, 132; Grant and, 133; Reagan and white evangelicals, 189–90, 318–19n16; repentance and participation in Black sacred spaces,

248–49; Social Gospel movement, 76, 79, 132, 304n10; Wells on, 86
Whiteness of Wealth, The (Brown), 265
Whitman, James Q., 76
Whitman, Walt, 116
"Who Divided This House?" (Franklin), 38
Wilcox, Walter, 114
Wilkerson, Isabel, 76, 101, 246–47
Wilkins, Roger, 204
Wilkinson, Bill, 189
Williams, Edward Huntington, 97
Wilson, Woodrow, 77, 95, 131
Women of the Ku Klux Klan (WKKK), 96
Wood, Fernando, 41
Wood, Gordon, 244
Wood, Henrietta, 70
Woods, Eliza, 86
Works Progress Administration, 156
World War I, 121, 124

World War II, 123–25, 135–36, 157, 159; Black Americans and, 124–25, 135–36; Germany's postwar process of repentance, 62, 255–56; Japanese American internment and reparations, 216–17, 227, 238; US refusal to admit Jewish child refugees, 123. *See also* Nazi Germany
Wright, Francis, 34
Wright, Hamilton, 96
Wright, Richard, 98–99
Wyman, Jane, 158, 189

Yale University, 102
Yarmolinsky, Adam, 313n17
Yerkes, Robert, 121
Young, Andrew, 189, 258, 327n27

Zellner, Bob, 258–59
Zinn, Howard, 326n1
Zucman, Gabriel, 265